Situating Spirituality

Situating Spirituality

Context, Practice, and Power

Edited by

BRIAN STEENSLAND, JAIME KUCINSKAS, AND ANNA SUN

OXFORD
UNIVERSITY PRESS

Oxford University Press is a department of the University of Oxford. It furthers
the University's objective of excellence in research, scholarship, and education
by publishing worldwide. Oxford is a registered trade mark of Oxford University
Press in the UK and certain other countries.

Published in the United States of America by Oxford University Press
198 Madison Avenue, New York, NY 10016, United States of America.

© Oxford University Press 2022

All rights reserved. No part of this publication may be reproduced, stored in
a retrieval system, or transmitted, in any form or by any means, without the
prior permission in writing of Oxford University Press, or as expressly permitted
by law, by license, or under terms agreed with the appropriate reproduction
rights organization. Inquiries concerning reproduction outside the scope of the
above should be sent to the Rights Department, Oxford University Press, at the
address above.

You must not circulate this work in any other form
and you must impose this same condition on any acquirer.

Library of Congress Cataloging-in-Publication Data
Names: Steensland, Brian, 1967– editor. | Kucinskas, Jaime, editor. |
Sun, Anna Xiao Dong, 1971– editor.
Title: Situating spirituality : context, practice, and power /
edited by Brian Steensland, Jaime Kucinskas, and Anna Sun.
Description: New York, NY, United States of America : Oxford University
Press, 2022. | Includes bibliographical references and index.
Identifiers: LCCN 2021033406 (print) | LCCN 2021033407 (ebook) |
ISBN 9780197565018 (paperback) | ISBN 9780197565001 (hardback) |
ISBN 9780197565032 (epub)
Subjects: LCSH: Spirituality. | Spirituality—Social aspects.
Classification: LCC BL624 .S543 2021 (print) |
LCC BL624 (ebook) | DDC 204—dc23
LC record available at https://lccn.loc.gov/2021033406
LC ebook record available at https://lccn.loc.gov/2021033407

DOI: 10.1093/oso/9780197565001.001.0001

Contents

Acknowledgments	vii
Contributors	ix

INTRODUCTION

Eminently Social Spirituality: Context, Practice, and Power   3
Brian Steensland, Jaime Kucinskas, and Anna Sun

PART I. CONTEXT

1. Social Practices and Cultural Contexts: Frameworks for
   the Study of Spirituality   33
   Nancy T. Ammerman

2. The Gods of Modern Spirituality   49
   Linda Woodhead

3. Fearful Asymmetry: Rethinking the Boundaries between
   Religion and Spirituality   72
   Anna Sun

4. Trumping the Devil!: Engendering the Spirituality of the
   Marketplace within Africa and the African Diaspora   97
   Afe Adogame

5. Methodological Innovations for the Study of Spirituality   113
   Bradley R. E. Wright

6. Shifts in Spiritual and Religious Self-Perceptions in the First Year
   of College   128
   Alyssa N. Rockenbach

7. Spirituality among African Americans: Interracial and Intraracial
   Differences across Followers of Various Religious Traditions   154
   Jason E. Shelton

vi CONTENTS

PART II. PRACTICE

8. The Microinteractive Order of Spirituality 179
   Michal Pagis

9. Ecstasies: Or, the Limitations of Vanilla Spirituality Studies 194
   Melissa M. Wilcox

10. Textures of Spirituality in Rural Malawi 210
    Ann Swidler

11. Gifts, Weapons, and Values: The Language of Spirituality in
    Twenty-First-Century Central America 227
    Robert Brenneman

PART III. POWER

12. Everything Is Connected: Relocating Spiritual Power from
    Nature to Society 245
    Stef Aupers

13. Yoga Spirituality in the Context of US Institutions 262
    Candy Gunther Brown

14. Training Spiritual Caregivers: Spirituality in Chaplaincy
    Programs in Theological Education 278
    *Wendy Cadge, Beth Stroud, Patricia K. Palmer, George Fitchett,
    Trace Haythorn, and Casey Clevenger*

15. Spirituality and Islam: Sufism in Indonesia 297
    Rachel Rinaldo

16. The Transmission of Spirituality in Broader Landscapes
    of Power 314
    Jaime Kucinskas

CONCLUSION

17. Three Questions about Spirituality: Its Meaning, Influence,
    and Future 335
    Brian Steensland

Index 345

Acknowledgments

Like many collaborations, this one began as a series of conversations over coffee and meals at academic conferences. As the three of us discussed thoughts for advancing the state of research on contemporary spirituality, ideas began to take shape that ended up providing a preliminary framework for this volume. We also started a running list of scholars we hoped to gather to help us formulate a forward-looking agenda on spirituality. In May 2019, we hosted the "Social Dimensions of Spirituality" conference at Indiana University–Purdue University Indianapolis (IUPUI) that yielded early versions of many of the chapters collected here. The conference was intellectually invigorating, and the collegiality was a lot of fun. The exchanges also impressed upon us the many stakes involved in the study of spirituality. These include the loaded assumptions inherent in many definitions of spirituality (most of which are rooted in the Christian and Western experience), the implied evaluations of both religion and secularism vis-à-vis spirituality, and the question of to what extent particular groups can be characterized as seeking or cultivating spirituality. These larger concerns extend beyond the confines of our volume, but the framework developed here is informed by and can provide purchase on them.

We have many people to thank for their contributions to the conference and the volume. Most centrally, we are grateful to our chapter authors. They were, amazingly, able to revise chapters and hit deadlines during the many challenges of a global pandemic. Thank you. We thank the Consortium for the Study of Religion, Ethics, and Society at Indiana University for generous funding and support. Leaders at IU, particularly Fred Cate, the Vice President for Research, and Faith Hawkins, the Associate Vice President for Research, have been stalwart supporters of research on religion and ethics within the IU system. We owe special thanks to Alicia MacDonald, the administrator of the Consortium, who handled all the conference planning related to travel, lodging, and hospitality. It was a pleasure to work with her. Geoffrey Ravenhall Meinke helped compile the volume; we are especially grateful for his help formatting the chapters and his fastidious attention to detail in copyediting the volume. Beyond the list of contributors, a number

viii ACKNOWLEDGMENTS

of other participants helped shape the discussion at the conference: Lynn Davidman, Andrea Jain, Amali Ibrahim, Trish Herzog, Dan Winchester, and Rob Saler. We also thank readers for their comments on iterations of our introductory chapter: Linda Woodhead, Mary Jo Neitz, and Evan Stewart. At Oxford University Press, we are grateful to Theo Calderara for his editorial guidance and support, to Drew Anderla for assistance with production, and to the reviewers for their constructive feedback and suggestions. Like our chapter contributors, Theo and Drew helped us move the volume forward during challenging times.

One of the genuine pleasures for us of working on this volume was getting together virtually for our Friday afternoon project meetings. While our intellectual and organizational work was always seeded with laughter and good cheer, the value of the camaraderie and friendship soon become all the more apparent during the turbulent year of 2020.

Closest to home, we give thanks for our families and loved ones. From Jaime: given the tumult of the pandemic, I am especially grateful to the women who have lovingly taken care of my children, Cynthia Muder and Mary Ellen Sigbieny—thereby enabling me to help complete this volume. I am also grateful to my husband Zack and daughter Adela, for their unconditional love and support. But above all, I want to acknowledge my son Rylee, who traveled the full journey of this book with me—from the start of our conversations to final edits—during the first several years of his life. From Anna: my deepest gratitude is always to my teachers, especially the first, my mother, who taught me to regard spirituality as essential to what it means to be human. I am grateful to inspiring colleagues at Kenyon College, my intellectual home for over a decade; at Harvard Divinity School, where I was welcomed as visiting faculty; and at Duke University, my new community of scholars of religion. From Brian: gratitude is indeed a spiritual practice. Every day I recognize my exceptional good fortune to share my life with my wife Shana and to have such incredible daughters, Minna and Maxine. They are the radiant lights of my life.

Contributors

Afe Adogame is the Maxwell M. Upson Professor of Religion and Society at Princeton Theological Seminary. His research interests focus on interrogating new dynamics of religious experiences and expressions in Africa and the African diaspora, and the interconnectedness between religion, migration, globalization, politics, economy, and media. He is the author of *The African Christian Diaspora: New Currents and Emerging Trends in World Christianity* (Bloomsbury Academic, 2013).

Nancy T. Ammerman is Professor Emerita of Sociology of Religion in the Department of Sociology and School of Theology at Boston University. A noted scholar of lived religion, religious congregations, and religious conflict, she has served as President of both the Society for the Scientific Study of Religion and the Association for the Sociology of Religion. Her books include *Sacred Stories, Spiritual Tribes* (Oxford, 2013) and *Everyday Religion: Observing Modern Religious Lives* (Oxford, 2006).

Stef Aupers is Professor of Media Culture at the Institute for Media Studies at the University of Leuven in Belgium. A cultural sociologist by training, most of his work deals with religion, spirituality, and "re-enchantment" in modern societies and, particularly, the way such cultural beliefs are mediatized. He has studied the elective affinity between information/communication technology and religion, spirituality in Silicon Valley, religious communities on the internet, and the manifestation of religion in online computer games.

Robert Brenneman is Professor of Criminal Justice and Sociology at Goshen College. His research focuses on the impact of violence on human flourishing. His book *Homies and Hermanos: God and Gangs in Central America* (Oxford, 2011) takes a close look at the lives of sixty-three former gang members, many of whom joined an evangelical congregation as part of their attempt to extricate themselves from gang violence. His latest book, *Building Faith: A Sociology of Religious Structures* (Oxford, 2020), coauthored with Brian Miller, examines the relationship between architecture and community.

Wendy Cadge is Professor in the Department of Sociology at Brandeis University. She has written two books, *Paging God: Religion in the Halls of Medicine* (Chicago, 2013) and *Heartwood: The First Generation of Theravada Buddhism in America* (Chicago, 2005), and coedited *Religion on the Edge: De-Centering and Re-Centering the Sociology of Religion* (Oxford, 2013). She has also published more than seventy-five articles on religion, spirituality, immigration, and healthcare.

X CONTRIBUTORS

Casey Clevenger is the author of *Unequal Partners: In Search of Transnational Catholic Sisterhood* (Chicago, 2020) and has published research on global Catholicism, transnational organizations, and women's agency in conservative religious traditions.

George Fitchett is Professor and the Director of Research in the Department of Religion, Health & Human Values at Rush University Medical Center. He also holds an appointment in the Department of Preventive Medicine at Rush.

Candy Gunther Brown is Professor of Religious Studies at Indiana University, Bloomington, and past President of the American Society of Church History. A historian and ethnographer, she has published six books on contemporary Christian, Buddhist, and Hindu spiritual traditions. Her most recent book, *Debating Yoga and Mindfulness in Public Schools* (University of North Carolina Press, 2019), draws on her extensive research and experiences as an expert witness in legal cases on yoga and mindfulness.

Trace Haythorn is Executive Director/CEO of the Association for Clinical Pastoral Education.

Jaime Kucinskas is Associate Professor and Chair of the Department of Sociology at Hamilton College. She is the author of *The Mindful Elite: Mobilizing from the Inside Out* (Oxford, 2019) and has published on spiritual and religious movements, inequalities, and the importance of situating studies of spirituality, religion, and morality in specific temporal, group, institutional, and national settings.

Michal Pagis is Associate Professor of Sociology at Bar-Ilan University, Israel. She is the author of *Inward: Vipassana Meditation and the Embodiment of the Self* (Chicago, 2019). She studies transformations of self and identity in contemporary culture and has published on meditation, life-coaching, spirituality, and the intersection of religion and popular psychology.

Patricia K. Palmer is Manager of Research at Woodruff Health Sciences Center, Emory University. Ms. Palmer is a board-certified chaplain with master of divinity and master of public health degrees from Emory University and over five years of clinical experience.

Rachel Rinaldo is Associate Professor of Sociology at the University of Colorado, Boulder. She is a cultural sociologist interested in gender, globalization, social change, and religion, with a special focus on the developing world and Muslim societies. She is the author of *Mobilizing Piety: Islam and Feminism in Indonesia* (Oxford, 2013) and articles on gender and Islam in Indonesia. Her current research projects include a study of marriage and divorce in Indonesia as well as a study of working parents and the Covid-19 pandemic in the United States.

Alyssa N. Rockenbach is Alumni Distinguished Graduate Professor of Higher Education at North Carolina State University. Her current interdisciplinary research centers on college students' learning and development, equity and social justice

CONTRIBUTORS   xi

issues in education, and religious pluralism on college campuses. She is the coeditor of *Spirituality in College Students' Lives* (Routledge, 2012) and coauthor of *How College Affects Students: 21st Century Evidence That Higher Education Works* (Jossey-Bass, 2016).

Jason E. Shelton is Associate Professor of Sociology and Director of the Center for African American Studies at the University of Texas, Arlington. His primary research interests concern the sociology of religion, as well as the intersections of race, class, and social attitudes in the post-civil rights era. He is currently working on his next book, which focuses on religious diversity among African Americans. He also chairs the City of Arlington's Unity Council, an inaugural racial equity task force that will produce a comprehensive report on ways in which the mayor and city council can reduce racial disparities.

Brian Steensland is Professor and Chair of Sociology at Indiana University–Purdue University Indianapolis. He is the coeditor of *The New Evangelical Social Engagement* (Oxford, 2014) and author of *The Failed Welfare Revolution* (Princeton, 2008). A scholar of American religion, culture, and politics, his current research interests focus on contemporary spirituality and religious pluralism.

Beth Stroud is Guest Professor of Religion at Sarah Lawrence College.

Anna Sun is Associate Professor of Religious Studies and Sociology at Duke University, and Cochair of the Chinese Religions Unit at the American Academy of Religion. She is the author of *Confucianism as a World Religion: Contested Histories and Contemporary Realities* (Princeton, 2013), which received book awards from the American Sociological Association and the American Academy of Religion. Her publications focus on the revival of ritual life in contemporary urban China, the development of global Confucianism, and theoretical and methodological issues in the social scientific study of East Asian religions, such as the problem of religious identity. She is the guest editor of the special issue "Confucianism and Daoism: From Max Weber to the Present" for *Review of Religion and Chinese Society* (2020).

Ann Swidler is Professor of Sociology at University of California, Berkeley. She studies the interplay of culture and institutions. She asks how culture works—both how people use it and how it shapes social life. She is best known for her books *Talk of Love* (Chicago, 2001) and the coauthored works *Habits of the Heart* (California, 1985) and *The Good Society* (Knopf, 1991) as well as her classic article, "Culture in Action: Symbols and Strategies" (*American Sociological Review*, 1986). Swidler's most recent work examines African religion and the institutions of African chieftaincy in order to understand the cultural and religious sources of collective capacities for social action.

Melissa M. Wilcox is Professor and Holstein Family and Community Chair of Religious Studies at the University of California, Riverside, and specializes in the study of gender, sexuality, and religion in the global North / global West. Dr. Wilcox is the author of seven books and numerous articles, including *Queer Nuns: Religion, Activism, and Serious Parody* (2018), *Queer Religiosities: An Introduction to Queer and Transgender Studies in Religion* (2020), and, with Nina Hoel and Liz Wilson, *Religion, the Body, and Sexuality* (2020). Dr. Wilcox's current research is on spirituality in leather and BDSM communities.

Linda Woodhead is Distinguished Professor of Sociology of Religion in the Department of Politics, Philosophy and Religion at Lancaster University. She researches the growth, decline, and transformation of religions in modern times. *The Spiritual Revolution* (with P. Heelas, Blackwell, 2005) is a study of holistic spirituality in an English town that offers an explanation of its widespread growth after the 1980s. *That Was the Church That Was* (with A. Brown, Bloomsbury 2017), examines the rapid decline of the Church of England during the same period. Woodhead's latest book is *Gen Z, Explained: The Art of Living in a Digital Age* (with R. Katz, S. Ogilivie, J. Shaw, Chicago 2021).

Bradley R. E. Wright is Professor of Sociology at the University of Connecticut. He has published widely in the areas of religion and spirituality, methodology, social psychology, and social stratification. He was Principal Investigator of SoulPulse, a real-time research project on daily spirituality among Americans.

INTRODUCTION

Eminently Social Spirituality

Context, Practice, and Power

Brian Steensland, Jaime Kucinskas, and Anna Sun

Spirituality is in the spotlight. While levels of traditional religious belief and observance are declining in much of the Western world, the number of people who consider themselves spiritual but not religious is on the rise. Spiritual practices such as yoga, meditation, and pilgrimage are prevalent and growing. Innumerable "wellness" regimes impart spiritual experiences and vocabularies to practitioners. Books on cultivating spiritual life proliferate. People are delving into non-Christian and premodern traditions for insights into spirituality, while global migration encourages hybrid practices that are both transnational and unique. Writers talk of a new spiritual awakening "after religion."

This current interest in spirituality has a lineage. A "spiritual revolution" has been underway since the middle of the twentieth century. After a revival of sorts after World War II, organized religion—and its associated identities, beliefs, and practices—began to weaken under the influence of the 1960s counterculture. In an era that placed greater value on individualism, freedom, and authenticity, people began to move away from commitment to organized religion toward spiritual seeking, which often happened outside religious institutions. This turn toward spirituality, fed by the rapid social transformations of the 1960s, was an acceleration point in a longer trajectory. Writing at the opening of the twentieth century, Émile Durkheim predicted the decline of religious authority and the complementary rise of the self as the center of sacredness. Even before that, pietist movements of the seventeenth and eighteenth centuries challenged religious institutions with their emphasis on interior experience, individual devotion, and emotional states over doctrine and conformity. Seen in this light, the contemporary embrace of spirituality can be viewed as the latest stage in a movement toward the subjectification of transcendent experience.

Brian Steensland, Jaime Kucinskas, and Anna Sun, *Eminently Social Spirituality* In: *Situating Spirituality.*
Edited by: Brian Steensland, Jaime Kucinskas, and Anna Sun, Oxford University Press. © Oxford University Press 2022.
DOI: 10.1093/oso/9780197565001.003.0001

4   BRIAN STEENSLAND, JAIME KUCINSKAS, AND ANNA SUN

Given the high degree of interest in spirituality, now is a valuable time for a new appraisal. While the historical trajectory that brought us here seems clear enough, common understandings of contemporary spirituality have limitations. As we outline in the sections to follow, the dominant assumptions embedded in much of our thinking about spirituality are only partially correct. Though spirituality is associated with individualism, it is not predominantly individuated and idiosyncratic; it is socially influenced, enabled, and patterned. There are not highly generalizable forms of spirituality; spirituality, both as a lived experience and as an analytic category, is shaped by context and therefore quite variable. Spirituality should not be solely associated with belief, transcendent states, and sentiments of awe and wonder; it is rooted in social practice and physical embodiment, and oriented toward pragmatic action. Spirituality does not float above human power relations; it is also contested, strategically framed, and shaped by institutional forces.

None of the foregoing denies the positive benefits commonly associated with spirituality. This view of spirituality is warranted, but its scope is narrower than supposed. We show the inescapably social foundations of spirituality. These foundations help explain spirituality's positive associations, but, more broadly, account for its multifaceted nature. While definitions of spirituality have an individual locus, and while spirituality is often grounded in a discourse of Western individualism, it nonetheless has sociological antecedents, variations, and consequences. Definitions and discourse aside, spirituality is just as "eminently social" as Durkheim ([1912] 1995) showed that religion was over a century ago. It should be socially situated.

Below we outline the insights and assumptions of what we refer to as first-wave scholarship on spirituality. Then we lay out a framework for second-wave scholarship on spirituality that is more oriented by context, practice, and power. Our hope is that this framework contributes to more socially embedded and comparative understandings of spirituality within and outside of organized religion and religious populations.

First-Wave Perspectives on Spirituality

There have long been spiritual groups and movements—metaphysicals, Transcendentalists, occult followers, and New Age practitioners, just to name a few (see Albanese 2007; Schmidt 2005). And there have long been scholars who studied them. What was distinctive about first-wave scholarship on

INTRODUCTION 5

spirituality was its attention to the *society-wide* shift away from religion and toward spirituality. The work of this first wave, which began in the 1990s, was crucial to better understanding spirituality. It carved out analytic space for spirituality that was distinct from religion, documented spiritual trends in the general public, analyzed factors that accounted for its growth, and assessed its impact.

In *After Heaven*, Robert Wuthnow (1998) argued that a fundamental shift from religious "dwelling" to spiritual "seeking" occurred in the decades following World War II. Dwelling involved an enduring commitment to a stable religious tradition, while seeking was characterized by restless movement between religious groups and traditions and by a more individualized assembly of personal beliefs and practices (what become known as "tinkering" or "bricolage"). Slow-moving social changes created fertile grounds for this shift: among them, an increasingly postindustrial economy, rising levels of education, occupational and geographical mobility, and the growth of a consumerist mindset. But it was the 1960s counterculture, with its emphasis on freedom, critique of existing institutions, mood of openness, influx of Eastern religious groups, and therapeutic discourse that accelerated the trend toward spiritual seeking. Wade Clark Roof's *The Spiritual Marketplace* (1999) specifically tied the trend toward spirituality to generational change. The spirituality of the baby boomers, who came of age in the 1960s or later, was based on seeking, questing, and expressive individualism. Religious traditions provided spiritual resources from which boomers eclectically drew for their own purposes. Roof argued that baby boomer spirituality was the vanguard of American religious life and would soon become the mainstream. Not long thereafter, Paul Heelas and Linda Woodhead (2005) documented similar trends in the United Kingdom. Their book's title, *The Spiritual Revolution: Why Religion Is Giving Way to Spirituality*, telegraphed their argument and its scope. The authors distinguished between religion and spirituality and the logics of conformity/transcendence and authenticity/immanence associated, respectively, with each. They argued that a spiritual revolution was underway in the contemporary West, a revolution rooted in the cultivation and sacralization of internal subjective significance.

With spirituality ascendant, researchers turned their attention to conceptual and descriptive matters. Exploring the definitional and empirical relationship between "religion" and "spirituality" proved to be complex and became a virtual cottage industry (e.g., Hill et al. 2000; Marler and Hadaway 2002). Documenting the spread of new forms of spirituality was another important objective. In the Western European case, Houtman and Aupers (2007) documented the growth of "post-Christian spirituality" between 1981 and 2000. Along similar lines to Heelas and Woodhead, they argued that this represented a trend away from the authority of external tradition and toward that of the self and subjective life. While people in the United States were more religiously observant than their European counterparts, the term "spiritual but not religious" entered the lexicon (e.g., Fuller 2001) and became a significant descriptive category in the analysis of US religious trends (Mercadante 2014; Parsons 2018).

Other attention turned to the personal impact of spirituality. Much of this research sought to explore the links between individual spirituality and mental and physical health (George et al. 2000). In the field of psychology, where much of this work was located analytically, research focused on determining the best measures of spirituality, raising numerous questions about definitions and dimensions. Health research found positive associations between spirituality and mental health, physical resilience, and life satisfaction. As this line of research proliferated, scholars raised questions about a potential bias toward positive findings. If spirituality was defined and measured in reference to inherently positive qualities, as was often the case, studies would inevitably find positive outcomes (Koenig 2008). Nevertheless, given spirituality's positive cultural connotations and empirical associations, it became something that healthcare providers sought to incorporate into patient care (see Koenig 2013).

First-wave scholarship on spirituality accomplished a number of important things. It created analytic space for attention to spirituality as distinct from religion, identified factors that led to the societal shift toward spirituality, and looked at the impact of spirituality in various areas of life. Yet it did not displace, and may have reinforced, a number of assumptions about spirituality that remain common. The first is that the trend away from organized religion leads to individuated spirituality. This draws an overly sharp boundary between religion and spirituality; in many contexts, religion and spirituality overlap considerably. It is also bound up with an overly sharp contrast between religion as social and communal and spirituality as cultivated outside of social relationships and influences. This contrast has been reinforced by definitions of spirituality, which have an individual locus, by psychological measures and scales that assess spirituality as a property of individuals, and by long-standing associations between spirituality and religious individualism (e.g., Bellah et al. 1985).

A second assumption is that spirituality plays a positive role in personal cultivation. This is reflected in spirituality's growing role in treatment and interventions of various types. Medical professionals see spirituality as enhancing mental health and physical well-being, prison systems host spiritual development programs for their inmates, schools have meditation and yoga programs for their students, and workplaces sponsor spiritual programming aimed toward improved employee satisfaction and productivity. As commentators have noted, these types of programs treat the individual, rather than systems, as the locus of personal and societal wellness (e.g., Carrette and King 2005) and assume that spirituality is positive or at least benign. This assumption overlooks the fact that seeking connection with transcendent sources of meaning may also lead to melancholy, despondence, or anger. These emotions, and feelings of failure, are not uncommon in spiritual life (Johnston 2017).

A third assumption is that the rise of spirituality has been largely uncontested and not a product of struggle or strategy. This view bears the mark of classical secularization theory, in which the rise of contemporary spirituality is the outgrowth of modernization processes (Bruce 2011), not a product of group interests and conflict (e.g., Smith 2003). Some first-wave studies tried to counter this view by showing, for example, how prominent women were in the rise of spirituality, how much it aligned with and supported changing gender roles, and how contested these changes were (Sointu and Woodhead 2008).

A fourth, and overlapping, assumption is that there is a master trend toward spirituality that follows a single path of societal modernization, modeled on North America and Europe, rather than a variety of ways that spirituality might manifest itself in modern settings (see Eisenstadt 2000). This assumption privileges a particular set of historical processes that serve as the foundation for theoretical generalizations. What constitutes "spirituality" for people in North America is not necessarily the same as, for instance, in East Asia or North Africa.

All of these assumptions require revision.

Second-Wave Perspectives on Spirituality

First-wave scholarship on spirituality laid a crucial foundation that subsequent work builds upon. But it was necessarily focused on early-stage problematics and foils involved in clearing conceptual ground. There have been compelling forays beyond the framework of first-wave perspectives, some coming from within the first wave itself. Here we consolidate a number of these insights to propose new conceptual perspectives that hold promise for a deeper understanding of contemporary spirituality.

The foundation of what we describe as second-wave perspectives is the recognition that, against the individuated view of spirituality, spirituality is thoroughly social. This recognition extends beyond first-wave analyses that identified the sociological factors driving the rise in spirituality. Newer work of the second wave centers on the *collective processes*—such as socialization, group gatherings, common affordances, shared narrative—that are constitutive of contemporary manifestations of spirituality. For instance, Aupers and Houtman (2006) showed that the growth of New Age spirituality in Western Europe not only took place against a backdrop of skepticism toward mainstream institutions but involved active socialization processes and ideological legitimations that produced a coherent form of "individuated" spirituality. The authors were early in calls for a "sociologization" of the study of spirituality and its legitimating structures. In an exemplary ethnographic study of "new metaphysicals," with metaphysicals serving as an exemplar of William James's "individual" religious experience, Bender (2010) explored how metaphysical spirituality was suffused with sociality—shared discourses and collective practices shaped by group settings. Ammerman's (2014) rich study of spirituality from a "lived religion" perspective likewise generated important insights about the social foundations of spirituality. Among them, she showed that a person's "sacred consciousness," which is at the center of a spiritual outlook, is often based in and nurtured through social conduits, including religious organizations, small groups, and diverse media. Pagis's (2019) ethnographic analysis of vipassana meditation illustrated how the cultivation of interior (and seemingly personal) spiritual experience is enabled by shared social practices, intersubjective understandings, and community affirmation.

In order to better situate spirituality in the social, and oriented by like-minded work, such as that of our chapter contributors here, we focus our attention on three angles of vision in particular: context, practice, and power. We also expand beyond the culturally Christian settings of the United States and Western Europe. Doing so helps to illustrate how a narrow and arguably provincial understanding of spirituality should be recast in light of a broader range of contexts. The contributors conduct research in North America,

INTRODUCTION 9

Central America, East Asia, South Asia, Africa and the African diaspora, Western Europe, and the Middle East. They study not only Christian, Jewish, and Islamic societies, but also non-Abrahamic societies with native as well as transnational sacred traditions.

As we elaborate further below, these analytic angles and expanded cases help to demonstrate that spirituality, both as analytic concept and as lived experience, is a relational phenomenon, embodied and practical, and shaped by power relations, even if these dynamics go unrecognized by practitioners (and perhaps analysts) themselves. Second-wave understandings of spirituality are also as attentive to the relationship between the spiritual and the secular as to the spiritual and the religious.

Context

Although the term "spirituality" is often used as if it refers to a stable, easily identifiable substance, we recognize that, like the term "religion," it does not have an innate, universal essence, the way H_2O is the chemical formula of water wherever water may be found. Thus, it is misguided to search for an overarching definition of spirituality that would work transhistorically, transnationally, and transculturally: "There is no view from nowhere—no Archimedean point outside of history—from which one could determine a fixed and universal meaning for the term 'spirituality'" (Carrette and King 2005, 3).

Instead of "a view from nowhere," a "view from somewhere"—or context—is how we approach the concept of spirituality. Context refers to two aspects of spirituality research: conceptual and substantive. How we understand spirituality is standpoint dependent (where we view spirituality from) and situation dependent (where spirituality is situated). The act of definition is itself a social process and practice, one related to institutional and political—such as postcolonial—structures of power. Context is the concrete as well as symbolic social space in which the embodied, intersubjective, discursive, and pragmatic spiritual practice takes place. By identifying contexts and emphasizing the significance of standpoints, we are following in the footsteps of feminist theorists to privilege the traditionally less powerful, invisible, and overlooked (Harding 2009).

The conceptual dimension of the context of spirituality must start with its historical embeddedness. In this, spirituality is very similar to the concept of religion, which is subject to myriad historical forces such as the development of different religious traditions; social and cultural changes; capitalism and colonialism; diverse modes of modernity; and the politics of academic knowledge production, among many others (Asad 1993; Chakrabarty 2000; King 1999; Sun 2013). As Nietzsche famously puts it in *On the Genealogy of Morals*, "Only that which is without history can be defined" ([1887] 2009, 60).

Any attempt at a genealogy of the concept of "spirituality" would yield a very complex history. In the Western tradition, the term goes back to the "spiritual" in Greek religion (*pneumatikos*), denoting both the spirit that resides in humans and what belongs to the divine spirit. The latter was used extensively in Greek biblical texts in early Christianity. By the thirteenth century, the term was used to refer to the jurisdiction of the church, the ecclesiastical sphere, and ecclesiastical authority. The idea of "spiritual exercise," referring to the rigorous cultivation of the spirit and the mind, also has ancient roots, practiced by the Stoics in the third century BC before it became part of early Christian monastic tradition (Hadot 1995). Ignatius of Loyola revived and reinvented spiritual exercise in the sixteenth century, and it remains a venerable practice in contemporary Catholicism.

In America in the nineteenth century, discourses on spirituality and transcendentalism captured the religious imagination of several generations of Americans, with the "new metaphysicals" engaging in new forms of spiritual practice in the twenty-first century (Bender 2010). The rising wave of non-Western religious practices such as meditation and yoga since the late nineteenth century resulted in the notion of "Eastern spirituality" (Ellwood 1979), although these diverse "Eastern traditions" have had vastly different processes of transformation once they were transplanted to America (Palmer and Siegler 2017; Seager 2012; Tweed 2000).

The concept of "spirituality" cannot be properly understood without knowledge of how the dominant form of religious life in North America functions in this context. It is the changing reality of Christianity—historically dominant and thoroughly institutionalized, now gradually evolving into a more porous presence in some quarters and a more rigid one in others—that shapes how spirituality is defined and comprehended there. The conceptualization of spirituality is relational, for its usage always corresponds to the historical developments of religion in societies where religious membership has been the norm.

Outside of such contexts, the term "spiritualty" has a very different set of connotations. For instance, it is not easy to find a Chinese or Hebrew translation of "spirituality" that is its exact functional equivalent in the Christian West, for the simple yet deep reason that there is no functional equivalent of a concept in societies where there have been very different religious, social, and political realities. This explains why, although the concept is much employed in the sociological study of religion in North America and in Europe, "spirituality" is not nearly as commonly used in studies from other parts of the world. The solution is not to ride off in all directions seeking a catchall definition of "spirituality," but rather to begin with an analysis of what counts for spirituality in a given society. Only then can we proceed from this nuanced and historically grounded understanding to undertaking empirical projects that may shed light on the specific conditions of a particular form of religious life.

Another aspect of spirituality as a concept is its boundary work (Gieryn 1999; Lamont and Molnar 2002). It is defined and understood in relation to both the religious and the secular. This is not unlike the contrasting and corresponding concepts such as the sacred and the profane in Durkheim, or "the proletariats as the negation of the capitalist class" in Marx (Lamont and Molnar 2002, 167), or the master-and-slave dialectic in Hegel. How are the symbolic and social boundaries between the three entities—religion, spirituality, and the secular—drawn and maintained? And which takes priority? Does the experience of spirituality come first? Or do we find first the boundaries that separate spirituality from religion and the secular?

Abbott makes the bold claim that "social entities come into existence when social actors tie social boundaries together in certain ways. Boundaries come first, then entities" (1995, 860). We suggest that the boundary work of spirituality often entails similar processes. Boundary-making is a social process that involves institutions, social actors, and material as well as symbolic objects. And in the case of spirituality, it also includes ritual activities. The making of "boundaries into entities" occurs in particular times and places: there is no universal pattern for how such a process of boundary work is carried out. For instance, in societies where the boundaries between the secular and the religious are long-standing and strong, such as in the United States and France, the boundaries of spirituality are likely to be under pressure to be clearly demarcated, therefore creating a social space for the existence of the entity of "spirituality." In these circumstances, the boundary work results in a stronger sense of the spiritual as a distinct entity, as a thing in itself. But the hard boundary between religion and spirituality comes first— people and institutions have stakes in the boundary's existence—and makes the bounded entity possible. In societies where the secular and the religious do not have strong boundaries and are often diffused, such as in Africa or in China, people are unburdened of the need to have clearly defined religious identities (Adogame, this volume; Sun 2021). In such cases, spirituality may not become a full-fledged social entity because boundary work is not needed. People will be more likely to speak of their practices rather than of their "spirituality" in the abstract, and indeed they may be puzzled when asked about spirituality detached from practices.

Once we are explicit about the situated nature of the conceptual frame we adopt, the ensuing empirical work allows us to examine the lived experiences of "spirituality," defined in whatever terms are meaningful to the specific contexts. This is the study of spirituality as lived experience, which aims to understand how spiritualty is practiced differently in different micro- and macrocontexts. This is what we call "situated spirituality," which refers to the way spirituality is always part of the social world, and always conditioned by cultural, political, and legal contexts. Spirituality can be—and should be—studied in terms of its substantive characteristics and variations, as long as we recognize that conceptualizations of spiritualty are always context dependent. As Talal Asad suggests, "there cannot be a universal definition of religion, not only because its constituent elements and relationships are historically specific, but because that definition is itself the historical product of discursive processes," rather than abstract systems of meaning (Asad 1993: 29). The same may be said about spirituality.

To situate spirituality means examining it in relation to other features of context, looking for patterns, variations, and significant comparisons. Valuable work has already been done in this direction, with empirical research looking for the impact of race and ethnicity, education, politics, religious membership, gender, sexuality, cross-national differences, interreligious differences, and many other social factors in the lived experience and practice of spiritualty. Notably, the general insight that one's individual spirituality has a sociological basis lays the groundwork for expecting variation but seeing it as patterned. At the individual level, the meaning and experience of spirituality are shaped by sociodemographic and ideological traits. In the United States, views of spirituality fall into distinct clusters that are associated with age, education, and political orientation, and changes in these contexts affect the way people identify themselves as "religious" or "spiritual" (Ammerman 2013; Rockenbach, this volume; Steensland et al. 2018). A study of daily spiritual experience found that people's spiritual awareness is

INTRODUCTION   13

influenced by a host of sociological factors—for example, it is typically higher in the presence of friends and family, which is evidence that solitude is not necessarily the most conducive setting for spiritual experience (Kucinskas et al. 2018). Research by Jason Shelton (this volume) also shows that blacks and whites differ in their identifications as "a spiritual person."

In cross-national comparisons, we see variation across entire societies. In regard to the meaning that spirituality holds for people, Ammerman (2013) and Steensland and colleagues (2018) both find that spirituality and religion overlap considerably in the United States. Theism of some type is the dominant reference point in American spirituality, and wholly immanent modes of spirituality are fairly limited. Studies in Western Europe that use similar research methods find that spirituality is markedly more immanent or "this-worldly." In an Italian study, spirituality was much more likely to connote things such as harmony, life's meaning, and inner peace than belief in God or other references to organized religion or transcendence (Palmisano 2010). Likewise, a Dutch study showed that people in Holland were considerably more likely to conceptualize spirituality in terms of inner feelings, the human mind, or a life philosophy than Americans are (Berghuijs et al. 2013).

Taken together, these micro- and macro-level comparisons illustrate an essential point: While spirituality feels personal to people, it is fundamentally sociological in its antecedents and manifestations. The situated discourses of spirituality and its attendant culture are what produce its individualistic connotations. This recognition opens up possibilities for expanding our understanding of spirituality in a host of ways. Ammerman's framework (this volume) for examining spiritual practices in four different contexts—entangled, established, institutionalized, interstitial—charts a promising course. Many of the other chapters further illustrate the value of studying spirituality in varied settings across the religious and secular landscape and in relation to religious and nonreligious groups.

Practice

Now is also the time to pay greater attention to practice in the study of spirituality. Robert Wuthnow (2020) surveyed the recent "practice turn" in the social sciences and highlighted its implications for the study for religion. He described the shift in focus as one from *classification concepts* to *structuring processes*. This, in essence, is a shift from *what* to *how*—from definitions and conceptual categories to the temporal and processual dynamics that undergird religion as it is actually lived. Religious leaders and institutions themselves have long recognized the centrality of practice in religious formation. Many traditions are in fact characterized as much by orthopraxy (right practice) as orthodoxy (right belief). In the study of religion, attention to practice is reflected in examinations of activity like private prayer, corporate worship, devotional pilgrimage, sacramental rites, dietary strictures, and acts of charity. Research in the lived religion perspective (e.g., Ammerman 2007; McGuire 2008) has been on the forefront of this agenda. The benefit to this attention to practice is that it situates religion in its everyday contexts while simultaneously demonstrating how practices constitute religious life itself (Ammerman 2020).

The study of spirituality is beginning to make this same shift toward practice. First-wave scholarship was largely oriented by the classificatory phase of study, as early work in a new area typically is. It focused more on questions concerning definitions, distinctions, and measurement. What is the nature of spirituality? How is spirituality related to religion? How should we conceptualize the dimensions of spirituality? To what extent does spirituality impact other aspects of life? This is necessary and important work. But it shaped our conceptualization of spirituality by centering on spiritual experience and spiritual identity (see Sheldrake 2012). For instance, numerous studies have focused on people who identify as "spiritual but not religious" and the growth of this group. Yet most of these studies shed little light on what sustains spirituality or what it does in the lives of respondents. Even Mercadante's (2014) illuminating analysis of this group focuses on beliefs and meaning structures over spiritual activities. Along similar lines, large national studies assess spiritual dispositions with questions about whether one has experienced a state of awe or wonder or harmony. But the field has devoted less attention to spiritual practices, which are the underlying engines that produce meaningful experiences and robust identities. Such experiences do not necessarily come easily or without intentionality. This neglect of practice could be due to the fact that spirituality connotes something that is deinstitutionalized and therefore less rooted in shared ritual. Spirituality has ostensibly fewer established behavioral expectations, is less prescriptively rooted in time and place, and, for scholars, is more challenging to observe outside established institutions. With prominent exceptions from research in the lived religion and ethnographic traditions, exemplified by a number of the contributors to our volume, the study of spirituality has yet to fully take the practice turn.

Yet understanding the role of practice in spirituality is arguably even more important than for religion. To the extent that spirituality is cultivated and lived outside of religious institutions, it is largely left up to individuals to assemble the components of their spiritual selves. As Wuthnow (1998) observed, this places the burden of spiritual formation on individuals that religious institutions have historically borne. Once institutions stop doing the "thinking" (Douglas 1986), individuals are left to improvise, choose, and tinker. Spiritual practice becomes the foundation that sustains the spiritual self.

Here and in the chapters to follow we and our contributors offer five angles of vision on the role of practice in spirituality based on insights from existing work in the field. The first is the most fundamental. Practices, while they may happen outside religious institutions, are social. Even as people cultivate an authentic-feeling and individualized spiritual self, they do so through collective processes. They meditate with others at retreat centers. They read books, listen to lectures, and participate in discussions. They internalize collectively produced narratives and aspirations that form and reshape their spiritual sensibilities (Johnston 2016). Recognizing the sociality of practice helps to move us beyond the mythos of the solitary spiritual individual. As Bender (2010) argues, even though observers in the modern West tend to think about the "autonomy of spirituality," there are few spiritual experiences are that sociologically unmediated. Even so-called spiritual virtuosi, who are devoted to personal practices and seem to represent extreme cases of sui generis spiritual individualism, are shaped by their immediate communities—who provide interpretation, discipline, and purpose—and their broader societal and historical contexts (Goldman and Pfaff 2018).

Second, spiritual practices are embodied. In the case of postural yoga, this is self-evident, but embodiment is much more broadly relevant. Daily routines, dietary habits, modes of dress, gestures of kneeling and prostration, tattoos—these and many more are techniques of the body that allow spirituality, metaphorically and physically, to get under the skin. Winchester (2016) examined the embodied nature of spiritual formation by showing the linkages between fasting and spiritual desires. Bodily experiences of hunger and appetite become embodied metaphors for understanding sin and virtue. Beyond the realm of overt spiritual practices, such as fasting, grasping the significance of embodiment also helps us see how everyday practices like gardening can take on the significance of spiritual disciplines (McGuire 2008). Attention to spirituality and the body also provides valuable points of entrée for conceptualizing the intersections of gender or race/ethnicity with sacred experience (e.g., Davidman 2015).

Third, practices include discourse. Speech is part of embodiment at the somatic level, such as the recitation of scriptures through lectio divina. But more broadly, spiritual meanings and identities are constructed and maintained through discourse: conversations, texts, media, and so on. Besecke (2014) showed how people cultivate a discourse of "reflexive spirituality," one that is akin to its own language, to help them navigate the tensions they experienced between faith and rationality. Along different lines, experiences as seemingly personal and idiosyncratic as spiritual awakenings are shaped by collective discursive conventions (DeGloma 2014). In the wider culture, to describe something as spiritual is to legitimate it as such. The discursive aspect of spirituality is part of the plausibility structure that sustains and legitimates it and, perhaps now even more so, broadens its appeal.

Fourth, practice is empowering. It can be a conduit for feelings of divine power and efficacy. McGuire (2008) described how this played out in medieval folk practices, where everyday spiritual powers were understood to be widespread. Practices gave people a sense of control in otherwise hard and uncertain circumstances. Beyond the mundane world of the everyday, practices provide spiritual resources that can lead people to engage in extraordinary ways during extraordinary times. Chappell (2004) identified practices oriented by divine power as a key spiritual resource in the southern civil rights movement. Because leaders and everyday participants believed in the power of miracles, they engaged in collective action that took on the appearance of the miraculous.

Fifth, spiritual practice is often pragmatic. While spirituality, at least in the modern West, is stereotypically associated with transcending everyday concerns, spirituality as practiced is also directed toward everyday goals and struggles. Smith (2017) has recently sought to reorient the study of religion toward the study of practices premised on the existence of superhuman powers that are oriented toward realizing human goods. These human goods are fundamentally practical (as opposed to otherworldly) concerns. In contrast to religion, spirituality may or may not reference superhuman powers, but we share Smith's view that both religion and spirituality are often oriented toward pragmatic problem-solving.

All told, practices are critical to have at the center of our understanding of spirituality. They are formative, sustaining, and expressive. Practices heighten spiritual awareness and open "doors to an experience of the sacred"

(Kucinskas et al. 2017, 434). Closer attention to spiritual practice in everyday life should (minimally) focus on its collective, embodied, discursive, empowering, and pragmatic dimensions.

Power

To recognize the social dimensions of spirituality is to create analytic space for power, influence, and contestation in ways that have yet to be adequately explored (Wood and Bunn 2009). Overt power is exercised through marshaling and utilizing resources for influence (Clark 1973). Opaque power operates in more subtle and diffused ways, through knowledge, normative influences, subjective development, and the structures in which we live (Foucault 2001). Spirituality is enmeshed in the dynamic relations between power and social practices, rather than operating outside of power dynamics, as some people assume.

Popular, romanticized interpretations of spiritual experience depict it as private and transcendent—a haven from the tainted world. Yet contemporary spirituality is deeply intertwined with powerful, resource-rich religious and secular institutions, such as healthcare, education, business, and government, as well as political dynamics locally and globally. While theorists of religion have long explored the powerful impacts of these forces on religion, recent attention to spirituality, based in psychology, medicine, and public health, has largely neglected how spiritual understandings, practices, and experiences are shaped by fields of power.

Despite a long-standing and rich literature on the organizational and institutional foundations of social life, the bulk of scholarship on spirituality has yet to acknowledge the depth and breadth of such influences. Charles Perrow (1991) declared that we live in a "society of organizations," which are constitutive of human experience through their structures, cultural logics, repertoires, and resources. Neil Fligstein and Doug McAdam (2012) conceptualize society as comprised of multi-institutional fields that exert social power across different levels, ranging from macro to micro-level influences. States, for example, provide public and legal infrastructure, tax citizens directly and indirectly, and provide resources and services in return to citizens and organizations alike, while businesses supply what we eat and wear and dictate when we work and how we travel. In addition, as Roger Friedland and Robert Alford (1991) explain, each institutional domain has its own "logics of action" and behavioral repertoires that shape individual and organizational preferences and actions within their purview. Jürgen Habermas (1984) suggested that in modern society, certain institutional logics, such as that of capitalism, have come to colonize the lifeworld of everyday interactions across domains.

While it may be challenging to discern spirituality in secular or multi-institutional contexts, its complicated relationship with the different contexts in which it abides make it all the more worthy of exploration. As Wendy Cadge and Mary Ellen Konieczny (2014) wrote, spirituality can often be "hidden in plain sight," and, as scholars, we need to try harder to make "invisible religion" and spirituality visible (551). To do so, it is necessary to examine how spiritual practitioners forge together religious, secular, political, and other cultural meanings, practices, and beliefs, in specific historical moments and places with their own constraints and affordances.

By incorporating how organizations and fields affect spirituality, we can better understand the nuanced ways spirituality manifests in relation to social and institutional power psychologically, in interactions with others, as well as across organizations and fields. Under what conditions does spirituality draw upon and come to reinforce powerful social forces such as individualism/collectivism, capitalism, nationalism, science, or ideologies like racism and sexism? And when and how can spirituality instead operate as an empowering or transformative force? In what follows, we start to broach these questions by focusing on five aspects of the relationship between spirituality and power: spiritualities by contexts of secularization; capitalism; organizational dynamics; hegemonic influences and contestation of boundary objects; and social movements and societal change.

Spiritualities by Contexts of Secularization
Nations' and locales' particular historical and cultural pasts lead to "different paths to modernity and secularization," making religion and secularity "inevitably bundled with distinct cultural meanings" (Di et al. 2021, 16). Depending on these histories and contexts, spirituality can operate either in alignment or opposition to the powers that be. Geopolitically, whether spirituality arises in post-Reformation, post-Enlightenment Western countries, in countries colonized by European nations, or in locations elsewhere in the world shapes people's understandings of spirituality. Is spirituality part of religious practice in states favoring a particular tradition or in pluralistic states, like the United States? Or is it part of a search apart from and

in partial opposition to religious institutions (e.g., Ammerman, this volume; Di et al. 2021; Ecklund and Di 2017)? Is spirituality instead a way to maintain relationships with ancestors and local cultures in the face of competing global colonial, economic, or political forces (e.g. Sun, this volume)? Or rather, is spirituality a utilitarian means of self-development, which can enhance one's social prowess and productivity at work (Kucinskas 2019)? It depends on the context in which spirituality is invoked and its relationship to hegemonic cultures and institutions.

While spirituality in Western countries is often intertwined with a culture of individualism, in other places it may be subject to other modernizing influences. Di and her colleagues (Di and Ecklund 2017; Di et al. 2021), for example, show how science and institutional and national contexts affect how spiritual practitioners construct alternative spiritualities. Historical relationships between religion and politics, and countries' subsequent secular and religious landscapes, enable, constrain, and otherwise influence what forms of spirituality emerge. Both French and Taiwanese spiritual scientists, living in societies governed by elite discourses that considered "superstition anathema to civil society" (Di et al. 2021, 17), distanced themselves from the supernatural. Instead, building upon historical cultural streams in their respective locations, Taiwanese spiritual scientists understood their folk religious practices to be spiritual, while the French espoused humanism. By contrast, in the United States and United Kingdom, which had stronger civil religions and historically powerful Christian majorities, spirituality most often was described as "an alternative value system," unaffiliated with a specific religious tradition and at times oppositional to Christianity (Di et al. 2021, 16). Rachel Rinaldo's chapter in this volume further demonstrates how national and international political and religious authorities and opportunity structures shape when, how, and what forms of Sufi spirituality emerged in Indonesia over the past century.

Capitalism

Capitalism and political affordances shape spirituality in both explicit and subtle ways. Whether spirituality is economically supported by being part and parcel of national churches, or whether it receives national recognition, tax exempt status, and a host of other forms of political support, shapes how spirituality evolves. If spiritual teachers need to support themselves in a capitalist market, their teachings and practices will likely differ from those who are financially supported by a state or other groups. For example, Tibetan

Buddhist teachings look quite different today, when traveling Tibetan lamas convey their teachings around the world supported by private donations and book sales, than when monks learned and taught Buddhist teachings under the Tibetan theocracy. As a burgeoning scholarship on mindfulness, yoga, and other forms of spirituality in the West show, such contemporary programs are influenced in manifold ways by neoliberal capitalism (Carrette and King 2005; Jain 2020). Along these lines, Candy Gunther Brown's chapter in our volume shows how laws and economic motives influence how yoga is defined and portrayed in court cases in the United States.

Organizational Climates and Multi-Institutional Fields

There is interplay between spirituality and the organizations and institutions in which it is embedded. Within secular organizations and fields, spirituality may bring in religiously derived cultures or manifest as people sacralize daily activities. Spiritual practitioners' incorporation of spirituality into their daily lives in secular workplaces and institutions may challenge the secular status quo and generate conversation in such locations (Ammerman 2013; Lindsay and Smith 2010) or be used to uphold and reinforce the status quo (Islam et al. 2017).

These processes through which spirituality is locally constituted in secular contexts are "both constrained and enabled by particular organizational climates," occupations, and other hegemonic influences (Di and Ecklund 2017, 2). Secular pressures can operate in many ways, at different levels or "subspheres," of an institution. As Di and Ecklund (2017) found, for example, most Taiwanese scientists largely kept religion and spirituality separate from their research in their labs, which was a core part of their scientific work. Yet some spiritual scientists were willing to raise religious and spiritual concerns more openly in a "nonscientific" tier of their work where they did secondary parts of their job, such as mentoring students. These examples suggest that extant professional, organizational, and other normative social hierarches, which esteem certain tasks and places, shape where spirituality can be brought and how it manifests. In this volume, Cadge and colleagues' chapter on chaplaincy education and Kucinskas's chapter on the movement of spiritual practices into secular institutions further show how spirituality morphs as it moves, in part to appeal to new audiences and fit within new institutions.

Engaging in communal spiritual practices contributes to one's likelihood of breaching secular norms to talk about spirituality at work (Ammerman 2013). Di and Ecklund (2017) also found that those who regularly attended religious services were more likely to talk about spiritual and religious life with colleagues, while those who prayed (mainly privately) were less likely to do so. Thus, it is important to track not only the organizational hierarchies and norms in which spirituality manifests, but also practitioners' religious and spiritual backgrounds, and the interplay between the two.

Hegemonic Power and Contestation of Boundary Objects

Contestation may arise over spiritual content based on the group, institutional, and national settings in which spiritual practitioners abide. Spirituality is a "porous" cultural boundary object that senders transmit and translate for receivers across social space and time and is "open to a wide range of interpretations and debates" (Pagis et al. 2018, 596). As an "empty signifier" (Laclau 1996, 36), it draws upon, encodes, and bridges "oppositional organizational elements" (Islam et al. 2017, 1). Spirituality is also polysemic; it can have different meanings, which teachers and practitioners can strategically employ in distinct ways to different audiences (Brown, this volume; Kucinskas 2019; Lindsay and Smith 2010). Spiritual and religious adherents can also creatively "circumnavigate moral dilemmas and conflicts of allegiance rather than incite conflict borne of religious conviction" (Lindsay and Smith 2010, 742). Due to the flexible, adaptive nature of spirituality, in some organizational contexts, such as corporate business, it can ultimately reinforce neoliberalism and other dominant professional cultures (Islam et al. 2017; Purser 2018). Spirituality is also often rooted in movements, organizations, and broader systems marked by gendered, racialized, and heteronormative hierarchies (Acker 1992; Jain 2018; Kucinskas 2020; Perry 2012; Ray 2019; Wilde 2018; Yukich and Edgell 2020). Despite the best of intentions, as Sam Perry (2012) contends, such systems can be integral to the moral habitus in which practitioners are a part, which may delimit or infiltrate the forms of spirituality possible.

Spirituality, Social Movements, and Societal Change

Spirituality can ground, infuse, and fortify social change efforts as well. Nonviolent activists in the American civil rights movement, for example, such as Rev. Martin Luther King and those trained in the Nashville schools, drew upon spiritual resources from the black church, Christianity, and Gandhi's philosophy of nonviolence (Isaac et al. 2012; Morris 1986). Mary Pattillo-McCoy (1998) similarly showed how black spirituality infused political organizing in Chicago. More recently, Extinction Rebellion, a spiritually

22 BRIAN STEENSLAND, JAIME KUCINSKAS, AND ANNA SUN

oriented British climate change protest group, made headlines in 2019 with their traffic-stopping meditation practices (Abrahams 2019).

Spirituality may also operate as an innovative cultural force. As Andrea Jain (2018) shows, in recreating "exotic" Indian devotional practices, early twentieth-century yoga challenged the American Protestant moral establishment's "mainstream cultural templates for sexuality" with its emphasis on "family-centered, reproductive marital sexuality," by instead promoting "starkly contrasting sacred sexual values: sexual renunciation on the one hand or sexual liberty on the other" (34). However, Jain concludes that by the century's end, yoga instead came to typify mainstream American cultural ideals of physical and spiritual well-being, rather than provide alternatives to them. Mindfulness has followed a similar trajectory. While it was promoted as "orthogonal" to mainstream capitalism as it gained popularity, it came to align more closely with the status quo in many places (Kucinskas 2019; Islam et al. 2017).

A common assumption among spiritual practitioners is that internal spiritual transformation will lead to social transformation. Scholarship on religion and spirituality suggests otherwise. Movements such as mindfulness and evangelicalism, which center upon personal growth and relational spiritual perspectives, rather than directly addressing systems, often have limited efficacy in addressing complex social problems (Emerson and Smith 2000; Kucinskas 2019; Marti et al. 2020; Perry 2017; Smith and Emerson 1998). Ultimately spirituality often tilts toward accommodating and reinforcing hegemonic cultural systems, unless maintained in minority or countercultural communities (e.g., Shelton, this volume) or bridging practices are developed to directly connect spiritual practices with social problems through movement tactics (Isaac et al. 2012).

Previewing the Chapters to Come

The first part of the book examines spirituality in context, both in terms of how the notion of "spirituality" is conceptualized in different global contexts, and in terms of its contextualization in the fabric of lived social experiences. Nancy Ammerman's chapter discusses situated spirituality and its diverse expressions in various contexts of lived religious practice, and suggests that lived religion is "a fused whole where spirituality is but one dimension." Linda Woodhead's analysis of the reconceptualization of spirituality in contemporary Britain focuses on the re-emergence of the polytheistic gods in the process of what she terms the "dereformation" of Europe. Anna Sun's examination of the boundary work between the concepts of "religion" and "spirituality" in Chinese society centers on the relational nature of these concepts, whose dynamics are determined by the social and historical conditions of the Chinese religious landscape. Afe Adogame's discussion of African spirituality shows how it is "a spirituality of the marketplace that encompasses a matrix of worldviews, belief systems and ritual practice," influencing not only African life, but also "African diasporic communities in their new sociocultural locations." Bradley Wright's chapter suggests that methodological choices shape our understanding of spirituality and offers innovative new approaches for empirical studies of spirituality. Alyssa Rockenbach's analysis of the changes in the "spiritual but not religious" identification among college students demonstrates that it is closely related to the context of one's social and cultural environment. Jason Shelton's examination of the racial differences in the way blacks and whites view themselves as "spiritual persons" offers an important account of the racial and ethnic context of spirituality in our everyday experience.

The second part of the book situates spirituality in distinct dimensions of practice. In her study of a vipassana meditation retreat center, Michal Pagis explores the social dimension of spiritual cultivation. She documents the microdynamics of "collective solitude," showing the ways that shared spiritual settings—meditation centers, yoga studios, pilgrimages—create private experiences of transcendence that are facilitated by group practices. Melissa Wilcox examines embodiment in her chapter on leather/BDSM spirituality. She draws out the significance of embodied spiritual practices, including sexual ones, and embodied and affective empiricism for expanding our perspective on spirituality beyond belief and identity. In her chapter on rural Malawi, where spirituality can be easily subsumed by religion, Ann Swidler teases out the differences between the two. She argues that spirituality as lived is sought out when the demands of ordinary life become difficult to bear, links people to transcendent sources of power and meaning, and replenishes inner strength and vitality. Robert Brenneman looks at the discourse of spirituality in Central America, particularly how the terminology of spirituality is used in the context of efforts to reduce youth violence. He identifies four central meanings that, while distinct, all provide resources for describing and addressing complex social problems.

The third part of the book shows some of the manifold ways in which spirituality is influenced by the social hierarches and fields in which it is embedded. Stef Aupers's chapter brings attention to how the overwhelming influence and power of institutions in shaping contemporary life can leave individuals feeling powerless and suspicious of the greater forces shaping their lives. As a result, spiritual seeking and conspiracy theories become appealing sources of sense-making and meaning. Candy Gunther Brown shows how yoga is socially constructed in different and sometimes contradictory ways in American courts. Yoga advocates define their practices as religious or secular, with different spiritual valences, based on what serves their interests in each particular case. Wendy Cadge and her colleagues describe how spiritual chaplaincy programs are constructed in an effort to bridge religious training with secular workplaces in pluralistic settings. Based on their respective religious traditions, these programs create distinctive curricula to help their students bridge differences and relate to people from other backgrounds. Moving across the world, Rachel Rinaldo's chapter discusses Sufism's contested status in Muslim countries generally, and shows in Indonesia specifically how its relation to powerholders has changed throughout the country's history. Spirituality and Sufism have experienced revival and increased appeal in recent years, in part due to their alignment with conventional Islamic practice. Jaime Kucinskas's chapter conceptualizes spirituality as a porous boundary object—or empty signifier—which changes as it moves from transmitters to receivers, in part based on their contexts. As an intermediary object, spirituality often maintains hegemonic power when situated in secular institutions. In the volume's concluding chapter, Brian Steensland develops a framework based on our volume's themes and our relational perspective on spirituality for addressing three persistent questions: What is spirituality? How does spirituality influence? And where is spirituality headed?

References

Abbott, Andrew. 1995. "Things of Boundaries." *Social Research* 62(4): 857–82.
Abrahams, Matthew. 2019. "The Buddhists of Extinction Rebellion." *Tricycle*, September 16. https://tricycle.org/trikedaily/extinction-rebellion-buddhists/.
Acker, Joan. 1992. "From Sex Roles to Gendered Institutions." *Contemporary Sociology* 21(5): 565–69.

INTRODUCTION 25

Albanese, Catherine L. 2007. *A Republic of Mind: A Cultural History of American Metaphysical Religion*. New Haven, CT: Yale University Press.

Ammerman, Nancy, ed. 2007. *Everyday Religion: Observing Modern Religious Lives*. New York: Oxford University Press.

Ammerman, Nancy. 2013. "Spiritual but Not Religious? Beyond Binary Choices in the Study of Religion." *Journal for the Scientific Study of Religion* 52(2): 258–78.

Ammerman, Nancy. 2014. *Sacred Stories, Spiritual Tribes: Finding Religion in Everyday Life*. New York: Oxford University Press.

Ammerman, Nancy. 2020. "Rethinking Religion: Toward a Practice Approach." *American Journal of Sociology* 126(1): 6–51.

Asad, Talal. 1993. *Genealogies of Religion: Discipline and Reasons of Power in Christianity and Islam*. Baltimore: Johns Hopkins University Press.

Asad, Talal. 2014. "Thinking about Tradition, Religion, and Politics in Egypt Today." *Critical Inquiry* 42(1): 166–214.

Aupers, Stef, and Dick Houtman. 2006. "Beyond the Spiritual Supermarket: The Social and Public Significance of New Age Spirituality." *Journal of Contemporary Religion* 21(2): 201–22.

Bellah, Robert, Richard Madsen, William Sullivan, Ann Swidler, and Steven Tipton. 1985. *Habits of the Heart: Individualism and Commitment in American Life*. Berkeley: University of California Press.

Bender, Courtney. 2010. *The New Metaphysicals: Spirituality and the American Religious Imagination*. Chicago: University of Chicago Press.

Berghuijs, Joantine, Jos Pieper, and Cok Bakker. 2013. "Being 'Spiritual' and Being 'Religious' in Europe: Diverging Life Orientations." *Journal of Contemporary Religion* 28(1): 15–32.

Besecke, Kelly. 2014. *You Can't Put God in a Box: Thoughtful Spirituality in a Rational Age*. New York: Oxford University Press.

Bruce, Steve. 2011. *Secularization: In Defence of an Unfashionable Theory*. New York: Oxford University Press.

Cadge, Wendy, and Mary Ellen Konieczny. 2014. "'Hidden in Plain Sight': The Significance of Religion and Spirituality in Secular Organizations." *Sociology of Religion* 75(4): 551–63.

Carrette, Jeremy, and Richard King. 2005. *Selling Spirituality: The Silent Takeover of Religion*. New York: Psychology Press.

Chakrabarty, Dipesh. 2000. *Provincializing Europe: Postcolonial Thought and Historical Difference*. Princeton, NJ: Princeton University Press.

Chappell, David L. 2004. *A Stone of Hope: Prophetic Religion and the Death of Jim Crow*. Chapel Hill: University of North Carolina Press.

Clark, Terry Nichols. 1973. *Community Power and Policy Outputs*. Beverly Hills, CA: Sage Publications.

Davidman, Lynn. 2015. *Becoming Un-Orthodox: Stories of Ex-Hasidic Jews*. New York: Oxford University Press.

DeGloma, Thomas. 2014. *Seeing the Light: The Social Logic of Personal Discovery*. Chicago: University of Chicago Press.

Di, Di, and Elaine H. Ecklund. 2017. "Producing Sacredness and Defending Secularity: Faith in the Workplace of Taiwanese Scientists." *Socius* 3: 1–15. https://doi.org/ 10.1177/2378023117733739.

Di, Di, Simranjit Khalsa, Robert A. Thomson, and Elaine Howard Ecklund. 2021. "Alternative Spirituality among Global Scientists." *Sociological Quarterly* 62(1): 187–208.

Douglas, Mary. 1986. *How Institutions Think*. Syracuse, NY: Syracuse University Press.

Durkheim, Émile. [1912] 1995. *The Elementary Forms of Religious Life*. Translated by K. Field. New York: Free Press.

Ecklund, Elaine H., and Di Di. 2017. "A Catholic Science? Italian Scientists Construct Religious Identity during Religious Shifts." *Philosophy, Theology and the Sciences* 4(1): 94–114.

Ellwood, Robert S. 1979. *Alternative Altars: Unconventional and Eastern Spirtualty in America*. Chicago: University of Chicago Press.

Emerson, Michael O., and Christian Smith. 2000. *Divided by Faith: Evangelical Religion and the Problem of Race in America*. New York: Oxford University Press.

Eisenstadt, S. N. 2000. "Multiple Modernities." *Daedalus* 129(1): 1–29.

Fligstein, Neil, and Doug McAdam. 2012. *A Theory of Fields*. New York: Oxford University Press.

Foucault, Michel. 2001. *The Essential Works of Michel Foucault 1954–1984*. Vol. 3, *Power*. Edited by J. D. Faubion. New York: New Press.

Friedland, Roger, and Robert R. Alford. 1991. "Bringing Society Back In: Symbols, Practices, and Institutional Contradictions." Pp. 232–66 in *The New Institutionalism in Organizational Analysis*, edited by W. W. Powell and P. J. DiMaggio. Chicago: University of Chicago Press.

Fuller, Robert C. 2001. *Spiritual but Not Religious: Understanding Unchurched America*. New York: Oxford University Press.

George, Linda, David B. Larson, Harold G. Koenig, and Michael E. McCullough. 2000. "Spirituality and Health: What We Know, What We Need to Know." *Journal of Social and Clinical Psychology* 19(1): 102–16.

Gieryn, Thomas F. 1999. *Cultural Boundaries of Science: Credibility on the Line*. Chicago: University of Chicago Press.

Goldman, Marion, and Steven Pfaff. 2018. *The Spiritual Virtuoso: Personal Faith and Social Transformation*. New York: Bloomsbury Academic.

Habermas, Jürgen. 1984. *The Theory of Communicative Action*. Vol. 2, *Lifeworld and System: A Critique of Functionalist Reason*. Translated by T. McCarthy. Boston: Beacon Press.

Hadot, Pierre. 1995. *Philosophy as a Way of Life*. London: Wiley-Blackwell.

Harding, Sandra. 2009. "Standpoint Theories: Productively Controversial." *Hypatia* 24(4): 192–200.

Heelas, Paul, and Linda Woodhead, with Benjamin Seel, Bronislaw Szerszynski, and Karin Tusting. 2005. *The Spiritual Revolution: Why Religion Is Giving Way to Spirituality*. Malden, MA: Blackwell.

Hill, Peter C., Kenneth I. Pargament, Ralph W. Hood Jr., Michael E. McCullough, James P. Swyers, David B. Larson, and Brian J. Zinnbauer. 2000. "Conceptualizing Religion and Spirituality: Points of Commonality, Points of Departure." *Journal for the Theory of Social Behavior* 30(1): 51–77.

Houtman, Dick, and Stef Aupers. 2007. "The Spiritual Turn and the Decline of Tradition: The Spread of Post-Christian Spirituality in 14 Western Countries, 1981–2000." *Journal for the Scientific Study of Religion* 46(3): 305–20.

Isaac, Larry W., Daniel B. Cornfield, Dennis C. Dickerson, James M. Lawson, and Jonathan S. Coley. 2012. "'Movement Schools' and Dialogical Diffusion of Nonviolent Praxis: Nashville Workshops in the Southern Civil Rights Movement." Pp. 155–84 in *Research in Social Movements, Conflict, and Change*, vol. 34, *Nonviolent Conflict and Civil Resistance*, edited by S. E. Nepstad and L. R. Kurtz. Bingley, UK: Emerald Group Publishing.

Islam, Gazi, Marie Holm, and Mira Karjalainen. 2017. "Sign of the Times: Workplace Mindfulness as an Empty Signifier." *Organization*, November, 1–27. https://doi.org/10.1177/1350508417740643.

Jain, Andrea. 2018. "Subversive Spiritualities: Yoga's Complex Role in the Narrative of Sex and Religion in the Twentieth Century U.S." Pp. 34–53 in *Devotions and Desires: Religion and Sexuality in the Twentieth Century United States*, edited by G. Frank, B. Moreton, and H. R. White. Chapel Hill: University of North Carolina Press.

Jain, Andrea. 2020. *Peace, Love, Yoga*. New York: Oxford University Press.

Johnston, Erin. 2016. "The Enlightened Self: Identity and Aspiration in Two Communities of Practice." *Religions* 7(7): 92. https://doi.org/10.1177%2F2378023117733739.

Johnston, Erin. 2017. "Failing to Learn, or Learning to Fail? Accounting for Persistence in the Acquisition of Spiritual Disciplines." *Qualitative Sociology* 40(3): 353–72.

King, Richard. 1999. *Orientalism and Religion: Postcolonial Theory, India, and "The Mystic East"*. London: Routledge.

Koenig, Harold G. 2008. "Concerns about Measuring 'Spirituality' in Research." *Journal of Nervous and Mental Disease* 196(5): 349–55.

Koenig, Harold G. 2013. *Spirituality in Patient Care: Why, How, When, and What*. West Conshohocken, PA: Templeton Press.

Kucinskas, Jaime. 2019. *The Mindful Elite: Mobilizing from the Inside Out*. New York: Oxford University Press.

Kucinskas, Jaime. 2020. "Racial and Class Gaps in Buddhist-Inspired Organizing." Pp. 178–200 in *Religion Is Raced: Understanding American Religion in the Twenty-First Century*, edited by G. Yukich and P. Edgell. New York: New York University Press.

Kucinskas, Jaime, Bradley R. E. Wright, D. Matthew Ray, and John Ortberg. 2017. "States of Spiritual Awareness by Time, Activity, and Social Interaction." *Journal for the Scientific Study of Religion* 56(2): 418–37.

Kucinskas, Jaime, Bradley R. E. Wright, and Stuart Riepl. 2018. "The Interplay between Meaning and Sacred Awareness in Everyday Life: Evidence from a Daily Smartphone Study." *International Journal for the Psychology of Religion* 28(2): 71–88.

Laclau, Ernesto. 1996. *Emancipation(s)*. London: Verso Books.

Lamont, Michelle, and Virag Molnar. 2002. "The Study of Boundaries across the Social Sciences." *Annual Review of Sociology* 28: 167–95.

Lindsay, D. Michael, and Bradley C. Smith. 2010. "Accounting by Faith: The Negotiated Logic of Elite Evangelicals' Workplace Decision-Making." *Journal of the American Academy of Religion* 78(3): 721–49.

Marler, Penny Long, and C. Kirk Hadaway. 2002. "'Being Religious' or 'Being Spiritual' in America: A Zero-Sum Proposition." *Journal for the Scientific Study of Religion* 41(2): 289–300.

Martí, Gerardo. 2020. "White Christian Libertarianism and the Trump Presidency." Pp. 19–39 in *Religion Is Raced: Understanding American Religion in the Twenty-First Century*, edited by G. Yukich and P. Edgell. New York: New York University Press.

McGuire, Meredith B. 2008. *Lived Religion: Faith and Practice in Everyday Life*. New York: Oxford University Press.

Mercadante, Linda A. 2014. *Belief without Borders: Inside the Minds of the Spiritual but Not Religious*. New York: Oxford University Press.

Morris, Aldon D. 1986. *The Origins of the Civil Rights Movement*. New York: Free Press.

Nietzsche, Friedrich. [1887] 2009. *On the Genealogy of Morals*. Translated by D. Smith. Oxford: Oxford University Press.

Pagis, Michal. 2019. *Inward: Vipassana Meditation and the Embodiment of the Self*. Chicago: University of Chicago Press.

Pagis, Michal, Wendy Cadge, and Orly Tal. 2018. "Translating Spirituality: Universalism and Particularism in the Diffusion of Spiritual Care from the United States to Israel." *Sociological Forum* 33(3): 596–618.

Palmer, David, and Elijah Siegler. 2017. *Dream Trippers: Global Daoism and the Predicament of Modern Spirituality*. Chicago: University of Chicago Press.

Palmisano, Stefania. 2010. "Moving Forward in Catholicism: New Monastic Organizations, Innovation, Recognition, Legitimation." *International Journal for the Study of New Religions* 1(2): 49–64.

Parsons, William B, ed. 2018. *Being Spiritual but Not Religious: Past, Present, and Future(s)*. New York: Routledge.

Pattillo-McCoy, Mary. 1998. "Church Culture as a Strategy of Action in the Black Community." *American Sociological Review* 63(6): 767–84.

Perrow, Charles. 1991. "A Society of Organizations." *Theory and Society* 20(6): 725–62.

Perry, Samuel L. 2012. "Racial Habitus, Moral Conflict, and White Moral Hegemony within Interracial Evangelical Organizations." *Qualitative Sociology* 35(1): 89–108.

Perry, Samuel L. 2017. *Growing God's Family: The Global Orphan Care Movement and the Limits of Evangelical Activism*. New York: New York University Press.

Purser, Ron E. 2018. "Critical Perspectives on Corporate Mindfulness." *Journal of Management, Spirituality and Religion* 15(2): 105–8.

Ray, Victor. 2019. "A Theory of Racialized Organizations." *American Sociological Review* 84(1): 26–53.

Roof, Wade Clark. 1999. *Spiritual Marketplace: Baby Boomers and the Remaking of American Religion*. Princeton, NJ: Princeton University Press.

Schmidt, Leigh Eric. 2005. *Restless Souls: The Making of American Spirituality*. San Francisco, CA: HarperCollins.

Seager, Richard Hughes. 2012. *Buddhism in America*. New York: Columbia University Press.

Sheldrake, Philip. 2012. *Spirituality: A Very Short Introduction*. Oxford: Oxford University Press.

Smith, Christian, ed. 2003. *The Secular Revolution: Power, Interests, and Conflict in the Secularization of Public Life*. Berkeley: University of California Press.

Smith, Christian. 2017. *Religion: What It Is, How It Works, and Why It Matters*. Princeton, NJ: Princeton University Press.

Smith, Christian, and Michael Emerson. 1998. *American Evangelicalism: Embattled and Thriving*. Chicago: University of Chicago Press.

Sointu, Eeva, and Linda Woodhead. 2008. "Spirituality, Gender, and Expressive Selfhood." *Journal for the Scientific Study of Religion* 47(2): 259–76.

Steensland, Brian, Xiaoyun Wang, and Lauren Chism Schmidt. 2018. "Spirituality: What Does It Mean and to Whom?" *Journal for the Scientific Study of Religion* 57(3): 450–72.

Sun, Anna. 2013. *Confucianism as a World Religion: Contested Histories and Contemporary Realities*. Princeton, NJ: Princeton University Press.

Sun, Anna. 2021. "To Be or Not to Be a Confucian: Explicit and Implicit Religious Identities in the Global Twenty-First Century." Pp. 211–35 in *Annual Review of the Sociology of Religion*, vol. 11: *Chinese Religions Going Global*. Leiden: Brill.

Tweed, Thomas A. 2000. *The American Encounter with Buddhism, 1844–1912: Victorian Culture and the Limits of Dissent*. Chapel Hill: University of North Carolina Press.

Wilde, Melissa J. 2018. "Complex Religion: Interrogating Assumptions of Independence in the Study of Religion." *Sociology of Religion* 79(3): 287–98.

Winchester, Daniel. 2016. "A Hunger for God: Embodied Metaphor as Cultural Cognition in Action." *Social Forces* 95(2): 585–606.

Wood, Matthew, and Christopher Bunn. 2009. "Strategy in a Religious Network: A Bourdieuian Critique of the Sociology of Spirituality." *Sociology* 43(2): 286–303.

Wuthnow, Robert. 1998. *After Heaven: Spirituality in America since the 1950s*. Berkeley: University of California Press.

Wuthnow, Robert. 2020. *What Happens When We Practice Religion? Textures of Devotion in Everyday Life*. Princeton, NJ: Princeton University Press.

Yukich, Grace, and Penny Edgell, eds. 2020. *Religion Is Raced: Understanding American Religion in the Twenty-First Century*. New York: New York University Press.

PART I
CONTEXT

1

Social Practices and Cultural Contexts

Frameworks for the Study of Spirituality

Nancy T. Ammerman

Spirituality and religion seem to be in something of a battle for rhetorical high ground. Both the battle and the phenomena themselves, however, are situated in ways that demand careful attention. Research has begun to demonstrate, for example, that in the United States, religion as an identity and practice is highly implicated in spirituality as an identity and practice (Steensland et al. 2018). I will argue here that if we are to situate spirituality as a part of the social world, we need to understand it, first, as *one dimension* of religious practice, but the dimension that makes religious practice distinctive from other social practices. And second, spirituality as part of religious practice must be understood as a phenomenon that is shaped by the *cultural and legal contexts* in which it exists. That is, I will argue for the utility of understanding spirituality as a distinct aspect of, not a pale replacement for, religion. But more importantly, I will elaborate four macrosocial contexts (plus one important variation) that each shape quite differently the practice of religion and its spiritual dimensions.

Religion as Multidimensional Practice

The study of spirituality has been considerably advanced by the advent of emphasis on "lived religion." By pointing to everyday practices and ordinary people, new generations and populations of researchers have shown us how everything from home altars to tattoos needs to be in the purview of the social scientific study of religion. By focusing on nonelites and practices in everyday life, however, lived religion has often missed the embodied experience and shared religious understanding that exists inside religious institutions as well. Having pointed to the importance of what ordinary people *do*, rather

Nancy T. Ammerman, *Social Practices and Cultural Contexts* In: *Situating Spirituality.* Edited by: Brian Steensland, Jaime Kucinskas, and Anna Sun, Oxford University Press. © Oxford University Press 2022.
DOI: 10.1093/oso/9780197565001.003.0002

34 NANCY T. AMMERMAN

than just what they think and believe, scholars have also failed to take advantage of the opportunity to link the study of religious practice to more general theories of social practice. What I have elaborated elsewhere (Ammerman 2020) is how that theoretical link can be made; what I want to show here is how that can make a difference in the study of spirituality.

Social practices of all kinds are, in the words of Theodore Schatzki (2001, 11), "embodied, materially mediated arrays of human activity centrally organized around shared practical understanding." If religion is a kind of social practice, we can look for it wherever it happens and see both its social dimensions and the distinctive patterns that make it religious. Studying religion as practice means recognizing that every social situation requires practical know-how. People have to retrieve expectations from their cognitive storehouse of patterns that have been formed by previous interactions (DiMaggio 1997; Lizardo and Strand 2010). Subtle cues are constituted by the social object at hand, a set of relationships, and the action called forth (Martin 2011). Beginning with religion as practice means that we start with the patterned regularities in what situations people recognize as religious and how they do what they do in response. We look for the shared practical understanding—rather than a presumed set of beliefs or worldview—that enables people to act together in ways they define as spiritual or religious. Lived religious practice is religious social knowledge in action.

Practices do not require a comprehensive "worldview"; indeed they may happen seemingly without thinking, lodged in habitual patterns (Bourdieu 1990) such as touching a mezuzah or crossing oneself. But practices are not only the taken-for-granted patterns in a given setting, but also the improvisations of the actors. This is so, in part, because all social interaction is inherently hybrid (Decoteau 2016; Sewell 1992). Patterns from one part of social life are always available in other parts of life, to be called on for new uses. Using Swidler's terms (1986), we can examine culture, in this case religion, that is present both in the "settled" habitual patterns that require no rationalized explanations and in the rituals and discourses and strategies that are consciously created to achieve collective goals. Religious practices are, that is, both habitual and emergent, structured and agentic. Likewise, because fields of interaction intersect, lived religious practices are not confined to a single institution. While it may be useful to think about distinct structural domains and the cultural logics they sustain, the reality of everyday life is that practices travel across those boundaries. Practices can be found across contexts and mutually constitute the way those contexts are structured and experienced.

Studying religion as practice allows us to draw more systematically on both practice theory and the accumulated body of research in lived religion to set out an orienting framework. This framework starts with a set of aspects that we might describe as foundational to human action in the cultural world. While a practice itself may be experienced as a fused whole, as Levi Martin (2011) argues, it has dimensions that can be recognized and partitioned out for study. Theories of culture and cognition have, for example, paid attention to knowledge that emerges from bodily, emotional, moral, and aesthetic judgments (Martin 2010), just as Schatzki's definition begins with the assertion that practices are embodied and materially mediated.

Likewise, recent overviews of the lived religion literature have pointed to common multidimensional themes. Penny Edgell's (2012) outline of a cultural approach to the sociology of religion lists emotion, embodiment, and narratives as the typical foci of study. Mary Jo Neitz (2011) pointed to materiality and locality, embodiment, and spirituality as domains that should continue to be addressed. Also, in an analysis of sixty-four journal articles published since David Hall's 1997 book, I (2016) identified embodiment, materiality, and discourse as consistent themes. These overviews provide a starting point for examining lived religion's intersections with practice theories. They allow us to identify a set of salient qualities that religious practice shares with all social practice, as well as what distinctively makes a practice religious. Those shared qualities, I am proposing, include *embodiment, materiality, emotion, aesthetics, moral judgment*, and *narrative*, with *spirituality* as the distinctively religious dimension.[1] The first six dimensions are common to all social practice. It is embodied and emotional, takes place in material contexts, involves aesthetic and moral judgments, and is structured (and explained) by narratives. What distinguishes religious practice from other social practices is its spiritual dimension. When we assess lived religious practices, our attention can fruitfully be drawn to the full range of qualities of those practices, including but not limited to spirituality, analyzing how they are combined and interrelated.

The Spiritual in Religious Practice

The shared human activity that concerns us here is *religious* practice, that is, patterns of action that presume a shared understanding that is perceived by the actors and/or can be analyzed by observers as including a spiritual, beyond-the-ordinary dimension.[2] It may or may not be personified or all-powerful or relied on for assistance. Spirituality is simply the inhabiting of a reality that goes beyond ordinary empirical perceptions. This is a notion that builds on Alfred Schutz's (1945) phenomenology. Human beings, he asserts, can act within multiple realities in addition to and alongside what he identifies as the foundational reality of shared everyday action.[3] The contents of these "finite provinces of meaning," in turn, can be communicated, shared, and acted within; they are not merely subjective experiences, but social ones. Indeed, the spiritual connections being analyzed may be indirect, invoked by way of participation in institutions, identities, and groups that claim to represent a spiritual presence and that create and maintain settings and routinized practices to sustain (and control) it. The key identifying element is simply the pattern of reference—either subjectively experienced or institutionalized—to a more-than-ordinary reality.

This sort of "etic" approach to recognizing religious practice can be useful to an analyst across multiple cultural contexts where definitions and language differ and things may not even be called "religion." But our analysis of the spiritual dimension of religious practice must be "emic," as well; that is, it must include attention to the use of native social categories and the experiences they reference. How are terms like "religious" and "spiritual" used across cultural contexts? Rather than positing an essential core that universally constitutes spirituality, the study of religious practice needs a lens that can adjust both to the variations in the spiritual dimensions of religious practice and to the variations in how religion and spirituality are perceived to be related to each other. Settings will vary in the degree to which they evoke or expect any particular spiritual state as part of religious practice. They will also vary in the degree to which they identify "spirituality" as part of or competing with "religion."[4] Rather than assuming that spirituality is a shorthand or substitute for religion, we must situate that distinction in its own cultural context.

Religious social practice, then, is multidimensional and includes both direct and indirect participation in action and with actors that are nonordinary. It happens across institutional sectors and encompasses both indigenous understandings and the official impositions of categories on that interaction. It may be habitual or creative, but it is constituted by socially recognizable configurations of material, embodied interactions, configurations that include or reference a spiritual dimension.

SOCIAL PRACTICES AND CULTURAL CONTEXTS 37

When we analyze spirituality as a dimension of lived religious practice, we can note, for example, that it varies in intensity and form and in the degree to which it is the dominant dimension of the practice. Some religious practices may barely reference anything spiritual, while others may be primarily centered on achieving a particular spiritual state. Those states can themselves vary from a quiet sense of awe to a completely alternative state of awareness. From meditating mystics to whirling dervishes to charismatic tongue speakers and shamans performing healing rituals, extraordinary spiritual experiences surely must be included in any understanding of religion. The "taming" of spirituality in Western middle-class culture threatens to blind us to vast realms of the spirit. Whether or not observers believe in the reality or authenticity of such experiences, they are seen as real by the participants and are foundational to many religious communities.

Paying attention to the spiritual dimension of religious experience can also allow us to understand social actions that are not explainable in other terms. Without taking account of perceived spiritual power, we cannot explain why otherwise powerless people act in powerful ways. McGuire (2008) points to the way lived religious practices in many communities assume that divine power is accessible and efficacious. People may invoke sacred words or mantras or touch sacred objects, expecting that divine power will bless or heal or purify. Individual and communal action is then premised on that perceived power and insight. This is a relational and a cognitive experience—a sense of being in intimate relationship with divine beings and equally a sense of knowing something that is not derived from immediate sense experience.[5] Studying spirituality as a distinct dimension of religion will entail attention to the substantive differences in its expression, the social structures of its interpretation, and the varying consequences of those expressions.

These kinds of extraordinary spiritual connections can also convey power and authority to the bearer of them—what Weber called charisma ([1922] 1946). And as he pointed out, authority derived in this way is inherently disruptive to the institutional powers that are based on tradition or bureaucratic rationality. The spiritual dimension of lived religious practice can have dramatic effects. Attention to the nature and variation within this dimension of religious practice can open sociological possibilities that extend far beyond the "spiritual" pursuits of middle-class Western seekers who reject "religion."

Religious Practice and Its Contexts

Recognizing that religion and spirituality are contextually specific categories means that we would do well to identify the macro- and microstructural variations in how religious practice is named and organized. At the macro level, what is named and authorized as religious? What sorts of experiences of the sacred are included and excluded, and how do authorities police the use of the category?[6] What are the pervasive cultural norms that encourage or discourage religious and spiritual practice? And how is religious practice situated in relation to systems of power? The shared knowledge that structures everyday practice includes larger cultural expectations about where and how religious practices can and should be enacted. That shared knowledge is also conditioned by intersecting systems of power. Not all actors have equal access to schemas from diverse settings or tactics for resisting exclusion. Available practices follow lines of power and influence that are structured by class, race, gender, and religious authority. When actors assess their possible actions in a religious practice, those intersecting statuses are likely to be in play (Avishai et al. 2015).

The dynamics of race and gender have often been on the agenda of those studying religious and spiritual practice, but most lived religion research has concerned micro-level social processes, largely ignoring questions of larger structural constraints. That has had the unfortunate consequence of perpetuating sociologists' focus on religion in Western democracies, where institutional religion is now relatively weak and individual choice is taken for granted. Spirituality is imagined as a replacement for what once was. However, everyday spirituality must be understood in the very different legal and cultural contexts around the world. If we are to understand religious and spiritual practice, we need a framework for thinking beyond the North Atlantic. The framework I propose here begins with four ideal-typical macro-level contexts, and one significant combination of them. These types of context are not mutually exclusive, nor are they necessarily descriptive of an entire society or nation-state. Rather, they identify differences in modal expectations for the fields within which religious practices and attendant spiritualities will be found and the modes of regulation that will constrain or encourage religious action.

The first kind of context is one I call *entangled*. People in many societies engage in religious and spiritual practices that are so highly entangled with everyday practical affairs that it is impossible to think of them as distinct

SOCIAL PRACTICES AND CULTURAL CONTEXTS   39

forms of social life, and they certainly are not formally organized into modern institutions or subject to official credentialing. *Spirituality is fused with action that is also economic, political, or familial.* There is, in fact, something like a "sacred canopy" (Berger 1967), but one of practice rather than ideas. Such fully entangled societies may be relatively rare, but it is useful to remind ourselves that Western notions about where religion belongs are not always applicable. Ellis and ter Haar (2007, 386), for example, argue that understanding politics in Africa requires an approach that recognizes "distinctive modes of acquiring knowledge about the world, characterised by a holistic approach in which the sacred and the secular can be said to constitute one organic reality."

Perceiving and acting on spirit-infused understandings of the world is not confined to Africa, of course, nor is it exclusively the domain of "traditional" societies. There may be religiously entangled times and places in the social life in any society. Small groups can organize themselves as religious communal societies and attempt to bring all of life into a similarly entangled religious whole (Davidman 1991; Kraybill and Bowman 2001). It is therefore useful to think about a continuum of religious entanglement, but to recognize that one end of that continuum is anchored by a widely shared high degree of overlap between religion and everyday social action, with spiritual presence everywhere. Even within such entangled contexts, however, the spiritual dimension of practice can vary widely. What matters in religious practice may be material or bodily engagements as much as any extraordinary spiritual encounters. Religious practice is fully multidimensional, even as it intersects with other domains of social practice.

A second, rather different sort of entanglement exists where there is an organized, *established* religious tradition. In these contexts there is both an organized entity that claims authority over religious practice and an organized state that legitimizes that authority.[7] Again, there is a continuum, since every state regulates religion in some measure (Hurd 2015), and religious minorities nearly always exist alongside officially recognized religious groups. But where there is an establishment (even an unofficial or legally "disestablished" one), both minorities and the majority are fundamentally shaped by the majority's religious ritual and tradition. From registering a birth to burying the dead to setting the calendar of holidays, majority religious culture imposes itself on everyone (Beaman et al. 2016). To the extent that states establish a national religion, many activities of everyday life may be at once civic and religious, and legacies of establishment religious culture can linger

40   NANCY T. AMMERMAN

without individuals believing official doctrines or expressing much of a spiritual sense (Davie 2015). In monopoly or postmonopoly societies, family, culture, education, politics, and civic life are entwined with religious identity and religious practice, but spirituality may be relatively absent. While religion is pervasive, *spirituality is optional.*

The spiritual dimension of established religions may be more apparent as it is revived and redefined—in different ways—by ethnic groups and by nationalists. Religious symbols and rituals can come to express ethnic identities, and here *spirituality expresses collectivity.*[8] The Virgin of Guadalupe, for example, is a manifestly religious symbol, surrounded by a wealth of religious practice, at the same time that she is a representation of being Mexican, especially for those who have left their homeland behind. Other religion-state links are more explicitly political and often contentious (Friedland 2001; Soper and Fetzer 2018; Whitehead and Perry 2020). Religious identity can become a highly contested political assertion about the legitimacy of one's place and power, a legitimacy that is entangled in religious practice and can have an intensely spiritual character in the veneration of religio-nationalist symbols (Sells 2003). Religious nationalists operate within the structure of modern nation-states but attempt to fill the state with religious cultural content, some of which may have already been present and some of which may have been invented or reinvented. It is worth paying attention to the particular effects of the spiritual dimension of these religious nationalist practices, as well as to the ways immigrant ethnicity may be reinforced by the spiritual intensity of rituals and material reminders.

A significant variation on the establishment context is present when the establishment was imposed as part of a colonial empire.[9] When indigenous religious practice (usually of the entangled variety) met colonial rule (usually of the established variety), both sides adapted, but *spirituality remains political.* In most cases preexisting sacred traditions persisted in some form, more or less tolerated. Sometimes colonists co-opted local religious leaders as agents of indirect rule.[10] And colonial culture was carried by the religious schools, hospitals, and churches that provided pathways for some local populations to advance in the colonial state. Then, with the exit of colonial rulers, political struggles over the role of religious institutions and identities have followed. What will properly count as religion becomes a part of political and national self-definition. In the process, colonial religious institutions have often been transformed by local populations into their own indigenous forms (Kollman 2012; Meyer 2004; Olupona 2011). Throughout the

SOCIAL PRACTICES AND CULTURAL CONTEXTS   41

postcolonial world, the practice of religion continues to bear the combined marks of its long local history and the overlay of establishment colonial religion, often visible in today's explosion of indigenous Pentecostal religious forms. Variations in the expression of spirituality are part of the story of colonial and postcolonial religion.

The third kind of setting for religious belief and practice is the one most commonly assumed in existing research (especially survey based), namely plural, formal, *institutionalized* traditions and organizations to which one can belong. "Modern" societies have organized themselves so that there are recognized and bounded organizations, professionals, activities, and memberships that constitute the religious organizational field, and *spirituality is therefore compartmentalized.*[11] There is overlap here with the "established" religious traditions, since they, too, take on these modern organizational forms. But in the disestablished, institutional context, there are multiple religious traditions existing on a roughly level legal playing field. Each has internal cultures and rules that shape practice, as well as internal resources and mechanisms for producing and reinventing ways of being religious. Congregations and denominations and religious nonprofits are, for example, the places in the United States where we expect religious action to take place and where spiritual experience is seen as appropriately housed. The spirituality of what happens inside sanctuaries is no less analyzable than what happens in individual life.

Individual life is, however, the domain of spirituality in the fourth macrostructural context, namely the less-institutionalized, diffuse, and fluid situations that exist in *interstitial* settings. As a result of diminished institutional religious expectations in the West, many analysts (and ordinary observers) have identified this as the "spiritual" domain that exists in lieu of the religious action of yore (Heelas and Woodhead 2005; Roof 1999). *Spirituality is individualized.* Lighting candles, meditating, walking labyrinths, doing yoga, even undertaking pilgrimages or getting a tattoo can make up a bricolage that is seemingly untethered to institutional authority and subject only to the individual's creative imagination. The seemingly noninstitutionalized character of such individualized religious practice is further magnified by new communication technologies that make a cornucopia of religious ideas and practices readily available. With the click of a mouse, one can discover compatriots and teachers and can join Facebook and YouTube communities that are as easily disengaged as engaged (Campbell 2013).

42   NANCY T. AMMERMAN

This experimentation, of course, is not utterly divorced from existing religious traditions or communities. Even for people who think of themselves as "exes" (e.g., ex-Catholic), there is a religious identity after the hyphen that has supplied a way of narrating who they are, even as they leave it behind. And when they create hybrids—Jewish Buddhists, for example (Sigalow 2019)—they draw on the traditions they combine and on the modes of spirituality contained within those traditions.

It is critical, however, to see the cultural particularity of these forms of religious practice and the limitations of defining spirituality only in these terms. This view of religion's place in the social world overlooks other macrostructural arrangements where religious cultural practices are located very differently. It also fails to acknowledge the particular political economy to which this form of religious practice is best suited. As Carrette and King (2005) argue, if the Enlightenment displaced "religion" from the public sphere, neoliberalism has displaced it further into the individual psyche. Having stripped out the ethical demands of public religious traditions, personal "spirituality" can be welcomed back into workplaces and other public space. When we examine practices labeled "spiritual but not religious," we will do well to pay attention to the social and economic supports for those practices (Aupers and Houtman 2006; Kucinskas 2019).

Nevertheless, it is useful to recognize the reality of social contexts in which religion is found in the margins. Also interstitial, for example, are the individual and collective adaptations and innovations resulting from migration.[12] When religious practices are transported across cultures and geographies, they inevitably change. Like others at the social margins, people who migrate—from one nation to another or from one kind of community to another—often engage in religious practices that mix and match or simply invent. Paying attention to the cultural work being done in these interstitial spaces of migration is likely to uncover a wide range of expectations about the spiritual dimensions of religiosity. Just as migrants reconstruct material, emotional, narrative, and other dimensions of their religious practice, the presence and intensity of the spirits change as well (Brown 1991; Crocker 2017).

Spirituality, then, can be found in the deinstitutionalized spaces carved out by seemingly unconstrained cultural seekers and bricoleurs, but that is just one dimension of the practices those seekers engage. Paying attention to the spiritual should not obscure a full measure of the embodied, material, emotional, and other dimensions of their practice, nor of the socially structured arrays of activity that constitute these practices. Nor are Western neoliberal spaces the only interstitial ones, and interstitial settings are not the only way religious practice is located in the social world. Religious practices in interstitial settings have to be understood differently than those in entangled wholistic cultures, in regulated national systems, or in bureaucratized organizations. Lived religious practices can happen in any of those settings, and in each, the spiritual dimension of shared religious practice is both variable and worth attention as part of the whole.

At the micro level, context matters, as well. Peter Berger introduced the notion of "plausibility structures" as a way to elaborate the social processes from which religious and spiritual practices emerge and are sustained. In Berger's (1967) rendering, a plausibility structure is not a logical schema or argument (as it is often misunderstood), but rather the social context in which religion is recognized, named, and taken to be real. This suggests that we should pay attention to the micro-level conversations and interactions of everyday life, asking how and when those interactions are understood by actors as religious in character and what role spirituality plays in them. As we have already noted, lived religious practice is not confined to a single organizational space, but it does take place in social settings. Those settings make religious practices more and less possible and expected. Both subtle norms and overt power can constrain or encourage the expression of religion.

The socially patterned practices that include spirituality exist in myriad social settings, including those specifically designated as religious or spiritual. Yoga classes, retreat centers, online forums, and pilgrimages are but a few. Within each context there are expectations for how things should happen and what sort of spiritual experience should be part of the picture. Participants engage in practice that is embodied, material, aesthetic, and spiritual; and the collective nature of their action and conversation provides it with ongoing plausibility. It may be individually chosen and part of a pastiche, but each practice is socially structured, enacted, and maintained. That shows up in the degree to which participation in organized religion matters in determining the presence of spiritual practices in a person's life (Ammerman 2013b). Congregations and other organized sites of religious interaction are critical components of the plausibility structures that sustain religious culture production and thereby set the stage for spiritual expression. Lived religious practice depends on plausibility structures, and some such interactional spaces will call forth a wider and deeper range of religious practice than others, with each practice calling on the particular shape of spiritual expression the community teaches and expects.

Conclusion

Lived religious practice, like all social practices, exists as socially situated action. Those social situations are defined both by the macrostructures of law and culture and by the microstructures of conversation and interaction. Those interactions and conversations create cognitive patterns that can then shape action whenever situational cues call them forth. Those cues may happen in institutionalized religious settings or in the shifting interactions of mundane life. In the world of everyday life, practices recognized as religious happen throughout the social world.

What sets religious practice apart is the presence of a spiritual dimension that exists alongside all the characteristics it shares with other human social practice, each varying in content and intensity. Socially patterned practices of religion define and use human embodiment and material surroundings in myriad ways. They shape and deploy emotion and aesthetics in equally various configurations. They take narrative forms and implicate moral expectations, as well. And the range of spiritual expressions of religion in practice is just as broad. It is useful to pay attention to where and when societies set spirituality and religion up as separate or opposing knowledge categories, but it is also useful to stay attuned to lived religious practice as a fused whole where spirituality is but one dimension. Doing so, ironically, may allow a wider, less culturally constrained view of spiritual experiences. If spirituality is a property of all religious practice, not just of middle-class Western seekers, we will be challenged to develop analyses that can describe that broader range and that are situated in a wider array of human communities.

Notes

1. This approach is elaborated in Ammerman 2020.
2. This admittedly sometimes includes ideas and practices like Big Foot followers or astrology practitioners that we might not usually think of as religious. But it is critical

SOCIAL PRACTICES AND CULTURAL CONTEXTS 45

not to impose presuppositions on what counts. On this see Ellis and ter Haar's (2007) insistence on calling African beliefs "religion" and not superstition or occult or magic.

3. Berger (2014) and Steets (2014) each offer accounts of how Schutz's ideas apply to religion, as did Mary Jo Neitz's earlier examination of the Catholic charismatic movement (Neitz 1987).

4. On popular uses of these terms in the United States, see Steensland et al. 2018 and Ammerman 2013a, and in Europe, see Berghuijs et al. 2013 and Palmisano 2010.

5. Ellis and Ter Haar (2007) offer an African example, while Luhrman (2012) documents a middle-class American example.

6. McCutcheon (2004) points out that this sort of deconstruction of the religion category—"What gets to count as religion and why?"—has been central to important strands in recent work in religious studies.

7. State-imposed atheism might also be said to follow this pattern, although with mixed success (Froese 2004b; Yang 2012).

8. On ethnic immigrant religion in the United States, see, for example, Joshi 2006 on Hindus and Warner et al. 2012 on Mexicans and Muslims.

9. An important variation on this dynamic can be seen in the political struggles of post-Soviet societies. Here, too, reemergent religious practices and authorities tangle with both communist and secular liberal powers for legitimacy and everyday relevance (Froese 2004a; Muller and Neundorf 2012).

10. The long and complicated political histories and current situations are treated in a variety of sources (Chidester 1996; Comaroff 1991; Fields 1985; Swidler 2010).

11. As many have noted, this bounding of the religious field runs alongside the establishment of a "secular" public domain that is supposed to be religion free (Asad 2003; Casanova 1994).

12. See for example, Levitt 2007; Warner 1997; or Murillo 2009, as well as Jeung 2012 and Knott 2016.

References

Ammerman, Nancy T. 2013a. "Spiritual but Not Religious? Beyond Binary Choices in the Study of Religion." *Journal for the Scientific Study of Religion* 52(2): 258–78.

Ammerman, Nancy T. 2013b. *Sacred Stories, Spiritual Tribes: Finding Religion in Everyday Life.* New York: Oxford University Press.

Ammerman, Nancy T. 2016. "Lived Religion as an Emerging Field: An Assessment of Its Contours and Frontiers." *Nordic Journal of Religion and Society* 29(2): 83–99.

Ammerman, Nancy T. 2020. "Rethinking Religion: Toward a Practice Approach." *American Journal of Sociology* 126(1): 6–51.

Asad, Talal. 2003. *Formations of the Secular: Christianity, Islam, Modernity.* Palo Alto, CA: Stanford University Press.

Aupers, Stef, and Dick Houtman. 2006. "Beyond the Spiritual Supermarket: The Social and Public Significance of New Age Spirituality." *Journal of Contemporary Religion* 21(2): 201–22.

Avishai, Orit, Afshan Jafar, and Rachel Rinaldo. 2015. "A Gender Lens on Religion." *Gender & Society* 29(1): 5–25.

Beaman, Lori G., Winnifred Fallers Sullivan, Rebecca Catto, and Linda Woodhead. 2016. *Varieties of Religious Establishment*. Abingdon, Oxon, UK: Taylor & Francis Group.

Berger, Peter L. 1967. *The Sacred Canopy*. Garden City, NY: Anchor Doubleday.

Berger, Peter L. 2014. *The Many Altars of Modernity: Toward a Paradigm for Religion in a Pluralist Age*. Boston: De Gruyter.

Berghuijs, Joantine, Jos Pieper, and Cok Bakker. 2013. "Conceptions of Spirituality among the Dutch Population." *Archive for the Psychology of Religion* 35(3): 369–97.

Bourdieu, Pierre. 1990. *The Logic of Practice*. Translated by Richard Nice. Stanford, CA: Stanford University Press.

Brown, Karen McCarthy. 1991. *Mama Lola: A Vodou Priestess in Brooklyn*. Berkeley: University of California Press.

Campbell, Heidi, ed. 2013. *Digital Religion: Understanding Religion in a New Media World*. New York: Routledge.

Carrette, Jeremy R., and Richard King. 2005. *Selling Spirituality: The Silent Takeover of Religion*. London: Routledge.

Casanova, Jose. 1994. *Public Religions in the Modern World*. Chicago: University of Chicago Press.

Chidester, David. 1996. *Savage Systems: Colonialism and Comparative Religion in Southern Africa*. Chicago: University of Chicago Press.

Comaroff, Jean. 1991. *Of Revelation and Revolution: Christianity, Colonialism, and Consciousness in South Africa*. Chicago: University of Chicago Press.

Crocker, Elizabeth Thomas. 2017. "Moral Geographies of Diasporic Belonging: Race, Ethnicity, and Identity among Haitian Vodou Practitioners in Boston." PhD dissertation, Boston University.

Davidman, Lynn. 1991. *Tradition in a Rootless World*. Berkeley: University of California Press.

Davie, Grace. 2015. *Religion in Britain: A Persistent Paradox*. Malden, MA: Wiley Blackwell.

Decoteau, Claire Laurier. 2016. "The Reflexive Habitus: Critical Realist and Bourdieusian Social Action." *European Journal of Social Theory* 19(3): 303–21.

DiMaggio, Paul. 1997. "Culture and Cognition." *Annual Review of Sociology* 23: 263–87.

Edgell, Penny. 2012. "A Cultural Sociology of Religion: New Directions." *Annual Review of Sociology* 38: 247–65.

Ellis, Stephen, and Gerrie ter Haar. 2007. "Religion and Politics: Taking African Epistemologies Seriously." *Journal of Modern African Studies* 45(3): 385–401.

Fields, Karen E. 1985. *Revival and Rebellion in Colonial Central Africa*. Princeton, NJ: Princeton University Press.

Friedland, Roger. 2001. "Religious Nationalism and the Problem of Collective Representation." *Annual Review of Sociology* 27: 125–52.

Froese, Paul. 2004a. "After Atheism: An Analysis of Religious Monopolies in the Post-communist World." *Sociology of Religion* 65(1): 57–75.

Froese, Paul. 2004b. "Forced Secularization in Soviet Russia: Why an Atheistic Monopoly Failed." *Journal for the Scientific Study of Religion* 43(1): 35–50.

Heelas, Paul, and Linda Woodhead, with Benjamin Seel, Bronislaw Szerszynski, and Karin Tusting. 2005. *The Spiritual Revolution: Why Religion Is Giving Way to Spirituality*. Malden, MA: Blackwell.

SOCIAL PRACTICES AND CULTURAL CONTEXTS 47

Hurd, Elizabeth Shakman. 2015. *Beyond Religious Freedom: The Global Politics of Religion*. Princeton, NJ: Princeton University Press.

Jeung, Russell. 2012. "Second-Generation Chinese Americans: The Familism of the Nonreligious." Pp. 208–33 in *Sustaining Faith Traditions: Race, Ethnicity, and Religion among the Latino and Asian American Second Generation*, edited by Carolyn Chen and Russell Jeung. New York: New York University Press.

Joshi, Khyati Y. 2006. *New Roots in America's Sacred Ground: Religion, Race, and Ethnicity in Indian America*. New Brunswick, NJ: Rutgers University Press.

Knott, Kim. 2016. "Living Religious Practices." Pp. 71–90 in *Intersections of Religion and Migration: Issues at the Global Crossroads*, edited by Jennifer B. Saunders, Elena Fiddian-Qasmiyeh, and Susanna Snyder. New York: Palgrave Macmillan.

Kollman, Paul. 2012. "Generations of Catholics in Eastern Africa: A Practice-Centered Analysis of Religious Change." *Journal for the Scientific Study of Religion* 51(3): 412–28.

Kraybill, Donald B., and Carl F. Bowman. 2001. *On the Backroad to Heaven: Old Order Hutterites, Mennonites, Amish, and Brethren*. Baltimore: Johns Hopkins University Press.

Kucinskas, Jaime. 2019. *The Mindful Elite: Mobilizing from the Inside Out*. New York: Oxford University Press.

Levitt, Peggy. 2007. *God Needs No Passport*. New York: New Press.

Lizardo, Omar, and Michael Strand. 2010. "Skills, Toolkits, Contexts and Institutions: Clarifying the Relationship between Different Approaches to Cognition in Cultural Sociology." *Poetics* 38(2): 205–28.

Luhrmann, Tanya M. 2012. *When God Talks Back: Understanding the American Evangelical Relationship with God*. New York: Alfred A. Knopf.

Martin, John Levi. 2010. "Life's a Beach but You're an Ant, and Other Unwelcome News for the Sociology of Culture." *Poetics* 38(2): 229–44.

Martin, John Levi. 2011. *The Explanation of Social Action*. New York: Oxford University Press.

McCutcheon, Russell T. 2004. "Religion, Ire, and Dangerous Things." *Journal of the American Academy of Religion* 72(1): 173–93.

McGuire, Meredith B. 2008. *Lived Religion: Faith and Practice in Everyday Life*. New York: Oxford University Press.

Meyer, Birgit. 2004. "Christianity in Africa: From African Independent to Pentecostal-Charismatic Churches." *Annual Review of Anthropology* 33: 447–74.

Muller, Tim, and Anja Neundorf. 2012. "The Role of the State in the Repression and Revival of Religiosity in Central Eastern Europe." *Social Forces* 91(2): 559–82.

Murillo, Luis E. 2009. "Tamales on the Fourth of July: The Transnational Parish of Coeneo, Michoacan." *Religion and American Culture* 19(2): 137–68.

Neitz, Mary Jo. 1987. *Charisma and Community*. New Brunswick, NJ: Transaction.

Neitz, Mary Jo. 2011. "Lived Religion: Signposts of Where We Have Been and Where We Can Go from Here." Pp. 45–55 in *Religion, Spirituality and Everyday Practice*, edited by Giuseppe Giordan and William H. Swatos Jr. New York: Springer.

Olupona, Jacob K. 2011. *City of 201 Gods: Ilé-Ifè in Time, Space, and the Imagination*. Berkeley: University of California Press.

Palmisano, Stefania. 2010. "Spirituality and Catholicism in Italy." *Journal of Contemporary Religion* 25(2): 221–41.

Roof, Wade Clark. 1999. *Spiritual Marketplace: Baby Boomers and the Remaking of American Religion*. Princeton, NJ: Princeton University Press.

48   NANCY T. AMMERMAN

Schatzki, Theodore R. 2001. "Introduction." Pp. 10–24 in *The Practice Turn in Contemporary Theory*, edited by Karin Knorr Cetina, Theodore R. Schatzki, and Eike von Savigny. New York: Routledge.

Schutz, Alfred. 1945. "On Multiple Realities." *Philosophy and Phenomenological Research* 5(4): 533–76.

Sells, Michael. 2003. "Crosses of Blood: Sacred Space, Religion, and Violence in Bosnia-Hercegovina." *Sociology of Religion* 64(3): 309–31.

Sewell, William H., Jr. 1992. "A Theory of Structure: Duality, Agency, and Transformation." *American Journal of Sociology* 98(1): 1–29.

Sigalow, Emily. 2019. *American Jewbu: Jews, Buddhists, and Religious Change*. Princeton, NJ: Princeton University Press.

Soper, J. Christopher, and Joel S. Fetzer. 2018. *Religion and Nationalism in Global Perspective*. Cambridge: Cambridge University Press.

Steensland, Brian, Xiaoyun Wang, and Lauren Chism Schmidt. 2018. "Spirituality: What Does It Mean and to Whom?" *Journal for the Scientific Study of Religion* 57(3): 450–72.

Steets, Silke. 2014. "Multiple Realities and Religion: A Sociological Approach." *Society* 51(2): 140–44.

Swidler, Ann. 1986. "Culture in Action: Symbols and Strategies." *American Sociological Review* 51(2): 273–86.

Swidler, Ann. 2010. "The Return of the Sacred: What African Chiefs Teach Us about Secularization." *Sociology of Religion* 71(2): 157–71.

Warner, R. Stephen. 1997. "Religion, Boundaries, and Bridges." *Sociology of Religion* 58(3): 217–38.

Warner, R. Stephen, Elise Martel, and Rhonda Duggan. 2012. "Islam Is to Catholicism as Teflon Is to Velcro." Pp. 46–68 in *Sustaining Faith Traditions: Race Ethnicity, and Religion among Latino and Asian Second Generation*, edited by Carolyn Chen and Russell Jeung. New York: New York University Press.

Weber, Max. [1922] 1946. "The Sociology of Charismatic Authority." Pp. 245–52 in *From Max Weber*, edited and translated by Hans Gerth and C. Wright Mills. New York: Oxford University Press.

Whitehead, Andrew L., and Samuel L. Perry. 2020. *Taking America Back for God: Christian Nationalism in the United States*. New York: Oxford University Press.

Yang, Fenggang. 2012. *Religion in China: Survival and Revival under Communist Rule*. New York: Oxford University Press.

2

The Gods of Modern Spirituality

Linda Woodhead

My starting point is the observation that what I will refer to as the theosphere of modern spirituality is worthy of attention in its own right, even before we go on to consider its social dimensions. The latter tend to preoccupy sociologists like myself to such an extent that there is a danger we turn into the caricature of a social scientist who analyzes sport in terms of race, class, gender, and politics and fails to mention the game itself: the sine qua non is forgotten. Thus we end up studying spirituality without considering Spirit and spirits, God or gods.

I will anchor this investigation in three sites in Great Britain and the United States, each of which reveals a different facet of the changing theosphere of anglophone spirituality. By spirituality I mean the whole spiritual milieu—from Wicca to New Age to ethnic forms of paganism—as manifest not only in groups but in popular culture and solitary practice. The sites are chosen because each has a somewhat representative quality by virtue of being a gathering point for a wide range of different spiritual practitioners, groups, and currents, and because each one opens a window onto a different period, from the late nineteenth century through to the present. They are sites I have researched over the course of my career, the oldest by way of historical documents and studies, and the two more recent ones by way of direct empirical observation.

I will suggest that four different approaches to the divine within modern, Western spirituality emerge from this exploration. I refer to them as "theologies" in the broadest sense, using that term, as well as others like "divinity," without any special reference to Christianity. The four theologies are, first, paternalist monotheism; second, formless mysticism; third, Energetic spirituality; fourth, pagan polytheism. My intention is not to suggest some sort of evolutionary progress over time from one theological stance to another, but to outline the characteristic features of each stance and consider how they may coexist and influence one another. The three typologies I offer at the end

---

Linda Woodhead, *The Gods of Modern Spirituality* In: *Situating Spirituality*. Edited by: Brian Steensland, Jaime Kucinskas, and Anna Sun, Oxford University Press. © Oxford University Press 2022. DOI: 10.1093/oso/9780197565001.003.0003

50 LINDA WOODHEAD

of the chapter consolidate this reflection and are offered as an aid to further exploration.

First Sounding: The World's Parliament of Religions, Chicago, 1893

Organized by a group of liberal-minded Christians, the World's Parliament of Religions of 1893 was a self-consciously progressive and ecumenical gathering that sought to showcase the world's religions and gather their leading representatives from around the world. It rested on the idea that there was a fundamental unity of mankind and all religions based on the Fatherhood of God and the brotherhood of man (*sic*). The parliament formed part of the much-larger world's fair held in Chicago in 1893, and matched the latter's confident global ambitions. Both took place at a time of great optimism about the global and civilizational progress that was thought by many involved in the event to be driven by Protestant powers and undergirded by colonialism, industrialism, trade, and commerce (Woodhead 2001).

The parliament's slogan, drawn from the Bible and embossed on the weighty two-volume account of its proceedings compiled by the chairman of the parliament, the Reverend John Henry Barrows (1893), summed up its official theological stance: "Hath we not all one Father? Hath not God Created Us?" (Malachi 2:10). This is a version of paternalist monotheism that pivots around belief in a solitary, universal, all-sufficient, all-good, all-powerful paternal Creator God. There are ethical as well as metaphysical implications: because this universal omni-god is Father of all, it follows that all men are brothers, whatever their race or creed.

Owing something to earlier Enlightenment deism with its search for a rational, ethical, universal religion, such paternalist monotheism is simultaneously both open and inclusive *and* Protestant and exclusive. It is inclusive because it implies that religious and spiritual leaders of all faiths can share a platform, but exclusive because a particular Protestant Christian approach is normative. The latter enshrines a progressivist, imperialist, paternalist view of God and man in the context of a world's fair where white racial supremacy was actively bolstered by ideologies of racial, cultural, and religious evolution and civilizational hierarchy (Seager 1993). Barrows wrote,

The Parliament has shown that Christianity is still the great quickener of humanity, that it is now educating those who do not accept its doctrines, that there is no teacher to be compared with Christ, and no Saviour excepting Christ. . . . The non-Christian world may give us valuable criticism and confirm scriptural truths and make excellent suggestion as to Christian improvement, but it has nothing to add to the Christian creed. (1893b, 1581)

The tension between exclusivism and inclusivism at the World's Parliament had unintended consequences. By offering a public platform for a wide range of religious views from across the world, a theological debate was initiated that spun out of the organizers' control. Barrows proclaimed God the Father as the universal and inclusive God, referred to the "Our Father" as the "universal prayer," and insisted that the whole parliament should recite it. But other speakers had different ideas. Of these, the unexpected celebrity was Swami Vivekananda from colonial India. He used the parliament's platform to present a neo-Hindu account of God that was subtly subversive of liberal Christian monotheism and its implicit support of paternalism and colonialism.

The divine, Vivekananda told the parliament in his address, is "everywhere the pure and formless one" (Vivekananda 1893, 972). Universally accessible, this supreme being can be approached without need of priesthood, scripture, ritual, or organization. This was formless mysticism rather than paternalist monotheism, and it had very different ethical and political implications from Barrow's theology. Although Vivekananda agreed with Barrows that all religions point to the one God, he suggested that it was in the East, particularly in India, that the deepest spiritual truth was to be found. "Every other religion," he told the Parliament, "lays down a certain amount of fixed dogma, and tries to force the whole society through it." But to the Hindu,

The whole world of religion is only a travelling, a coming up, of different men and women, through various conditions and circumstances, to the same goal. Every religion is only an evolving of a god out of the material man; and the same God is the inspiration of them all. . . . It is the same light coming through different colors. (Vivekananda 1893, 976–77)

Explicitly addressing women as well as men, Vivekananda spoke of the divine in and around us all. It is beyond name and form. It is formless Spirit.

52   LINDA WOODHEAD

The implicit message was that so-called subject races—and women—have a closer connection to the Spirit and to genuine spirituality than those who consider themselves their religious and political superiors.

Vivekananda was not the only person at the World's Parliament to argue that a mystical, universalist theological stance—what I refer to as formless mysticism—trumped Christian theism. Buddhist, Quaker, Swedenborgian, and Theosophist delegates offered different versions of the same message. Subsequently, the battle lines between formless mysticism and the paternalist theism of Barrows and others would harden, as each presented itself as representing universal truth and supporting global unity. For example, the Theosophist Annie Besant (1847–1933), also present at the parliament, later locked horns with the British Roman Catholic poet, philosopher and polemicist G. K. Chesterton. Chesterton painted Besant's version of spirituality as the dangerous antithesis of Christian theism. "By insisting especially on the immanence of God," he said,

> We get introspection, self-isolation, quietism, social indifference—Tibet. By insisting on the transcendence of God we get wonder, curiosity, moral and political adventure, righteous indignation—Christendom. Insisting that God is inside man, man is always inside himself. By insisting that God transcends man, man has transcended himself. ([1908] 1961, 133)

Besant retaliated in her book *Mysticism*, published in 1914. The Christian dogmas, she said, "must be broken into pieces . . . they are outgrown when the unfolding Spirit of man begins to know for himself, and no longer needs testimony from outside" ([1914] 1941, 21). It was a swipe at the idea that people need male, Christian priestly mediators and religious institutions to know God.

This struggle between formless mysticism and paternalist monotheism would weave its way through the cultural history of the twentieth century. As it did so, it took on the distinctive concerns and hues of different times, places, and protagonists (Schmidt 2005). To take just one mid-century example, the Anglo-American guru Alan Watts (1915–1973) rejected the faith of the Church of England and his priestly ordination therein in favor of a version of formless mysticism that he traced back to his mother's influence. She, despite a "wretched fundamentalist Protestant upbringing," lived in "a world of magic beyond that religion . . . inhabited not by domineering prophets and sentimental angels . . . but by sweet peas, scarlet-runner beans, rose trees, crisp apples, speckled thrushes . . . the South Downs, dew-ponds and wells of chalk-cool water" (Watts 1972, 8). Intellectually, it was Theosophy that first helped Watts to escape, followed by a growing immersion in Asian philosophy. Watts migrated to California, where he became an important figure in a spiritual counterculture that drew on Daoism, Zen Buddhism, and California cool. "God," he said, "is what there is and all that there is," the "happening" of life, "beyond all possible conception, to be found by "getting with it and going with it" and abolishing a sense of a separate "I" (1972, 223–224, 451).

In an interesting twist, the formless mystical started to enter the mainstream of Christianity itself in the 1960s and 1970s, though the roots of this development go back to the Edwardian period and books like Evelyn Underhill's *Mysticism* ([1910] 1993) (see Shaw 2018). In Britain, the last great public controversy about God was generated in 1963 with the publication of the book *Honest to God* by the Anglican bishop John Robinson. Presenting ideas from Dietrich Bonhoeffer, Paul Tillich, Rudolph Bultmann, and other modernizing Christian theologians, Robinson contended that the old God in the sky was no longer credible in the scientific age (Clements 1988). Instead of looking for a God above, we should encounter God as the ground of being. Robinson's ideas were part of a wider development within liberal Christianity, both Catholic and Protestant, where they were often combined with initiatives of social reform and political action that sought to realize the kingdom of God in the here and now rather than in a future heavenly realm. Social and theological progressivism combined to create a "social gospel" that was quasi-mystical and socially concerned, but somewhat removed from the immediate, practical, and worldly concerns of individuals—as indeed was the formless mysticism of Vivekananda or even Watts (Chapman 2015).

Despite the efforts of Robinson and other Christian liberals, however, the mainstream Catholic and Protestant churches, along with the dominant currents in academic Christian theology, took a decidedly more antimystical and postliberal stance after the 1970s, reaffirming belief in a Trinitarian deity mediated by ecclesiastical authority and labeled "orthodoxy." The effect was to drive a wedge between popular spirituality and Christian life and thought. Shut out of the churches by these developments, formless mysticism grew in influence outside them, at the expense of the mainline churches (Brown and Woodhead 2016, 179–203).

By the 1990s formless mysticism was well on the way to being institutionalized in parts of public life where the churches had once held sway, including

54   LINDA WOODHEAD

healthcare, prisons, schools, and colleges (Sullivan 2014; Tusting and Woodhead 2018). This process has gone further in Britain than the United States because of a long historical entanglement of state, society, and religion, and the absence of a legal obligation to maintain separation. In a recent study of the town of Kendal in northern England, we found that every primary school in the town took seriously the spiritual education of its pupils and had a well-developed strategy to do so (Tusting and Woodhead 2018, 130–31). Similarly, spirituality has now been integrated into healthcare training and prison chaplaincy. In 2010 the *Journal for the Study of Spirituality* was founded to cater for the growing audience of professionals interested in applied spirituality (Hunt 2020). An important reason for the success of formless mystical spirituality in such public settings is that it is universal and inclusive enough to cater to an increasingly multicultural clientele, and to people of all religions and none. It goes hand in hand with the idea that every individual has a spiritual identity, and it appeals to a sensibility and legal regime that eschews proselytism in favor of individual human rights, liberty, and mutual respect.

Second Sounding: Kendal, England, 2000–2002

Between 2000 and 2002 I was involved in a large research project that investigated every manifestation of religion and spirituality with a public face in the medium-sized, somewhat typical market town of Kendal in Cumbria.[1] Findings were presented in the book *The Spiritual Revolution* (Heelas and Woodhead 2005). In total, we discovered twenty-five churches and chapels and congregations and 126 different spiritual groups or one-to-one therapies and activities (we only counted those where practitioners confirmed that their work had a spiritual dimension). The 126 separate activities in this single small town offered fifty-three different kinds of spiritual approach, from acupressure to paganism to reiki and yoga (full list in Heelas and Woodhead 2005, 156–57). Throughout the spiritual milieu, the concepts and language of "mind, body, spirit" and "holistic" were prominent (Heelas and Woodhead 2005, 156–57). There was a strong emphasis on the importance of relationship and improving relationships—with self, others and the planet — and 80 percent of those active in the holistic milieu were women.

When it came to theology in Kendal, we found that "God" and paternalist monotheism were largely confined to the churches and chapels, whereas in

THE GODS OF MODERN SPIRITUALITY   55

the burgeoning spiritual milieu all the talk was of "spirit," "energy," and "chi." Thus 82 percent of respondents to a survey distributed within the holistic milieu expressed belief in "some sort of spirit or life force that pervades all that lives" (Heelas and Woodhead 2005, 98). At first sight, this might easily be classified as formless mysticism, and there were indeed some clear threads of influence, particularly via the New Age movement.[2] However, we found the spiritual energy put to work in Kendal to be rather different: more rooted in everyday, mundane concerns of women and men than the "spirit" or the "what there is" invoked by Vivekananda and Watts. The latter is more metaphysical; the energy being tapped into in Kendal was more accessible and useful in dealing with everyday, practical concerns. It was harnessed to heal, comfort, guide, remove obstacles, protect, repair relationships, and help people realize their potential. Such "helpful energy," as I will call it, was thought of as integral to the body, mind, and spirit of each and every individual, as well as being the connective tissue between all beings and things. Contrary to the idea that such spirituality is purely individualistic, the bodily and relational aspects were usually to the fore in both theory and practice (Sointu and Woodhead 2008).

By the early twentieth century, spirituality in places like Kendal had been taken out of the hands of religious virtuosi and appropriated by a much broader spread of the population, in a vibrant marketplace of well-being practices. The majority of practitioners and participants were white British women, of all socioeconomic classes, many with a background in either teaching or healthcare, especially nursing. They spoke openly about their frustrations with the overly rationalized, managerial, and restrictive contexts in which they had found their efforts to care being frustrated. They left them in order to set up their own enterprises in which they could relate to people in what they believed to be more appropriate, humane, and healing ways. The many different kinds of practice and spiritual retailing they offered catered to different classes, right across the socioeconomic spectrum, often with a flexible pricing structure that aimed to be inclusive.

Of the many different spiritual practices on offer in Kendal, yoga and reiki were the two that were most popular there at the start of the twentieth century. Reiki provides a particularly revealing glimpse into Energetic spirituality because it is a kind of healing that works without direct physical contact. Connection with healing energy is central. Healers hold their hands a small distance (sometimes a great distance, in remote healing) from the person or other animal or object that needs to be healed. In doing so, they explain, they

56 LINDA WOODHEAD

are tapping into the energetic "Source" and acting as a channel. Healers often speak of sensations in their hands as they move them over those parts of the body where a person's energy is blocked; clients may also experience heat or tingling. The analogy with electricity is obvious and often explicit. Reiki is said to be dangerous work if you don't know what you are doing and are tempted to draw on your own energy. In that case, you are in danger of being depleted and harmed. You have to plug into higher energy.

In such ways, the divine becomes more down-to-earth, practical, and demotic than in formless mysticism (or than in nineteenth- and twentieth-century manifestations of ritual magic and occultism). This very practical version of spirituality abandons the idealist tendencies in earlier formless mysticism that suggested the necessity of escaping from material and bodily entrapment in order to ascend to more mystical realms and material realms through contemplation. The kind of practical spirituality that we found to be widespread in Kendal is more readily accessible and relevant to mental and physical disease. Although an emphasis on contemplation was retained in meditation practices, it was their practical, immediate mental and bodily benefits that were given the most emphasis. And of course, this kind of Energetic spirituality requires no priestly mediators, occult knowledge, cosmological speculation, high ritual, or purificatory practices—or paternalism.

Although Charles Taylor (1989, 2002) may be right to point out the connection between contemporary "expressive" spirituality, as he calls it, and the Romantic movement's idea of an inspiring and animating élan vital, to leave it at that is to miss the important reinterpretations that have taken place since the origins of such spirituality. These reinterpretations and popularisations must be credited not to male cultural elites, but to nonelite, mainly female practitioners offering friends, family, and clients spiritual remedies, guidance, and help (Sointu and Woodhead 2008). As a Rebirthing practitioner said of what she offered, "It's very much based in the body, it's not going off somewhere. So although there's the spiritual element, it's not going off into the clouds. It is a wonderful sense people get, they're filling their bodies" (Sointu and Woodhead 2008, 266). The idea is that energy that is trapped or blocked will manifest in mental and physical disease and spiritual malaise. The goal is to unblock energy so that it can flow more freely. The result can be spiritual or physical or both—as one informant said, rather wonderfully: "The divine gives you a basis for meaning and boosting the immune system" (Sointu and Woodhead 2008). What counts as evidence in this kind of spirituality is what works. Practitioners, groups, and techniques that do

THE GODS OF MODERN SPIRITUALITY   57

not get results do not survive long in a milieu that depends upon paying clients and their recommendations to others. Today, with the advent of the internet, there are stars to be awarded and reviews to be shared online.

We found very little overlap or cooperation between the churches and holistic spirituality in Kendal, despite the fact that they have a potential theological meeting point in the concepts of "spirit" and "spirituality," and in an intertwined history (Woodhead 2011). In the early twentieth century in Kendal, however, both the theological understanding and the practice of the Christian and holistic domains were clearly separate. Only the fringe Christian denominations, the Quakers and the Unitarians, had built common ground. By contrast, the Roman Catholic Church, echoing recent magisterial teaching, was actively hostile to New Age notions, and the leadership and ethos of the main Protestant denominations found it hard to make much common cause with female spiritual practitioners. This is not to deny the possibility of overlap and experimentation between the two realms, but in practice these were found to be the exception rather than the rule. In some spinoff research carried out in 2006 with Helen Berger in Asheville, North Carolina,[3] to take an example of the exception, we attended the nondenominational Christian-pagan experimental church, the Jubilee Community, which consciously brings together the Christian, the alternative, and the pagan. Its current website says: "We are a creative and inclusive spiritual community that celebrates the divine mystery in all of creation."[4] Incorporation of healing practices and the pagan calendar and ritual elements reinforce the linkage. But such attempts at synthesis between the Christian "God" and post-Christian "spirit" or "energy" are still rather rare. In the first quarter of the twenty-first century, it was the differences between Christian theism and "alternative" conceptions of the divine that were more apparent than their overlap.

Third Sounding: Glastonbury, England, 2010–2020

Glastonbury in Somerset, England, is a much smaller town than Kendal, with a population of nine thousand. Unlike Kendal, it is a well-known sacred site that attracts pilgrims from around the world. Today a plethora of different kinds of religion and spirituality are active and represented there, from conservative Roman Catholic Christianity to various kinds of paganism and magical practice. I have been a regular visitor for over twenty years, and over that period there has been a noticeable growth in practically oriented engagements with a plethora of different deities, spiritual entities, forces, and beings—a pagan polytheistic turn. I select Glastonbury as my third site for discussion because it offers a rich glimpse of how the theosphere has changed in the two decades since the research carried out in Kendal.

It is certainly not the case that monotheism and formless mysticism have disappeared from Glastonbury. There are still several active churches, as well as the central and imposing ruin of the medieval abbey, and various forms of historic and contemporary formless mysticism and Christian spirituality all retain a presence.

One interesting and prominent example of formless mysticism is the distinctive brand of Goddess spirituality that has developed in Glastonbury since the 1980s. By the 2010s it was institutionalized in a priestly hierarchy, training courses, a growing suite of temples and buildings, and an annual Goddess Festival that attracts participants from around the world and which was held online for the first time in the summer of 2020 due to the pandemic. In 2012 I took part in the festival as a participating observer. Glastonbury Goddess theology is monotheist in the sense that there is a single deity— the Mother Goddess—with many manifestations. The original "Goddess Temple," situated above a shop in the main street, has at one end a sanctuary area with large statues of the Goddess in different manifestations, including the Lady of Avalon (Glastonbury being identified with the ancient Isle of Avalon). Regular daily offerings of food are made to the deities and then distributed to visitors. The atmosphere is warm, informal, and maternal. The Goddess is encountered as creative, nurturing, and powerful. She is the creative, infusing Spirit of the universe, nature, and life itself. She takes different forms, is found in all cultures, and may be worshiped in the many different historic or modern manifestations in which she appears to her followers. She is there for all who turn to her, offering peace, joy, creative inspiration, and purpose.

Much of this is familiar from liberal Christian theism, with some mystical elements added. What has changed—dramatically—is the gender of the deity. God has become Goddess; Father has become Mother; beards have given way to long flowing locks. It is an example of what Salomonsen (2001) calls "enchanted feminism." Behind this obvious and important reversal, however, there are shared theological themes between paternalist monotheism and this kind of formless mysticism: the unity and all-sufficiency of the deity; her loving, nurturing, and benevolent qualities; divine creation; the

THE GODS OF MODERN SPIRITUALITY   59

human duty of loving care for one another; universalism. Goddess spirituality, Christian theism, and formless mysticism also share an indifference or hostility to magic, from which they distinguish themselves.

When we move to the many forms of paganism that have become increasingly prominent in Glastonbury in the first part of the twenty-first century, however, there is far less evidence of overlap with either paternalist monotheism or formless mysticism. To a visitor walking down the main street in Glastonbury in the late 2010s or early 2020s, or browsing the shops and activities online, what is most striking is the sheer variety of spiritual and magical goods on offer. The Cat and Cauldron offers English magic supplies and quite a highbrow collection of books; the Sacred Cove Hoodoo a North African style of magic; Man, Myth and Magick something more occult and eclectic. Wyrdraven caters to all things heathen, Viking and Asatru; several crystal shops cater to all incomes and needs. In addition, there are several bookstores catering to different tastes, and the Library of Avalon, the "only public access esoteric library in the country."[5] Here Christian monotheism has ceased to be a reference point.

Glastonbury is representative of wider trends. In her "Pagan Census" of 2009–2010, Helen Berger discovered twenty-two separate pagan paths or identities, and all have a presence in Glastonbury (Berger 2019). She finds that the three most popular are "Wiccan" or "Witch" (combined), "Eclectic" and "Goddess Worshipper," followed by "Magic Worker," "Spiritual no labels," "Shaman," "Druid," and "Heathen." The fastest-growing of these are eclecticism and all forms of ethnic paganism (Berger 2019). She also notes the greater prevalence of solitary practice over group involvement but notes that the growth of ethnic forms of paganism means that their stronger emphasis on the value of family and community may start to change that solitary orientation (Berger, private correspondence).

Within this increasingly diverse and eclectic scene, polytheism has become the theological norm. In Glastonbury as elsewhere, pagans recognize many different deities and powers: of both sexes and none; good, evil, and amoral; with varying powers and potentials. Some are distinctive to particular versions of paganism, while others cross between different strands. Pagan deities are distinct beings, not one Being in different manifestations and guises, as in formless mysticism and much Energetic spirituality. No one pagan deity is supreme, omnipotent, omniscient, and omnipresent. The gods operate within limits and have particular areas of concern and operation. They are active within this world and interact in a personal way with human and nonhuman beings, objects, and sites. Some of these deities move between earth and heavens, some between earth and underworld, some between all three. They may blur the boundaries of the human, the nonhuman, and the divine. One Wiccan pagan in Glastonbury whom I interviewed told me that she was currently very engaged with Sekhmet, the Egyptian lion-headed goddess, warrior, and healer. This had been important to her at a time when her husband has been very ill; he is now making an excellent recovery. The gods come and go, she says. They are not always what you wanted or expected. It amuses her to recount that rough-and-tough men often find themselves being visited by elfin deities. She talks about her home altar and her daily practices of visualization and meditation. She is an experienced magician.

Typically, pagan polytheists, like other polytheists past and present, do not claim to know all the gods or even a small portion of them, nor do they deny the reality of deities who make themselves known to others but not to them. Increasingly, there is a suspicion of "cultural appropriation," and weight is given to considerations of place, tradition, and sometimes race—hence the rise of various forms of ethnic paganism. The gods are more closely tied to place, time, and sometimes a people. Here the theological basis of toleration is likely to lie in embracing theistic pluralism (Mavrodes 2000), rather than assimilating all deities into a monotheistic or mystical unity in the style of universalist monotheism or formless mysticism.

The gods of contemporary paganism are also more involved in mundane concerns than a monotheist high God or a formless Spirit. There is a similarity here with the practical usefulness of Energetic spirituality, but magic is much more important in paganism, both in Glastonbury and beyond. When I ask people in Glastonbury how magic works, some give explanations in terms of tapping into natural forces, some speak about the power of human intention, some make reference to invoking deities and supernatural forces, and some combine these responses. Around 40 percent of the pagans who responded to Helen Berger's census agreed that magic taps into "an impersonal force that is not supernatural," and around 60 percent that it involves "spiritual entities," with only around 10 percent agreeing that it is "nothing more than human psychology" (not exclusive options) (Berger 2019, 99). Several people in Glastonbury spoke about the power of human intention concentrated through magical ritual and objects having effects in its own right or by blending with other forces, both natural and divine. Magic can be turned to good or ill and aligned with forces and purposes both benevolent

THE GODS OF MODERN SPIRITUALITY   61

and harmful. In the spiritual marketplace and event-scape of the town, things like curses, the evil eye, bad spells, black magic, and evil spirits are taken seriously—albeit with a dollop of humor and skepticism when appropriate. Many people I spoke to are more interested in what works than in intellectual coherence or system. As one said to me of magic: "I wouldn't believe it if it didn't work."

In the practical and down-to-earth tendencies of their theology, the different varieties of pagan polytheism thus have much in common with the Energetic spirituality that was so prevalent in the holistic milieu in Kendal. Nevertheless, these polytheistic theologies are not identical with those of Energetic spirituality, nor with nature mysticism, pantheism, and animism, all of which overlap with formless mysticism and remain somewhat influential, including in the bookstores of Glastonbury. For example, animism, as Graham Harvey defines it, is the belief that "all that exists lives" (2005, 81). This overlaps with pagan pantheism in the sense that it finds soul or spirit in rock, bird, and plant (Taylor 2010; Wallace 2010), but pagans more typically experience supernatural powers in more singular, personal, relational ways: as beings that are encountered in this tree, not that one; this particular sacred spring; that unique coincidence of events; this moment, not that one. The pagan deities are distinct beings with agency who can enter into relationship with humans. Although some pagans in Glastonbury tell me that they choose their own deities, more say that the gods come to them, often unbidden. Pagans may speak of a supreme power, spirit, or deity, but it is rarely the focus, let alone sole focus, of their everyday devotion and piety: for that you need more relatable deities.

Heathenism, or Asatru, whose presence in Glastonbury is increasingly visible, is an example of the increasingly popular ethnic paganism whose differences from formless mysticism and Energetic or Goddess spirituality are striking. Heathens worship the indigenous, pre-Christian deities to whom they believe themselves linked by ancestral as well as cultural ties. The old Norse and Germanic gods are often prominent. Heathens are attentive to historical sources and archaeological evidence, and their reverence for the past means they are sometimes labeled "reconstructionist." In a recent study of American heathens, Snook (2015) distinguishes between strict reconstructionists and neo-heathens, showing how disputes over historical authenticity and precedent precipitate fractures and disputes. Greater authority is typically accorded to tradition and community than to individual experience; it is conventional to signal that knowledge of the divine is based purely on individual revelation by referring to it in parenthesis as "UPG" (unverified personal gnosis) in order to distinguish it from more authoritative knowledge of the gods that has the backing of tradition. To give too much weight to individual experience is considered too "New Agey" and eclectic. Heathenism runs the gamut from right- to left-wing groups, and there is currently a passionate ongoing discussion among the liberal wing of paganism on how best to combat anti-Semitism and other kinds of racism and violence within the movement (Strmiska 2020). The political dimensions are increasingly clear: in the Ukraine, for example, heathenism has become a mobilizing force against Russian incursion; in the United States some white supremacists in the Charlottesville "Unite the Right" rally of 2017 carried symbols of Odin, while the storming of the US Capitol in 2021 brought other versions to prominence.

Although it is possible that alliances on the far right will now start to develop between Christians and heathens, in theological terms heathenism also departs from Christian monotheism, which evacuates earth and underworld of supernatural entities and concentrates divinity in a transcendent heavenly Father—or his Son, Jesus Christ. It moves in the opposite direction: repopulating the heavens, earth, and underworld with gods and goddesses, ancestors and ghosts, elves and creatures of the deep—in other words, with many different spiritual "races." Many are dangerous, especially if you cross them. Here Christianity's typical close-coupling of God, goodness, and morality fades or disappears altogether.

With heathenism, then, we have traveled far from the theism of the World's Parliament of Religions, far from formless mysticism and Goddess spirituality, and quite a distance from Wicca. Heathen identity is sometimes constructed in active disavowal of one or more of these different paths and pantheons. The fact that heathens are busy reviving gods that Christianity once dishonored and supplanted is not lost on those involved.

Typologies

The fact that I have presented this account of "God-change" within modern spirituality by way of soundings across time does not imply evolution from one theological stage to another. The different types of theology that I have identified are better thought of as distinguishable categories or ideal types.

Each one may rise, fall, and combine with others at different times and in different social settings and individual lives.

In individual autobiography, a shift or conversion from one theological stance to another sometimes occurs in early or later adulthood, even though religious or secular attitudes in general seem to be formed earlier and in relation to parental belief (e.g., Manning 2015). I have spoken to many Christians who have fallen out of love with the father God and into the arms of Goddesses or formless Spirit, and have occasionally heard of the opposite journey, away from formless mysticism or Energetic spirituality to theism— as in Otterbeck's (2013) account of a young male European Muslim who for whom mind-body-spirit practices in the holistic milieu led him to greater involvement and interest in more Islamic prayer and piety. Personal journeys into or away from various forms of pagan pantheism will no doubt become more common as these forms of spirituality become increasingly influential, and a second and third generation is raised.

A typographical approach can make more sense of this kind of complexity and choice—and the wider cultural context—than an evolutionary one. Cultures are always in surplus, with vast possibilities and potentials, some or several of which can be activated in particular social settings and called upon by different actors (Swidler 1986). In multicultural and digitized societies, it is quite easy for people to come into contact with different deities—or for them to make contact with us. Devotion may be incubated in subcultures, appropriated by commercial interests and mainstream culture, then circulated and absorbed back again into religious life and subcultures with even greater conviction, as illustrated by the teenage witchcraft studied by Berger and Ezzy (2007).

The first typology that is immediately familiar and relevant to making sense of this is that of "monotheism and polytheism." For historical and political reasons, the former has more often been the dominant term, with a great variety of different but "other" theological stances being categorized as polytheistic. In evolutionary accounts like the one that shaped the World's Parliament in 1893, monotheism was believed to drive out polytheism in the course of civilizational evolution and progress—a supercessionist account that often justified monotheistic expansionist activity. Less commonly, and often in reaction, polytheism has been defended as the evolutionary telos (e.g., Greer 2014). Rather than rely on such politically and culturally freighted accounts of cultural and religious evolution, however, it is possible to think of monotheism and polytheism as extreme ends of a very widely

64   LINDA WOODHEAD

populated theological spectrum. At one end is the religious purist's ideal of monotheism; at the other is a polytheism that is not qualified by any hint that there may be a supreme deity or unifying principle lying behind or above the plurality of different spiritual entities. Between these extremes lie the more common and varied realities of real-life operative and reflective theologies.

Some historians comment on what they see as the rarity of genuine monotheism (e.g. Korte and de Haardt 2009). Even in medieval Ireland, when Christian power was extensive, for example, the situation is described by one historian as only "monotheistic to a certain extent" (Borsje 2009). Christianization of "pagan" lands in the past called for a depopulation of the theosphere that was only ever partially achieved. Rather than deny the reality of other gods, demons, earth spirits, and other entities, evangelists tended to denounce them or relegate them to subordinate positions: shrines were repurposed, deities renamed, festivals repurposed (Woodhead 2012). The Reformation was, in part, an attempt to do better: its theistic cleansing involved masculinizing the heavens as well as winnowing them, throwing out the Virgin Mary and a plethora of female saints/goddesses in the process (Roper 1989). The extent to which the monotheistic project has ever really succeeded remains open for debate.

And just as monotheism can be said to exist in different degrees, so the same can be said of polytheism. One version of polytheism, for example, has been labeled "henotheism," denoting the worship of one deity without denying the reality of others. But there are many other kinds of polytheism, the word itself being, after all, no more than a clumsy attempt to signify a huge complexity of belief, identity, and practice (Paper 2005).

Formless mysticism can be considered as a distinct theological type, separate from polytheism and monotheism, or as a mystical version of one or other of them. This ambiguity reflects the fluid and adaptable nature of formless mysticism itself. When it emphasizes unity rather than difference within the theosphere and combines this with an apophatic rejection of attempts to personalize the deity and give God attributes, it draws closer to monotheism or at least to monism. By contrast, in Graham Harvey's version of animism referred to above, we have a kind of formless mysticism-cum-polytheism. It is therefore helpful to introduce a second typology, or theological spectrum, that runs between apophatic kinds of theology (whether polytheistic or monotheistic), on the one hand, and cataphatic forms in which God/s are ascribed name, form, narrative, and agency, on the other.

To express this visually, Table 2.1 depicts three ideal types of theology: polytheistic, monotheistic, and formless-mystical. Figure 2.1 adds more nuance

Table 2.1 Ideal types of theology

Polytheism	Monotheism	Mysticism
Many gods and other spiritual entities (both dangerous and benevolent)	God / the Omni-God	Formless spirit

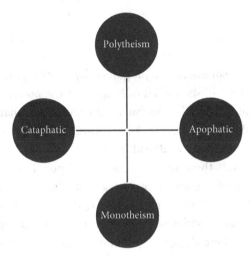

Figure 2.1 A 2 × 2 matrix of god-belief

by visualizing this as a spectrum between monotheistic and more polytheistic kinds of god-belief, depicted by the vertical axis. In addition, we can visualize a spectrum between more cataphatic and apophatic kinds of theology, depicted by the horizontal axis.

Thus Figure 2.1 offers a two-by-two matrix on which many different varieties of real-world god-belief can be located. For example, Graham Harvey's apophatic animism would be located in the top right-hand corner, whereas the theological vision of Wiccans would typically be in the opposite, top left-hand, corner. A strictly formless mysticism would fall in the right-hand bottom corner, but the left-hand bottom corner is the domain of different kinds of theistic monotheism with a personal God.

These typologies allow some precision in thinking about different representations of God/s. The soundings into the theosphere made above suggest that they need to be supplemented and refined by a scheme of classification that has more to do with how and why people relate to God/s. The

Metaphysical religion	Practical religion (including magic)
Abstract, intellectual, cosmological, ethical	Worldly, personal, immediately efficacious uses

Figure 2.2 Spectrum of metaphysical to practical religion

Father God of William Burrows, for example, is a deity to be worshiped, studied, reverenced, and treated with deferential respect. He is a source of moral guidance, inspiration, and judgment. By contrast, the helpful energy drawn upon in the holistic milieu of Kendal, or the powerful forces called upon in practical magic in Glastonbury, have more immediate and practical uses. In Michel de Certeau's terms, the first kind of theology is more strategic, the second more tactical (Woodhead 2013).

Figure 2.2 depicts these relational and "use" possibilities in terms of a spectrum. On the left are the more strategic, intellectual, metaphysical, and ethico-political forms of theology. On the right are more worldly, practical, and immediately useful kinds of theology. In reality, much religion and spirituality falls somewhere along the spectrum, or has different wings, factions, and elements located at different points.

By employing all three of these different classificatory schemes, alone or in combination, it is possible to focus attention not only on what kind of deities and spirits are being invoked in any particular instance of spirituality, but also on whether the primary concern is metaphysical and moral or pragmatic and magical, and what balance of power and agency there is between divine and human. It is also easier to consider the plurality and coexistence of different theologies at play in personal, group, or cultural contexts, rather than trying to force everything into a simple scheme.

Conclusion

Characteristically, the sociology of religion tries to understand religious phenomena by considering their social aspects and relation to wider social identities, domains, and developments. To do so, it is necessary to be two-eyed, paying close attention both to religion and to wider society and trying to discern the links between them. In disciplinary terms, however, the notoriously secular field of sociology can offer no help in understanding religion or theology, while the discipline of theology, the most focused on the divine, is rarely mined for information by sociologists. The result is relative neglect within sociology of religion of Gods and Spirits compared with topics like class, gender, race, identity, the body, and material culture. Reacting against this bias, the geographer Sara MacKian (2012) argues in a recent study of spirituality that "we must remember that spirituality is essentially about spirit." I believe that we need to remain two-eyed, but because my previous work on spirituality has followed the general bias of the field, I have deliberately tipped the balance toward the theological aspects of modern American and British spirituality in this chapter.

I have approached the topic by taking historical soundings from across the last century and a quarter. They hint at some significant theological developments in anglophone spirituality since the late nineteenth century. In 1893, at the World's Parliament of Religions, an omnipotent Father God was still the main reference point, but alternative, more mystical conceptions were already visible, and they were to become increasingly influential in the first part of the twentieth century. This finding is supported by polling after the World War II that reveals a shift from belief in "a personal God" to a "higher power" (Field 2021). By the start of the new millennium, the growing importance of a somewhat different Energetic spirituality with a practical orientation is confirmed by the research carried out in Kendal. In Britain this shift has now been institutionalized in public services from education to healthcare to the point where, by the late twentieth century, it has often displaced Christian theism in public life. The final sounding, taken in Glastonbury in the 2010s, reveals the recent growth of various forms of polytheistic paganism, their influence now evident in film, fiction, and other forms of more mainstream culture as well.

The chapter paints a picture of growing theological diversity, creativity, and choice, responding to multiple influences. Although it may suggest certain overall trends—from monotheism to polytheism, or toward more relatable deities who offer practical and worldly benefits—these are far from uniform or universal, even with the United Kingdom or United States. The sociological question that I have deliberately avoided concerns social causes and correlates of this theological change and diversity. The decline of the Christian churches and their influence is one obvious factor, as is a wider deregulation of the theosphere in which secular as well as religious authorities are losing their ability to control theology and ritual. What is not yet clear is whether these changes are better understood as "post-Christian" or perhaps "postsecular" developments in which new forms of spirituality are diffused through consumer culture and the internet; or as the bubbling up of older forms of vernacular religion that never really went away but remained largely hidden when regulated theism held sway (or both). This in turn raises interesting questions about the adequacy of existing categories of official, folk, popular, everyday, lived, and vernacular religion, and about changing forms of religion and religious socialization in the digital age. Putting God and gods, Spirit and spirits back into the picture is an important step in raising and addressing these issues, and in refining our concepts and theories so that they become more sensitive to the changing contours of modern and contemporary religion and society.

Notes

1. Research in Kendal was carried out as part of a team comprising Paul Heelas (PI), Ben Seel, Bronislaw Szerszynski, and Karin Tusting, and was supported by a grant from the Leverhulme Trust.
2. Closer in heritage to formless mysticism, New Age retains a monism that posits an inner, unifying cosmic principle. New Age thinking characteristically proclaims that the boundaries between human and divine have broken down and that enlightenment is dawning. Holistic spirituality Kendal placed more emphasis on immediate concerns than on cosmological and apocalyptic speculation.
3. Research in Asheville carried out in collaboration with Helen Berger and supported by a British Academy grant.
4. Home page of the website for the Jubilee Community, Asheville, NC, accessed October 18 2020, (http://www.jubileecommunity.org/).
5. Front page, "The Library of Avalon," accessed October 18, 2020, (https://www.unitythroughdiversity.org/the-library-of-avalon.html).

References

Achuthananda, Swami. 2013. *Many, Many, Many Gods of Hinduism*. North Charleston, SC: Create Space Independent Publishing.
Barrows, Henry, ed. 1893. *The World's Parliament of Religions*. 2 vols. Chicago: Parliament Publishing.
Besant, Annie. [1914] 1941. *Mysticism*. London: Theosophical Publishing Society.
Berger, Helen. 2019. *Solitary Pagans: Contemporary Witches, Wiccans, and Others Who Practice Alone*. Columbia: University of South Carolina Press.

Berger, Helen, and Doug Ezzy. 2007. *Teenage Witches: Magical Youth and the Search for the Self*. New Brunswick, NJ: Rutgers University Press.

Besecke, K. 2005. "Seeing Invisible Religion: Religion as a Societal Conversation about Transcendent Meaning." *Sociological Theory* 23: 179–96.

Borsje, Jacqueline. 2009. "Monotheistic to a Certain Extent: The 'Good Neighbours' of God in Ireland." Pp. 53–82 in *The Boundaries of Monotheism: Interdisciplinary Explorations into the Foundations of Western Monotheism*, edited by Anne-Marie Korte and Maaike de Haardt. Leiden: Brill.

Brown, Andrew, and Linda Woodhead. 2016. *That Was the Church That Was: How the Church of England Lost the English People*. London: Bloomsbury.

Chapman, Mark D. 2015. "Theology in the Public Arena: The Case of South Bank Religion." Pp. 92–105 in *Redefining Christian Britain: Post-1945 Perspectives*, edited by Jane Garnett, Matthew Grimley, Alana Harris, William Whyte, and Sarah Williams. London: SCM Press.

Chapman, Mark D., Shuruq Naguib, and Linda Woodhead. 2012. "Go-Change." Pp. 173–95 in *Religion and Change in Modern Britain*, edited by Linda Woodhead and Rebecca Catto. London: Routledge.

Chesterton, G. K. [1908] 1961. *Orthodoxy*. London: Fontana.

Clements, Keith. 1988. *Lovers of Discord*. London: SPCK.

Field, Clive D. 2021. *Counting Religion in Britain, 1970–2020: Secularization in a Statistical Context*. Oxford: Oxford University Press.

Greer, Michael. 2014. *A World Full of Gods*. Shorewood, IL: ADF Publishing.

Harvey, Graham. 2005. "Animism—a Contemporary Perspective." Pp. 81 in *The Encyclopedia of Religion and Nature*, vol. 1, edited by Bron Taylor. New York: Continuum.

Heelas, Paul, and Linda Woodhead, with Benjamin Seel, Bronislaw Szerszynski, and Karin Tusting. 2005. *The Spiritual Revolution: Why Religion Is Giving Way to Spirituality*. Malden, MA: Blackwell.

Hunt, Cheryl. 2020. "The Best of Times, the Worst of Times?" *Journal for the Study of Spirituality* 10(2): 109–13.

Ivakhiv, Adrian. 2001. *Claiming Sacred Ground: Pilgrims and Politics at Glastonbury and Sedona*. Bloomington: Indiana University Press.

Korte, Anne-Marie, and Maaike de Haardt. 2009. *The Boundaries of Monotheism: Interdisciplinary Explorations into the Foundations of Western Monotheism*. Leiden: Brill.

MacKian, Sara. 2012. *Everyday Spirituality: Social and Spatial Worlds of Enchantment*. London: Palgrave MacMillan.

Manning, Christel. 2015. *Losing Our Religion: How Unaffiliated Parents Are Raising Their Children*. New York: New York University Press.

Mavrodes, George. 2000. "Polytheism." Pp. 139–60 in *The Philosophical Challenge of Religious Diversity*, edited by P. Quinn and K. Meeker. New York: Oxford University Press.

Otterbeck, Jonas. 2013. "Experiencing Islam: Narratives about Faith by Young Adult Muslims in Malmô and Copenhagen." Pp. 115–34 in *Everyday Lived Islam in Europe*, edited by Nathal Dessing, Nadia Jeldtoft, and Jørgen Nielsen. Aldershot, UK: Ashgate.

Paper, Jordan. 2005. *The Deities Are Many*. Albany: State University of New York Press.

Roper, Lyndal. 1989. *The Holy Household: Women and Morals in Reformation Augsburg*. New York: Oxford University Press.

Salomonsen, Jone. 2001. *Enchanted Feminism: Ritual Constructions of Gender, Agency and Divinity among the Reclaiming Witches of San Francisco*. London: Routledge.

Schmidt, Leigh E. 2005. *Restless Souls: The Making of American Spirituality*. New York: HarperSanFrancisco.

Seager, Richard Hughes. 1993. *The Dawn of Religious Pluralism: Voices from the World's Parliament of Religions*. LaSalle, IL: Open Court.

Shaw, Jane. 2018. *Pioneers of Modern Spirituality. The Neglected Anglican Innovators of a "Spiritual Not Religious" Age*. London: Darton, Longman and Todd.

Snook, Jennifer. 2015. *American Heathens: The Politics of Identity in a Pagan Religious Movement*. Philadelphia: Temple University Press.

Sointu, Eeva, and Linda Woodhead. 2008. "Holistic Spirituality, Gender, and Expressive Selfhood." *Journal for the Scientific Study of Religion* 47(2): 259–76.

Stringer, Martin. 2008. *Contemporary Western Ethnography and the Definition of Religion*. New York: Continuum.

Strmiska, Michael F. 2020. "Arguing with the Ancestors: Making the Case for a Paganism without Racism." Pp. 1–21 in *Paganism and Its Discontents: Enduring Problems of Racialized Identity*, edited by Holli S. Emore and Jonathan M. Leader. Newcastle upon Tyne, UK: Cambridge Scholars Publishing.

Sullivan, Winnifred Fallers. 2014. *A Ministry of Presence: Chaplaincy, Spiritual Care, and the Law*. Chicago: University of Chicago Press.

Swidler, Ann. 1986. "Culture in Action: Symbols and Strategies." *American Sociological Review* 51(2): 273–86.

Taylor, Bron. 2010. *Dark Green Religion: Nature Spirituality and the Planetary Future*. Berkeley: University of California Press.

Taylor, Charles. 1989. *Sources of the Self*. Cambridge, MA: Harvard University Press.

Taylor, Charles. 1991. *The Ethics of Authenticity*. Cambridge, MA: Harvard University Press.

Taylor, Charles. 2002. *Varieties of Religion Today: William James Revisited*. Cambridge, MA: Harvard University Press.

Tusting, Karin, and Linda Woodhead. 2018. "Kendal Revisited: The Study of Spirituality Then and Now." Pp. 120–34 in *Spaces of Spirituality*, edited by N. Bartolini, S. MacKian, and Steve Pile. London: Routledge.

Underhill, Evelyn. [1910] 1993. *Mysticism: The Nature and Development of Spiritual Consciousness*. 12th ed. Oxford: OneWorld.

Vivekananda, Swami. 1893. "Hinduism." Pp. 968–78 in *The World's Parliament of Religions*, vol. 2, edited by Henry Barrows. Chicago: Parliament Publishing.

Wallace, Mark I. 2010. *When God Was a Bird: Christianity, Animism and the Re-enchantment of the World*. New York: Fordham University Press.

Walter, Tony. 2015. "The Dead Who Become Angels: Bereavement and Vernacular Religion." *Omega* 73(1): 3–28.

Watts, Alan. 1972. *In My Own Way: An Autobiography*. New York: Vintage Books.

Woodhead, Linda. 2001. "The New Spirituality and the World's Parliament of Religions." Pp. 81–96 in *Reinventing Christianity: Nineteenth Century Contexts*, edited by Linda Woodhead. Aldershot, UK: Ashgate.

Woodhead, Linda. 2011. "Christianity and Spirituality: Untangling a Complex Relationship." Pp. 3–21 in *Religion, Spirituality, and Everyday Life*, edited by Giuseppe Giordan and William Swatos. Chicago: Springer.

Woodhead, Linda. 2012. "Mind, Body, Spirit: It's the Dereformation of Religion." *The Guardian*, May 7. https://www.theguardian.com/commentisfree/belief/2012/may/07/mind-body-spirit-dereformation-religion.

Woodhead, Linda. 2013. "Tactical and Strategic Religion." Pp. 9–22 in *Everyday Lived Islam in Europe*, edited by Nathal Dessing, Nadia Jeldtoft, Jørgen Nielsen, and Linda Woodhead. Aldershot, UK: Ashgate.

3

Fearful Asymmetry

Rethinking the Boundaries between Religion and Spirituality

Anna Sun

Tyger Tyger, burning bright,
In the forests of the night;
What immortal hand or eye,
Could frame thy fearful symmetry?

—William Blake, "The Tyger," 1794

When we speak of "spirituality" and "religion" today, there is often an implicit assumption that there is a structural symmetry between them: religion and spirituality seem to exist side by side as social facts[1]. They appear to be definable independently of each other, each having properties that sets it inherently apart. This is the framework often assumed by survey researchers when they ask whether one is religious, or spiritual, or simply "not religious" (Nones), or "spiritual but not religious" (SBNR).

The seemingly symmetrical opposition of "religious" and "spiritual" allows us to view some people as living a life within the boundaries of a particular religion and others as living a life within the boundaries of a particular form of spirituality. The latter may be less clearly defined than the first, but it is nevertheless with its own intrinsic properties, something we are able to recognize as being characteristic of spirituality. Outside of these two spheres we have "the secular," the world in which neither the religious nor the spiritual has significant social, political, or epistemological authority. Here, then, in brief is the framework of which I am speaking: on the one hand we have the dichotomy of religion versus spirituality; on the other hand we have the

---

Anna Sun, *Fearful Asymmetry* In: *Situating Spirituality.* Edited by: Brian Steensland, Jaime Kucinskas, and Anna Sun, Oxford University Press. © Oxford University Press 2022. DOI: 10.1093/oso/9780197565001.003.0004

FEARFUL ASYMMETRY 73

trichotomy of religion and spirituality, each clearly distinct from the other, but both opposed to the secular.

In this chapter, I suggest that, as analytical concepts, religion and spirituality are in fact *relational*, and that their relational nature is connected to the larger social and political context in which they are used and understood. In other words, religion and spirituality are concepts defined *in relation to* each other, rather than independently. What they have in common is their intentional engagements with the sacred that have immense richness and extraordinary diversity across human societies.[2] Such reconsideration is not unlike the kind of critical thinking that has been done with the concept of "religion" or "the secular" (Asad 2003; King 1999; King 2013; McCutcheon 1997). As Talal Asad puts it in his comparative exegesis, the secular "is neither continuous with the religious that supposedly preceded it (that is, it is not the latest phase of a sacred origin) nor a simple break from it (that is, it is not the opposite, an essence that excludes the sacred)" (2003, 25).

By "fearful symmetry," the poet William Blake meant the coexistence and mutual necessity of innocence and experience, beauty and terror, heaven and hell. His symbol for symmetry is the tiger, created by the "immortal hand or eye" of God. For Blake, *symmetry* is a theological conception, whereas for us, asymmetry is a sociological and epistemological one.

This has two implications. First, instead of treating "spirituality" in perpetual contrast to its symmetrical counterpart, "religion," we need to examine "spirituality" —however one defines it—in its "thick" rather than "thin" historical and cultural contexts, examining comparatively its ever-evolving expressions of practice in vastly different global social realities. The kind of deeply nuanced analysis of practice given to the study of religion (Wuthnow 2020) needs to be given to the study of spirituality. Second, we need to be aware of the epistemological asymmetry of the very concepts of "spiritualty" and "religion," which reflects the historical productions of knowledge and the complex relations of power embedded in the processes of the making and maintenance of these concepts. Such relations of power reside in often implicit yet long-standing hierarchies that privilege understandings of "religion" that are based predominantly on Western experiences, that is, Christianity, a monotheistic and Abrahamic religious tradition that emerged from Judaism and is related to Islam. As a result, the concept "religion" implies a form of engagement with the sacred that empathizes belief, religious identity, and religious affiliation, as well as sets of institutionally sanctioned practices that are characteristic only of monotheistic traditions.

74 ANNA SUN

What is left out of this framework are the unfamiliar expressions of non-Western engagements with the sacred, which are seen either as "spiritual" or "*not* religious." But what if we rethink our conceptualization of both concepts, not out of *ressentiment* but out of the desire to do justice to the multivariate engagements with the sacred that take place outside of the realm of Euro-American experience? What if we treat the concept of spirituality not as the subordinating "Other" to the all-encompassing norm of religion, but rather, view monotheistic "religion" as the exceptional "Other" to the more general norm of spirituality? What if this overturning of our conceptual imagination might help us see better not only the experiences of people in far-away places, but also people's experiences here and now?

The Boundary Work of "Religion" and "Spirituality"

The boundaries of spirituality seem to be changing perpetually across time and place, but perhaps there is a certain pattern at work. The boundaries of "spirituality" are in relation to the boundaries of "religion" in a given society, and its changing meaning depends on the reality of the ever-changing course of religion. This may be a good example of the merging and shaping of social and symbolic boundaries, as defined by Michele Lamont and Virag Molnar:

> Social boundaries are objectified forms of social differences manifested in unequal access to and unequal distribution of resources (material and nonmaterial) and social opportunities. They are also revealed in stable behavioral patterns of association, as manifested in connubiality and commensality. Only when symbolic boundaries are widely agreed upon can they take on a constraining character and pattern social interaction in important ways. Moreover, only then can they become social boundaries, i.e., translate, for instance, into identifiable patterns of social exclusion or class and racial segregation. . . . But symbolic and social boundaries should be viewed as equally real: The former exist at the intersubjective level whereas the latter manifest themselves as groupings of individuals. (2002, 168–69)

In the case of the United States, for example, where there is the long-standing tradition of highly institutionalized and congregational religious life as the dominant form of religion, spirituality is often (though not always) defined, symbolically, as what is left out of religion's boundaries, by which we mean diverse beliefs and varied everyday practices outside of—or on the margins of—existing religious institutional norms. These norms of religion emphasize belief in theological doctrines, congregational membership, and the attendance at formal religious services. Scholars have argued for a new approach to the study of religious life—the "lived religion" approach—which emphasizes diverse practices in everyday experiences, making spirituality part of a more inclusive understanding of religion (Ammerman 2013, 2020; Hall 1997). This important intervention allows scholars to account for aspects of religious life that do not fit easily into existing boundaries of religion and its related institutions.

Scholars have pointed out, in various ways, that the boundary between religion and spirituality has been constantly shifting (Smith 2009). Research has shown that the SBNR population has been steadily increasing, partly because "people are less likely to say they are religious," but also because "a larger share of nonreligious people say they are spiritual" (Chaves 2017, 38). These who are SBNR show openness to "non-monotheistic, spiritual traditions" (McClure 2017, 64), although "the centrality of theism" is still "the most prominent referent in American spirituality" (Steensland et al. 2018, 469). The religious Nones are not necessarily secular, with a significant percentage engaging regularly in prayers, as well as believing in God (Drescher 2016; Lipka 2015).

The boundaries of religion/spiritual/secular are indeed blurry. Analyzing public debates over religion in Quebec, Peter Beyer suggests that the classification of a religion and the "performance of religion" are social and cultural constructs, "a matter of political contestation" as well as "a matter of power assertion and distribution" (Beyer 2020, 2). In other words, the line between what is religious and what is secular is often a contested one serving culture and political purposes, and its settlement reflects relations of power rather than inherent boundaries. In terms of the line between religion and spirituality, Nancy Ammerman suggests that "spiritual-but-not religious . . . is more a moral and political category than an empirical one," and proposes four spiritual discourses: "the theistic package," "the extra-theistic package," "the ethical spirituality," and the "belief and belonging spirituality" (Ammerman 2013b, 275). In her work on spiritual experience and lived religion, Ammerman (this volume) views spirituality as an essential part of religious practice. These nuanced takes on religion, spirituality, and the secular are much-needed paradigms for empirical research in North America and elsewhere. In societies where having a "religion" and a "religious identity" as well as a "religious affiliation" are taken-for-granted actions in social life, the dynamics between religion and spirituality are anchored in their interchange, with the boundaries porous, mutable, yet always functionally in place.

Yet these basic assumptions about what having a religion means are characteristic of *predominantly monotheistic religious worlds*. In such worlds—genuinely pluralistic and inclusive as they might be—one is supposed to have an exclusive religious identity (one cannot be a Protestant and a Catholic at once, for instance), a set of beliefs and practices that are implicitly if not explicated exclusive (one cannot—or at least one should not—offer prayers to both Jesus Christ and the Guanyin Bodhisattva), and religious affiliation that is aligned with one's religious identity (a Muslim would attend a mosque, but not a church). There is plenty of spiritual space in these worlds, so to speak, where an observant Jew might practice Buddhist meditation outside of the synagogue, or a practicing Episcopalian might take a Catholic retreat in a monastery, or a Quaker might contemplate Hindu or Confucian ethics in a Friends' meeting. Such creative "spiritual" actions both in and outside of the boundaries of monotheistic religious traditions are common today, and sometimes people might even break free all together and discover gods and goddesses buried in the deep past of a monotheistic world (Woodhead, this volume). But no matter how much "spirituality" there is and how diverse it might be, it needs to be understood in relation to what "religion" is and means in these societies.

Let us now consider how to understand "religion" and "spirituality" in a different kind of religious world, such as China. It is a world in which polytheistic religious practices and beliefs are the norm, even when there are sizable populations who are monotheists. Scholars such as Asad have pointed out that the Protestantism-informed framework for the understanding of religion—focusing especially on belief—has been the foundation of the academic knowledge of religion, which cannot do justice to religious life in most parts of the world (Asad 2003). The problem goes beyond the emphasis on belief; the emphasis on exclusive religious identity and religious affiliation is also part of what I call "the monotheistic assumptions" (Sun 2016). The issue here is not religious politics—religious tolerance or religious conflicts, for example—but *religious epistemology*.

The nonmonotheistic/polytheistic imagination is necessary for understanding societies in which historically there has not been a significant separation between what is "religious" and what is "secular"; in which religious life and other aspects of life experiences are constantly intertwined; in which ritual activities involving gods and spirits are not, for the most part, tied to religious affiliations or memberships; in which ritual time is an integral part of social time, even in highly developed urban centers; in which ritual relations are integral parts of social relations, binding families and clans; and in which ethical demands are often embodied in and connected to diverse ritual activities rather than singular religious identity.

Here I am thinking of societies such as China, where "religion" and "religious identity" as categories of classification have histories very different from those of societies such as the United States. In the case of China, the notions of the set-apart "religion" and the exclusive form of "religious identity"—as formed in the monotheistic context and much deployed by scholars globally in the nineteenth and twentieth centuries—have been intimately connected with the modernization agenda of the state since the turn of the twentieth century (Palmer and Goossaert 2011). Today, over a hundred years later, having a self-avowed religious identity is still mostly correlated to being a Christian or Muslim, who is seen as "having a religion" (according to recent surveys, about 2 percent of Chinese are Muslims and about 5 percent Christians). Most people who follow polytheistic religious traditions such as Confucianism or Daoism claim no religious identity (Sun 2020a).

But in traditional as well as in contemporary China, it is not the case that the Chinese are "less religious"; the issue is that, as can be seen in survey and ethnographic data, they engage with the sacred *differently*. These facts require us to reconsider the very concepts of religion and spirituality in the context of Chinese society, or perhaps any society that does not share the predominantly Christian—or monotheistic—religious history of North America and Europe.

It is time to turn to a sketch from my fieldwork in contemporary China, as a way of offering a sense of the actual lived experience of prayer and ritual life in Chinese society.

Notes from the Field

It was a bright October morning when I joined the Chen family to observe their most important ritual day of the year.[3] We were in Lan County, Shanxi (*shanxi*山西) Province, known as much for its coal production as for its long cultural and religious history. This antique region is very much the heartland

78 ANNA SUN

of ancient China. Autumn is usually the most beautiful season in the north, and this warm and luminous October was no exception.

By car, L. County is about four hours south of the famous Yungang Grottoes (*yungang shiku* 云冈石窟), a UNESCO World Heritage Site with extraordinary Buddhist sculptures carved into the mountains and caves during the Northern Wei dynasty (386–535), when Buddhism was becoming an important religious and social force in East Asia. The nearby city of Datong (*datong* 大同), the ancient capital of Northern Wei, has many imposing and ritually active Buddhist monasteries and temples, serene yet powerful testaments to the continued influence of Buddhism in China today. Datong also has sacred sites of other religious traditions, such as the graciously renovated Confucius Temple, where I talked to young people praying for examination success, and the grand old mosque with its magnificent grey stone facade, founded in Ming Dynasty (1368–1644) and the center of a proud and devout local Muslim community. During my visit there, the women were welcoming and cheerful, showing me their embroidered hijabs that they obviously took delight in.

To the north of L. County, three hours by car, is the city of Ping Yao (*pingyao* 平遥), another World Heritage Site. It is a well-preserved city founded in the fourteenth century, with its original city walls and architectural structures still intact, including many religious ones. I visited Ping Yao right before I went to Lan County and found the ancient city a tourist destination with a lively religious scene, not at all unusual in China, for the main attractions of historical tourist sites tend to be monasteries and temples, and people take the touring opportunity to pray to deities in famous temples. In Ping Yao, not only were the temples well preserved and clearly well managed, but they were also well attended, with a bustling stream of visitors touring the sites and paying respects to the various deities they encounter, for the most part indiscriminately. A middle-aged man visiting the temples with his family said to me, "After all, who am I to say which deity deserves to be prayed to, and which ones do not?" This was the logic followed by most people I interviewed, unless they were Muslims or Christians. People would make offerings to deities along the route of their visit, even though the gods or goddesses they prayed to might be in temples that belong to widely diverse religious traditions. Buddhist and Daoist monastics or professionals do mark the distinctions between different religious traditions, but even for them the lines are often porous. I have observed two Buddhist monks offering prayers and incense while visiting the White Clouds Temple in Beijing, an important

Daoist site. They expressed their ritual action as "paying respect to all the deities."

The Confucius Temple was wholly majestic, one of the earliest and largest Confucius temple complexes in the country. One enters through a grand wooden crimson gate, crosses a classical fishpond on decorative bridges, and passes through a large hall venerating Confucian sages whose lives exemplified Confucian virtues of filial piety, courage, wisdom, and justice, before reaching the Great Hall, reserved for major ritual activities. I learned from the woman working at the bookshop of the Ping Yao Confucius Temple that, for the locals, it was important to pray to Confucius in the beginning of the Lunar New Year for blessings in educational success, followed by prayers to the God of Fortune for blessings in business affairs in another temple nearby. She said that during the first month of the Lunar New Year, there would be hundreds and even thousands of people praying there, mostly from nearby counties.

The God of Fortune resided in the City God Temple, along with the City God himself, the deity blessing the particular locality of which he is in charge. The temple houses other significant deities as well, such as the Kitchen Gods, who are often depicted as a couple in elaborate formal court robes, as well as "assorted gods in the side halls," the official description of lesser deities. To pray to the God of Fortune was an act very similar to praying to Confucius: one would offer incense, prayers (verbal prayers or prayers written on cards purchased in the temple), objects such as flowers, fruits, or other food items, and often monetary donations. Most people conducted these rituals with fluency. There were also parents teaching young children how to hold up incense or how to bow in prayer, and there were roughly equal numbers of women and men making offerings.

As I was leaving Ping Yao, I came across a Catholic church marked on the map but not in tourist materials. It was clearly in need of repair; the structure looked as if it were built at least a hundred years ago and not touched since. I learned from talking to the elderly woman sitting in the church that, even though there were no formal services, people would still come in to pray, sometimes a few dozens a day. A donation box for church repair was placed in a visible place near the entrance, and to my surprise—since this was not something formally sanctioned by the Chinese Catholic Church—a small photo of Pope Francis was hanging on a side wall.

The many religious sites of Ping Yao were still fresh in my mind when I arrived in L. County. Unlike Ping Yao, L. County is not a tourist hub, nor a place with a notable religious culture. Situated in the heartland of coal production, it has a solid economy based on mining and agriculture, and today a rising middle class. I met the friend who invited me to join the Chen family rituals in a sunny and spacious apartment in one of the most desirable highrises, overlooking a calm river flowing by.

My friend Lin is a warm and vivacious woman in her fifties. A professor at an Ivy League university, she left China thirty years ago to study for her PhD in the United States and stayed on. This was the first time in more than ten years that she had come back to L. County, the birthplace of her deceased father. Of her four siblings, the oldest two were the offspring of her father's long-deceased first wife. Lin's two other siblings were the children of Lin's own mother. The younger brother lived in Canada and was unable to join this important family occasion. The younger sister lived in Sichuan Province, and she came to L. County specifically for the purpose of joining her older sister in this long-hoped-for grave visitation.

The eldest sister, already in her seventies, was the host of this gathering. She could not join the grave rituals because of health, but she insisted that we all have breakfast together—the famed handcrafted noodles of the region that she made for the "family and guest from afar" —before we set off. Logistics were discussed during breakfast: where to purchase ritual objects for the offering, whose car to drive, whether the rules for death anniversaries would apply to this ritual date. I learned that the date was chosen through an ancient almanac, with the explicit purpose of accommodating Lin's visit from the United States.

Lin's younger sister explained, "Someone might say, 'You are a scientist— how could you observe the almanac?' But these are two totally separate matters." Her pregnant daughter wanted to join her for this visit, but she said it was a bad idea: "Graves are not good for unborn babies; there is too much *yinqi* [energy of the Underworld] in such places." She seemed to be well versed in matters of rituals. During the discussion of what objects to bring to the grave offering, she said that, within the first three years of a family member's death, there were many rules one must follow. But afterward it was mainly about "following your heart's desire." Around the table, all agreed that these grave rituals came from the Confucian tradition, and filial piety was the foundation of a decent life. Lin was clearly moved when her siblings commended her for her return to be part of the grave visitation, which showed her filial love for her father.

We set off in the car of Lin's cousin—the first son of her eldest sister—who was the director of the local branch of a major bank. He was in his forties, low-key, knowledgeable about local customs, and fully engaged in the preparations for the rituals. Under his direction, we stopped on a commercial street specializing in religious ritual objects. There were several shops selling grave-related ritual items, and the Chen family made purchases that they thought appropriate for today: two huge wreaths—as tall as fix feet—made with paper flowers; large piles of "spirit money," which were colorful papers printed as currency to be burned in front of the grave as a way of sending money to the spirit of deceased family members in the Underworld; fruits and pastries to be offered to the spirits of the deceased. Lin ordered some bananas and oranges, which her father enjoyed while alive— "it has to be four pieces of each rather than eight," the woman in the shop said, "for four are meant for funerals and eight for weddings" —while her younger sister ordered a few sets of pastries, each set representing the household making the offering on that day.

On this clear October day, the leaves were just beginning to change, and the air was crisp. After an hour on the highway and another half an hour on a smaller road into a wooded area, we parked the car by the side of the hill and proceeded to climb up through wild sorghum and dense bushes and trees, carrying all the items the family had purchased. The family bought this parcel of land because of its excellent feng shui, and it was an expensive undertaking to build the grave here. The site was discreet and not easy to access, which added to its sacrality.

As we came to the top of the hill, we emerged from the trees and were greeted with a view of green valleys in all directions. In the far distance could be seen the pale contour of an enormous industrial plant. The grave itself was impressive: the heavy headstone was at least seven feet tall, with a long text caved onto its gray surface, a narrative in classical Chinese of the deceased's many achievements, as well as declarations of filial love from his children and their spouses. The Chen clan belonged to the local elite, and the gravestone reflected the confident representation of a patriarch's successful life. The commemorative narrative stated that he joined the Communist Party early, participated in the anti-Japanese war in the 1930s, and became the first party official in the county. His subsequent positions were all bureaucratic and substantial.

As I was reading about his many official accomplishments, I wondered what he might think of all the religious elements surrounding his burial and the scene of his afterlife. Would he have cared about the feng shui of his grave? Would he have sanctioned the ritual objects we carried up the hill to be offered to him? Would he have approved of the prayers addressed to him? I turned around to see what the Chen family was doing, who had been talking cheerfully until now. A hush had fallen among them, as a warmer light shone on the grass and fallen leaves of this autumnal hill. I was reminded that such grave rituals in China were often not sorrowful but warm and peaceful; it was a chance to connect with the loved ones who were no longer in this world yet still, somehow, within reach.

My friend Lin was putting white paper ribbons on the vibrant paper-flower wreaths, on which she had written couplets in classical Chinese about her gratitude to her father, signing not only her own name but also the names of her American husband and her son. Her cousin the bank director was setting up the food offerings in front of the grave, arranging the fruits and pastries as objects for the dead on an altar. Stretching to reach, Lin's younger sister was cleaning the gravestone with a soft cloth, a gesture essential to the ritual of *saomu*: cleaning the grave of the deceased. Soon, the gray stone shone. She then traced an invisible circle with her fingers on the ground in front of the grave, next to the food offerings, and gathered all the "spirit money" inside it to be burned, the circle a designated safe space for the spirit to return without disturbance. "We are back to see you now, Father," she said.

Spirituality as a Relational Concept

The preceding vignette is an example of how, in the case of contemporary China, a different kind of dynamics is at work in relation to the sacred—to deities, gods, and spirits. Why do the concepts of "religious" or "spiritual" seem inadequate to give an account of the members of the Chen family, who conducted ritual activities with no concern for religious member-ship or spiritual consciousness? To understand their experience in terms of the trichotomy of concepts that we use—the secular, the religious, and the spiritual—it is necessary to have a sense of the historical context of Chinese life, particularly in the past century.

From the beginning of the twentieth century China has gone through pro-found economic and political changes and transformed itself from a prein-dustrial imperial dynasty—1911 marked the end of imperial China—to an industrialized modern state. From the outset, many leading political and social reformers believed that, in order for China to become a modern nation, it needed not only to adopt scientific knowledge and republican politics, but also to renounce traditional ways of life, things that belonged to the old, "feudal" Chinese society. The "old ways" included "magic," "superstition," "primitive" beliefs and practices, as well as Confucian values, which had dominated Chinese society for over two thousand years. Although there were individuals who took exception to this attitude, such as Kang Youwei, a leading reformer who unsuccessfully promoted Confucianism as the Chinese national religion, the reform had a strong agenda of establishing an entirely modern and secular state (Palmer and Goossaert 2011; Sun 2013).

We can see clearly today how such a radical rejection of the past profoundly influenced China's modern encounters with the West. Eager to be a modern nation-state yet lacking the economic, technological, and military power of European countries and the United States, China suffered humiliating military defeats in the two Opium Wars in the nineteenth century (1839–1860). As China emerged from this national trauma in the twentieth century, its intellectual elites vowed to achieve Western-style modernity in China at all cost (Wang 2014).

The May Fourth Movement was a watershed moment in modern Chinese history. It started on May 4, 1919, in Beijing as a student demonstration against colonialism and the Treaty of Versailles, as well as the backward-looking Chinese national politics. It demanded the Chinese state "close the shop of the Confucians" and "invite Mr. Democracy and Mr. Science to China." This modernizing attitude was inherited by the Chinese communists, who established the Chinese Communist Party in 1921. Throughout this turbulent process, traditional ritual practices were distrusted and often vilified by Enlightenment-minded antisuperstition campaigners (Schwartz 1972). With the founding of the People's Republic in 1949, all things "primitive," "feudal," and "antiquated" were condemned.

Although traditional Chinese ritual practices were deemed antimodern, by a curious twist the idea of "religion" —a late nineteenth-century "loan word" from Japanese—still had its peculiar political allure, for "religion" seemed to be a necessary part of being a modern nation-state, as exemplified by Christianity in the West. After all, the great Western nations all had "religion," and a modern state is one that has "religious freedom." This idea of "religion," informed mostly by the example of modern Protestantism, was the operational definition of "religion" for the Chinese state when it started the Bureau of Religious Affairs in the 1950s. It was also behind the creation

84 ANNA SUN

of the "Five Major Religions" classification scheme in the same period, which include Buddhism, Daoism, Islam, Protestantism, and Catholicism (Confucianism did not make the cut) (Sun 2013).

In the seventy years of the People's Republic of China, all forms of religious life have been regulated and controlled by the state. During the Cultural Revolution (1966–76), denunciation of religions and rituals reached a fever pitch, with temples, churches, and shrines all suffering great damage during that destructive decade. Things stated to change in the 1990s, however, after the beginning of China's economic reform. In the first decade of the twenty-first century, mostly for the purpose of political legitimation, the Chinese state started paying increasing attention to traditional cultural and religious traditions, especially Confucianism (Bell 2008; Billioud 2018; Billioud and Thoraval 2015; Hammond and Richey 2015; Sun 2013). This opened the door—or floodgates—to the revival, reinvention, and overall renaissance of traditional Chinese ritual life, even though organized religions such as Christianity and Islam remained under tight control, with increasingly severe repression of Uyghur Muslims (Buckley and Ramzy 2020; Madsen 2011; Vala 2017; Yang 2011).

But how about spirituality in China?

If we were to follow the contemporary scholarly convention of treating religion as the norm and spirituality as the Other, we would classify those who formally belong to institutionalized religions in China as religious (Christian, Muslims, and officially converted Buddhists). People who fall into this category—namely the ones who claim religious affiliations in surveys—are certainly in the minority in China. According to surveys, they are under 25 percent of the population.[4] Indeed, the notion of "religion," as understood in the West, does not adequately address the lived religious reality of China.

However, if we treat spirituality as the norm, we can see that the majority of the Chinese conduct ritual activities regularly: according to the 2007 Horizon survey, 68 percent of Chinese participated in ancestral rites in the past year, regardless of their religious affiliations. In the 2016 Horizon survey, this number had risen to nearly 80 percent.

There is something else that makes the discussion of religion in China quite different from, say, the discussion of religion in the United States. The dominant form of religious life in China—as in most of East Asia—is not one that stresses belief, membership, or attendance at formal services. This is a historical reality that long preceded the repression of organized religions by the Chinese state. For centuries the dominant form of religious life in China has been one that emphasizes diverse beliefs, everyday ritual activities, and diffused attachments to multiple religious traditions. C. K. Yang's term for Chinese religions without clear institutional structures and boundaries is "diffused religion" (Yang 1962). In other words, what is seen as distinct from American religious life is instead the norm in China, with the exception of followers of monotheistic religions such as Christianity and Islam, which, though numerous and growing, are still a minority of the Chinese population (Christians and Muslims combined count for under 8 percent by most accounts) (Horizon 2007; Pew 2012). This means that we have to be open to new ways of thinking about what it means to be religious in China.

Looking for Spirituality in the Chinese Context

To paraphrase Wilfred Cantwell Smith, the question "How do we understand 'spirituality' in the Chinese context?" is "one that the West has never been able to answer, and China never able to ask" (Smith 1963: 86). People do not speak of "spirituality" in the sense that we may use the term in Europe or North America, as something in contrast to "religion," something defined in relation to a more dominant form of highly organized and institutionalized religious life. Furthermore, even if one attempts to introduce the term in interviews in China, there is no full equivalent of the English word "spirituality" in Chinese (Lippiello 2018). The closest transliteration is *jingshen* (精神), but it has multifarious meanings that have to be unpacked.

There are essentially three usages of the term *jingshen* (精神):

1. The "life of the spirit," or the spiritual life: it refers to an ethical life, or life of the soul. This is a term frequently used in government propaganda on the importance of civility:
   Jingshen shenghuo (精神生活)　the life of the spirit
   Jingshen wenming (精神文明)　civilizing the life of the spirit
   Jingshen jiaohua (精神教化)　cultivation of the life of the spirit

2. Psychological and emotional state, or mental health:
   Jingshen hao (精神好)　in good spirts
   Jingshen buhao (精神不好)　in ill spirits
   Jingshen bing (精神病)　mentally ill

86   ANNA SUN

3. Engagement with something beyond the everyday world:
   Jingshen jituo (精神寄托)   resting spirit/hope on something beyond

In fact, the best translation of "spirituality" might be terms that are not direct translations of the English word, but express a sense of engagement with the world of spirits as well as the cosmos:

Tongling (通灵)   having connections with the spiritual world
Youling (有灵)   having the aura of spirits
Lingxing (灵性)   having a spiritual nature; in tune with the spiritual world

In order to denote the connection with spirits, people indeed use terms such as *lingxing* 灵性 or *tongling* 通灵 to describe someone who is in tune with the world of gods and spirits, or the divine forces in the cosmos (*ling* 灵 is one of the words used for spirits).

The concept of "spiritual milieu," or "the milieu of spirituality," may be useful in speaking of the spheres covered by these examples (Campbell 2002; Heelas and Woodhead 2005). The term highlights the way spirituality and the social are profoundly interconnected, as well as the relational nature between the concepts of "spirituality" and "religion." The word "milieu" has a strong connotation of social environments. To be spiritual is to be engaged with the spiritual milieu. It is indeed a person's environment, one that includes not only the living, but also the gods and spirits, all in harmony with the cosmos.

Daoist practice is a good example of how one becomes in tune with this spiritual milieu. Palmer and Siegler speak of Daoist bodily cultivation as "cosmological attunement," which is a process "in which spirituality consists in the harmonization of the dynamic structure and forces of the body/mind with the corresponding dynamic structure and forces of society and of the cosmos" (2017, 9). Such spiritual exercise is what Palmer and Siegler call "spiritual subject formation." Although Daoist practices seem to align "with 'holistic' approaches" to healing and well-being, and seem to attune "to the spiritual sensibilities of a hyper individualistic, postmodern West," Palmer and Siegler suggest that it is not so:

And yet, these practices emerged in China over 2,500 years ago, and have evolved in a religious field structured by the dynamic tensions between the imperial center and local societies, between the canonical traditions of Confucianism, Buddhism, and Daoism, and between communal ritual traditions and salvationist movements. . . . [T]hese forms are deeply embedded within border cultural and social practices, institutions, and contexts. (2017, 10)

Is this religion or spirituality in our conceptual scheme? If we bear in mind the fact that traditionally only Daoist monastics have a clearly defined Daoist religious identity, not their lay followers, then we might see both groups as being in the spiritual milieu, with the monastic drawing an institutional boundary around themselves. As Andrew Abbott puts it, "Social entities come into existence when social actors tie social boundaries together in certain ways. Boundaries come first, then entities" (1985, 860). This might be the case for Chinese religious life in general: religion, "a social thing," exists only when its boundaries are tied together by social actors under specific historical, cultural, and political circumstances (Sun 2020b). To speak metaphorically, they become visible islands in the sea of the spiritual milieu.

The "Spiritual Milieu" of Contemporary China

There is one thread that runs through all these elements, which is that they all engage with something *outside this world*. When people address God or gods, it is an engagement with something beyond, some divine force that holds power over us. When people address ancestral spirits, it is an engagement with something in the underworld, where the spirits dwell (whatever it might mean to the actors conducting rituals). Scholars have proposed different ways of studying these entangled arrays of beliefs and practices engaging with the spiritual realm (Chau 2011; Dean 1998; Lagerwey 2019; Sun 2016), with increasing attention paid to the transnational and global nature of the "Chinese religious field" or "Chinese religious systems" (Dean 2020; Sun 2020b; Yang 2016).

The spiritual milieu is what the Chinese religious systems mean to individual actors. What we think of as the "Chinese religious systems" is the view from above, an aerial perspective that allows us to see the entirety of the landscape from a distance. And the "spiritual milieu" is the lived reality of people who inherit and thrive in these complex ecological systems of practices, beliefs, institutions, and ethics. The spiritual milieu is something most of these social actors take for granted, the way water is to fish who dwell in it.

88 ANNA SUN

In the Chinese spiritual milieu, the following components are key:

- Ritual practices
- Sacred texts and oral transmissions
- Religious institutions (churches, temples, mosques, religious academies, etc.)
- Religious professionals (monks, priests, pastors, shamans, healers)
- Ethical frameworks informed by religious traditions (Confucian, Buddhist, Daoist, Islamic, Christian, Baha'i, etc.)
- God; gods; spirits of deceased persons; spirits of the natural world (places, animals, etc.)
- Beliefs (often expressed implicitly through practice) in the presence of *tian* (or Heaven, a divine presence that ensures a moral cosmos), and *ming* (fate of individuals, communities, nations, dynastic changes, etc.)
- Individual actors who practice rituals and engage with the elements above

What these elements have in common is their being all connected to something beyond this world. There is no apparent unity to this "something beyond," for there is no well-defined theology that fully articulates the Chinese spiritual milieu: it is too diverse and vast. It consists of "toolkits" people use to engage in ritual activities and to make sense of life experiences through various ethical systems of meaning; it produces spiritual habitus that is embodied and often gendered; it maintains a shared cosmology and sacred ritual calendar—what I call the Chinese "*Fasti,*" as in the Roman fast (Rüpke 2013; Sun 2016) —which is shared by the majority of the Chinese people.

It is important to note that the engagement with the world beyond does not negate the actors' commitment to rational scientific reasoning in this world. These are different milieus: the physical reality of this world stays on one plane, and the spiritual reality of the other world stays both above (heaven) and under (the underworld of afterlife). The actors who engage in ritual activities know that their hands, hearts, and minds are reaching out to something that is at least partially beyond our everyday world. When one prays and makes offerings to the spirits of deceased ancestors, one does not need to denounce the validity of claims made by the logic of scientific reasoning, or turn one's back on this-worldly realities, with their increasing dependency on technology. One simply steps into the spiritual milieu while conducting rituals and steps back when the ritual is complete.

If we were to use the term "religion" as defined with implications of certain norms that are typical of Protestantism, such as the centrality of belief, congregational belonging, and clear religious identity, we may say that the sphere of "religion" is only one part of what we term the spiritual milieu. In this context, "religion" denotes a specific expression and form of spiritual life, with stricter boundaries, firmer religious identities, and a professional class that guides and polices the adherents' beliefs and behaviors. To the people who belong to the same spiritual milieu but not the more restricted spheres of "religion," this may be seen as a sterner, and more explicit, form of spiritual life, though not fundamentally different from what they know and experience.

Conclusion

In our current vocabulary, the relation between "religion" and "spirituality" is not unlike the relation between other dichotomies of power, such as "men" and "women," or "West" and "East." Simone de Beauvoir was the first to point out the "asymmetrical" relation between men and women:

> The categories masculine and feminine appear as symmetrical in a formal way on town hall records or identification papers. The relation of the two sexes is not that of two electrical poles: the man represents both the positive and the neuter to such an extent that in French *hommes* designates human beings. . . . "The female is female by virtue of a certain *lack* of qualities," Aristotle said. "We should regard women's nature as suffering from natural defectiveness." . . . Humanity is male, and man defines woman, not in herself, but in relation to himself; she is not considered an autonomous being. "Woman, the relative being," writes Michelet. ([1949] 2011, 5)

A structurally similar argument can be found in Edward Said's analysis of the East and the West: "Orientalism is a style of thought based upon an ontological and epistemological distinction made between 'the Orient' and (most of the time) 'the Occident'" (Said 1979, 2). Although these dichotomic concepts seem evenly balanced, like yin and yang, symmetry only exists in their logical forms, not in historical empirical reality, in which the two parts are always in an asymmetrical relation of unequal influence and power.

And this may be true with the historical usage of the concepts of "religion" and "spirituality" as well. What is at stake here is not gendered hierarchy or

90 ANNA SUN

colonial power, but epistemological dominance. Dipesh Chakrabarty makes a similar point about the importance of postcolonial knowledge production:

> A key question in the world of postcolonial scholarship will be the following. . . . There was a time—before scholarship itself became globalized—when the process of translating diverse forms, practices, and understandings of life into universalist political-theoretical categories of deeply European origin seemed to most social scientists an unproblematic proposition. That which was considered an analytical category (such as capital) was understood to have transcended the fragment of European history in which it may have originated. At most we assumed that a translation acknowledged as "rough" was adequate for the task of comprehension. (2007, 17)

What we gain from the effort of "provincializing" our concepts through the reconsideration of analytical categories, however, is not only a better understanding of non-Western "forms, practices, and understandings of life." What we gain is also a potentially better conceptualization of lived religious experiences globally. The mobility of religious life—of people as well as of ideas and practices—has been our shared reality for centuries. What is often referred to as "spirituality" in the West has long been connected to the transmission of Eastern religious traditions, from Buddhism to Daoism (Jaffe 2014; Palmer and Siegler 2017). In the United States, we have been deeply entangled in a web of profoundly transnational forms of religious life ever since Thoreau and Emerson started engaging with Hindu and Buddhist ideas in their small New England village, and certainly now, when we are turning to Zen and mindfulness practices for both personal and corporate needs (Bender 2010; Kucinskas 2018; Versluis 1993). We also must mention the experiences of Asian immigrants who have been struggling to fit their culturally embedded and ritually embodied religious experiences into the rigid boxes of religious identities (Chen 2014; Jeung et al. 2019).

However, if we cease to see "religion" as the dominant form and "spirituality" as the subordinate one, new possibilities emerge (Figure 3.1). To make a bold move, we might consider taking the spiritual milieu as the default landscape, and developments such as Protestantism as exceptional cases, with their strong boundaries, exclusive identity, and emphasis on conscious and explicit belief. In other words, we could see the spiritual milieu and its constantly changing landscapes of interactions among practices, beliefs,

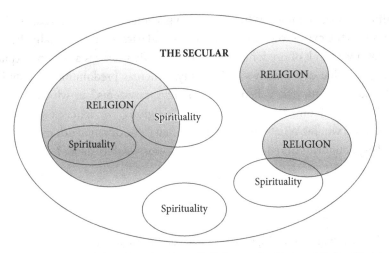

Figure 3.1 Mapping Our Assumptions: Religion as the Norm, Spirituality as the Other

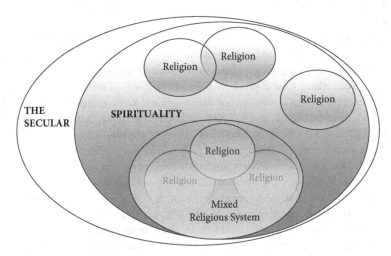

Figure 3.2 Rethinking the Boundary of Religion and Spirituality

institutions, and individual actors as the norm, and view the formal or explicit religions as adding new dynamics and elements to the mix.

"Clarifying the terms" (*zhengming*) is as much a hermeneutic practice as an ethical one in the Confucian tradition. What if we define the "the secular" in relation not to "religion" but to "spirituality"? What if we define the

92   ANNA SUN

diffused spiritual milieu as the norm of engagement with the sacred, and "religion" as the exceptional case in which boundaries are intentionally drawn? What if we think of predominately monotheistic societies as having explicit "religion" that overshadows "spirituality," whereas predominantly polytheistic societies may be called "mixed religious systems," in which diffused "spirituality" looms larger than explicit "religions," yet all coexisting as an ecological whole? What if the spiritual milieu is the ocean of our *religious life*, and explicit forms of religion are merely its most visible islands?

Notes

1. The early drafts of this chapter were written during my year at the Women's Study in Religion Program at Harvard Divinity School. I thank my colleagues there for their insightful comments and intellectual companionship. I am grateful to Professor Jin Li of Brown University, colleague and friend, for receiving me into her family in Shanxi during my fieldwork there. It was a privilege not only to be welcomed among them but also to be accorded their trust. Lastly, I thank Brian Steensland and Jaime Kucinskas, great friends-in-thinking.

2. Here I am not following the well-known definitions of the sacred from Émile Durkheim or Mircea Eliade. Both emphasize the dichotomy between the sacred and the profane, with Durkheim highlighting the homogeneous moral communities that are united by the sacred. What I have in mind are the more open-ended definitions derived from studies of early Chinese religions and early Greek and Roman religions, which emphasize communications with deities/spirits or the divine presence. In the context of examining Chinese sacred writing, Yuri Pines defines religion and the sacred as follows: "I define a text, or an aspect thereof as 'religious' insofar as it is related to communication with deities (particularly ancestral spirits), or insofar as it is supposed to have a certain sacral power of influencing the world through a proper choice of wording or proper arrangement of the material. Alternatively, I treat the text as 'secular' if it lacks the above traits and is intended either for political education of the elite or for their entertainment" (2009, 315). In the context of Greek and Roman religions, Émile Benveniste states, "The study of the designation of the 'sacred' confronts us with a strange linguistic situation: the absence of any specific term in common Indo-European on the one hand, and a two-fold designation in many languages (Iranian, Latin, and Greek) on the other. The investigation, by throwing light on the connotations of the historical terms, has the aim of clarifying the structure of a notion, the expression of which seems to demand not one but two terms. The study of each of the pairs attested—Av. *spənta: yaoždāta* (cf. also Got. *hails: weihs*); Lat. *sacer: sanctus*; Gr. *hierós: hágios*—lead us to posit, for the prehistorical period, a notion with a double aspect: positive 'what is charged with divine presence,' and negative 'what is forbidden for men to contact'" (Benveniste 1973, 453).

3. This vignette is from my fieldwork in Shanxi Province in October 2016, with the names of people interviewed changed. The fieldwork was part of my ethnographic project on prayer life in urban China (2008–18). My interviews were conducted at diverse religious sites, including Buddhist, Daoist, and Confucian temples; Protestant churches (both official and unregistered); Catholic churches and pilgrim sites; mosques (including a woman's mosque); and other sacred sites such as cemeteries and other gravesites, and altars in private homes.
4. See 2007 Horizon Survey, "The Survey of Spiritual Life of Chinese Residents," ARDA (http://www.thearda.com/Archive/Files/Descriptions/SPRTCHNA.asp).

References

Abbott, Andrew. 1985. "Things of Boundaries." *Social Research* 62(4): 857–81.
Ammerman, Nancy T. 2020. "Rethinking Religion: Toward a Practice Approach." *The American Journal of Sociology* 126(1): 6–51.
Ammerman, Nancy T. 2013a. *Sacred Stories, Spiritual Tribes: Finding Religion in Everyday Life*. New York: Oxford University Press.
Ammerman, Nancy T. 2013b. "Spiritual but Not Religious? Beyond Binary Choices in the Study of Religion." *Journal for the Scientific Study of Religion* 52(2): 258–78.
Asad, Talal. 1993. *Genealogies of Religion: Discipline and Reasons of Power in Christianity and Islam*. Baltimore: Johns Hopkins University Press.
Asad, Talal. 2003. *Formations of the Secular: Christianity, Islam, Modernity*. Palo Alto, CA: Stanford University Press.
Bell, Daniel. 2008. *China's New Confucianism: Politics and Everyday Life*. Princeton, NJ: Princeton University Press.
Bender, Courtney. 2010. *The New Metaphysicals: Spirituality and the American Religious Imagination*. Chicago: University of Chicago Press.
Benveniste, Emile, and Elizabeth Palmer, trans. [1973] 2016. *Dictionary of Indo-European Language and Society*. Chicago: HAU Books.
Beyer, Peter. 2020. "Religion in Interesting Times: Contesting Form, Function, and Future." *Sociology of Religion* 81(1): 1–19.
Billioud, Sébastien, ed. 2018. *The Varieties of Confucian Experience: Documenting a Grassroots Revival of Tradition*. Leiden: Brill.
Billioud, Sébastien, and Joël Thoraval. 2015. *The Sage and the People: The Confucian Revival in China*. Oxford: Oxford University Press.
Buckley, Chris, and Austin Ramzy. 2020. "Night Images Reveal Many New Detention Sites in China's Xinjiang Region." *New York Times*, September 24.
Campbell, Colin. 2002. "The Cult, the Cultic Milieu and Secularization." Pp. 12–25 in *The Cultic Milieu: Oppositional Subcultures in an Age of Globalization*, edited by Jeffrey Kaplan and Helene Loow. Walnut Creek, CA: AltaMira Press.
Chakrabarty, Dipesh. 2007. *Provincializing Europe: Postcolonial Thought and Historical Difference*. Princeton, NJ: Princeton University Press.
Chau, Adam Yuet. 2011. "Modalities of Doing Religion." Pp. 67–87 in *Chinese Religious Life*, edited by David A. Palmer, Glenn Shive, and Philip Wickeri. New York: Oxford University Press.

Chaves, Mark. 2017. *American Religion: Contemporary Trends*. 2nd ed. Princeton, NJ: Princeton University Press.

Chen, Carolyn. 2014. *Getting Saved in America: Taiwanese Immigration and Religious Experience*. Princeton, NJ: Princeton University Press.

China Daily. 2017. "Qingming Brings Rush of Rail Travel." *China Daily*, April 5. https://www.chinadaily.com.cn/china/2017-04/05/content_28793551.htm

Dean, Kenneth. 1998. *Lord of the Three in One: The Spread of a Cult in Southeast China*. Princeton, NJ: Princeton University Press.

Dean, Kenneth. 2020. "Religion and the Chinese Diaspora in Southeast Asia." *Review of Religion and Chinese Society* 7(2): 220–249.

de Beauvoir, Simone. [1949] 2011. *The Second Sex*. Translated by Constance Borde. New York: Vintage Books.

Drescher, Elizabeth. 2016. *Choosing Our Religion: The Spiritual Lives of America's Nones*. New York: Oxford University Press.

Fuller, Robert C. 2001. *Spiritual but Not Religious: Understanding Unchurched America*. New York: Oxford University Press.

Hadot, Pierre. 1995. *Philosophy as a Way of Life*. London: Wiley-Blackwell.

Hall, David, ed. 1997. *Lived Religion in America: Toward a History of Practice*. Princeton, NJ: Princeton University Press.

Hammond, Kenneth, and Jeffrey Richey, eds. 2015. *The Sage Returns: Confucian Revival in Contemporary China*. Albany: State University of New York Press.

Harding, Sandra. 2009. "Standpoint Theories: Productively Controversial." *Hypatia* 24(4): 192–200.

Heelas, Paul, and Linda Woodhead, with Benjamin Seel, Bronislaw Szerszynski, and Karin Tusting. 2005. *The Spiritual Revolution: Why Religion Is Giving Way to Spirituality*. London: Wiley-Blackwell.

Horizon Survey. 2007. "The Spiritual Life of Chinese Residents Survey." Association of Religion Data Archive.

Jaffe, Richard. 2014. "Introduction." Pp. xi–lvi in *Selected Works of D. T. Suzuki*, vol. 1, *Zen*, edited by Richard Jaffe. Berkeley: University of California Press.

Jeung, Russell M., Seanan S. Fong, and Helen Jin Kim. 2019. *Family Sacrifices: The Worldviews and Ethics of Chinese Americans*. Oxford: Oxford University Press.

King, Richard. 1999. *Orientalism and Religion: India, Postcolonial theory and the "Mystic East"*. London: Routledge.

King, Richard. 2013. "The Copernican Turn in the Study of Religion." *Method & Theory in the Study of Religion* 25(2): 137–59.

Kucinskas, Jaime. 2018. *The Mindful Elite: Mobilizing from the Inside Out*. New York: Oxford University Press.

Lamont, Michelle, and Virag Molnar. 2002. "The Study of Boundaries across the Social Sciences." *Annual Review of Sociology* 28: 167–95.

Lagerwey, John. 2019. "The Continent of the Gods." *Review of Religion and Chinese Society* 2019(6):188–208.

Lipka, Michael. 2015. "Religious 'Nones' Are Not Only Growing, They're Becoming More Secular." *Fact Tank*, Pew Research Center. https://www.pewresearch.org/fact-tank/2015/11/11/religious-nones-are-not-only-growing-theyre-becoming-more-secular/.

Lippiello, Tiziana. 2018. "The Paradigm of Religious and Philosophical Plurality: The Return of 'Spirituality' in China Today." *Philosophy and Social Criticism* 44(4): 371–81.

Madsen, Richard. 2011. "Religious Renaissance in China Today." *Journal of Current Chinese Affairs* 40(2): 17–42.

McClure, Paul K. 2017. "Something besides Monotheism: Sociotheological Boundary Work among the Spiritual, but Not Religious." *Poetics* 62: 53–65.

McCutcheon, Russell T. 1997. *Manufacturing Religion: The Discourse on Sui Generis Religion and the Politics of Nostalgia.* New York: Oxford University Press.

Palmer, David A., and Vincent Goossaert. 2011. *The Religious Question in Modern China.* Chicago: University of Chicago Press.

Palmer, David A., Glenn Shive, and Philip Wickeri, eds. 2011. *Chinese Religious Life.* Oxford: Oxford University Press.

Palmer, David A., and Elijah Siegler. 2017. *Dream Trippers: Global Daoism and the Predicament of Modern Spirituality.* Chicago: University of Chicago Press.

Pew Research Center. 2012. *The Global Religious Landscape: A Report on the Size and Distribution of the World's Major Religious Groups as of 2010.* Washington, DC: Pew Research Center.

Pine, Yuri. 2009. "Chinese History Writing between the Sacred and the Secular." Pp. 315–40 in *Early Chinese Religion, Part One: Shang through Han (1250 BC–220 AD),* edited by John Lagerwey and Marc Kalinowski. Leiden: Brill.

Roof, Wade Clark. 1999. *Spiritual Marketplace: Baby Boomers and the Remaking of American Religion.* Princeton, NJ: Princeton University Press.

Rüpke, Jörg. 2013. *Religion: Antiquity and Its Legacy.* Oxford: Oxford University Press.

Said, Edward. 1979. *Orientalism.* New York: Vintage Books.

Schwartz, Benjamin, ed. 1972. *Reflections on the May Fourth Movement: A Symposium.* Cambridge, MA: Harvard University Asia Center.

Smith, Christian, and Patricia Snell. 2009. *Souls in Transition: The Religious and Spiritual Lives of Emerging Adults.* New York: Oxford University Press.

Smith, Wilfred Cantwell. 1963. *The Meaning and End of Religion: A New Approach to the Religious Traditions of Mankind.* New York: Macmillan.

Steensland, Brian, Xiaoyun Wang, and Lauren Chism Schmidt. 2018. "Spirituality: What Does It Mean and to Whom?" *Journal for the Scientific Study of Religion* 57(3): 450–472.

Sun, Anna. 2013. *Confucianism as a World Religion: Contested Histories and Contemporary Realities.* Princeton, NJ: Princeton University Press.

Sun, Anna. 2016. "The Study of Chinese Religions in the Social Sciences: Beyond the Monotheistic Assumption." Pp. 51–72 in *Religion and Orientalism in Asian Studies,* edited by Kiri Paramore. London: Bloomsbury.

Sun, Anna. 2020a. "To Be or Not to Be a Confucian: Explicit and Implicit Religious Identities in the Global Twenty-First Century." *Annual Review of the Sociology of Religion* 11: 210–235.

Sun, Anna. 2020b. "Weber's 'Religion of China' in the 21st Century." *Review of Religion and Chinese Society* 7: 250–70.

Teiser, Stephen. 1996. *The Ghost Festival in Medieval China.* Princeton, NJ: Princeton University Press.

Vala, Carsten T. 2017. *The Politics of Protestant Churches and the Party-State in China: God above Party?* Leiden: Brill.

Versluis, Arthur. 1993. *American Transcendentalism and Asian Religions.* New York: Oxford University Press.

Wang, Zheng. 2014. *Never Forget National Humiliation: Historical Memory in Chinese Politics and Foreign Relations*. New York: Columbia University Press.

Warner, R. Stephen. 2014. "In Defense of Religion: The 2013 H. Paul Douglass Lecture." *Review of Religious Research* 56(4): 495–512.

Woodhead, Linda. 2011. "Spirituality and Christianity: The Unfolding of a Tangled Relationship." Pp. 3–21 in *Religion, Spirituality and Everyday Practice*, edited by G. Giordan and W. H. Swatos. New York: Springer.

Wuthnow, Robert. 2020. *What Happens When We Practice Religion? Textures of Devotion in Everyday Life*. Princeton, NJ: Princeton University Press.

Yang, C. K. 1962. *Religion of Chinese Society: A Study of Contemporary Social Functions of Religion and Some of Their Historical Factors*. Berkeley: University of California Press.

Yang, Fenggang. 2011. *Religion in China: Survival and Revival under Communist Rule*. New York: Oxford University Press.

Yang, Fenggang. 2016. "Exceptionalism or Chinamerica: Measuring Religious Change in the Globalizing World Today." *Journal for the Scientific Study of Religion* 55(1): 7–22.

4

Trumping the Devil!

Engendering the Spirituality of the Marketplace within Africa and the African Diaspora

Afe Adogame

On a sizzling summer afternoon in 1995, during a research trip from Germany to Nigeria, I boarded a city taxi cab in Lagos to one of my field sites, Makoko, a Lagos suburb. No sooner did the cab driver start off than I was attracted to the front and rear windshields and bumper sticker inscriptions: "Jesus is the Way, the truth and the life," "Jesus is Lord," "Allah is the Greatest," "Smile, Allah loves you," and "Nigerian by Birth, saved by the Grace of God," competing for meager space, almost blocking visibility, and rendering the windscreen opaque. Closer scrutiny led to further unanticipated revelation, as I found a charm-amulet substance tied beneath the car's steering wheel. This mélange of religious aesthetics led me to pose a question to the driver. I queried: "Are you a Christian, Muslim, or adherent of the indigenous religion?" His rhetorical response, "Why did you ask?" led to my probing further. When I pointed to the religious insignias that adorned the car's interior, he retorted instantaneously: "*Aaahhh* [exclamation], *Ọga* [Sir], it is better to hold on to the three faiths. Just in case one fails, then the other will work." This phrase is akin to a popular Yoruba aphorism: *Ọna kan o wọ ọja*, literally translated, "The marketplace usually has multiple entranceways."

Several inferences and symbolizations can be drawn from the above. First, the car sticker insignias allude to the visual face of religiosity, the public visibility, and overt dramatization of spirituality through apperception. The public and private objectification of spirituality in concrete paraphernalia, physical structures, billboards, bumper stickers, audiovisual-sonic templates is often internalized by individuals to reflect and shape their everyday life exigencies, experiences, and expressions. The everyday lived encounters of the cab driver and others in this sociocultural milieu are situated within a cosmological tradition mostly perceived as populated by antagonistic

Afe Adogame, *Trumping the Devil!* In: *Situating Spirituality.* Edited by: Brian Steensland, Jaime Kucinskas, and Anna Sun, Oxford University Press. © Oxford University Press 2022. DOI: 10.1093/oso/9780197565001.003.0005

benevolent and malevolent spiritual entities, with humans at the receiving end. Following this combative encounter, the ritual act of trumping the malevolent entity (Devil/Satan) becomes an important antidote for ensuring cosmic balance and harmony. Second, the inscriptions and maxim suggest openness to, tolerance for, and synthesis of different aspects of multiple faiths. Such reasoning, controversial as it may be, can be better understood against the backdrop of local religious sensibilities and popular appropriations that are contextual in nature.

My vivid reminiscence of the taxi driver, with his car stickers and concrete object indicators, invokes emblematic symbols of belief and iconic representations of Christianity, Islam, and the indigenous religions. It is not uncommon within African religious landscapes to observe that people (un)consciously sustain multiple religious affiliations through intrafaith traditions or even interfaith allegiances, such as Catholicism and Pentecostalism, Christianity and indigenous religions, or indigenous religions and Islam. This complicates the discourse on religious membership, belonging, and identity, but demonstrates how religious eclecticism makes sense within African religious sensibilities. More importantly, the quest for and use of multiple resources avail religious profundities and perhaps a multiplex know-how that is mutually intelligible and fungible. It is against this backdrop that we can decipher commonalities in ways of knowing, in what Ali Mazrui (1986) calls "Africa's triple religious heritage." The question of agency or medium through which new knowledges are contested and funneled is quintessential. For instance, there is a complementarity in the roles of Muslim clerics, *alfas/mallams* (Islam), prophets/ prophetesses/pastors (Christianity), and diviners/spirit mediums (indigenous religions) in that they all function in a cosmos not unfamiliar to the wider society. These ritual specialists are vested with special spiritual powers; they serve as repositories of esoteric knowledge and pharmacology. They prognosticate into the future in the quest for panaceas to life exigencies, through processes of "explanation, prediction and control" (Horton 1971, 373). The similitude maintained with regards to agency, function, and method makes it easy to conjecture religious clientalism. Clients hardly consider incongruous the practice of patronizing different religious brokers contemporaneously, as the end often justifies the means. Such behavior, in a landscape with robust religious resources and preferences, is suggestive of spiritual fluidity and mobility. Such an environment also provokes religious innovation and competition.

Ama McKinley's blog article "Beyoncé Serves African Spirituality in 'Lemonade'" in the *Huffington Post* (2016) depicts Beyoncé Knowles Carter as "an artist of the Earth, using her stage and global influence to teach about the human condition, using symbology and language that is sacred and pronounced beyond a few approved circles." This view partly epitomizes the resilience of African spirituality in the diaspora, where she in *Lemonade* invokes so much of the Yoruba tradition, grounded in African tradition, by offering a musical and visual journey through the African diaspora. In an ensuing crisis of modernity, Africa does not seem to experience a quandary with regards to the dualisms that starkly compartmentalize secular and mundane identities. African spiritualities touch on and imbue every facet of life and thus cannot be separated from quotidian, mundane thought. But how does African spirituality contrast with other social dimensions of spirituality? In what ways is spirituality encountered and experienced within and beyond the confines of religion? This chapter explores African spirituality as a spirituality of the marketplace that is mostly concerned with the pursuit of cosmic balance, harmony, and human flourishing through a matrix of worldviews, belief systems, and ritual praxis. Through exploring the diversity of African spirituality and cosmologies—the forms, meanings, and expressions that link them—I demonstrate how and to what extent the religious, moral values and imaginaries pervading indigenous worldviews in Africa and the African diaspora are continually contested and negotiated.

Permit me to conclude my preliminary reflections with some caveats that will provide a historiographical backdrop and a significant template for grasping, deconstructing, and redefining indigenous epistemologies and spiritualities. The growth and development of old/new forms of religions and spiritualities in Africa, and the discourses they engender, are laced with interpretational powers that are often conflictual in nature.

First, I do not intend to homogenize or villagize Africa, a gigantic continent with several "worlds" covering one-fifth of the earth's land mass and comprising more than fifty countries, nor suggest an African diaspora with one history and experience. The eight hundred million people of Africa have evolved a cultural milieu that is a study in contrast and has several dimensions. Africa is a vast continent characterized by complex cultural, religious, and linguistic varieties, as well as diverse historical experiences. It is home to innumerable ethnic, social groupings whose diverse cultures represent the mosaic of cultural diversity of Africa. Sub-Saharan Africa (also Africa south of the Sahara, or tropical Africa) represents countries of predominantly black indigenous population not often considered within the North Africa geographical ambit. There are no clear-cut, defined boundaries between North and sub-Saharan Africa regions, owing to discontinuous, blurred break points between national boundaries, ecologies, and ethnicities. Nevertheless, sub-Saharan Africa seems to produce the most profound religious vitality, with interactions of the various indigenous religions with Christianity, Islam, and other Eastern- and Western-related religions producing new religious constellations that attract more scholarly attention than anywhere else on the continent. North Africa has witnessed a more ingrained history and imprint of Islam in a way that renders its interlocking with the indigenous religions less visible. The Islamic onslaught on the former Christian strongholds in North Africa has largely stripped it of much contemporary significance as a context for Christianity.

Second, the discourse on and definition of African religion and African spirituality has a long history that is characterized by denial, ignorance, misconception, and misunderstanding. I prefer to talk about African spiritualities and African religions in recognition of their profound affinities and remarkable particularities. I use the terms—religion, religions, religiosity, religiosities, spirituality, spiritualities—interchangeably in relation to the history of their appropriations in the academy, while recognizing their limitations in meaning. The very concept "religion," like "Africa," is a Western invention, an academic construct involving both misconceptions and changing perceptions (Mudimbe 1988), that hardly does justice to the complexity of African spiritualities. The perception of religion as a phenomenon separate from culture is not a suitable reflection of the embedded nature of "religion" in African cultures (Adogame 2007, 534). In most African societies, religion is variously conceptualized as a spiritual, epistemological, and philosophical phenomenon. Beyond the typical focus on religion as a coterie of belief and ritual patterns, the treatment of religion as an epistemological phenomenon sheds new light on studies of African cultures and societies. We need to pay attention to the significance of cosmological ideas as expressions of moral values in relation to the material conditions of life and the total social order. As a category of analysis for the study of societies, religion is, therefore, quintessential to our understanding of African cultures in a global context. While we continue to use the concept "religion" to embrace African spiritualities, one should be aware of its limitations and tendency to obscure its dynamism. It is against this backdrop that the exploration of spirituality inside and outside of religion can be better undertaken. As a broader domain of action, spirituality encompasses religion as well as other spheres of life and social structure. Thus, to explain African spiritualities and religious life in Western categories can be illuminating and offer useful insights, just as it can be misleading and obscuring. Modes of thought, ritual patterns, and symbolism that are integral to African spiritualities are sometimes puzzling to Western ethnography.

Religions, spiritualities, societies, and cultures are hardly static and unchanging; they are dynamic and are constantly in flux. Spiritualities are not museum pieces or tourist-trod monuments, but vibrant forces in the lived expressions and experiences of African and African diaspora peoples. African spiritualities are usually not thought out in the agora of "desk" theology but lived out in the spiritual marketplace. Africans generally celebrate life, their spirituality, their religion; they dance it, sing it, and act it. For instance, prayer repertoire and song texts are seldom written down in books and recited or sung. Prayers are mostly rendered extempore rather than from a prayer book or a formal compilation of prayer genres. Songs/choruses are often sung spontaneously rather than from hymn/song books. African religions are living, expressive spiritualities. Through rituals, people act out their spiritualities. Therefore, to understand and interpret their complex ritual worlds would require methodologies that seek to unearth and conceptualize their day-to-day ritual dimension and how this is informed by cosmology, rather than look out for any stereotyped theology of a sort.

Toward Redefining African Spiritualities and Epistemologies

Jacob Olupona (2015) puts it succinctly: "African spirituality simply acknowledges that beliefs and practices touch on and inform every facet of human life, and therefore African religion cannot be separated from the everyday or mundane." As he notes,

> For starters, the word "religion" is problematic for many Africans, because it suggests that religion is separate from the other aspects of one's culture, society and environment. But for many Africans, religion can never be separated from all these. It is a way of life, and it can never be separated from the public sphere. Religion informs everything in traditional African

102   AFE ADOGAME

society, including political art, marriage, health, diet, dress, economics, and death. (Olupona 2015)

In fact, Olupona cautions that "this is not to say that indigenous African spirituality represents a form of theocracy or religious totalitarianism, but simply that African spirituality is truly holistic." In an influential book, *African Spirituality: Forms, Meanings and Expressions* (2000), Olupona captures the misconception among Western scholars who assumed an absence of spirituality in Africa, by focusing on many elements of Africans' spiritual and cultural heritage that puzzle both foreigners resident in Africa and more broadly the global community. The book's content under the following categories—cosmologies and sacred knowledge; authority, agencies, and performance; Africans' encounter with other religions; and African spirituality in the Americas—underscores how the historicity of African spirituality has always been in flux, negotiating resilience, transformation, and change. As Olupona remarks: "Though larger religions have made big inroads, traditional belief systems, which are based on openness and adaptation, endure" (Olupona 2015). This dynamism and fluidity undergird indigeneity in African spiritualities.

One external import into indigenous African spiritualities that deserves deconstructing is the subtle compartmentalization of sacred and mundane domains. Just as the dichotomy between sacred and secular is sometimes blurred, it is problematic to pigeonhole indigenous epistemologies. African spiritualities embrace beliefs, practices, technologies, values, and ways of knowing and sharing, in terms of which communities have survived. They are informed by and relate to all domains of life and the environment, including the creative and artistic aspects of music, dance, and oral traditions. Spiritualities also includes philosophy, ethics, and worldview—concepts of life, death, religious cosmos, divination, transfer of religious knowledge, rites of passage, etiologies of sickness and disease, and traditional healing systems.

African spiritualities are concerned with memory. There are varied ways in which the discourse on memory is embedded and has always been integral to understanding religious sensibilities and lifeworlds in Africa. Memory is approached as mnemonic devices employed in the oral preservation of sacred texts. Myths and legends, stories, folktales, proverbs, riddles, and songs found in large numbers among African societies are repositories of memory and serve as sources for indigenous values and spiritualities. They are handed down or transmitted orally. Some are a record of actual historical events, while others are created by people's imaginations. They serve many purposes: some entertain; others warn, teach morals, stimulate the imagination of the listener; some are told as a commentary on people's lives in a given period, and they are often a way of explaining certain things. For instance, the values of myths include the creation of humans, divine/human separation (cosmogonic), the social order, creation of the world—sky/earth (cosmological). They also help to convey the origins of agriculture, death, and priesthood/sacral kingship. While it is important to explore the relationship between myth and memory, there is also a link between myth, history, and ritual. Myths of origin refer to the creative time of the beginnings when the first ancestors established society and when the creator deity distanced himself from the world. There is a major division in this time represented by the period before and the period after the separation between the sky world of the deities and the human world. This helps to explain the distinction between mythical time and ritual time, cosmogonic time and temporal time (Mbiti 2015).

In addition to creation myths that explain the nature of the human condition, there are myths that explain the origins of important ritual institutions and practices. The events of these myths are often enacted in ceremonial activity, thereby linking the creative powers of the deities, divinities, and ancestors with the present needs of the people. For instance, Orunmila is the oracular deity linked with divination among the Yoruba of West Africa. African indigenous spiritualities or Africans' entire life cycles are dotted with innumerable rituals and ceremonies, including personal/individual rituals, communal rituals, agricultural rituals (seasonal), health rituals, professional rituals, and festivals. Rituals and festivals are religious ways of implementing the values and beliefs of society. The memorialization and routinization of myths and rituals are indicative of the dynamism of indigenous religious cosmologies. Ancestral veneration and rites of passage are at the center of memory and commemoration. Burial and funeral obsequies are emblematic of rituals of memory, memorialization, and remembering.

Ancestors play an intermediary role between the mundane and supersensible realms; and they are the guardians and custodians of moral and religious values of society. "The influence of ancestral spirits in Africa is very pervasive, and devotional concerns over them loom so large in the primal religious structures that emergent religious forms must perforce reflect the encounter with ancestral covenants" (Kalu 2000, 54). The concept of ancestorhood is better understood with the African concept of time, which is cyclical and not linear. Death does not write a finis to life; it is a kind of recycling of life. Death is considered as a mere passage or transition from the human world to the spiritual world. Thus, the life cycle would involve birth, death, ancestral world, and reincarnation. Ancestors could also be reborn as children, thus evidencing the belief in reincarnation. Among the Yoruba peoples in West Africa, reborn children are identified by their names, such as *Babatunde* (Father has returned or is reborn) or *Iyetunde* (Mother has returned or is reborn). Rites of passage are central within the indigenous worldviews and point to the ritual attitude in maintaining cosmic harmony and balance.

Benjamin Ray (1999) has argued that rites of passage create a bond between temporal processes and archetypal patterns to give form and meaning to human events. The African religious cosmos covers the entire life span from the cradle to the grave. To Africans life is worth living and death worth dying. Rites and ceremonies therefore characterize each stage of existence and as circumstances require. The definite intent of the passage rites is to develop fixed and meaningful transformations in life cycles, ecological cycles, and temporal cycles and in the accessions of individuals to high office (Ray 1999). The rapidity of these rites and ceremonies even in contemporary African socioreligious milieux makes clear the strength of the belief that humans are in active touch with the supersensible world and that a right relationship with these benevolent powers is a prerequisite for social harmony and human flourishing. Elaborate rituals and ceremonies for the remembrance of the dead are therefore characteristic of most African religious cultures.

Historicizing and Deconstructing African Spiritualities and Epistemologies

The historiography of African religions and spiritualities provides a significant template for understanding and deconstructing indigenous epistemologies within global academic studies (Adogame 2015, 1813–26). "African religions" is used here as a generic term to embrace the triple religious heritage—indigenous religions, African Christianities, and African Islam (Mazrui 1986). This historiography is burdened on the one level by competing claims for the power of interpretation between African and non-African scholars, the different academic approaches and historical phases aimed at defining, explaining, interpreting, and (de)legitimizing African religious beliefs and ritual systems.

The historical trajectory of the study of religions in Africa has evolved through several phases, each involving different purposes and points of view. Jan Platvoet (1996, 105) best categorizes these overlapping epochs paradigmatically, as "Africa as Object" and as "Africa as Subject" when its religions were studied virtually exclusively by scholars, and other observers from outside Africa; and as "Africa as Subject" when the religions of Africa began to be studied also, and increasingly, by Africa scholars. Descriptions and theories of Africa's religious history have been essential elements of the cultural contacts since the very first encounters with European imperialism and remain so up to the present (Ludwig and Adogame 2004, 2; see also Adogame, Chitando, Bateye 2012). Within these historical phases, the colonial and missionary machineries invented and produced ways of knowing and meaning-making that anchored and facilitated processes of subjugation, exploitation, and expropriation. Alien forms of reasoning were entrenched while also laying claims to supporting a "civilizing mission." The "European" knowledge that was introduced into Africa was on collision course with indigenous knowledge systems, leading to a spate of ideological contestations culminating in a bricolage of knowledges. The knowledge funneled through the colonial process took center stage, assuming a dominant epistemology that marginalized and almost silenced alternative worldviews and conceptualizations of the universe. Such a hegemonic way of knowing and meaning-making was even presumed to be capable of turning indigenous epistemologies on their head (Adogame 2015, 1815).

Legacies of the European Enlightenment filtered thought patterns that legitimized tropes of otherness and binaries of difference, espoused as tradition versus modernity, primitive versus civilized, superiority versus inferiority, in the very fabric of the dominant knowledge. It was characteristic of the forms of reasoning that it privileged and superimposed on other cultures. This dominant knowledge was liberating, transforming, but also entrapping. The contestation that ensued in the production of religious knowledge produced a chasm of epistemological richness and bankruptcy at the same time. Indigenous religious epistemologies hardly witnessed their obituary in the face of the knowledge-encounter that ensued. This scenario produced multiple discourses and theories of knowledge within the academic study of religion in Africa, and knowledge production is continually negotiated in ways that result in the reification of some meaning-making systems and the invention of others, and in "hybridized" epistemologies. This (re)production and contestation of ways of knowing and meaning-making has dire implications for unpacking and decolonizing indigenous religious epistemologies.

The experience of colonization and sustained interaction with the West has produced and continues to perpetuate an imagined culture in transition from tradition to modernity. The chasm created between tradition and modernity is now being turned on its head, as such binaries of opposition are no longer very convincing. It is more useful in some sense to talk of the modernity of African cultures, traditions, and religions in an era of social-cultural flux. A proper grasp of indigenous spiritualities and religious epistemologies is central to the conceptual issues that modernization (then) and globalization (now) raise. A historical explication of the distortion needs to be balanced with an explanation of why redressing the distortion and suppression is an imperative. Processes of transformation and change are not merely driven by sociopolitical agendas but are informed distinctly by the knowledge closest to the people. The socio-cultural landscape, including indigenous knowledge and technologies of diverse communities and groups, correlates directly with the dynamics of change and the transformation of individuals' as well as groups' cultural meaning systems and senses of belonging. The spiritual, physical, and animal worlds and local geographies are central in this consideration too. Therefore, any analysis or interpretation of existing or changing cultural patterns and societal institutions, of terrestrial and extraterrestrial worlds, of how they are conditioned and who conditions them, cannot claim validity without full recognition of the important role indigenous knowledge systems play—a fact largely discarded by colonial knowledge hegemony.

In the intellectual enterprise highlighted here, it is important to underscore that Western, European scholars not only dominated this endeavor, namely the academic study of religions in Africa, but imposed their methodologies and brought their worldviews and epistemologies to bear. In fact, the academic study of religion in Africa has its roots outside the continent, just as the very category of religion itself has a European history. Undoubtedly, Western scholars have contributed significantly to the understanding of African religions, but they have also paved paths into obscurity and public misunderstanding.

African Spiritualities and the African Diaspora

The African diaspora is one theoretical construct with which to describe the global dispersal of indigenous African populations at different phases of world history. "African diaspora" was employed starting from the mid-1950s and 1960s, when the discourse on the historical phenomenon of dispersion and settlement of Africans abroad began to lay claim to *diaspora* as a descriptive label. Employing the term "Black Atlantic," Paul Gilroy (1993) contextualizes the voluntary and involuntary migration of Africans to Europe and the Americas since the purported age of "discovery." However, the breadth of the African diaspora transcends the popular geographical fixation to Europe and the New World, embodying the voluntary and forced dispersion of Africans, their descendants, their cultures at different historical phases and in diverse directions, not just to the Americas and Europe but to Asia, the Mediterranean, and Arab and former Soviet worlds, and cross-migration within the African shores. Thus, the African diaspora assumes the dynamic character of an ongoing, complex process located across space-time.

The historiography of the African diaspora encompasses enduring experiences of struggles and victories; displacements and dehumanization; frustrations and hope; depravity and survival; resilience and transformation; but also a stark narrative that offers inroads into Africans' peculiar expressions and sustained cultural, religious, and philosophical legacies to the "Old" and "New" worlds (Adogame 2016). It is an unending sojourn characterized by the mobility of individuals, small groups, large groups, and extensive relocations, over long periods of time, leading to global dispersal of Africans and their descendants. The historical journey of the African diaspora is characterized by people of African descent who, involuntarily and voluntarily, found themselves living either outside of African shores or in contexts within Africa were territorially distant from their original homelands or places of birth. The uniqueness of the African diaspora lies in its formation and in narratives transcending several continents, resulting in a complex pattern of communities and cultures with contrasting local and regional histories (Adogame 2016, 137). A better grasp of African cultural influences in the various regions in the Americas and other diasporas requires an exploration of the pattern of introduction of Africans over time and place.

The historical, cultural import and peregrination of African religious epistemologies is discerned in their plurality and multivocality in Africa and

108   AFE ADOGAME

its diasporas (Adogame 2009). The global dimension manifests in varied forms, being introduced to new, varied geocultural contexts through migration, tourism, and new communication technologies. The African diaspora adapted to, and shaped, the sociocultural universe of the Americas, Europe, and elsewhere partly through African religions and spiritualities. For instance, in Brazil, Candomblé and Umbanda have remained resilient in the face of racism and public criminalization, just as majority of Afro-Brazilians continue to encounter injustice and sociopolitical marginalization. Despite threats against survival, Africans and their descendants strive to preserve their cultural heritage and religious identity. African and African-derived religions have continued to impact other societies and world religions, while they have been influenced by them as well. Brazil is home to the largest black population (African diaspora) in the world, besides Nigeria. Brazil's recent demographics show African-Brazilians in the majority for the first time, with 2010 census showing over 50.7 percent black/mixed race, compared to 47.7 percent white population (IBGE 2011). Brazil is home to Candomblé and Umbanda, two of the largest African-derived religions. Brazilian Portuguese was richly influenced by people of African descent and their languages, even as a new Afro-Brazilian vocabulary emerged. Candomblé rituals have been incorporated into the fabric of Brazilian national identity from New Year's Eve offerings to the ocean (*revellion*), capoeira dance, samba (*rodas*), and culinary preferences such as *acarajé* fritters. In Umbanda, there is a loose affinity of Roman Catholic saints with African and indigenous deities.

The resilience produced an epistemological reservoir that shaped the sufferance, resistance, adaptation, creativity, and innovation of African descendants in new milieus. These epistemologies partly shape global art, sculpture, painting, and cultural artifacts, which populate the world's museums, galleries, libraries, and exhibitions, just as horticultural, culinary, and medical knowledges are also impacted. English vocabulary has been further enriched through loaned words such as "taboo" and "voodoo" and creolization from Africa and its diaspora. The commodification of African music, art, and religious objects is on the increase. How and to what extent have African indigenous and derived religions shaped the local contexts, cultures, and societies within which they are practiced; and how have they been influenced by other religions and cultures globally? The character of indigenous and African-derived spiritualities in conditions of globality will continue to be shaped by how and to what extent they negotiate continuity, identity, and change. A proper grasp of their complex religious cosmologies, traditions, and cultures will improve understanding of African peoples and their descendants in conditions of globality.

Gwendolyn Hall (2005, xv) shows that the diverse peoples who met and mingled in the Americas all made major contributions to its economy, culture, aesthetics, language, and survival skills. The impact of Africans on patterns of creolization varied greatly over time and among different places, depending on several factors (2005, 166). People of African descent are located in all walks of life, with their achievements in some instances unparalleled. Michael Gomez (2005) aptly observes that they have made foundational and extensive contributions to the "old," "new," and "modern" worlds through slave, plantation, agriculture, and mining economies, particularly in Europe and the Americas. The clearest example of African technology transfer to the Americas is the production of rice. Mining was another important technology transferred from Africa to the Americas (Hall 2005, 66–67). Also, people of African descent have made deep imprints in the sciences and arts in fundamental ways.

Perhaps the aspect that has received the most profound attention is their cultural influence, involving theater, painting, sculpture, dance, music, athletics, and religion. Jazz, blues, reggae, and hip-hop are now global phenomena. As Ronald Segal (1995) shows, it is "a diaspora of wondrous achievement. It has enriched world culture in music, language and literature; in painting and sculpture; made sport a form of art and given religion an ecological relevance." He maintains that "whatever else Africans lost in being transported as slaves, it was not their musical attachment and aptitude, which came to be valued especially in providing entertainment at the parties and dances that were the main source of colonial diversion" (Segal 1995, 375). At various times and places within the reaches of the diaspora, blacks have been central to creative developments in the fine arts of painting, sculpture, and architecture. Nonetheless, these contributions largely contrast with the public perception of Africans in the diaspora and the continent itself, mental images that are almost always negative (cf. Gomez 2005).

The journey of African religious and philosophical ideas is best charted through the longue durée of African diaspora history (Adogame 2016, 139). Although the African diaspora is complex and diverse, its peoples share affinities, such as the idea of an original home, Africa as the land of origins; the dehumanizing experience of enslavement that characterizes the first waves of African diaspora; and deprivation and xenophobia that have confronted African descendants throughout history and today. Other commonalities include the resilience of cultural, religious, and philosophical worldviews against the backdrop of adaptation to new geocultural environments and the mutual transnational significance of Africa and the African diaspora. Religion, what Segal (1995, 428–40) has dubbed "the Soul of the Diaspora," is a constant identity variable within African diaspora communities, where many Africans and their descendants carry traits of their religio-cultural identity. Africans of diverse origins largely retained their religious symbolisms, worldviews, and spiritualities.

Marsh-Locket and West's *Literary Expressions of African Spirituality* (2013) builds a critical framework for exploring the presence and import of African spirituality in black Ameri-Atlantic artistic musings. Through the prism of the connected spiritual legacy of the black Atlantic and the memorialization of African spirituality, the book analyzes shared cosmology and spirituality through transnational precincts. In its three main sections— "African Faith Systems in the Postmodern World," Integrations of the African and the Western in New World Black Atlantic Writing," and "African Deities and Divinations as Forces in New World Black Works"—the book highlights expressions of African spiritual ethos in the artistic realm and demonstrates "how creative persons in the diaspora use African spirituality overtly and at times subconsciously in their work to give meaning to their world" (Manning 2017, 419). These essays "illustrate the intricate network of African spiritual transportations and transformations among New World and continental African literatures" (Manning 2017, 421). While the book illuminates significant discourses in African spirituality, gender, history and criticism, it also provides an understanding of aspects of African spirituality such as journey motifs. In another vein, Manning aptly suggests that "spirituality in the New World facilitated survival for the enslaved Africans; participation in specific rituals strengthened connections to ancestors and fortified their inner being. For good reasons, African spirituality was deemed an act of defiance, as it provided direct connections to aspects of the human spirit that will always remain free" (Manning 2017, 419). Ackah, Dodson, and Smith's *Religion, Culture and Spirituality in Africa and the African Diaspora* (2017) explores the ways in which religious ideas and beliefs continue to play a crucial role in the lives of people of African descent. The book responds to the question to what extent ideas of spirituality emanating from Africa and the diaspora are still influenced by an African aesthetic. They reveal how spirituality weaves and intersects with issues of gender, class, sexuality, and race across Africa and the diaspora.

Conclusion

This chapter has briefly demonstrated how African spirituality is a spirituality of the marketplace that encompasses a matrix of worldviews, belief systems, and ritual practices, and whose main quest is in the realization of cosmic balance, social harmony, and human flourishing. African spiritualities are a distinctive system of thought and praxis necessary for grasping the African lifeworld. Thus the everyday lived encounters and religious sensibilities of the cab driver are better understood within this broader frame of reference. African spiritualities permeate every aspect of human life and its exigencies, and thus cannot be fully separated from commonplace, mundane thought. Even in the face of secularism and modernity, African spiritualities continue to be embedded in the cultural, political, social, and religious lives of Africans on the continent and in the African diaspora. The chapter also interrogated ways in which African spiritualities; religio-cultural, philosophical, and social values; and political forms influence African diasporic communities in their new sociocultural locations. This helps to tease out how and to what extent such forms and values change and transform through interaction with non-African cultures; but also to consider the transnational relationships between African diasporic communities that are geographically separated or culturally distinct.

References

Ackah, William, Jualynne E. Dodson, and R. Drew Smith, eds. 2017. *Religion, Culture and Spirituality in Africa and the African Diaspora*. New York: Routledge.

Adogame, Afe. 2007. "Religion in Sub-Saharan Africa." Pp. 533–554 in *Religion, Globalization and Culture*, edited by P. Beyer and L. Beaman. Leiden: Brill.

Adogame, Afe. 2009. "Practitioners of Indigenous Religions in Africa and the African Diaspora." Pp. 75–100 in *Religions in Focus: New Approaches to Tradition and Contemporary Practices*, edited by G. Harvey. London: Equinox.

Adogame, Afe. 2015. "Calling a Trickster Deity a 'Bad' Name in Order to Hang It? Deconstructing Indigenous African Epistemologies within Global Religious Maps of the Universe." Pp. 1813–26 in *The Changing World Religion Map: Sacred Places, Identities, Practices and Politics*, edited by S. D. Brunn. Dordrecht: Springer Science + Business Media.

Adogame, Afe. 2016. "The Journey of African Religious and Epistemological Ideas to the New World—Diaspora." Pp. 137–49 in *The Interwoven World: Ideas and Encounters in History*, edited by B. Avari and G. G. Joseph. Champaign, IL: Common Ground Publishing.

Adogame, Afe, Ezra Chitando, and Bolaji Bateye, eds. 2012. *African Traditions in the Study of Religion in Africa: Emerging Trends, Indigenous Spirituality and the Interface with Other World Religions*. Burlington, VT: Routledge.

Gilroy, Paul. 1993. *The Black Atlantic: Modernity and Double Consciousness*. Cambridge, MA: Harvard University Press.

Gomez, Michael A. 2005. *Reversing Sail: A History of the African Diaspora*. Cambridge: Cambridge University Press.

Hall, Gwendolyn Midlo. 2005. *Slavery and African Ethnicities in the Americas: Restoring the Links*. Chapel Hill: University of North Carolina Press.

Horton, Robin. 1971. *Patterns of Thought in Africa and the West: Essays on Magic, Religion and Science*. Cambridge: Cambridge University Press.

Instituto Brasileiro de Geografia e Estatística (IBGE). 2011. *Sinopse do Censo Demográfico: 2010*. Rio de Janiero: Instituto Brasileiro de Geografia e Estatística.

Kalu, Ogbu. 2000. "Ancestral Spirituality and Society in Africa." Pp. 54–84 in *African Spirituality: Forms, Meanings and Expressions*, edited by J. K. Olupona. New York: Crossroad Publishing Company.

Ludwig, Frieder, and Afe Adogame, eds. 2004. *European Traditions in the Study of Religion in Africa*. Wiesbaden: Harrassowitz Verlag.

Manning, D. P. 2017. "Literary Expressions of African Spirituality." *Caribbean Quarterly* 63(2–3): 419–21.

Marsh-Locket, Carol P., and Elizabeth J. West, eds. 2013. *Literary Expressions of African Spirituality*. Plymouth, UK: Lexington Books.

Mazrui, Ali A. 1986. *The Africans: A Triple Heritage*. Boston: Little, Brown.

Mbiti, John S. 2015. *Introduction to African Religion*. 2nd ed. Long Grove, IL: Waveland Press.

McKinley, Ama. 2016. "Beyoncé Serves African Spirituality in 'Lemonade.'" *Huffington Post*, 24 April. https://www.huffpost.com/entry/beyonce-serves-african-spirituality-in-lemonade_b_9774668.

Mudimbe, V. Y. 1988. *The Invention of Africa: Gnosis, Philosophy, and the Order of Knowledge*. Bloomington: Indiana University Press.

Olupona, Jacob K. 2000. *African Spirituality: Forms, Meanings, and Expressions*. Spring Valley, NY: Crossroad.

Olupona, Jacob K. 2011. *City of 201 Gods: Ilé-Ifè in Time, Space, and the Imagination*. Berkeley: University of California Press.

Olupona, Jacob K. 2015. "The Spirituality of Africa." *Harvard Gazette*, October 6. http://news.harvard.edu/gazette/story/2015/10/the-spirituality-of-africa/.

Platvoet, Jan G. 1996. "From Object to Subject: A History of the Study of the Religions of Africa." Pp. 105–38 in *The Study of Religions in Africa: Past, Present and Prospects*, edited by J. G. Platvoet, J. Cox, and J. K. Olupona. Cambridge: Roots & Branches.

Ray, Benjamin C. 1999. *African Religions: Symbol, Ritual, and Community*. 2nd ed. Upper Saddle River, NJ: Pearson.

Segal, Ronald. 1995. *The Black Diaspora*. London: Faber & Faber.

William, A., D. Dodson, and D. Smith, eds. 2017. *Religion, Culture and Spirituality in Africa and the African Diaspora*. New York: Routledge.

5

Methodological Innovations for the Study of Spirituality

Bradley R. E. Wright

Researchers who study spirituality have their methodological choices influenced by multiple factors. Their choices reflect personal interests and aptitudes. They are influenced by graduate school training. In addition, these choices are rooted in an understanding of spirituality. How researchers understand spirituality guides how they study it.

Understanding of spirituality → methodological choices

Although easily overlooked, research methods also shape an understanding of spirituality. Each method makes its own assumption about the world. It is a lens with which to view spirituality. How researchers study spirituality shapes how they think about it.

Methodological choices → understanding of spirituality

The Value of Methodological Innovation

This interplay between understanding and methodology underscores the value of methodological innovation in the study of spiritualty. Each method teaches us something about spirituality. It might be how spirituality is experienced by the person, how spiritual phenomena vary across types of people, or what are the antecedents and consequences of a spiritual phenomenon. More is learned about spirituality using different methodologies across studies than would be learned if all researchers used the same methodology.

Bradley R. E. Wright, *Methodological Innovations for the Study of Spirituality* In: *Situating Spirituality*. Edited by: Brian Steensland, Jaime Kucinskas, and Anna Sun, Oxford University Press. © Oxford University Press 2022. DOI: 10.1093/oso/9780197565001.003.0006

This puts a premium on using new methodologies. All else being equal, the marginal return in knowledge is greater when using an innovative method than it is with a frequently used method.

The history of natural science illustrates the principle of methodological innovation prompting conceptual insights. In countless instances, scientists have developed new ways of observing natural phenomena which result in new knowledge. In the early 1600s, Galileo Galilei improved the design of the telescope, and he applied it to astronomy. His observations of Jupiter, Venus, and the Sun provided powerful new evidence to support a Copernican view of the solar system (Wootton 2010).

Likewise, in the study of spirituality, methodological innovation can add to, modify, and even overturn currently understandings. This chapter reviews three research methodologies that are relatively new, or otherwise underutilized, in the study of spirituality. It will explain how they work, give an example of their use, and explore what can be learned with them.

Innovation 1: Smartphone-Based Experience Sampling

We can understand research methods by the assumptions they make about spirituality.

A first assumption is about the stability of spirituality. Does it change within a person over short periods of time? If spirituality does not change, then it ought to be studied as a stable characteristic, a fixed trait. Researchers should use methodologies that examine differences between types of people. If within-person spirituality changes slowly over time, it would be preferable to use methods that capture long-term change. This could mean longitudinal data with waves of data collection spaced years apart. If, however, within-person spirituality changes at a more accelerated rate—across weeks, days, and even moments—methods should capture this short-term state change. Studying spirituality becomes more like studying emotions, moods, or attitudes—all things that change rapidly.

The study of lived religion, as pioneered by Nancy Ammerman (2014), illustrates an understanding of spirituality as quickly changing. The lived religion paradigm assumes that religion, and the spiritual experiences that it entails, takes new forms at different times and places within a person's life. It is the study of "embodied and enacted forms of spirituality that occur in everyday life" (Ammerman 2014, 189). Conventional research methods did not fit well with this view of spirituality. So Ammerman (2003) and others developed a narrative methodology. This entailed collecting stories about how sacred moments are woven into everyday, mundane life. These narratives were collected in a variety of ways, including life histories, interviews, photograph elicitation, interviews, and oral diaries (Ammerman 2014).

The use of this new method, in turn, sparked new insight into how spirituality is lived in everyday life. Researchers in this paradigm found that spirituality involves eating, dressing, personal spaces, habits, and rituals. In sum, "Non-ordinary sensibilities weave in and out of mundane reality" (Ammerman 2014, 194).

While Ammerman and colleagues applied qualitative methods to the study of quickly changing spirituality, quantitative methods can be used as well. One approach is experience-sampling methodology (ESM) with smartphones. In the 1980s, Mihaly Csikszentmihalyi and colleagues developed the experience-sampling method to study the psychological experience of flow. They used beepers and paper diaries to measure flow and its correlates multiple times a day for days and weeks (Csikszentmihalyi and Larson 1987). Killingsworth and Gilbert (2010) used smartphones to conduct experience-sampling research. They texted study participants two short surveys a day to study momentary variations in happiness. This innovation can be referred to as the smartphone-based experience-sampling method, or S-ESM (Wright et al. 2017).

From 2013 to 2017, I worked with a team to conduct the SoulPulse study. Participants signed up for a two-week study. They started by filling out an intake survey that asked about psychological, demographic, and religious characteristics. For the next fourteen days, they were texted two brief surveys a day at random times during waking hours. These daily surveys took two to three minutes to fill out. They included survey questions about what participants were experiencing at the moment that they received the survey. The questions asked about what they were feeling, doing, and thinking, with many of the questions regarding spirituality. The questions also asked the study members about where they were and whom they were with.

Over a three-and-a-half-year span, SoulPulse enrolled about seven thousand participants. The participants represented a diverse convenience sample. People signed up from all fifty states as well as a dozen other countries. Compared to the general American population, the sample trended toward being more educated, white or Asian, and religious (Wright et al. 2017).

ESM studies generate a significant amount of data. The average SoulPulse respondent filled out twenty of the twenty-eight daily surveys, and each survey had twenty to twenty-five questions. In addition, there were forty to fifty questions on the intake survey. Altogether, this generated several million points of data.

The data collected by SoulPulse were time-ordered. The software recorded both when participants received the daily survey and when they filled it out. This timing allowed for examination of how people change by day over the fourteen-day study period. In addition, because two daily surveys were collected each day, it allowed for examination of the timing of changes throughout the day.

SoulPulse also asked about participants' location and activity during each daily survey. There was even a question about the weather outside. This type of contextual data is a classic strength of ESM data (Csikszentmihalyi and Larson 1987). In contrast, other survey collection methods fix respondents to a particular location, such as being on the phone or sitting at a table filling out the survey. This contextual information allowed for analysis of the interplay between people's characteristics and their immediate environment.

The structure of the data lent itself to multilevel modeling. At the lower level are the daily surveys. They capture data about a single moment in a participant's day. At the higher level are the intake questions. They regard a participant's stable characteristics.

One analytic approach was to take a daily survey question and calculate the average of each respondent's answers to it across the two-week study. This represented the participant's baseline of that measure. Then, for each daily survey, the value of the response given for that survey was subtracted from the two-week baseline measure. This created a deviation score. The deviation score represented participants' level on that measure relative to their two-week average. Statistical analysis included both the deviation score and the two-week baseline in the same equation. This approach estimates both the trait and state effect of the independent variable (McCrae et al. 2008).

A 2017 paper by noted spirituality scholar Jaime Kucinskas, with several colleagues, illustrates the power of using S-ESM data to study spirituality (Kucinskas et al. 2017). With SoulPulse data, Kucinskas et al. examined variation in spiritual awareness throughout the day. They used a question that asked participants to rate how true the following statement was for them: "I am aware of God at this moment." Participants responded on a scale from 1 ("not at all") to 10 ("very much"). Before the question was asked the first time, participants were told that if the word "God" did not fit with their belief systems, they should substitute another word that called to mind the divine, holy, or significant for them. Kucinskas et al. (2017) analyzed over fifty thousand participant responses to this spiritual awareness measure. The median score of the 1–10 scale was 6.8.

Spiritual awareness was examined as it varied by time. By day, the researchers found that within-person deviation scores (i.e., a participant's survey score on a particular daily survey minus their two-week average) were highest on Sundays and lowest on Mondays and Fridays. This pattern, however, significantly varied by participants' religiosity. Those who regularly attended church displayed this pattern. Those who did not attend church had spiritual awareness scores on Saturdays that were as high as those on Sundays. Spiritual awareness also varied by time of day. On average, spiritual awareness was highest in the morning, peaking at 11:00 a.m. It was lowest in the afternoon, with its nadir being at 5:00 p.m.

Kucinskas et al. (2017) also examined the variation of within-person deviations of spiritual awareness by activity. SoulPulse included a checklist of twenty-four common daily activities. Participants checked off which, if any, of the activities they were engaging in at that moment. The activities associated with the highest levels of spiritual awareness were prayer and meditation, exercising, and walking. The activities associated with the lowest were resting, watching television, shopping, and watching the news.

Finally, Kucinskas et al. (2017) examined variation in spiritual awareness by social context. SoulPulse included questions about how many people participants were with when they took the survey and the nature of their relationships with those people. The number of people in a participant's situation had relatively little association with spiritual awareness. When participants were with others, especially three or more people, they reported slightly higher levels of spiritual awareness than when they were alone. Though statistically significant, the magnitude of this difference was trivial. More variation in spiritual awareness was observed in whom the study participants were with. They reported the highest levels of spiritual awareness when they were with friends, acquaintances, and customers. They reported the lowest when they were with coworkers and their parents.

The study by Kucinskas et al. (2017) demonstrated the power of S-ESM research to study spirituality. It captured short-term changes in spirituality levels and examined how these changes related to the immediate context. While the momentary-variation measured by S-ESM is not as rich as could be gained with qualitative, observational methods, S-ESM provides much richer data than other forms of survey data collection. In addition, compared to qualitative methods, it allows for the collection of data from larger samples as well as statistical analysis using methods such as multilevel modeling.

While the SoulPulse study illustrates the power of S-ESM, it is not the only way to collect such data. SoulPulse was designed for a specific purpose. The goal was to collect data nationwide from thousands of people with more than one hundred daily survey variables. It entailed creating a website for the study as well as customized software. Furthermore, the study ran for several years.

A researcher could conduct a scaled-down version for a fraction of the cost and effort that SoulPulse required. The first task would be to select a dozen or so survey questions for analysis. With these questions, the researcher could create an online survey using Google Forms or another software survey. Two hundred study participants could be recruited with the promise of $50 each for participating in the study. The study runs for two weeks and, after a brief intake survey, participants would receive two surveys a day. Twice a day, for two weeks, the researcher could text the participants a link to the online survey at randomly selected times during normal waking hours. Participants would be instructed to fill out the survey when they received it, or if they were unable to do so at that time, fill it out as soon thereafter as possible. This simple S-ESM survey design would generate almost fifty thousand data points, and it would cost only $10,000. It could be done by a graduate student as paid for by a small dissertation grant. It would also make for an inexpensive side project for an established researcher. Furthermore, it could be done for free if the researcher could motivate participation for extra credit or by being especially persuasive.

Innovation 2: Field Experiments

A second question about spirituality relevant to methodology is whether aspects of spirituality can be intentionally and ethically changed by the researcher. If this is not the case, researchers are limited to analysis of observational data. If, however, a researcher can directly change people's spirituality, or change their exposure to spirituality-related phenomena, this opens up a new class of research methods: experiments.

The great majority of studies on spirituality do not use experiments. Rather, they rely on observational methods—both quantitative and

METHODOLOGICAL INNOVATIONS 119

qualitative. Observational methods have important advantages in studying spirituality. They provide rich description of spiritual activities. Whether it is a nationwide survey or an in-depth interview, observational methods tell us a lot about what people are currently doing. In addition, observational methods identify associations. Levels of multiple phenomena can be measured and tested for correlation. This can be done statistically, in the case of quantitative analyses, or impressionistically, as with qualitative analyses.

Problems with observational methods arise when they are used to infer causality. In observational studies, researchers observe the naturally occurring fluctuations of phenomena. From associations of those fluctuations, researchers infer causal relationships. The fundamental problem here is that the concept of causality is rooted in change. If one variable, A, changes, what is the impact of this change on another variable, B (Gerber and Green 2012)? An observed correlation is open to multiple interpretations. It could be that A causes B. It could be that B causes A. It could be that some prior factor causes both. And selection could generate the correlation (Schutt 2016).

These problems of causal interpretation of observational data are well known. Various strategies are used to work around them. For example, phenomena can be measured at multiple times to impose time ordering. Additional measures can be used as control variables. In multilevel modeling, higher-level characteristics can be controlled for. These approaches clarify causality, but they require making additional assumptions about the observed association. These assumptions are usually untested. As a result, there is an inherent level of ambiguity when causality is inferred from observational data (Gelman 2014).

In contrast, experiments have a more direct, defensible approach to testing for causality. The levels of one variable, A, are randomly assigned. Resulting changes in another variable, B, are observed. Within estimated confidence levels, the effect of A on B can be known. As Box et al. (1978) put it, to find out "what happens when you change something, it is necessary to change it" (404).

With random assignment, experiments impose a clear temporal ordering. They lessen the probability of third variables creating a spurious correlation. They provide stronger, clearer tests of causality than do observational studies.

The limitations of experiments come with their usability. Experimentation is possible only when the treatment can be randomly assigned. Some treatments are logistically infeasible to assign. For example, suppose a researcher wanted to examine the effect of driving distance to a place of worship on the frequency of attendance. As an experiment, this would require randomly assigning how far people live from their place of worship.[1] This would be infeasible.

Also, experiments can only be used when it is ethical to randomly assign the treatment. There are various experimental interventions that researchers could do but ought not due to ethical concerns. For example, it would be logistically possible to randomly assign people to undergo forcible conversion to a different spiritual belief system, but it would be unethical.

If treatment can be suitably randomly assigned, experiments are a powerful research option.[2] There are a variety of experimental principles and strategies that have been developed for the study of religion (Wright 2018) that could also be applied to the study of spirituality. The study of spirituality readily lends itself to experimentation. Spiritual experiences and practices are deemed good by many people, so it's possible to find people who will willingly participate. Also, spiritual practices are often inexpensive and easy to do, so it's logistically feasible to assign them.

An example of the suitability of experimentation for the study of spirituality is provided by Trammel's (2018) study of Christian mindfulness. For this study, Trammel recruited 127 undergraduate and graduate students from two universities. She randomly divided them into two groups. The control group received no mindfulness training. The treatment group was sent twenty- to thirty-minute recorded practices. These practices incorporated elements of centering prayer, guided images, and mindful reading of scripture. Treatment group members received these recorded practices twice a week for six weeks.

Over the course of the study, about a third of the initial participants dropped out. After six weeks, the remaining eighty participants were given two outcome measures. The participants who practiced mindfulness scored significantly higher on a common mindfulness scale. This showed that the mindfulness intervention did indeed increase levels of mindfulness. In addition, the treatment participants scored significantly lower on a perceived stress scale. This experiment made a strong causal statement. With a high degree of certainty, we can know that Christian mindfulness practices lowered levels of perceived stress among the study members.

In contrast, suppose that the study was done with conventional survey data. It would be open to causal second-guessing. Mindfulness might lower stress, or maybe having less stress results in more mindfulness. Or maybe the type of people who practice mindfulness are also the type of people who experience less stress.

In addition to randomly assigning spiritual phenomena, experiments can be used in other ways to learn about spiritualty. For example, a researcher can randomly assign factors that affect spirituality. For example, if one thought that happiness affected spiritual experiences, a happiness intervention could be assigned, with spirituality measured as dependent variables. Experiments can study spirituality as both a cause and a consequence.

A promising approach is to test the impact of existing spiritual training programs. This saves the researcher the difficulty of having to create a program from scratch, as Trammel (2018) did. This works especially well if the program is already oversubscribed. In this situation, there are more people wanting to participate in the program than there are spaces to do so. For example, maybe the meeting room is too small to accommodate everyone. Or maybe there aren't enough mentors. In this type of situation, the researcher can contact the person or organization to see if some of the applicants may be selected randomly by the researcher. If so, an experiment emerges in which the organization is randomly applying an intervention, and the researcher collects outcome measures.

Innovation 3: Big Data

A third question about spirituality relevant to methods is whether expressions of it can be easily and inexpensively observed across many people. Is it possible, however, to observe expressions of spirituality at little or no cost? Existing methods, such as participant observation, require considerable time and effort. This limits both the number of people who can be observed as well as the number of observed places and contexts.

A promising approach is to study spirituality using big data. Big data are large sets of existing data that can be statistically analyzed to reveal treads and associations in a broader population (NIST Big Data Public Working Group 2015). There are various strategies with which big data can be used to study spirituality. One strategy is to study word choice in online verbal expression and code it for spiritual content. People verbally express themselves online in various ways. They enter search terms into Google. They post tweets on Twitter. They write updates on Facebook. In varying degrees, these online expressions can be made available to the researcher. Sometimes companies release such data in anonymous format. Researchers can use search algorithms to scrape data off the web.

Once collected, algorithms can be written to code this online language in terms of spirituality-related emotions, thoughts, and behaviors. In a Google search people might ask if God exists. In tweets, they might refer to their soul. In a post, they might tell their friends that they meditated that morning.

Once coded, online spiritual language can be analyzed in various ways. Trends over time can be established and linked to external events. For example, do online spiritual expressions vary by season of the year or by publicized events such as a school shooting or presidential election? Online spiritual language can be linked to known characteristics of the person who posted it. For example, if it were possible to establish the city, state, and country in which the owner of a phone resides, regional analyses would be possible. Online spiritual language can be associated with other language expressions made by the same person. It is possible to code for emotional states, social activities, political expressions, and more. This makes possible analysis of a wide range of correlates of online spiritual language.

Eichstaedt et al. (2015) demonstrate the feasibility and power of studying online language to learn about inner states. They collected hundreds of millions of tweets. They coded these tweets for positive and negative emotions, engagement, and relationships. For example, the use of words such as wonderful, great, and hope were coded as representing positive experiences. Many of the Twitter users reported where they lived in their profile. This information was used to establish which county they lived in. To this was added county-level data about the mortality risk of heart diseases. The resulting data set covered 1,347 counties that had at least fifty thousand tweets in the data set as well as data on heart disease and morality risk. These counties represent 88 percent of the national population. Eichstaedt et al. (2015) then calculated the correlation, at the county level, between emotions, engagement, and relationship language and heart disease risk. They found that frequent use of words reflecting negative emotion (especially anger), disengagement, and negative relationship language correlated with increased risk of heart disease. In contrast, words reflecting positive emotions and engagement correlated with decreased risk.

It would be possible to do something similar with expressions of spirituality. For example, there are various words that are used in expressions of spirituality. They include words like "soul," "spirit," "karma," "sacred," "holy,"

METHODOLOGICAL INNOVATIONS   123

and so forth. They could be correlated with other types of words, such as positive emotions.

Another strategy involves the GPS function of smartphones. With study participants' permission, researchers can access GPS information from their phone. This identifies the exact location of the phone at any given time—within a matter of feet. And since most people keep their phone with them most of the time, this, by extension, gives the location of study participants. These location data can be linked to spiritual activities, such as going to a church, temple, or mosque. Some years ago, a series of studies debated how often Americans attend religious services (Hadaway et al. 1993). These studies found that most people overestimated their religious attendance in self-reported surveys. Using the location function of study members' smartphones could give valuable insight into this issue. This use of locational data fits with a broader methodological push in the social sciences to examine the temporal sequence structures of everyday life (Cornwell et al. 2019).

Smartphone location data can also be coupled with other types of spirituality data to create other analytic options. For example, suppose a study kept track of participants' location and also collected short surveys from them using S-ESM. The surveys would measure spirituality. The location function could be used to measure various correlates of spirituality. They could include how much time subjects have spent at home versus out and about, how much they walked, how far they drove, whether they were in a rural or urban setting, and so on.

MacKerron and Mourato (2013) did something like this with happiness. They used a smartphone app that gave study members a several-question survey while at the same time using GPS to record their exact location. Twenty thousand people participated in this study, generating over a million points of data. Studying within-person variation of location, the authors discovered that study members were significantly happier when they were outdoors than when they were in urban settings.

Another strategy for using big data to study spirituality would be to analyze the use of spiritually related apps. There are various smartphone apps that guide users in spiritual practices. It would be possible to measure how people use these apps and to link this usage to other aspects of their lives. For this, researchers would need access to data about use of the app—knowing when, how often, and for how long people used it. It might be possible to work with an existing app manufacturer to study their users. Researchers could also create their own spiritual practice apps. If study members are willing to incorporate such an app into their daily practice, it would give researchers a concrete, objective measure of the patterning of a spiritual behavior. This could be coupled with S-ESM survey data, location data, in-depth interviews, or other methods to produce rich data about when and why people engage in spiritual practices.

A last strategy to mention is the use of records previously collected by denominations, congregations, and other religious groups. These records can be voluminous, span many years, and cover many aspects of a group's experience. For example, denominations might record the initiation, dissolution, and size of individual congregations over time. Congregations themselves might track attendance, donations, and other measures of participation. To illustrate, one known congregation has all Sunday service attendees sign a logbook, and they have practiced this recordkeeping for decades. The analysis of such church records would give unique and powerful insight into individual and organizational religious persistence and transformation.[3]

Conclusion

The guiding assumption of this chapter is that methodological innovation brings knowledge to the study of spirituality that cannot be obtained with standard methods—no matter how well they are implemented. Surveys, participant observation, in-depth interviewing, and similar methods have been used in the great majority of spirituality studies to date. These research methods have a long history of usage in the social sciences. They are powerful and will, and probably should, continue to be mainstays in the study of spirituality.

In addition, there is much to be gained by incorporating new, innovative research methods. They make different assumptions and collect different kinds of data. This gives them the potential of generating new insights into spirituality. For some research questions, it might be more productive to conduct one study using an innovative method than a dozen studies using mainstays.

In short, there is a premium on methodological innovation in the study of spirituality. This chapter fosters this innovation by identifying three types of research methodologies that are underutilized in the study of spirituality—S-ESM, field experiments, and big-data analysis. These methodological innovations not only apply to new ways of studying spirituality, but also point to different conceptualizations of spirituality itself.

S-ESM emphasizes spirituality as having a dual nature. It is both a stable characteristic and a constantly changing experience. Its trait-and-state characteristics coexist and influence one another. In this way, spirituality is like an electron, which exists as both a particle of matter and a wave of energy. Methods that focus solely on between- or within-person change in spirituality overlook this duality. S-ESM moves the researcher to this richer conceptualization.

Field experiments emphasize spirituality as a powerful force in individuals' lives. It is something that when randomly assigned will have significant, measurable consequences for the individual. It will have this effect independent of other psychological or social factors. Furthermore, its effects are salubrious (Gonçalves et al. 2015; Akbari and Hossaini 2018; Johnson 2018). Other research methods emphasize people's creation of spirituality through perceptions and identification. Spirituality becomes embodied in and reflective of many other factors. Field experiments highlight the unique and discreet power of spirituality.

Big data emphasize spirituality as a macro-social characteristic. It has salient differences between regions of the country, groups of people, even periods of time. Though it is experienced at the individual level, the macrosocial aspect of spirituality means that it must be taken into account in understanding the workings of society as a whole. The summation of spirituality into larger groups matters. Other research methods focus on individual and interpersonal aspects of spirituality. Big data alerts us to this larger-scale conceptualization of it.

In the end, research innovation is central to both the study and the understanding of spirituality.

Notes

1. Quasi experiments can be used for treatments that are not open to random assignment (Campbell and Stanley 1963).
2. This chapter emphasizes the use of field experiments to study spirituality. For a discussion of the relative merits of field experiments versus lab experiments see Gerber and Green 2012.
3. The author thanks an anonymous reviewer from Oxford University Press for the suggestion of this strategy.

References

Akbari, Mehdi, and Sayed Morteza Hossaini. 2018. "The Relationship of Spiritual Health with Quality of Life, Mental Health, and Burnout: The Mediating Role of Emotional Regulation." *Iranian Journal of Psychiatry* 13(1): 22–31.

Ammerman, Nancy T. 2003. "Religious Identities and Religious Institutions." Pp. 207–17 in *Handbook of the Sociology of Religion*, edited by M. Dillion. Cambridge: Cambridge University Press.

Ammerman, Nancy T. 2014. "Finding Religion in Everyday Life." *Sociology of Religion* 75(2): 189–207.

Box, George E. P., William G. Hunter, and J. Stuart Hunter. 1978. *Statistics for Experimenters*. New York: Wiley-Interscience.

Campbell, Donald T. and Julian C. Stanley. 1963. *Experimental and Quasi-Experimental Design for Research*. Boston: Houghton Mifflin.

Cornwell, Benjamin, Jonathan Gershuny, and Oriel Sullivan. 2019. "The Social Structure of Time: Emerging Trends and New Directions." *Annual Review of Sociology* 45: 301–20.

Csikszentmihalyi, Mihaly, and Reed Larson. 1987. "Validity and Reliability of the Experience-Sampling Method." *Journal of Nervous and Mental Disease* 175(9): 526–36.

Eichstaedt, Johannes C., et al. 2015. "Psychological Language on Twitter Predicts County-Level Heart Disease Mortality." *Psychological Science* 26(2): 159–69.

Gelman, Andrew. 2014. "Experimental Reasoning in Social Science." Pp. 185–95 in *Field Experiments and Their Critics: Essays on the Uses and Abuses of Experimentation in the Social Sciences*, edited by Dawn Langan Teele. New Haven: Yale University Press.

Gerber, Alan S., and Donald P. Green. 2012. *Field Experiments: Design, Analysis, and Interpretation*. New York: W.W. Norton.

Gonçalves, Juliane P. B., Giancarlo Lucchetti, Paulo Rossi Menezes, and Homero Vallada. 2015. "Religious and Spiritual Interventions in Mental Health Care: A Systematic Review and Meta-analysis of Randomized Controlled Clinical Trials." *Psychological Medicine* 45(14): 2937–49.

Hadaway, C. Kirk, Penny Long Marler, and Mark Chaves. 1993. "What the Polls Don't Show: A Closer Look at US Church Attendance." *American Sociological Review* 58: 741–52.

Johnson, Kirk A. 2018. "Prayer: A Helpful Aid in Recovery from Depression." *Journal of Religion and Health* 57(6): 2290–300.

Killingsworth, Matthew A., and Daniel T. Gilbert. 2010. "A Wandering Mind Is an Unhappy Mind." *Science* 330(6006): 932.

Kucinskas, Jaime, Bradley R. E. Wright, and Stuart Riepl. 2017. "The Interplay between Meaning and Sacred Awareness in Everyday Life: Evidence from a Daily Smartphone Study." *International Journal for the Psychology of Religion* 28(2): 71–88.

MacKerron, George, and Susana Mourato. 2013. "Happiness Is Greater in Natural Environments." *Global Environmental Change* 23(5): 992–1000.

McCrae, Christina S., Joseph P. McNamara, Meredeth A. Rowe, Joseph M. Dzierzewski, Judith Dirk, Michael Marsiske, and Jason G. Craggs. 2008. "Sleep and Affect in Older Adults: Using Multilevel Modeling to Examine Daily Associations." *Journal of Sleep Research* 17(1): 42–53.

NIST Big Data Public Working Group. 2015. *NIST Big Data Interoperability Framework*. Vol. 1: *Definitions*. Washington, DC: US Department of Commerce.

Schutt, Russell K. 2016. *Understanding the Social World: Research Methods for the 21st Century*. Thousand Oaks, CA: Sage Publications.

Trammel, Regina. 2018. "Effectiveness of an MP3 Christian Mindfulness Intervention on Mindfulness and Perceived Stress." *Mental Health, Religion, and Culture* 21(5): 500–514.

Wootton, David. 2010. *Galileo: Watcher of the Skies*. New Haven: Yale University Press.

Wright, Bradley R. E. 2018. "Field Experiments of Religion: A Dream Whose Time Has Come." *Journal for the Scientific Study of Religion* 57(2): 193–205.

Wright, Bradley R. E., Richard Blackmon, David Carreon, and Luke Knepper. 2017. "Lessons Learned from SoulPulse, a Smartphone-Based Experience Sampling Method (S-ESM) Study of Spirituality." Pp. 344–64 in *Faithful Measures: New Methods in the Measurement of Religion*, edited by Roger Finke and Christopher D. Bader. New York: New York University Press.

6

Shifts in Spiritual and Religious Self-Perceptions in the First Year of College

Alyssa N. Rockenbach

The spiritual and religious dimensions of college students' lives have received marked attention over the last two decades as education scholars have opened the door to new questions about the "inner" domains of experience that have historically received less attention than traditional educational outcomes, such as academic achievement, persistence, and career attainment (Astin 2004). Initial efforts to make meaning of spirituality and religion in the higher-education context led scholars to puzzle over terminology and definitions. This discourse resulted in some shared understandings that became foundational to subsequent educational research and practice.

Representative of perspectives on the meaning of "religion," Stamm (2006, 37) explained that religion is the "beliefs and practices delineated by established denominational institutions and framed through defined doctrines, theology, and historical narratives or myths." Although the meaning of spirituality is more elusive, Love and Talbot (1999) attempted to synthesize different conceptualizations in the field and offered that spirituality entails five components: the pursuit of wholeness and authenticity; self-transcendence; interconnectedness within and beyond the self; meaning and purpose; and relationship to and with transcendence or the divine. Adding further layers to evolving definitions, other scholars (Astin et al. 2011) contributed empirical evidence in support of various spiritual qualities exhibited by contemporary college students (e.g., spiritual quest, equanimity). College student religiosity, Astin et al. (2011) argued, consists of another distinctive set of dimensions (e.g., religious commitment, religious engagement).

While conceptual and empirical foundations have been critical to this emerging line of research, the terrain of religious and (especially) spiritual research is complicated by the fact that college students who participate in research carry their own assumptions and definitions about religious and

Alyssa N. Rockenbach, *Shifts in Spiritual and Religious Self-Perceptions in the First Year of College* In: *Situating Spirituality*. Edited by: Brian Steensland, Jaime Kucinskas, and Anna Sun, Oxford University Press. © Oxford University Press 2022. DOI: 10.1093/oso/9780197565001.003.0007

spiritual concepts. Importantly, the boundary between religion and spirituality is porous and fuzzy in the lives of young adults—and overly simple dichotomies often fall short. Smith and Snell (2009) provided evidence to suggest that internal, subjective religion (which some might call "spirituality") and external, public religion coincide more often than not, while Wuthnow (2007, 134) resolved that "the dominant pattern among young adults is not spirituality *or* religion, but spirituality *and* religion" (though a significant minority of young people in his study were "spiritual but not religious"). In the end, binary conceptions of religious and spiritual dimensions are far removed from the way most young adults live and experience these domains in everyday life.

Spiritual and Religious Identification and Change among College Students

The emergent stream of research on spirituality and religion in higher education has illuminated a number of insights regarding how college students understand, engage, and identify with religion and spirituality. For example, the first national, longitudinal study of college student spirituality—involving more than fourteen thousand students attending 136 institutions between 2004 and 2007—revealed that a considerable proportion of contemporary college students—a full 80 percent—do have interest in spirituality (Astin et al. 2005). Affirmations of spiritual interest among college students and young adults in the twenty-first century contrast to a certain degree with older studies that suggested patterns of less religiousness and spirituality within younger age cohorts (Marler and Hadaway 2002).

Following their matriculation, college students make considerable gains on spiritual qualities—spiritual quest, equanimity, and ecumenical worldview—from the first to the third year of college (Astin et al. 2011). Interestingly, students may underestimate the spiritual gains they make in college. While students on the whole become more inclined to report that "integrating spirituality into my life" is "essential" the longer they are in college, they become less likely to rate their spirituality as "above average" or "highest 10%" compared to their peers (Bryant 2007; Bryant et al. 2003). Perhaps students become more contemplative about what it means to be a spiritual person and therefore more critical in their self-evaluations (Mayhew, Rockenbach, Bowman, et al. 2016).

What about religious development during the college years? Although the assumption that higher education disrupts religious commitments is embedded in our societal narrative, the reality is much more nuanced. Longitudinal data have provided assurances that religious continuity is more often the norm—but it depends on the measure. For example, Astin et al. (2011) found that students' degree of religious commitment was relatively stable across three years of college. Smith and Snell (2009), reporting findings from the National Study of Youth and Religion, also traced patterns in religious identity, with continuity as the predominant pattern. Moreover, evidence of religious decline over time was more apparent among individuals who did *not* attend college, calling into question the notion that college necessarily has a secularizing influence. By contrast, changes in religious engagement were much more pronounced, according to Astin et al. (2011). Whereas 44 percent of first-year students reported frequent religious service attendance in their last year of high school, only 25 percent did so in their last year of college (Astin et al. 2011).

Evidence abounds within and beyond the literature on college student development that a number of personal and familial characteristics shape religious and spiritual qualities and change. Where one abides in one's religious and spiritual identity is tied to religious affiliation (Ammerman 2013 2014; Astin et al. 2011) and upbringing (Bengston et al. 2013), race and cultural background (Ammerman 2013, 2014; Astin et al. 2011; McClure 2017), gender (Ammerman 2013, 2014; Astin et al. 2011; Bryant 2007), and political orientation (Hirsh et al. 2013; Steensland et al. 2018).

The environmental and experiential influences of college on students' spiritual and religious development have been the focus of a number of studies. The religious emphasis of the campus appears to have a role in either promoting or curtailing growth. Protestant institutions (compared to Catholic and nonsectarian institutions) have been linked to both spiritual and religious development (Bowman and Small 2010; Small and Bowman 2011). Another study found more pronounced negative effects on religious service participation of attending mainline Protestant, Catholic, and nonreligious private institutions relative to evangelical institutions and public colleges and universities (Hill 2009). Hill (2009) suggested that a shared moral order at evangelical institutions may have attenuated religious declines, while the pluralistic nature of public institutions may serve to activate religious identity, particularly among students whose religious worldview is in the minority on campus. In a later study, Hill (2011) found an increase in skepticism toward "super-empirical religious beliefs" (e.g., belief in God, belief in an afterlife) among college students, particularly for those attending elite institutions. Yet college completion was actually tied to a stronger preference for institutionalized religion (despite reduced exclusivist religious belief).

The effects of institutional affiliation on students' religious and spiritual development are best explained by cultural and climatic factors that vary by affiliation. For instance, at institutions where faculty are focused on spirituality, students exhibit gains in spiritual quest (Astin et al. 2011), and on campuses where students are, on the whole, more religiously engaged, individual students become more inclined toward religious engagement. Religious conversion—arguably the most radical type of religious or spiritual change that students may undergo—is more likely for students attending campuses where other students are converting at higher than average rates (Starcke 2017). Finally, hostile campus climates—where students feel pressured and coerced—can stymie students' worldview commitments (Mayhew and Bryant Rockenbach 2013). In sum, peer and faculty cultures in higher education explain some of the change evidenced in students' spiritual and religious identification.

Beyond structural and cultural features of the campus environment, students' engagement patterns relate to their religious and spiritual growth. Notably, student engagement with faculty who encourage religious and spiritual discussions has a demonstrable impact on spiritual quest, equanimity, religious engagement, and religious commitment (Astin et al. 2011). So, too, do "religious reinforcers" (activities and relationships that connect students to their faith traditions and communities) have implications for development; reinforcers bolster religious commitments (Astin et al. 2011), but may diminish other spiritual traits, such as openness to people of diverse religions and cultures (Bryant 2011). Students' decisions regarding academic major may also influence them spiritually and religiously, with some evidence pointing to the negative effects of majoring in engineering (but not necessarily other scientific disciplines) (Astin et al. 2011; Scheitle 2011). Conversations with friends or family members play a role in conversion patterns among college students. Starcke (2017) noted that frequent conversations of a religious or spiritual nature with family members predicted that students would adopt, maintain, or grow more committed to a religious tradition. By contrast, frequent religious or spiritual discussions with friends tended to increase the likelihood of conversion.

132 ALYSSA N. ROCKENBACH

More recent work extends from explorations of college students' religious and spiritual development and asks new questions about the ways in which students of diverse religious and worldview identities learn to engage productively across those differences (Mayhew, Rockenbach, Correia, et al. 2016; Rockenbach et al. 2017). This research suggests that religious and spiritual dimensions of the campus climate (e.g., the extent to which the campus is religiously diverse, supportive of spiritual expression, welcoming, divisive, coercive) as well as "provocative" encounters that disrupt assumptions and stereotypes have critical implications as students develop thoughtful worldview commitments and positive attitudes toward religious and worldview diversity. In other words, we are starting to gain perspective on how campus climate and religious diversity exposure connect to students' attitudinal development and openness to diversity—foundational outcomes of college that will determine how productively they will engage others in the future. However, we know much less about how these particular collegiate experiences (campus climate, religious diversity exposure, and the like) potentially change how students see themselves religiously and spiritually.

Research Questions and Conceptual Framework

Despite accumulated research that has offered new insights on college students' religious and spiritual development across the last two decades, a number of critical questions remain. Contested definitions of "religion" and "spirituality" and their relationship to each other necessitate further inquiry into how everyday people (for this study's purpose, college students) understand and incorporate these domains into their lives. Moreover, empirical investigations show how students change (and why they change) on measures of spirituality and religion—but these measures that researchers have constructed tell us little about the choices students make to assume or cast aside these labels. Finally, although recent studies have illuminated the role of campus climate and religious diversity exposure in changing students' attitudes and outward expressions of those attitudes, how these experiences shape inward religious and spiritual self-perceptions remains to be seen. Thus, this study addresses the following research questions via the empirically based conceptual framework illustrated in Figure 6.1:

SHIFTS IN SELF-PERCEPTIONS 133

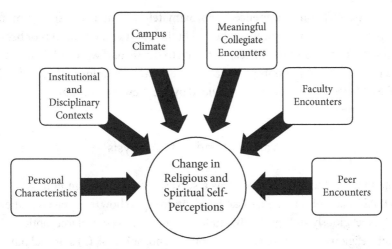

Figure 6.1 Conceptual framework

1. To what extent and how do college students change their religious and spiritual self-perceptions in their first year on campus?
2. How do personal characteristics, institutional and disciplinary contexts, meaningful collegiate encounters, faculty encounters, and peer encounters relate to changes in students' inclinations to identity as "both religious and spiritual," "religious but not spiritual," "spiritual but not religious," or "neither spiritual nor religious"?

Method

Instrumentation and Data Collection

The data for this study derive from the Interfaith Diversity Experiences and Attitudes Longitudinal Survey (IDEALS), a multiyear investigation of the educational experiences most conducive to students' developing the attitudinal and behavioral capacities to engage productively across religious and worldview differences. The first wave of the IDEALS project launched in summer and fall of 2015 at 122 colleges and universities. First-term students[1] attending participating colleges and universities across the country were invited to complete the survey in summer and/or fall 2015. A total of 20,436 students provided usable data in the first wave of IDEALS. The second wave

134 ALYSSA N. ROCKENBACH

of data collection commenced approximately a year later (spring or fall 2016) as students were nearing the end of their first year on campus or beginning their second year. The response rate to the second wave of IDEALS was 43 percent; 7,194 students provided usable data. More information about the IDEALS design and sample is provided by Mayhew et al. (2020).

Variables and Data Analysis

The focus of the present study was a survey item, included in both waves of IDEALS data collection, that asked students to report how they perceived themselves religiously and spiritually. Students could choose one of four options: (1) both religious and spiritual, (2) religious but not spiritual, (3) spiritual but not religious, or (4) neither religious nor spiritual. A variable was generated to indicate whether students had changed their self-perception by the second wave of data collection (i.e., the end of their first year on campus or the beginning of their second year). The new variable was coded as 0 = no change in religious and spiritual self-perception, 1 = change to "both religious and spiritual," 2 = change to "religious but not spiritual," 3 = change to "spiritual but not religious," and 4 = change to "neither religious nor spiritual." The generated variable served as the dependent variable. Six clusters of independent variables (*Personal Characteristics, Institutional and Disciplinary Context, Campus Climate, Meaningful Collegiate Encounters, Faculty Encounters,* and *Peer Encounters*), as depicted in Figure 6.1, were included in the analysis as predictors of change in religious and spiritual self-identification. Descriptive statistics for all variables can be found in Table 6.1. To address research question 1, cross-tabulations were used to examine students' movement between religious and spiritual categories across waves 1 and 2 of the IDEALS study. Multilevel multinomial logistic regression was used to address the second research question, predicting change in religious and spiritual self-perceptions.

Results

Cross-tabulations of students' religious and spiritual self-perceptions in 2015 and 2016 provided insight on patterns of change across their first year on campus in response to research question 1. Table 6.2 highlights net changes in students' baseline (2015) and end-of-first-year (2016) proclivities toward

Table 6.1 Descriptive statistics

	N	Min	Max	M	SD
Personal characteristics					
Gender identity					
Woman	7,194	0.000	1.000	0.690	0.462
Man	7,194	0.000	1.000	0.290	0.455
Another gender identity	7,134	0.000	1.000	0.010	0.106
Sexual orientation					
Bisexual	7,194	0.000	1.000	0.050	0.221
Gay	7,194	0.000	1.000	0.010	0.115
Heterosexual	7,194	0.000	1.000	0.840	0.371
Lesbian	7,194	0.000	1.000	0.010	0.111
Queer	7,194	0.000	1.000	0.010	0.098
Another sexual orientation	7,194	0.000	1.000	0.030	0.178
Race/ethnicity					
African American / black	7,194	0.000	1.000	0.050	0.223
Asian / Pacific Islander	7,194	0.000	1.000	0.130	0.340
Latinx	7,194	0.000	1.000	0.070	0.260
Native American	7,194	0.000	1.000	0.000	0.047
White	7,194	0.000	1.000	0.620	0.485
Another race	7,194	0.000	1.000	0.010	0.112
Multiracial	7,194	0.000	1.000	0.100	0.305
Religion/worldview					
Atheist	7,194	0.000	1.000	0.080	0.272
Buddhist	7,194	0.000	1.000	0.017	0.128
Catholic	7,194	0.000	1.000	0.205	0.404
Evangelical Christian	7,194	0.000	1.000	0.172	0.377
Hindu	7,194	0.000	1.000	0.014	0.115
Jewish	7,194	0.000	1.000	0.025	0.155
Latter-Day Saint	7,194	0.000	1.000	0.040	0.195
Mainline Protestant	7,194	0.000	1.000	0.112	0.315
Muslim	7,194	0.000	1.000	0.021	0.142
Another majority worldview	7,194	0.000	1.000	0.033	0.178

Continued

Table 6.1 *Continued*

	N	Min	Max	M	SD
Another minority worldview	7,194	0.000	1.000	0.038	0.192
Another nonreligious worldview	7,194	0.000	1.000	0.201	0.401
Another worldview	7,194	0.000	1.000	0.044	0.205
Political leaning (liberal)	7,157	−2.361	1.699	0.000	1.000

Institutional and disciplinary context

Institutional religious affiliation

	N	Min	Max	M	SD
Catholic	7,194	0.000	1.000	0.090	0.289
Evangelical Protestant	7,194	0.000	1.000	0.060	0.236
Mainline Protestant	7,194	0.000	1.000	0.170	0.378
Private-nonsectarian	7,194	0.000	1.000	0.240	0.425
Public	7,194	0.000	1.000	0.440	0.496
Selectivity	7,194	−2.873	1.541	0.000	1.000
Percentage of students changing religious and spiritual identification	7,194	−4.585	5.478	0.000	1.000

Academic major

	N	Min	Max	M	SD
Arts, humanities, or religion	7,194	−0.000	1.000	0.110	0.316
Social science or education	7,194	0.000	1.000	0.160	1.371
Health	7,194	0.000	1.000	0.110	1.310
Science, math, or engineering	7,194	0.000	1.000	0.300	0.460
Business	7,194	0.000	1.000	0.070	1.252
Undecided or another major	7,194	0.000	1.000	0.230	1.420

Campus climate

	N	Min	Max	M	SD
Structural worldview diversity	7,194	−3.000	1.000	0.000	1.000
Divisiveness on campus	7,161	−2.000	3.000	0.000	1.000
Welcoming on campus	6,959	−5.000	1.000	0.000	1.000

Meaningful collegiate encounters

	N	Min	Max	M	SD
Space for support and spiritual expression	7,161	−4.000	1.000	0.000	1.000

Table 6.1 *Continued*

	N	Min	Max	M	SD
Provocative encounters that challenge personal worldview	7,167	−1.601	2.647	0.000	1.000
Felt pressured by others on campus to change worldview	7,182	−0.843	2.902	0.000	1.000
Religious reinforcers	7,194	−0.811	3.151	0.000	1.000
Faculty encounters					
Frequency of insensitive comments from faculty	7,183	−0.752	3.547	0.000	1.000
Discussed religious or spiritual topics with faculty	7,194	0.000	1.000	0.280	0.447
Participated in contemplative practices in the classroom	7,194	0.000	1.000	0.210	0.405
Peer encounters					
Frequency of insensitive comments from friends/ peers	7,189	−1.307	2.333	0.000	1.000
Informal engagement with diverse peers	7,194	−3.000	1.000	0.000	1.000
Number of friends of a different worldview	7,164	−2.303	0.850	0.000	1.000
at least one friend who is spiritual but not religious	7,194	−0.000	1.000	0.600	0.490

Table 6.2 Frequency distribution of 2015 and 2016 religious and spiritual identification

	% 2015	% 2016	Difference
Both religious and spiritual	41.30	40.50	−0.80
Religious but not spiritual	9.80	8.50	−1.30
Spiritual but not religious	26.40	29.00	2.60
Neither spiritual nor religious	22.50	22.00	−0.50

religious and spiritual self-descriptions. "Both religious and spiritual" (41 percent) was the most popular selection among students as they began their first term on campus, followed by "spiritual but not religious" (26 percent), "neither spiritual nor religious" (23 percent), and "religious but not spiritual" (10 percent). Net changes in these categories suggest very little movement across the first year; in fact, the only category showing a small net increase was "spiritual but not religious," which grew slightly by three percentage points. All other categories showed slight net declines.

Importantly, net changes in the four categories mask the more substantial movement of individual students into and out of categories. As shown in Table 6.3, 28 percent of students changed their religious and spiritual self-perceptions. Thus, although the norm is stability, a significant minority of students adopted or relinquished "religious" and "spiritual" descriptors. The most common type of change was a shift toward being "spiritual but not religious" (10.5 percent), followed by "both religious and spiritual" (7.5 percent), "neither spiritual nor religious" (5.5 percent), and "religious but not spiritual" (4.6 percent). From which categories did students change? Students who ultimately changed to "both religious and spiritual" tended to originate from either the "religious but not spiritual" (8.4 percent) or "spiritual but not religious" (8.3 percent) categories. Students who made the shift to "religious but not spiritual" most often began their first year on campus as "both religious and spiritual" (37.0 percent). Those who moved into the "spiritual but not religious" designation drew in roughly similar numbers from the "both religious and spiritual" (14.9 percent) and "neither spiritual nor religious" (15.7 percent) categories. Finally, students who changed to "neither spiritual nor religious" in their first year came primarily from the "spiritual but not religious" (17.4 percent) category (see Table 6.4).

Table 6.3 Frequency distribution of 2016 religious and spiritual identification

	Frequency	Percent
No change	5,177	72.00
Change to both religious and spiritual	538	7.50
Change to religious but not spiritual	330	4.60
Change to spiritual but not religious	752	10.50
Change to neither spiritual nor religious	397	5.50
Total	7,194	100.00

SHIFTS IN SELF-PERCEPTIONS   139

Table 6.4 Change in religious and spiritual identification 2015–2016

2016 religious and spiritual identification	2015 religious and spiritual identification			
	Both religious and spiritual	Religious but not spiritual	Spiritual but not religious	Neither spiritual nor religious
Both religious and spiritual	81.50%	8.40%	8.30%	1.80%
Religious but not spiritual	37.00%	46.00%	8.20%	8.80%
Spiritual but not religious	14.90%	5.60%	63.80%	15.70%
Neither spiritual nor religious	4.00%	3.70%	17.40%	74.80%

Table 6.5 presents results from the multilevel multinomial logistic regression. The coefficients shown in the table are relative risk ratios (RR), which represent the "risk" (or probability) of changing one's religious and spiritual self-perceptions versus not changing as a result of the independent variable (holding all other independent variables constant). Coefficients that are less than 1 point to a reduced risk of change, whereas coefficients that are greater than 1 indicate a higher risk of change. To address research question 2, significant predictors of the four types of change are discussed in the following sections.

Change to "Both Religious and Spiritual"

The probability of shifting to "both religious and spiritual" (compared to not changing) is predicated on a number of personal characteristics. Students who identify as Native American (RR = 4.540, $p < .05$) are more likely to make the transition to "both religious and spiritual" than are white students (however, this finding is based on a small number of Native American students in the sample, $n = 16$). Students of several different worldview identities have a reduced likelihood of changing to "both religious and spiritual" compared to mainline Protestants: atheists (RR = 0.109, $p < .001$), students of another nonreligious worldview (RR = 0.172, $p < .001$), and students of another worldview (RR = 0.422, $p < .01$). Institutional context also makes an appreciable difference in the likelihood of becoming "both religious and

Table 6.5 Results of multilevel multinomial logistic regression models comparing religious and spiritual identification change to no change

	To both religious and spiritual		To religious but not spiritual		To spiritual but not religious		Neither religious nor spiritual	
	RR	SE	RR	SE	RR	SE	RR	SE
Personal characteristics								
Gender identity[a]								
Woman	1.091	0.120	0.963	0.12	0.998	0.084	0.887	0.126
Another gender identity	0.440	0.300	0.000***	0.000	1.059	0.391	1.100	0.589
Sexual orientation[b]								
Bisexual	0.803	0.227	0.818	0.316	1.024	0.179	0.805	0.196
Gay	0.805	0.381	0.000***	0.000	0.785	0.329	0.970	0.371
Lesbian	1.218	0.505	2.417	1.101	0.768	0.260	0.659	0.326
Queer	1.209	0.692	2.794	1.615	0.518	0.240	0.656	0.386
Another sexual orientation	1.291	0.382	0.813	0.447	1.221	0.246	0.836	0.287
Race/ethnicity[c]								
African American / black	1.470	0.306	1.216	0.342	1.163	0.217	1.324	0.311
Asian / Pacific Islander	1.311	0.205	1.500*	0.293	1.392**	0.167	0.977	0.171
Latinx	1.340	0.239	1.380	0.299	1.341	0.265	1.265	0.208
Native American	4.540*	3.117	2.228	2.264	0.997	1.191	3.254	2.826
Another race	0.701	0.291	0.784	0.453	1.143	0.398	0.458	0.296
Multiracial	1.357	0.247	0.656	0.160	1.159	0.194	1.321	0.249

Religion/worldview[d]								
Atheist	0.109***	0.037	0.050***	0.032	0.250***	0.064	0.705	0.180
Buddhist	0.876	0.278	0.483	0.217	0.828	0.247	1.488	0.697
Catholic	0.829	0.118	1.024	0.174	0.769	0.110	1.099	0.235
Evangelical Christian	0.851	0.145	0.482***	0.092	0.714**	0.097	0.745	0.232
Hindu	0.785	0.274	0.434	0.282	0.839	0.291	0.911	0.583
Jewish	1.528	0.407	1.043	0.368	0.902	0.260	2.880*	1.231
Latter-Day Saint	0.770	0.197	0.779	0.225	0.817	0.185	1.202	0.441
Muslim	0.756	0.268	1.157	0.462	0.631	0.189	1.219	0.673
Another majority worldview	0.963	0.263	0.963	0.274	0.637	0.227	1.319	0.512
Another minority worldview	0.644	0.176	0.173***	0.082	0.451**	0.118	0.714	0.261
Another nonreligious worldview	0.172***	0.038	0.145***	0.044	0.735*	0.107	1.36	0.230
Another worldview	0.422**	0.122	0.380*	0.153	0.763	0.164	1.742*	0.425
Political leaning (liberal)	0.985	0.050	0.991	0.078	1.131*	0.055	1.159	0.093
Institutional and disciplinary context								
Institutional religious affiliation[e]								
Catholic	1.019	0.143	0.916	0.150	1.036	0.113	0.788	0.197
Evangelical Protestant	1.438*	0.222	1.289	0.299	0.864	0.119	0.460*	0.162
Mainline Protestant	1.068	0.102	1.018	0.150	0.941	0.073	1.161	0.197
Private-nonsectarian	0.882	0.088	1.195	0.145	0.954	0.084	1.111	0.128
Selectivity	0.988	0.046	0.897*	0.043	1.023	0.034	1.015	0.052
Percentage of students changing religious and spiritual identification	1.407***	0.046	1.347***	0.056	1.309***	0.048	1.263***	0.069

Continued

Table 6.5 *Continued*

	To both religious and spiritual		To religious but not spiritual		To spiritual but not religious		Neither religious nor spiritual	
	RR	SE	RR	SE	RR	SE	RR	SE
Academic major[f]								
Social science or education	1.133	0.218	1.400	0.398	0.958	0.119	1.242	0.287
Health	1.109	0.264	1.411	0.48.	0.915	0.130	1.150	0.268
Science, math, or engineering	1.016	0.168	1.258	0.323	0.811	0.111	1.007	0.201
Business	1.297	0.253	1.183	0.479	0.845	0.155	1.034	0.281
Undecided or another major	1.077	0.208	1.606	0.425	0.917	0.122	1.000	0.200
Campus climate								
Structural worldview diversity	1.006	0.060	0.953	0.077	0.958	0.048	0.937	0.071
Divisiveness on campus	0.980	0.053	0.879	0.064	1.078	0.046	1.062	0.074
Welcoming campus	1.069	0.069	1.027	0.078	1.033	0.065	1.048	0.073
Meaningful collegiate encounters								
Space for support and spiritual expression	1.031	0.070	1.158	0.087	1.028	0.060	0.991	0.084
Provocative encounters that challenge personal worldview	1.149*	0.068	1.003	0.062	1.139*	0.059	1.120*	0.061
Felt pressured by others on campus to change worldview	0.994	0.058	1.152*	0.078	0.995	0.046	1.112	0.079
Religious reinforcers	0.955	0.056	0.911	0.059	0.732***	0.041	0.439***	0.051

Faculty encounters								
Frequency of insensitive comments from faculty	0.974	0.048	1.104	0.081	0.913	0.052	0.863	0.077
Discussed religious or spiritual topics with faculty	1.062	0.131	0.740*	0.113	0.967	0.099	0.748	0.112
Participated in contemplative practices in the classroom	0.949	0.130	0.830	0.141	1.074	0.109	1.083	0.170
Peer encounters								
Frequency of insensitive comments from friends/peers	1.116	0.071	1.030	0.096	1.056	0.050	0.943	0.070
Informal engagement with diverse peers	0.974	0.045	0.903	0.052	0.978	0.040	1.002	0.052
Number of friends of a different worldview	1.089	0.055	1.102	0.066	1.074	0.053	1.093	0.062
At least one friend who is spiritual but not religious	0.830*	0.079	0.492***	0.060	1.206*	0.101	0.752*	0.092

Note. RR is the relative risk of experiencing a particular type of spiritual and/or religious change relative to no change.

[a] Man is the reference group.

[b] Heterosexual is the reference group.

[c] White is the reference group.

[d] Mainline Protestant is the reference group.

[e] Public is the reference group.

[f] Arts, humanities, or religion is the reference group.

*$p < .05$ **$p < .01$ ***$p < .001$

144   ALYSSA N. ROCKENBACH

spiritual"; students who attend evangelical Protestant institutions (RR = 1.438, $p < .05$) and who are immersed in a peer environment where a higher percentage of students are altering their religious and spiritual self-perceptions (RR = 1.407, $p < .001$) are more inclined to shift their own religious and spiritual identification in this way. Turning to meaningful collegiate and peer encounters, provocative experiences that call into question students' understanding of their personal worldview appear to precipitate shifts toward "both religious and spiritual" (RR = 1.149, $p < .05$), while having at least one close friend who is "spiritual but not religious" (RR = 0.830, $p < .05$) makes such shifts less likely.

Change to "Religious but Not Spiritual"

Among the personal characteristics included in the full model, gender identity, sexual orientation, race/ethnicity, and (especially) worldview play a part in explaining the trajectories of students who transition to being "religious but not spiritual" in their first year on campus. Students who report a nonbinary gender identity (RR = 0.000, $p < .001$) and those who identify as gay (RR = 0.000, $p < .001$) have a lower likelihood of changing to "religious but not spiritual" relative to men and heterosexual students, respectively. By contrast, Asian / Pacific Islander (RR = 1.500, $p < .05$) students have a higher probability than white students of becoming "religious but not spiritual." Students of five different worldviews are less likely than mainline Protestants to assume a "religious but not spiritual" designation: atheists (RR = 0.050, $p < .001$), evangelical Christians (RR = 0.482, $p < .001$), students of another minority worldview (RR = 0.173, $p < .001$), students of another nonreligious worldview (RR = 0.145, $p < .001$), and students of another worldview (RR = 0.380, $p < .05$). With respect to institutional context, students attending more selective institutions (RR = 0.897, $p < .05$) are less inclined to become "religious but not spiritual," but where more students are changing their religious and spiritual self-identifications (RR = 1.347, $p < .001$), the shift toward "religious but not spiritual" is more probable. Regarding meaningful collegiate, faculty, and peer encounters on campus, feeling pressured to change one's worldview (RR = 1.152, $p < .05$) increases the likelihood that students will become "religious but not spiritual"; however, discussing religious or spiritual topics with faculty (RR = 0.740, $p < .001$) and having one close friend who is "spiritual but

SHIFTS IN SELF-PERCEPTIONS 145

not religious" (RR = 0.492, $p < .001$) reduce inclinations toward identifying as such.

Change to "Spiritual but Not Religious"

The personal characteristics predictive of students shifting to a "spiritual but not religious" identification are, for the most part, related to students' worldview and political leaning, but one significant finding with regard to race surfaced: compared to white students, Asian / Pacific Islanders (RR = 1.392, $p < .01$) are more likely to become "spiritual but not religious" during their first year on campus. Four worldview groups are less likely to move toward identifying as "spiritual but not religious," including atheists (RR = 0.250, $p < .001$), evangelical Christians (RR = 0.714, $p < .01$), students of another minority worldview (RR = 0.451, $p < .01$), and students of another nonreligious worldview (RR = 0.735, $p < .01$). Liberal-leaning students (RR = 1.131, $p < .05$) have a greater tendency to change their identification to "spiritual but not religious" than conservative students. Only one institutional variable, the percentage of students who changed their religious and spiritual identification (RR = 1.309, $p < .001$), is associated with an increased likelihood of changing to "spiritual but not religious." Turning to meaningful collegiate and peer encounters, I found that students who have provocative encounters that challenge their own worldviews (RR = 1.139, $p < .05$) and a "spiritual but not religious" close friend (RR = 1.206, $p < .05$) are more likely to become "spiritual but not religious." At the same time, religious reinforcers (e.g., attending religious services, participating in a student religious organization) (RR = 0.732, $p < .001$) reduce the likelihood of transitioning to a "spiritual but not religious" identification.

Change to "Neither Spiritual nor Religious"

Only two personal characteristics (both worldview identities) predict movement toward a "neither spiritual nor religious" identification: being Jewish (RR = 2.880, $p < .05$) and identifying with another worldview (RR = 1.742, $p < .05$). Institutional context also plays a role in that students who attend campuses where a higher degree of religious and spiritual change is happening among their peers (RR = 1.263, $p < .001$) are more

146 ALYSSA N. ROCKENBACH

inclined to become "neither spiritual nor religious," while students attending evangelical Protestant institutions (RR = 0.460, $p <$ .05) are less inclined to do so. Other experiences linked to becoming "neither spiritual nor religious" include provocative encounters that challenge one's worldview (RR = 1.120, $p <$ .05), which increase the likelihood of change, as well as religious reinforcers (RR = 0.439, $p <$ .001) and having a "spiritual but not religious" close friend (RR = 0.752, $p <$ .05), which reduce the likelihood of change.

Discussion

Although consistency in religious and spiritual self-perceptions across the first year of college is the norm for the majority of participants in the IDEALS study (reiterating findings from other national studies, e.g., Astin et al. 2011; Smith and Snell 2009), a significant minority—close to one in three students—undergoes changes in the ways they perceive themselves spiritually and religiously. That a number of first-term college students would assume or leave behind salient identity dimensions over a relatively short period of time raises important questions about higher education's role in the ways that emerging adults understand themselves and formulate commitments within religious and spiritual domains. The most common type of change was toward "spiritual but not religious" self-perceptions, while movement to a "religious but not spiritual" identity was the least common. More often than not, students who changed ordinarily embraced or rejected only one religious or spiritual label. For instance, students who began their first year on campus as "both religious and spiritual" and saw themselves differently a year later most often dropped either the "religious" or "spiritual" label, but typically did not make the more revolutionary type of change by dropping both at once. "Spirituality" seemed to be the middle path for students who were initially "neither spiritual nor religious" and made a change; these students took on the "spiritual" label if they changed but rarely the "religious" label or both. In short, when change happens among emerging adults in the first year on campus, it tends to be more incremental than radical in nature.

This study revealed a number of personal characteristics linked to changes in religious and spiritual self-perceptions. Students with certain queer identities—most principally, those who identify as gay or with a nonbinary gender identity—are less inclined than heterosexuals and men to adopt a "religious but not spiritual" self-perception. This finding highlights the identity-based conflicts that members of the LGBTQ community regularly endure (Love et al. 2005), as many faith traditions maintain doctrinal stances that reject queer people and fail to offer spaces of welcome and inclusion. For some queer students, these realities may present an obstacle to assuming an identity that is solely religious in quality. This finding also reiterates the importance of analytical practices that compare the experiences of minoritized groups to those that hold power and privilege in society; without such comparisons, continued oppressions may be left invisible and unchecked in our scholarship.

Regarding the role of race and ethnicity in religious and spiritual change, students identifying as Asian or Pacific Islander were more inclined than white students to shift toward a "religious but not spiritual" or a "spiritual but not religious" identification. That Asian and Pacific Islander students would simultaneously exhibit such different types of change suggests a great deal of within-group heterogeneity (affirmed in other studies of college students; e.g., Chan 2018) and presents an important opportunity for future research to address the inadequacies of aggregated racial/ethnic categories. In particular, future studies should investigate the nuanced ways that students of different Asian identities (e.g., East Asians, Southeast Asians, Native Hawaiians and Pacific Islanders, international and domestic Asian students, among others) navigate religious and spiritual change during college. Although gender identity, sexual orientation, and race/ethnicity were included in the models and surfaced as predictors of religious and spiritual change, the role of social class was not considered. Could it be that students of different socioeconomic backgrounds engage their religious and spiritual identities in different ways? To date, this question has received little or no attention in higher-education research, but it might prove to be a valuable direction for future studies.

Like gender identity, sexual orientation, and race/ethnicity, students' worldviews made them more or less likely to shift toward particular religious and spiritual self-identifications. Of all the worldviews included in the analysis, only Jewish students were more inclined than mainline Protestants to gravitate toward the "neither spiritual nor religious" identification. Other research has affirmed the variability in Jewish students' sentiments toward religion and spirituality; there are numerous cultural, religious, and spiritual expressions of Jewish identity—and for some, Jewish and nonreligious expressions go hand in hand (Ammerman 2014; Small 2011).

Intriguing similarities in patterns of change for atheists and evangelical Christians offer insight on how each group understands and relates to religious and spiritual concepts. Both groups are less likely than mainline Protestants to adopt the "religious but not spiritual" and "spiritual but not religious" monikers. It makes sense that atheists would avoid religious self-descriptors, but that they also keep their distance from spiritual labels suggests they see these concepts as intertwined. Evangelicals also seem to perceive the intersections between religion and spirituality and tend not to adopt labels that include one but not the other. Were these two in conversation, the atheist might explain, "Spirituality is linked to religion—I'd rather not identify with either one," while the evangelical might concur with the conceptualization and make a different life application: "Spirituality is linked to religion—I can't identify with one and not the other." Highlighting a fascinating parallel, two groups that are often at opposite ends of the religious continuum appear to share common ground in their perceptions of what religious and spiritual self-identification entails. An addendum to studies that explore meanings of spirituality (e.g., Ammerman 2013, 2014; Steensland et al. 2018) and the growing population of "nones" (e.g., Baker and Smith 2009; Drescher 2016; Lim et al. 2010), this study adds further dimension to our understanding of how emerging adults make meaning of spirituality in relation to religion, and how the expressly nonreligious might be engaging or disengaging from this domain.

The final personal characteristic with a significant relationship to religious and spiritual change—holding a left-leaning political ideology—was more common among those students who made the change to identifying as "spiritual but not religious." Other studies of spiritual identification have produced similar findings (e.g., McClure 2017). Developing a "spiritual but not religious" identity connotes breaking free from traditional religiosity, which may be more common among those with liberal inclinations, especially given that religious and political orientations are closely linked and influence one another (Putnam and Campbell 2010). In other words, emerging adults who hold to a liberal political ideology at the outset of college may simply be primed and open to the influence of a diverse student body; as they learn about other ways of being spiritual or religious, they may be more readily apt to change than students with more conservative leanings. Future research might further probe these connections—do political and religious or spiritual changes occur simultaneously, or does a shift in one domain typically happen before the other? Beyond political leaning, are there other value orientations that predict or result from changes in religious and spiritual identification?

One of two variables that was significantly predictive of all four types of change—the percentage of students on campus who changed their religious and spiritual identification in the first year of college—affirms the considerable impression that peer cultures make on individual students' development (Astin et al. 2011; Mayhew, Rockenbach, Bowman, et al. 2016; Starcke 2017). Where changing one's religious and spiritual self-perceptions is the norm, emerging adults consider new ways of understanding and relating to religion and spirituality. It is noteworthy that peer culture is a more prevalent source of change than other structural characteristics of the institution, such as religious affiliation (which predicted two types of change) and selectivity (which predicted just one type of change). As educators and leaders in postsecondary institutions consider the practical implications of these findings, it would be worth attending to how the characteristics and patterns of change evident in their student body affect the well-being and success of individual students. In campus environments where religious and spiritual change is more pronounced, for example, are emerging adults at risk for higher levels of distress and spiritual struggle?

The second variable that emerged as predictive of all four types of change—having a close friend who is "spiritual but not religious"—underscores the powerful impact of friendships on emerging adults. While the number of friends of different worldviews seems less important in regard to change, having a "spiritual but not religious" friend increases the likelihood of assuming a similar type of religious and spiritual self-identification while reducing the likelihood of the other three. Typically, the effects of friendships on college students have been studied in relation to intergroup attitudes and prejudice reduction (Mayhew, Rockenbach, Bowman, et al. 2016). Rarely have friendship patterns been examined as cultivators of religious and spiritual development. Yet we know that peer cultures—arguably a more distal force in students' lives—make a major impression on students—why wouldn't friendships have even more of an enduring impact? There is plenty of opportunity for future studies to unpack how intra- and inter-worldview friendships shape religious and spiritual development—and not merely attitudes toward others but how emerging adults see themselves.

It comes as no surprise that religious reinforcers (e.g., attending religious services, participating in student religious organizations) lessen the likelihood of switching to a "spiritual but not religious" or a "neither spiritual nor religious" identification. Students exposed to such reinforcing influences probably maintain their religious commitments (Bryant 2011). The effects of provocative encounters are a little less straightforward. When students are challenged to look closely at their own worldview—to question it and recognize the limits of their own understanding—they are more likely to undergo multiple types of change, sometimes toward religious and spiritual self-perceptions and sometimes away from them. The impact of these provocative encounters most likely depends on the identity of the individual student as well as the identity of the person they are engaging. The marginally religious student engaging a devoutly religious peer might be persuaded toward a stronger religious and spiritual identity. Conversely, a student questioning their religious identity might be further provoked toward reducing their religious commitments through conversations with an atheist faculty member. Given that survey data have their share of limitations in terms of uncovering the experiential features and meaning that individuals make of a particular phenomenon, further research employing qualitative designs would offer valuable insight on the nature and impact of these provocative moments. Also, while participating in religious organizations on campus appears to reinforce existing religious and spiritual identities, involvement in other types of student organizations (e.g., fraternities and sororities, athletics, service clubs, multicultural organizations) may have altogether different effects that should be explored in subsequent studies.

Surprisingly, institutional religious affiliation, campus climate, disciplinary context, and faculty interactions played little or no role in students' religious and spiritual changes. Other studies have shown considerable effects of many of these indicators (Astin et al. 2011; Mayhew, Rockenbach, Bowman, et al. 2016; Rockenbach et al. 2017), particularly faculty engagement. It may be that the faculty measures included in this study were not robust enough to illuminate the effects that these encounters can have on students. The last national study devoted explicitly to students' spiritual development (Astin et al. 2011), which was conducted more than ten years ago, incorporated national data on faculty spirituality. Scholars engaged in future efforts should consider doing the same. It may also be the case that faculty impact is contingent on the type of institution in which students are enrolled. Conceivably, faculty may feel more responsibility to engage students religiously and spiritually within campus contexts—like religious colleges—where such conversations are more salient and even expected. By contrast, faculty in public university settings may feel such dialogue is beyond their purview and off limits. Future research that considers the nuanced way in which faculty impact on students' spiritual identities varies by institution type would be instructive.

Conclusion

In the end, this study provides further insight on how first-year college students perceive the relevance of religious and spiritual qualities in their lives—and how their understanding of themselves changes as they encounter life on campus for the first time. This study highlights the environmental and experiential forces that provoke changes in self-perceptions among emerging adults as they are exposed to a new educational and social landscape. Change is more common in contexts where other students are wrestling with religious or spiritual identities and where students routinely enter into meaningful conversations and new friendships that push them toward self-reflection and critical questions about their own worldview.

Note

1. A small percentage of the sample (385 of 7,194 wave 1 and wave 2 respondents) had transferred from another institution; those were not "first-year" students per se, but in their first term on campus.

References

Ammerman, Nancy T. 2013. "Spiritual but Not Religious? Beyond Binary Choices in the Study of Religion." *Journal for the Scientific Study of Religion* 52(2): 258–78.

Ammerman, Nancy T. 2014. *Sacred Stories, Spiritual Tribes: Finding Religion in Everyday Life*. New York: Oxford University Press.

Astin, Alexander W. 2004. "Why Spirituality Deserves a Central Place in Liberal Education." *Liberal Education* 90(2): 34–41.

Astin, Alexander W., Helen S. Astin, and Jennifer A. Lindholm. 2011. *Cultivating the Spirit: How College Can Enhance Students' Inner Lives*. San Francisco: Jossey-Bass.

Astin, Alexander W., Helen S. Astin, Jennifer A. Lindholm, Alyssa N. Bryant, Shannon Calderone, and Katalin Szelényi. 2005. *The Spiritual Life of College Students: A National Study of College Students' Search for Meaning and Purpose*. Los Angeles: Higher Education Research Institute, UCLA.

Baker, Joseph O., and Buster Smith. 2009. "None Too Simple: Examining Issues of Religious Nonbelief and Nonbelonging in the United States." *Journal for the Scientific Study of Religion* 48(4): 719–33.

Bengston, Vern L., Norella M. Putney, and Susan Harris. 2013. *Families and Faith: How Religion Is Passed Down across Generations.* New York: Oxford University Press.

Bowman, Nicholas A., and Jenny L. Small. 2010. "Do College Students Who Identify with a Privileged Religion Experience Greater Spiritual Development? Exploring Individual and Institutional Dynamics." *Research in Higher Education* 51(7): 595–614.

Bryant, Alyssa N. 2007. "Gender Differences in Spiritual Development during the College Years." *Sex Roles* 56: 835–46.

Bryant, Alyssa N. 2011. "The Impact of Campus Context, College Encounters, and Religious/Spiritual Struggle on Ecumenical Worldview Development." *Research in Higher Education* 52: 441–59.

Bryant, Alyssa N., Jeung Yun Choi, and Maiko Yasuno. 2003. "Understanding the Religious and Spiritual Dimensions of Students' Lives in the First Year of College." *Journal of College Student Development* 44(6): 723–45.

Chan, Jason. 2018. "Geographic Constructions of Racial Identity: The Experiences of Asian American College Students in the Midwest." PhD dissertation, University of California, Los Angeles.

Drescher, Elizabeth. 2016. *Choosing Our Religion: The Spiritual Lives of America's Nones.* New York: Oxford University Press.

Hill, Jonathan P. 2009. "Higher Education as Moral Community: Institutional Influences on Religious Participation during College." *Journal for the Scientific Study of Religion* 48(3): 515–34.

Hill, Jonathan P. 2011. "Faith and Understanding: Specifying the Impact of Higher Education on Religious Belief." *Journal for the Scientific Study of Religion* 50(3): 533–51.

Hirsh, Jacob B., Megan D. Walberg, and Jordan B. Peterson. 2013. "Spiritual Liberals and Religious Conservatives." *Social Psychological and Personality Science* 4(1): 14–20.

Lim, Chaeyoon, Carol Ann MacGregor, and Robert D. Putnam. 2010. "Secular and Liminal: Discovering Heterogeneity among Religious Nones." *Journal for the Scientific Study of Religion* 49(4): 596–618.

Love, Patrick, Marianne Bock, Annie Jannarone, and Paul Richardson. 2005. "Identity Interaction: Exploring the Spiritual Experiences of Lesbian and Gay College Students." *Journal of College Student Development* 46(2): 193–209.

Love, Patrick, and Donna Talbot. 1999. "Defining Spiritual Development: A Missing Consideration for Student Affairs." *NASPA Journal* 37(1): 361–75.

Marler, Penny L., and C. Kirk Hadaway. 2002. "'Being Religious' or 'Being Spiritual' in America: A Zero-Sum Proposition?" *Journal for the Scientific Study of Religion* 41(2): 289–300.

Mayhew, Matthew J., and Alyssa N. Bryant Rockenbach. 2013. "Achievement or Arrest? The Influence of the Collegiate Religious and Spiritual Climate on Students' Worldview Commitment." *Research in Higher Education* 54: 63–84.

Mayhew, Matthew J., Alyssa N. Rockenbach, and L. S. Dahl. 2020. "Owning Faith: First-year College-Going and the Development of Students' Self-Authored Worldview Commitments." *Journal of Higher Education,* 91(6), 977–1002.

Mayhew, Matthew J., Alyssa N. Rockenbach, Nicholas A. Bowman, Tricia A. D. Seifert, and Gregory C. Wolniak, with E. T. Pascarella and P. T. Terenzini. 2016. *How College Affects Students.* Vol. 3, *21st Century Evidence That Higher Education Works.* San Francisco: Jossey-Bass.

Mayhew, Matthew J., Alyssa N. Rockenbach, Benjamin P. Correia, Rebecca E. Crandall, Mark A. Lo, and Associates. 2016. *Emerging Interfaith Trends: What College Students Are Saying about Religion in 2016.* Chicago: Interfaith Youth Core.

McClure, Paul K. 2017. "Something besides Monotheism: Sociotheological Boundary Work among the Spiritual, but Not Religious." *Poetics* 62: 53–65.

Putnam, R. D., and D. E. Campbell. 2010. *American grace: How religion divides and unites us.* New York, NY: Simon & Schuster.

Rockenbach, Alyssa N., Matthew J. Mayhew, Benjamin P. Correia-Harker, Laura Dahl, Shauna Morin, and Associates. 2017. *Navigating Pluralism: How Students Approach Religious Difference and Interfaith Engagement in Their First Year of College.* Chicago: Interfaith Youth Core.

Scheitle, Christopher P. 2011. "U.S. College Students' Perception of Religion and Science: Conflict, Collaboration, or Independence? A Research Note." *Journal for the Scientific Study of Religion* 50(1): 175–86.

Small, Jenny L. 2011. *Understanding College Students' Spiritual Identities: Different Faiths, Varied Worldviews.* Cresskill, NJ: Hampton Press.

Small, Jenny L., and Nicholas A. Bowman. 2011. "Religious Commitment, Skepticism, and Struggle among U.S. College Students: The Impact of Majority/Minority Religious Affiliation and Institutional Type." *Journal for the Scientific Study of Religion* 50(1): 154–74.

Smith, Christian, and Patricia Snell. 2009. *Souls in Transition: The Religious and Spiritual Lives of Emerging Adults.* New York: Oxford University Press.

Stamm, Liesa. 2006. "The Dynamics of Spirituality and the Religious Experience." Pp. 37–65 in *Encouraging Authenticity and Spirituality in Higher Education*, edited by A. W. Chickering, J. C. Dalton, and L. Stamm. San Francisco: Jossey-Bass.

Starcke, Matthew A. 2017. "Finding Their Way: The Predictors and Correlates of College Student Religious Conversion." PhD dissertation, North Carolina State University.

Steensland, Brian, Xiaoyun Wang, and Lauren Chism Schmidt. 2018. "Spirituality: What Does It Mean and to Whom?" *Journal for the Scientific Study of Religion* 57(3): 450–72.

Wuthnow, Robert. 2007. *After the Baby Boomers: How Twenty-and Thirty-Somethings Are Shaping the Future of American Religion.* Princeton, NJ: Princeton University Press.

7

Spirituality among African Americans

Interracial and Intraracial Differences across Followers of Various Religious Traditions

Jason E. Shelton

Spirituality is a fundamental feature of African American life. For centuries, the black church has defined spirituality within the context of Christianity and aimed to empower its members with otherworldly tools that reify their humanity and metaphysically protect them from consequences of slavery and segregation. This helps to explain why religion and spirituality are coterminous for most African Americans: spirituality is predominately viewed as a dimension of organized religion that manifests in people's personal lives (Frazier 1964; Lincoln and Mamiya 1990). From praying to singing, reading the Bible to a seemingly endless list of faith-based practices or convictions, "spirituality" is widely viewed as a method for establishing and developing a personal relationship with God (Voisin et al. 2016). It is individualistic with respect to the multitude of ways in which different people engage the sacred, yet corporate in that its parameters are delimited by religious institutions that sanction appropriate ways for expressing one's spirituality.

Consequently, there is strong reason to presume that African Americans widely differ in their beliefs about spirituality. One reason for this diversity is attributable to the range of denominational affiliations in which blacks adhere. To be sure, African Americans observe traditional and nontraditional liberal and conservative Protestant denominations with roots inside and outside of the black church (Shelton and Cobb 2017). Moreover, studies have shown that denominational differences drive strong and consistent variation among African Americans with respect to their beliefs about the Bible and how often they pray and attend worship services (Barnes 2004; Chatters et al. 1999; Edwards 2009; Shelton and Cobb 2017; Taylor 1993), for example. Such differences establish a basis for conceptualizing the variation in spirituality among African American Christians. However, another reason to presume

Jason E. Shelton, *Spirituality among African Americans* In: *Situating Spirituality.* Edited by: Brian Steensland, Jaime Kucinskas, and Anna Sun, Oxford University Press. © Oxford University Press 2022.
DOI: 10.1093/oso/9780197565001.003.0008

that blacks differ is due to growing faith-based diversity beyond organized religion. Indeed, findings from a recent Pew Research Center (2017) poll showed that 26 percent of African Americans now view themselves as "spiritual but not religious," up from 19 percent just five years earlier. Certainly, this major trend in American religion transcends racial and ethnic group memberships (Chaves 2011; Fischer and Hout 2006). However, the growing disconnection of spirituality from Christianity is especially important considering the preeminent role that the black church has played in establishing political, social, and cultural unity among African Americans. Increasing numbers of African Americans who view themselves as "spiritual but not religious" bolster arguments concerning growing ideological commitments to individualism within black America (Cose 2011; Dawson 2001; Hunt 2007; Lacy 2007; Shelton and Greene 2012).

This chapter examines the importance of spirituality among African Americans. More specifically, it assesses sociodemographic correlates of the extent to which study participants in a large, nationally representative survey view themselves as a "spiritual person." It makes three contributions to the literature on changing dynamics of spirituality in contemporary America. First, this chapter examines racial differences in spirituality among members of the same denominational family. This is important because existing studies have yet to determine if black Baptists, Methodists, or Catholics, for example, differ from white followers of these traditions in whether spirituality is a key feature of their personal identity. Second, this chapter assesses differences in beliefs about the centrality of spirituality among African Americans across various religious affiliations. While black Methodists may be more likely to view themselves as a spiritual person than white Methodists, they may be less likely do so than black Pentecostals. If so, the simultaneous impact of strong and consistent *interracial* variation as well as *intraracial* diversity further attests to distinctive features of the African American Protestant religious tradition.

Finally, this chapter examines the links between race and beliefs about spirituality among study participants who do not associate with an established religious faith. For instance, it aims to determine whether black nonaffiliates are more likely to view themselves as a spiritual person than white nonaffiliates. It also assesses racial differences among respondents who view themselves as "spiritual but not religious." This latter contribution is particularly notable considering blacks' long-standing commitment to organized religion. In sum, this chapter features the most comprehensive

156   JASON E. SHELTON

survey-based analysis to date of diversity in blacks' beliefs about the links between spirituality and one's self-concept. It offers new insights by assessing racial differences *within* various denominational families, and specifically among African Americans *across* various religious affiliations.

Existing Research on Spirituality among African Americans

Generally speaking, "religion" refers to group-based forms of worship within organized institutions and communities that emphasize particular beliefs, rituals, and traditions. It helps to make sense of the world, as well as reinforce conventional beliefs about meaning and commonality (Durkheim [1912] 1998; Emerson et al. 2011). Conversely, in today's world, "spirituality" refers to individual pursuits of sacred deities, knowledge, feelings, and/or relationships that do not necessarily require affiliation with an established faith or group of believers. That blacks increasingly separate these metaphysical modes of engaging a larger cosmic order reflects transformations taking place in the post-civil rights era. For most of American history, overt racial discrimination limited blacks' range of religious and spiritual options.

The black church's broad delineation of the combined effects of religion and spirituality affirmed blacks' humanity, nurtured cultural cohesion, developed future leaders, reinforced familial and communal bonds, and established a basis for confronting the politics and economics of their second-class citizenship. This helps to explain why the legendary theologian Dr. James H. Cone of Union Theological Seminary argued that "black people must use their spirituality to cope with all the racial contradictions in our society. . . . When you don't have control of the world, but whites do, your faith has to be flexible because it has to respond to so many different kinds of contradictions."[1] His statement implicitly attests to the coterminous relationship between religion and spirituality. However, a more explicit expression of this connection appears in Shelton and Emerson's (2012, 143) book *Blacks and Whites in Christian America: How Racial Discrimination Shapes Religious Convictions*. The following statement was communicated by Deacon Harris, the director of Christian counseling at a predominately African American megachurch in New York City: "African American spirituality tends to be very survival focused. God helps us through the problems of the vicissitudes of life. One of the themes in our [African American] theology is 'Hang in

SPIRITUALITY AMONG AFRICAN AMERICANS 157

there, God's going to bring you through. You're going to make it, don't give up. Don't throw in the towel. Believe in God, help is on the way. Your miracle is coming.'"

Both of the preceding statements—in combination with the faith-based institutional affiliations of the men who expressed them—suggest that organized religion establishes parameters for personal spirituality. Findings from various studies confirm this belief among everyday African American Christians (Berkel et al. 2011; Cohen et al. 2008; Taylor et al. 2004). For instance, an interviewee in Mattis's (2000, 115) study of black women's views of the links between religion and spirituality stated: "For me one of the ways that I get in touch with spirituality sometimes is *through practices of a religious organization* [emphasis added], or the choir that I sing in. It'll allow the spirit to fill me, and so I feel my spirituality on a deeper level. *I don't confuse spirituality with religiosity* [emphasis added], though religious practices are important for me." Similarly, a participant in Voisin et al.'s (2016, 18) study of African American college students declared: "Attending church is important to me, but I also find worship—singing, listening to gospel music, and prayer—to be a central aspect of my spiritual practice." These comments bolster a common finding across various studies: most African Americans believe that forms of corporal faith assist with developing a personal relationship with a higher external power and/or supreme being (Cohen et al. 2008; Mattis 2000; Voisin et al. 2016).

Individualized Conceptualizations of Spirituality

However, there is strong evidence of growing numbers of African Americans who completely separate spirituality from religion. For instance, one of Mattis's (2000, 117) study participants asserted: *"I'm not really religious. But, I have a weird spirituality* [emphasis added]. I believe in more of like destiny and kind of like a force kind of thing. But, I do believe that there's something out there that's greater than us, because I do believe that when things happen they are meant to be." Likewise, one of Voisin et al.'s (2016, 20) interviewees proclaimed: *"Listen, it [spirituality] has nothing to do with God, religion, or going to church* [emphasis added], but about doing the right thing when life presents you with private decisions." Both of these statements are consistent with a recent turn in American religion that people increasingly view spirituality as autonomous from organized faith (Ammerman 2013; Chaves

2011; Steensland et al. 2018). Furthermore, some Americans sharply disagree with the traditional assumption that personal spirituality is a dimension of collective faith. For example, a participant in Voisin et al.'s (2016:19) study contends that "some black people think they have an inside track with God, but it [spirituality] for me is really about getting up and doing things for me . . . trying to improve me and make life happen for me and *not waiting for God to rescue me . . . you have to rescue and save your own self* [emphasis added]." This latter sentiment is important because it challenges the notion of *divine rescue*, which asserts that God is attentive to the trials and tribulations facing black people in America (e.g., Deacon Harris's previous statement). It, along with *liberation theology* and other *theologies of suffering and evil* are distinct doctrinal features of the African American Protestant religious tradition.

The foregoing statements regarding alternative spiritualities within black America comprise the tip of the proverbial iceberg. To reiterate: quantitative (Berkel et al. 2011; Taylor et al. 2004), qualitative (Cohen et al. 2008), and theoretical studies (Coleman 1997) of blacks' contemporary beliefs reveal rich and diverse sets of meaningful findings. Some of these results attest to conflicts between spirituality and Christianity, while others reveal unique forms of individual spirituality that coexist with institutional faith. In addition to those mentioned earlier, some features of the new spirituality in black America focus on understanding one's inner self, a profound sense of personal meaning and purpose in life, responsibility to a broader community, personal morality, and resurgent attention to traditional African spiritualities (Mattis 2000; Steensland et al. 2018). This wide range of options permits people to "mix and match" various alternative spiritualities with organized faith (or not). For example, the following general sentiment is consistent with Christianity: "Spirituality means really being in touch with your inner self. Knowing what your fears are, what those may come from, what your beliefs, values, and those types of things are" (Mattis 2000, 116). The ensuing statement is also consistent with Christianity, although the interviewee clearly distinguishes individual spirituality from collective faith: "[Spirituality] for me has nothing to do with God. Hmm, *I do believe in God, that is religion. Spirituality is about what I can do for myself* [emphasis added]: the ability to get up and make things happen, set goals and do them, and be the kind of black man that society says we are not—educated, employed, raise a family, and not be locked up or high on drugs" (Voisin et al., 19).

SPIRITUALITY AMONG AFRICAN AMERICANS   159

However, other conceptualizations of the links between spirituality and religion are inconsistent with traditional Christian teachings. *Divination* is the pursuit of non-divinely ordained information or insights gained through astrology, fortune telling, magic, tarot card readings, sorcery, witchcraft, psychics, or other sources of esoteric understanding. These methods for engaging the supernatural—and the individuals and groups associated with them—are viewed as unacceptable because they seemingly undermine key features of Christ's teachings (Shelton and Emerson 2012). Consequently, most clergy would reject the following view of spirituality: "Spirituality has to do with energy. It is our spirit (mind), the part of us that is not biological. Psychological mechanisms, archetypes, after-death experiences, ESP, telekinesis (and more) all indicate that we have some sort of mind/energy that isn't always—or usually—tapped, but which still exists and will continue to exist after our bodies die" (Mattis 2000, 110). The following statement (Mattis 2000, 117) would probably also be viewed as divination since the respondent's perspective on "how the universe is run" lies beyond the boundaries of conventional Christianity: "Lately [spirituality] means to me—*I sort of developed this understanding that I'm in harmony with nature, and the universe* [emphasis added]. And, that sort of answers any questions that I have when I'm confused about a situation, and not knowing what to do. I think about what's natural in terms of how the universe is run."

Finally, it must be stated that blacks' expanding beliefs about spirituality aid individuals in pursing non-Christian religions. In today's world, 3 percent of African Americans now follow Islam, Judaism, Hinduism, or Buddhism, for example. While this is small as compared to the previously mentioned growth of religious nonaffiliates, the percentage of blacks adhering to such faiths has doubled since the turn of the twenty-first century. Consequently, one of Voisin et al.'s (2016, 20) respondents' recognition of "Karma" further attests to the spread of faith-based diversity in black America: "Spirituality is knowing that you do right because Karma is real—you get back what you put out into this world. . . . I try and treat and do right by people because it would eventually come back to me, *and that has nothing to do with God* [emphasis added], it is a universal truth . . . a fact of life . . . what goes around comes around." Lastly, it's worth noting that the changing dynamics of religion and spirituality have also impacted African American clergy. Shelton and Emerson's (2012) book *Blacks and Whites in Christian America* features an interview with Reverend Jenkins, an assistant pastor at a small Pentecostal congregation. Before "returning to Christ," Reverend Jenkins spent his

160   JASON E. SHELTON

teenage and young adult years exploring non-Christian faiths. The following comment further attests to the explosion of spiritual and religious diversity in black America in the post-civil rights era:

> As a young man who came of age in the 1960s and 1970s, I used to look around at various religious sects, you know, whether it be the spiritual churches, the little storefronts or whatever. . . . I went to Catholic churches, I went to Jewish temples. I was searching on this quest trying to find out which one of these is supposed to work, which one gets us there—to a profound level of understanding—the fastest or whatever the case might be, and I determined that people join certain churches or religious sects to help control what they cannot control themselves.[2]

Research Methods

The data examined in this study are from the 1998 and 2006–2016 General Social Surveys (GSS).[3] The GSS is a nationally representative data source featuring a multistage full probability sampling design that accounts for all US households. See Smith et al. (2016) for a complete discussion of the survey's sampling methodology. The average response rate across the GSS years examined here is 70 percent, and the data are weighted to account for methodological advancements in sampling beginning in 2004. These improvements enhance generalizability and produce more reliable statistical estimates. The aforementioned years of the survey were purposely selected because they include an item that assesses respondents' beliefs about whether they individually view themselves as a "spiritual person."

As previously mentioned, a goal of this study is to examine sociodemographic correlates of blacks' beliefs about spirituality. However, the data analyzed here are limited to American blacks—respondents who say that they themselves, as well as both of their parents and all four of their grandparents, were born in the United States.[4] These study participants are most likely to have had ancestors that experienced the hardships of slavery and segregation. This is important because historically, Backs' beliefs about religion and spirituality were established during these ignominious periods in American history (Cone 1969; Lincoln and Mamiya 1990; Wilmore 1973). Consequently, GSS data for American whites are included to help contextualize results for American blacks. Findings for Asians, Latinos, and members

SPIRITUALITY AMONG AFRICAN AMERICANS 161

of other racial and ethnic groups are omitted.[5] These groups' diverse histories and experiences with religion and spirituality in the United States and abroad are beyond the scope of the present study.

Dependent Variables

Table 7.1 presents detailed information for the dependent variables analyzed in this study, including survey questions, answer possibilities, codes, and percentage distributions by race. The primary outcome examined in this study is Q1. It asks whether GSS respondents view themselves as a "spiritual person." It is coded from 0 to 3 ("not spiritual at all" to "very spiritual"). As a result, odds ratios over 1 signal that spirituality is a central feature of respondents' self-concept, while odds ratios less than 1 signal that spirituality is less central to their personal identity.

Table 7.1 Survey questions, answer possibilities, codes, and percentage distributions by race for (1) whether the respondent views her- or himself as a spiritual person, and (2) whether the respondent views her- or himself as a religious person

	Blacks	Whites	T-value
Q1: "To what extent do you consider yourself a spiritual person? Are you . . ."			
Not spiritual at all (0)	6.5	10.8	−12.04***
Slightly spiritual (1)	15.1	23.7	
Moderately spiritual (2)	38.2	38.7	
Very spiritual (3)	40.2	26.8	
Total %	100	100	
N	1,714	6,995	
Q2: "To what extent do you consider yourself a religious person? Are you . . ."			
Not religious at all (0)	11.5	19.1	−13.05***
Slightly religious (1)	15.8	23.5	
Moderately religious (2)	44.7	39.7	
Very religious (3)	28.0	17.7	
Total %	100	100	
N	1,718	7,013	

Note: T-values assess differences between blacks and whites on the variable overall.
*** $p < .001$ (2-tailed tests)

162   JASON E. SHELTON

A second dependent variable is analyzed only among respondents who view themselves as "spiritual but not religious." These study participants are operationalized as follows: they selected option 2 or 3 to the question about whether they view themselves as a spiritual person, and option 0 for whether they view themselves as a religious person. Consequently, data for Q2 are included for context only. They are not analyzed as an outcome. The dependent variable analyzed among respondents who view themselves as spiritual but not religious is dichotomous since it is limited to study participants who view themselves as either "moderately spiritual" or "very spiritual." Odds ratios over 1 signal that respondents view themselves as "very spiritual," while odds ratios less than 1 signal that respondents view themselves as "moderately spiritual."

Independent Variable

Table 7.2 presents detailed information for all independent variables, including codes and percent distributions by race. The dependent variables are regressed on a set of sociodemographic indicators that are common in the literature on American religion (i.e., income, education, age, sex, region of residence, and the year respondents participated in the survey). REALINC converts the original GSS income categories into dollar amounts and then adjusts these values to account for inflation across all survey years by using 1986 as the base year for comparison.[6] Including this variable permits testing income differences across GSS modules. Lastly, it is important to control for frequency of worship service attendance because studies have shown that this variable strongly influences faith-based practices and convictions (Edwards 2009; Shelton and Cobb 2017; Shelton and Emerson 2012).

One final point must be addressed. Respondents' religious affiliations are operationalized by two separate and distinct coding schemes. Some tests for racial differences within particular denominational families are conducted with Lehman and Sherkat's (2018) measure for "religious identification," which distinguishes between liberal and moderate traditions within American Protestantism. However, other tests are administered with an adapted version of Shelton and Cobb's (2018) "Black Reltrad" syntax, which permits comparisons between various families of conservative Protestants, non-Christian faiths, and respondents with no religious preference. The adapted version utilized for

SPIRITUALITY AMONG AFRICAN AMERICANS 163

Table 7.2 Codes and percentage distributions by race for all independent variables

Independent variable	Blacks	Whites	T-value
Sociodemographics			
Income[a]			
Lowest Category (0)	35.1	16.6	38.54***
Second Lowest Category (1)	28.1	23.3	
Middle Category (2)	6.7	8.3	
Second Highest Category (3)	17.7	26.4	
Highest Category (4)	12.4	25.4	
Education[a]			
Less than High School (0)	31.2	20.5	25.69***
High School Degree (1)	53.1	54.4	
Some/Junior College (2)	5.7	5.0	
Bachelor Degree (3)	6.8	14.1	
Graduate/Advanced Degree (4)	3.2	6.0	
Age[a]	(43.15)	(44.14)	4.56***
Sex (women = 1, men = 0)	58.9	53.4	−8.45***
Region (South = 1, non-South = 0)	43.8	41.7	−3.28***
Year R Participated in the GSS[a]	(1993.57)	(1992.13)	−8.49***
Church Attendance[a]			
Never (0)	9.4	18.1	−24.64***
Less Than Once a Year (1)	5.2	8.5	
Once a Year (2)	9.2	14.0	
Several Times a Year (3)	12.4	12.3	
Once a Month (4)	8.4	6.6	
2 to 3 Times a Month (5)	16.6	7.7	
Nearly Every Week (6)	7.2	5.4	
Every Week (7)	20.3	19.3	
More Than Once a Week (8)	11.3	8.1	

Note: Means appear in parentheses.

[a] Analyzed as a continuous variable in the multivariate models.

** $p < .01$, *** $p < .001$ (2-tailed tests)

Table 7.3 includes Holiness, Pentecostal, and nondenominational affiliations specified by white GSS respondents. However, Table 7.5 features Black Reltrad's original typology. It is worth noting that nontraditional liberal and conservative Protestants are included as followers of "other faiths" (Steensland et al. 2000).

Table 7.3 Ordered logistic regressions assessing racial differences among followers of various evangelical Protestant traditions in whether they view themselves as a spiritual person

Independent variable	Baptists		Holiness		Pentecostals		Other evangelicals		Nondenominational	
	OR	SE	OR	SE	OR	SE	OR	SE	OR	SE
Blacks	1.22*	0.10	1.97†	0.40	1.19	0.32	1.22	0.35	1.73**	0.21
Income	1.11**	0.03	1.02	0.11	1.16	0.11	0.99	0.08	0.97	0.05
Education	1.20***	0.05	0.98	0.16	1.04	0.19	1.12	0.10	1.11	0.07
Age	1.02***	0.00	1.01	0.01	1.02	0.01	1.01	0.01	1.01*	0.00
Women	1.46***	0.09	1.26	0.30	1.21	0.32	1.28	0.21	1.23	0.14
South	1.17†	0.09	1.13	0.29	0.80	0.30	1.48†	0.21	1.15	0.14
Year	1.02**	0.01	1.05†	0.03	0.99	0.03	1.05**	0.02	0.99	0.02
Attendance	1.30***	0.02	1.52***	0.07	1.34***	0.06	1.57***	0.05	1.42***	0.03
Pseudo R^2	0.20		0.32		0.22		0.30		0.26	
X^2	374.36***		64.98***		44.39***		114.05***		216.77***	
N	1,860		194		215		370		806	

† $p < .10$, * $p < .05$, ** $p < .01$, *** $p < .001$ (2-tailed tests)

Findings

Descriptive statistics presented in Table 7.1 show that black and white respondents sharply differ in the extent to which they view themselves as a "spiritual person." More specifically, 40 percent of African Americans in the sample describe themselves as "very spiritual," while only 27 percent of whites feel this way. Moreover, only 7 percent of African Americans describe themselves as "not spiritual at all," while 11 percent of whites do so. These preliminary findings suggest that blacks and whites in the broader American population report contrasting beliefs about the role that spirituality plays with respect to their self-concept.

Results displayed in Table 7.2 attest to long-standing and widely known racial disparities in the United States. For instance, black GSS respondents earn less income and are less educated than whites. More specifically, 35 percent of African American study participants are situated in the lowest income category, while only 17 percent of whites are positioned so. Moreover, the percentage of whites in the highest income category is double that for African Americans. Other significant differences include that blacks in the sample are younger, more often female, and more likely to reside in the South. As for religion, American blacks and whites differ in the frequency of worship service attendance. For example, only 9 percent of blacks "never" attend services, while 18 percent of whites do not. In fact, a higher percentage of blacks attend church on a monthly and weekly basis than whites. Taken together, these findings help to establish a baseline for understanding more rigorous inferential results for racial differences in the extent to which GSS study participants view themselves as a spiritual person.

Table 7.3 presents findings for ordered logistic regressions assessing racial differences among followers of various evangelical Protestant traditions. These models aim to determine whether black and white members of the same denominational family report contrasting beliefs about whether they view themselves as a spiritual person. Separate tests were conducted by running the previously described statistical model among religious classifications specified by Lehman and Sherkat (2018) and Shelton and Cobb (2017). After adjusting for sociodemographic factors, black Baptists (OR = 1.22, $p <$. 05) are more likely than white Baptists to link spirituality with their personal identity. Black nondenominational Protestants (OR = 1.73, $p < .01$) also score significantly higher on the spirituality measure than white nondenominational Protestants. However, black members of the Holiness (OR = 1.97,

166   JASON E. SHELTON

$p < .10$) family are only slightly more likely to view themselves as a spiritual person than white members of the Holiness family. This finding could be attributable to the small sample size for this tradition. Regardless, results presented in this table reveal meaningful racial differences among some of Christianity's most ardent and charismatic followers.

Table 7.4 displays results for ordered logistic regressions assessing racial differences across a range of faiths, including mainline Christian traditions as well as respondents with no religious affiliation. Black Methodists (OR = 2.20, $p < .001$) are more than twice as likely as white Methodists to view themselves as a spiritual person, controlling for all other variables. However, this wide racial difference is comparatively small with respect to Catholics: blacks (OR = 2.97, $p < .001$) are nearly three times as likely as whites to link spirituality with their self-concept. In considering these results alongside previously discussed findings in Table 7.3, it appears that racial differences in whether respondents view themselves as a spiritual person are much wider in scope among mainline than among evangelical believers. Moreover, Baptists, Holiness, and Methodists help to comprise the denominational nucleus of the historic black church. Thus, save for Pentecostals, the most historically relevant families within the African American Protestant religious tradition are more likely than whites to view themselves as a spiritual person. Such findings expand our knowledge of the scope of racial differences in religious sensibilities among black and white Protestants.

The final result presented in Table 7.4 assesses beliefs about spirituality among black and white respondents with no religious preference. Black nonaffiliates (OR = 1.65, $p < .001$) score significantly higher on the spirituality measure than white nonaffiliates. This finding suggests that racial differences in faith-based sensibilities extend beyond the boundaries of established religious traditions. To be sure, findings not published show that 56 percent of black nonaffiliates view themselves as at least "moderately spiritual," while 66 percent of white nonaffiliates view themselves as no more than "slightly spiritual." (Indeed, 31 percent say they are "not spiritual at all.") These findings suggest that while a growing number of African Americans are departing organized religion, they are still more likely than whites to declare that spirituality is a key feature of their personal identity.

Despite these important findings, racial differences only tell half of the story of blacks' beliefs about spirituality. To repeat: findings from a growing number of studies document strong and consistent faith-based differences *among* African Americans (Brown 2009; Calhoun-Brown 1998; Ellison 1991;

Table 7.4 Ordered logistic regressions assessing racial differences among various mainline Protestant and Catholic traditions, as well as other faiths and nonaffiliates in whether they view themselves as a spiritual person

Independent variable	Methodists		Other mainliners		Catholics		Other faiths		No religious preference	
	OR	SE	OR	SE	OR	SE	OR	SE	OR	SE
Blacks	2.20***	0.24	1.54	0.40	2.97***	0.23	0.92	0.31	1.65***	0.14
Income	1.01	0.06	0.90†	0.06	0.92†	0.04	0.99	0.08	0.91*	0.03
Education	1.31***	0.08	1.22**	0.07	1.19***	0.05	1.27*	0.11	1.13**	0.05
Age	1.01*	0.01	1.01	0.01	1.01***	0.00	1.01*	0.01	1.01**	0.00
Women	2.18***	0.16	2.32***	0.16	1.86***	0.12	1.17	0.24	1.72***	0.10
South	1.07	0.16	0.93	0.15	1.27*	0.11	0.76	0.23	1.14	0.10
Year	1.02	0.02	1.02	0.02	0.98	0.01	1.04†	0.03	1.00	0.01
Attendance	1.27***	0.03	1.23***	0.03	1.26***	0.02	1.31***	0.04	1.30***	0.04
Pseudo R^2	0.22		0.16		0.19		0.19		0.09	
X^2	133.85***		97.06***		215.57***		54.31***		131.66***	
N	601		614		1,105		292		1,437	

† $p < .10$, * $p < .05$, ** $p < .01$, *** $p < .001$ (2-tailed tests)

168   JASON E. SHELTON

Shelton and Cobb 2017; Sherkat and Ellison 1991). Thus, a more complete understanding of the links between spirituality and one's self-concept cannot be achieved until blacks are analyzed separately from whites. Toward this end, Table 7.5 displays results from an ordered logistic regression assessing the extent to which African American followers of various religious traditions differ in whether they view themselves as a spiritual person. Nonaffiliates serve as the reference category for this model. Holding all other variables constant, black Holiness / Pentecostals[7] (OR = 2.77, $p < .001$) and nondenominational Protestants (OR = 2.94, $p < .001$) are nearly three times as likely

Table 7.5 Ordered logistic regressions assessing differences among African Americans across various religious traditions in whether they view themselves as a spiritual person

Independent variable	R views self as spiritual person	
	OR	SE
Holiness/Pentecostal	2.77***[512789]	0.25
White Evangelical	1.28[36]	0.40
Non-Denominational	2.94***[5124789]	0.23
Baptist	1.35†[369]	0.16
Methodist	1.49[36]	0.26
White Mainline	1.42[6]	0.42
Catholic	1.57†[369]	0.25
Other Faiths	1.67†[869]	0.28
Income	1.06	0.04
Education	1.12*	0.06
Age	1.02†	0.00
Women	1.21†	0.10
Southerners	1.11	0.10
Year	1.02†	0.01
Church Attendance	1.23***	0.02
Pseudo R^2	0.21	
X^2	306.80***	
N	1,482	

Note: No Religious Preference/Unaffiliated reference group (2-tailed tests). Results from separate models with each Black Reltrad classification as the respective reference group are significant at at least * $p <.10$: [1] Baptists, [2] Methodists, [3] Holiness/Pentecostals, [4] White Mainlines, [5] White Evangelicals, [6] Nondenominationals, [7] Catholics, [8] Others, [9] Unaffiliated.

† $p < .10$, * $p < .05$, ** $p < .01$, *** $p < .001$

SPIRITUALITY AMONG AFRICAN AMERICANS   169

as black nonaffiliates to view themselves as a spiritual person. Moreover, Holiness / Pentecostals and nondenominational Protestants sharply differ from observers of nearly all other traditions in the strong role spirituality plays in shaping their personal identity. Otherwise, Baptists (OR = 1.35, $p < .10$) and Catholics (OR = 1.57, $p < .10$) are the only other established traditions that at least marginally vary from black nonaffiliates. Neither black Methodists, members of historically white mainline, nor historically white evangelical Protestant denominations differ from black nonaffiliates (or one another, for that matter). Such findings bolster the evidence for high levels of spirituality among African Americans with no religious affiliation. For instance, a similar model including data for American whites only shows that adherents of all Protestant and Catholic traditions are significantly more likely than nonaffiliates to view themselves as a spiritual person.[8]

These findings, as well as the previously discussed result for racial differences among black and white nonaffiliates, raises the possibility for racial differences among the growing number of Americans who view themselves as "spiritual but not religious." In particular, (a) the high level of spirituality among black nonaffiliates and (b) consistent variation among whites across various religious traditions suggest that (c) black observers of this new trend in American religion are especially spiritual as compared to their white counterparts. Before we proceed, it must be stated that the growth of religious nonaffiliates and the movement of Americans who view themselves as "spiritual but not religious" are similar but distinct currents. As shown here, religious nonaffiliates may or not view themselves as "spiritual." However, individuals who view themselves as "spiritual but not religious" indeed proclaim a personal sense of spirituality. Additionally, it is worth noting that a similar percentage of black and white GSS respondents are operationalized as spiritual but not religious. Although it is not immediately apparent in Table 7.1, 88 (or 5.2 percent) of the 1,707 black respondents who answered both questions about spirituality and religion are captured as "spiritual but not religious." For whites, 426 (or 6.1 percent) of the 6,970 are analyzed as such.

Do black respondents who view themselves as spiritual but not religious score significantly higher on the spirituality measure than whites who view themselves as spiritual but not religious? Table 7.6 presents a logistic regression assessing racial differences among study participants operationalized as such. To reiterate, odds ratios over 1 signal that respondents view themselves as "very spiritual," while odds ratios less than 1 signal that respondents view

170   JASON E. SHELTON

Table 7.6 Logistic regression assessing racial differences in whether respondents who view themselves as spiritual but not religious are "moderately" or "very" spiritual

Independent variable	r views self as moderately or very spiritual person	
	OR	SE
Blacks	3.12***	0.29
Income	0.97	0.07
Education	0.91	0.09
Age	1.01	0.01
Women	2.16***	0.20
Southerners	1.14	0.20
Year	0.98	0.02
Church Attendance	1.22***	0.04
R^2	0.18	
X^2	69.77***	
N	517	

† p < .10, * p < .05, ** p < .01, *** p<.001 (2-tailed tests)

themselves as "moderately spiritual." Results show that blacks (OR = 3.12, $p <$ .001) are more than three times as likely as whites to view themselves as "very spiritual." This wide margin is partly attributable to fact that nonpublished findings show that 71 percent of black respondents who are operationalized as spiritual but not religious view themselves as "very spiritual," while only 40 percent of white respondents who are operationalized as spiritual but not religious do so. Furthermore, separate subgroup analyses show that changes over the years regarding the growth of respondents who view themselves as spiritual but not religious are much stronger in magnitude for blacks rather than whites. In combination, these findings suggest that race plays a critical role with respect to the movement of Americans who view themselves as spiritual but not religious.

Several supplemental statistical findings must be addressed. First, across the models under analysis, frequency of worship service attendance most strongly and consistently influences respondents' beliefs about whether they view themselves as a spiritual person. In fact, this variable is highly statistically significant and strong in magnitude across each of the twelve models shown here. Moreover, this variable moves in the same direction across all models regardless of the religious classification under analysis: study participants who attend worship services more often report stronger beliefs about the role that spirituality plays with respect to their personal identity. Significantly, this finding holds constant for religious nonaffiliates and members of the spiritual-but-not-religious movement.

Second, there is far more statistical variation among mainline Protestants and Catholics than among evangelicals in whether respondents view themselves as a spiritual person. For mainliners, higher levels of income and education operate differently in shaping beliefs about the links between spirituality and one's self-concept. As income increases, respondents score significantly lower on the spirituality measure, while respondents with higher levels of educational attainment score significantly higher. Moreover, in general, women are twice as likely as men to view themselves as a spiritual person. Interestingly, effects for these variables operate similarly among religious nonaffiliates. As for evangelicals, there is far more statistical variation among Baptists than other conservative Protestant traditions. Members of this denominational family vary across each of the independent variables examined in this study. Beyond this, however, the only consistent variation concerns at least slight changes in beliefs held by members of some traditions about spirituality over the years.

Conclusion

Results of this study indicate that spirituality is a key feature of many African Americans' personal identity. This is true for black adherents of established faiths, as well as those who have departed from organized religion. Regarding Christianity, multivariate tests reveal that black Baptists, Holiness, and nondenominational Protestants are more likely than white followers of these flocks to view themselves as a "spiritual person." Similarly, black Methodists and Catholics are more likely than white members of these denominational families to link spirituality with their self-concept. Taken together, these findings reveal strong racial differences among mainline and evangelical believers in the extent to which blacks and whites associate spirituality with their personal identity.

There are also strong faith-based differences in beliefs about spirituality among African Americans. Holiness / Pentecostals and nondenominational Protestants are far more likely than observers of nearly all other religious traditions to view themselves as a spiritual person. Interestingly, however, followers of mainline denominations do not differ from nonaffiliates. This important finding is attributable to the high level of spirituality among African Americans with no religious preference. In fact, blacks who view themselves as "spiritual but not religious" are far more likely to view themselves as "very spiritual" than whites who have joined the movement. This finding attests to the critical role that spirituality plays as a building block of African American life. In short, spirituality is important to blacks both inside and outside of organized religion.

Findings presented here enhance our awareness of racial differences in religious sensibilities. Researchers have established that African American Protestants pray, attend worship services, and engage in other faith-based practices and convictions more often than white Protestants (Barnes 2004; Chatters et al. 1999; Edwards 2009; Shelton and Cobb 2017; Taylor 1993). We can now add beliefs about the role that spirituality plays in shaping one's personal identity to this growing list. Moreover, this study pinpoints racial differences in the salience of spirituality within particular denominational families. This information can potentially enhance dialogues on racial reconciliation that are taking place within religious traditions. Lastly, results of this study further our knowledge on the growing number of African Americans who no longer associate with an established religious faith. Conventional wisdom presumes that blacks and whites who view themselves as spiritual but not religious would not meaningfully differ in the role that spirituality plays in shaping their personal self-concept. Yet they indeed do. This, as well as other findings presented here, indicate that race remains a critical factor for determining ways in which every day Americans engage the sacred.

Future research in spirituality among African Americans must further explore faith-based practices and convictions among religious nonaffiliates. A qualitative research method is better equipped to address this important issue than a quantitative method. For instance, are nonaffiliates departing the black church for political reasons related to controversial issues such as homosexuality and abortion? To what extent are they dissatisfied with traditional beliefs and/or motivated by perceived hypocrisy among clergy? Moreover, it is widely known that blacks lean on their faith as a supernatural call for help to protect against the consequences of contemporary racial discrimination and inequality (Cone 1969; Lincoln and Mamiya 1990; Wilmore 1973). Clearly, black nonaffiliates place similar calls. But what deity, entity, or force is the subject of these calls? Finally, there is reason to believe that some young, black nonaffiliates may have begun to re-embrace traditional African modes of spirituality (Malbroux 2017; Voisin et al. 2016). But how extensive is this trend? Have both older and younger black nonaffiliates begun to explore their African spiritual roots? These questions, as well as many others, are especially important considering that GSS data show that the percentage of blacks who describe themselves as spiritual but not religious grew from 1 percent in 1998 to 10 percent in 2016.

Finally, for three centuries, the black church has served as the institutional glue that has bound blacks together in confronting past and present racial discrimination. It has no institutional rival in black America, and is widely recognized for having galvanized victories of the civil rights movement and the election of the nation's first African American president. Consequently, future studies must determine whether blacks who do not affiliate with organized religion differ from those who do in their racial and political attitudes, as well as commitment to black unity and solidarity. Both quantitative and qualitative studies must engage this pivotal line of research. As shown here, a more profoundly personal sense of spirituality that is separate from corporal faith is taking hold within black America. However, scholars must determine the extent to which individualized spirituality reinforces the collective sense of peoplehood underlying political and social movements aiming to improve conditions for blacks in the United States.

Notes

1. Dr. Cone made this statement in an interview related to Shelton and Emerson's (2012) book, *Blacks and Whites in Christian America: How Racial Discrimination Shapes Religion Convictions*. It does not appear in the book.
2. Reverend Jenkins made this statement in an interview related to Shelton and Emerson's (2012) book. It does not appear in the text.
3. To be clear, the data analyzed in this study include the 1998, 2006, 2008, 2010, 2012, 2014, and 2016 GSS.
4. See the variables BORN, PARBORN, and GRANBORN for more information.
5. In 2000, the GSS began to include a wider range of variables and classifications for measuring respondents' racial and ethnic group memberships. Some of these indicators were used to specify the sample of GSS participants since 2006 to only those who *exclusively* view themselves as "black." For example, Latinos were jettisoned from the data by using the HISPANIC variable, and then respondents who consider themselves to be members of "more than one race" were removed by using RACECEN1.
6. REALINC was recoded into five categories to more clearly illustrate income inequality by race. The "lowest income category" captures those respondents who reported a total

174 JASON E. SHELTON

family income of approximately $11,200 or less. The "second lowest category" denotes those who reported approximately $11,201 to $23,000, while the "middle category" captures those whose income approximates $24,900 (within $1,900 below and $2,100 above this threshold). Each GSS module contains the exact same codes for the lower and middle areas of the income distribution. However, different codes are used at the higher end of the distribution to account for inflation. The final two income groups, the "second highest category" and the "highest category," were created by simply dividing the total number of remaining codes in half.

7. In black America, Holiness and Pentecostals are members of the same family of conservative Protestants. This is partly because the founder of the Church of God in Christ (COGIC), Elder Charles H. Mason, first spoke in tongues during the Azusa Street Revival, which was led by William Seymour, a black Holiness preacher from Louisiana. COGIC is now the largest and most influential denomination within the black Pentecostal tradition. Please see Shelton and Cobb (2017) and Lincoln and Mamiya (1990) for more information.

8. This nonpublished model was specified by utilizing Steenland et al.'s (2000) RELTRAD syntax. Interestingly, the magnitude of the odds ratio for white members of historically African American Protestant traditions is stronger than that for mainline Protestants and Catholics.

References

Barnes, Sandra. 2004. "Priestly and Prophetic Influences on Black Church Social Services." *Social Problems* 51(2): 202–21.

Brown, Khari R. 2009. "Denominational Differences in Support for Race-Based Policies among White, Black, Hispanic, and Asian Americans." *Journal for the Scientific Study of Religion* 48(3): 604–15.

Calhoun-Brown, Allison. 1998. "While Marching to Zion: Otherworldliness and Racial Empowerment in the Black Community." *Journal for the Scientific Study of Religion* 37(3): 427–39.

Chatters, Linda M., Robert J. Taylor, and Karen Lincoln. 1999. "African American Religious Participation: A Multi-sample Comparison." *Journal for the Scientific Study of Religion* 38(1): 132–45.

Chaves, Mark. 2011. *American Religion: Contemporary Trends*. Princeton, NJ: Princeton University Press.

Cone, James. 1969. *Black Theology and Black Power*. San Francisco: Harper & Row.

Cose, Ellis. 2011. *The End of Anger: A New Generation's Take on Race and Rage*. New York: HarperCollins.

Dawson, Michael. 2001. *Black Visions: The Roots of Contemporary African American Political Ideologies*. Chicago: University of Chicago Press.

Edwards, Korie L. 2009. "Race, Religion, and Worship: Are Contemporary African-American Worship Practices Distinct?" *Journal for the Scientific Study of Religion* 48(1): 30–52.

Ellison, Christopher. 1991. "Identification and Separatism: Religious Involvement and Racial Orientations among Black Americans." *Sociological Quarterly* 32(3): 477–94.

SPIRITUALITY AMONG AFRICAN AMERICANS 175

Fischer, Claude S., and Michael Hout. 2006. *Century of Difference: How America Changed in the Last One Hundred Years*. New York: Russell Sage Foundation.

Frazier, E. Franklin. 1964. *The Negro Church in America*. New York: Schocken Books.

Hunt, Matthew O. 2007. "African American, Hispanic, and White Beliefs about Black/White Inequality, 1977–2004." *American Sociological Review* 72(3): 390–415.

Lacy, Karyn. 2007. *Blue-Chip Black: Race, Class, and Status in the New Black Middle Class*. Berkeley: University of California Press.

Lehman, Derek, and Darren Sherkat. 2018. "Measuring Religious Identification in the United States." *Journal for the Scientific Study of Religion* 57(4): 779–94.

Lincoln, C. Eric, and Lawrence H. Mamiya. 1990. *The Black Church in the African American Experience*. Durham, NC: Duke University Press.

Malbroux, Luna. 2017. "Why More Young Black People Are Trading in Church for African Spirituality." *Splinter*, December 18. https://splinternews.com/why-more-young-black-people-are-trading-in-church-for-a-1821316608.

Pew Research Center. 2017. "More Americans Now Say They're Spiritual but Not Religious." September 6. http://www.pewresearch.org/fact-tank/2017/09/06/more-americans-now-say-theyre-spiritual-but-not-religious/.

Shelton, Jason E., and Ryon J. Cobb. 2017. "Black Reltrad: Measuring Religious Diversity and Commonality among African Americans." *Journal for the Scientific Study of Religion* 56(4): 737–64.

Shelton, Jason E., and Michael O. Emerson. 2012. *Blacks and Whites in Christian America: How Racial Discrimination Shapes Religious Convictions*. New York: New York University Press.

Shelton, Jason E., and Anthony D. Greene. 2012. "'Get Up, Get Out, and Git Sumthin': How Race and Class Influence African Americans' Attitudes about Inequality." *American Behavioral Scientist* 56(11): 1480–507.

Sherkat, Darren, and Christopher Ellison. 1991. "The Politics of Black Religious Change: Disaffiliation from Black Mainline Denominations." *Social Forces* 70(2): 431–54.

Smith, Tom W., Peter V. Marsden, Michael Hout, and Jibum Kim. 2016. *General Social Surveys, 1972–2012*. Chicago: University of Chicago, National Opinion Research Center.

Steensland, Brian, Jerry Z. Park, Mark D. Regnerus, Lynn D. Robinson, W. Bradford Wilcox, and Robert Woodberry. 2000. "The Measure of American Religion: Toward Improving the State of the Art." *Social Forces* 79(1): 291–318.

Taylor, Robert J. 1993. "Religion and Religious Observances." Pp. 101–23 in *Aging in Black America*, edited by James S. Jackson, Linda M. Chatters, and Robert J. Taylor. Newbury Park, CA: Sage Publications.

Voisin, Dexter, Dennis E. Corbin, and Camesha Jones. 2016. "A Conceptualization of Spirituality among African American Young Adults." *Western Journal of Black Studies* 40(1): 14–23.

Wilmore, Gayraud S. 1973. *Black Religion and Black Radicalism: An Interpretation of the Religious History of African Americans*. Maryknoll, NY: Orbis Books.

PART II
PRACTICE

8

The Microinteractive Order of Spirituality

Michal Pagis

Spirituality-related discourses emphasize personal, embodied experience while underplaying social institutions. This explains why writings on the spiritual turn tend to focus on the growing individualization that characterizes late modernity, understanding spirituality as an oppositional reaction to tradition and formal religion, and thus as a personal choice and endeavor (Heelas and Woodhead 2005; Luckman 1967; Wuthnow 1998). Following Bellah et al. (1985), American society is seen as pulling away from traditional religious communities, moving to a more privatized form of religion, one that is based on idiosyncratic bricolage that has little to do with communal and social arrangements.

The growing popularity of mindfulness-related meditations, often analyzed as being a part of the spiritual turn, can be seen as the epitome of this individualization processes. Western meditation practice is frequently understood as another indicator of contemporary preoccupation with the self. Studies on meditation tend to focus on its psychological and physical affects (e.g., Brown and Ryan 2003; Lutz et al. 2008) and tend to view meditation as an individual endeavor, which may stem from the notion that meditative silence is "noninteractive" (Saville-Troike 1985).

In this chapter I join recent efforts in the sociology of religion to challenge this individualistic view on spirituality (e.g., Bender 2010). I argue that spiritual spheres in general, and meditation spheres in particular, are based on microsocial dynamics that are central to the turn inward that characterizes contemporary spirituality and are not asocial and certainly not noninteractive. Yet, at the same time, this microsocial dynamic fosters "personal" and "private" experiences that are facilitated by the presence of others. Such a social dynamic is different from the overt group interaction that characterizes traditional religious rituals and thus requires nuanced ethnographic attention.

Michal Pagis, *The Microinteractive Order of Spirituality* In: *Situating Spirituality.* Edited by: Brian Steensland, Jaime Kucinskas, and Anna Sun, Oxford University Press. © Oxford University Press 2022.
DOI: 10.1093/oso/9780197565001.003.0009

180   MICHAL PAGIS

Based on in-depth ethnography of vipassana meditation practice in the United States and in Israel,[1] I illustrate how the unique interaction order of meditation spheres produces a delicate balance between being alone and being together, a balance I dub "collective solitude." I suggest that studies of spiritual practice should pay attention to the interaction modes and orders that are at the base of these practices, and how social togetherness produces and enhances spiritual experiences.

The Puzzle

The question I am asking is quite paradoxical: how do individuals discover the most "private" aspects of themselves precisely through being with others? Throughout my fieldwork among practitioners of vipassana meditation I heard phrases such as "I go to a meditation retreat to face myself" or "Meditation is something between me and myself." One of my informants even expressed his wonder out loud when asking, "Why would a sociologist study meditation?" Thus, practitioners understand meditation as something one experiences alone, in the privacy of one's body and mind.

This perspective stands in sharp contrast to a view of a meditation hall during group sitting. For one hour people sit side by side in close proximity, with their eyes closed, each concentrating on his or her own breath and bodily sensations. The breath of one's neighboring meditator can be easily heard, and other meditators' movements, coughs, crying, and on a rare occasion laughter disturb one's meditative focus. What can be further away from "facing oneself"?

Even though people may learn meditation from a book, there is a vast demand for meditation courses, retreats, and group sittings, where people meditate together, collectively. Moreover, when I asked people about their meditation experiences, they reported that their deepest and most significant experiences took place while being surrounded by other meditating bodies. Many said that they find it easier to meditate with others, and prefer group meditation to solo meditation.

How does the group facilitate individuals' "look inward"? What kind of interaction order, to use Goffman's (1983) phrase, produces deep meditation experiences? And what is the role of others even when practicing solo at home?

Meditation Retreats: A Break from Conventional Social Reality

The meditation center is not just a training space for meditation—it is a space where people train in an alternative social order. This social order, I argue, is key for understanding why meditation is experienced as private and personal even though participants are surrounded by others. As I shall show, in meditation people attempt to transcend their everyday social selves, and they do so through participation in a social interaction mode that encourages them to relax their tendency to focus on their social self as reflected from the eyes of others.[2]

Before the beginning of the twentieth century, the spaces we know today as Buddhist meditation centers did not exist, either in Buddhist or non-Buddhist locations (Gombrich 1983). In fact, until the twentieth century, Buddhist meditation was practiced mainly by monks as a way toward enlightenment. Following the mass-meditation movement in Southeast Asia (Jordt 2007), and the secularization and globalization of meditation practice (Kucinskas 2018; Pagis 2019; Wilson 2013), meditation centers have become an important space where the meditative spirit is introduced to a large audience.

The social order of meditation retreats invites and encourages people to leave outside their local identities and social roles. First, the retreat participants are asked to refrain from any connection to the outside world, including phones, newspapers, television, or internet. They are completely disconnected from their external lives. Second, for the majority of the retreat the participants are asked to keep silence, with minimal verbal and nonverbal communication. Retreat participants share the meditation center with fifty people or more, meet in the corridors, walk in the same trails, eat one next to the other in the dining hall, without openly and directly gesturing or talking to each other.[3]

Vipassana meditation centers in Israel, Illinois, Massachusetts (the centers I visited during this study) and in many other locations have similar physical environments. A meditation center consists of dorms, a dining hall, a kitchen, a meditation hall, and walking grounds. In the meditation hall the lighting is dim and individuals sit side by side in rows on the floor. The space between practitioners is minimal—enabling a single person to walk between the meditation cushions without touching anyone.

The meditation center provides a space where a silent community can be formed, yet while the notion of community may evoke connotations of intimate ties and mutual commitment, this silent community is different. If you arrive with a friend, you are asked to mention this to the organizing staff, since room sharing with friends is discouraged and so is sitting near friends in the meditation hall. When the meditation retreat ends, participants leave the silent community and return home to their everyday lives and rarely maintain contact with each other. A community therefore surrounds the participants, but this is a community of strangers who have gathered together for one purpose—to learn to meditate. This meditative community of strangers produces the oxymoronic state of *collective solitude*. Meditators have come to face themselves and to practice internal observation. The cultivation of these apparently subjective abilities, however, requires a supporting group.

The Meditative Interaction Mode

Even though meditation teachers advise students to focus on their inner feelings and "ignore others," when people begin their meditation training, they tend to focus on others, observing them and trying to guess what is happening in their minds. In fact, at the beginner's level of training, attention to others is important—as social mechanisms such as imitation, competition, comparison, and feelings of guilt all play an important role.

A vignette from a one-day vipassana retreat I observed illustrates the role of imitation and the search for role models. Most participants in this relatively short retreat were not very experienced in meditation. The person in charge was an advanced practitioner named Peter. In the afternoon, after the retreat was over and people began talking, one of the women asked Peter about his unfamiliar meditation posture, as she noticed that "he was slightly rocking back and forth." He looked at her surprised and answered— "Oh, I just fell asleep" and laughed. The woman started laughing as well and answered that it looked so intriguing she thought this might be some kind of unique meditation reserved for advanced students and tried imitating it herself but without success.

Even though meditation is considered a personal practice, when practicing in a group, practitioners report spending time in the minds of others, taking in consideration their judgments. Rachel, for example, was seated in the

THE MICROINTERACTIVE ORDER OF SPIRITUALITY   183

second row in one meditation retreat. Even though she had some experience in meditation, she still could not sit for one hour without moving. Sitting at the first row and knowing that others may observe her as a role model, she wondered, "What will they think of me? I keep moving all the time." Tom, on the other hand, was not aware of the fact that students were tracking him when he was sitting in the first row. Then he participated in a more advanced meditation course in which he sat in the third row. He found that in the third row, he tended to move more and had difficulty cultivating peacefulness. Thinking back, Tom felt that he had not been conscious of the fact that others were observing him from behind when he was in the first row, but somehow their presence behind him had been extremely influential.

The above reports confirm Goffman's (1981, 103) claim that "when nothing eventful is accruing, persons in each other's presence are still nonetheless tracking one another and acting so as to make themselves trackable." Yet practitioners quickly find that too much attention to others is destructive to meditation. Take Ben, for example, who was tormented by a pressing need to swallow saliva continuously during meditation. He was extremely bothered by this and was certain that others suffered from the sounds that his body generated. When the course was over, he went to the person who sat next to him and apologized for "making so much noise." His neighbor was extremely surprised and answered sincerely that he was not aware of any noise and was certainly not troubled by it. Instead of meditating, Ben was attending to "what my neighbor thinks of me" and was not able to turn his attention inward, away from others.

Thus, an important part of meditation training is to learn to balance between attention to others and attention to one's own breath and bodily sensations. This is not easy, as people are attracted to the habitual mode of interaction in which they attend to the people around them. Here the group is key in signaling others that the right interaction mode is not to engage with others. The following incident I observed in the meditation hall illustrates this well.

In the middle of the meditation session, a woman sitting in the first row started giggling. She tried to control her giggling but was not successful. She giggled, was silent for half a minute, and then giggled again. During the third round of giggling, a woman sitting behind her began giggling as well. They shared a short laugh together. To an outside observer, it looked as if they were acquainted with one another (as I later inquired, they were not). At the next giggle, a third woman joined in—her giggle was more restrained but could definitely be heard (all three were giggling while sitting with eyes closed and bodies still). The incident lasted a few minutes, and then they all returned to silence. Throughout the entire episode, the other students in the hall sat quietly.

The joint giggling episode is an excellent example of the mutual influence of physical proximity. Though these women were not concentrating on the same amusing object, they were certainly influenced by emotional contagion (Hatfield et al. 1994). Yet this mutual influence is quite distinct from everyday interactions, in which the feeling of togetherness is based on talk, movement, eye contact, and joint attention on an external object. The gigglers did not open their eyes and did not gesture to one another. At the same time, by continuing their own silence, the other people in the room conveyed to the gigglers that they were expected to end their interruption and return to meditation. Through their silence, they indicated that too much attention to others was an obstacle to overcome, that they were there to help one another to synchronize in silence and internal observation.

When retreat participants reduce their attentiveness to others, they feel that they can completely "ignore" the happening in the meditation hall. Yet such ignoring is actually based on synchronization with others, of which practitioners are only tacitly aware. Imagine a meditation hall, full of meditating bodies. The general sight is quiet and devoid of any movements or gestures. Perhaps sixty bodies sit quietly without moving. You observe their faces, sitting there with their eyes closed; some appear filled with concentration and others with a relaxed look of calmness. Once in a while you can see or hear a movement, but by and large the students sit quietly. After many long observations, I have come to realize that despite the apparent lack of communication, a pattern emerges out of the silence, connecting the movements of different meditators. Following the movements closely, I noticed that movements cluster and form bundles of noise: the movement of one woman leads to a reaction of a few others. One person's cough triggers others to join. It is clear that the movement of one person tends to lead to the movement of another.

For example, in one incident a loud cough was heard from the left side. As the man continued coughing, a woman in the third row moved her leg and changed her posture. Her movement was loud and activated two other movements—another woman moved her hand, and another straightened her

THE MICROINTERACTIVE ORDER OF SPIRITUALITY 185

back. In another incident, fifteen minutes before the end of a one-hour sitting, a woman moved her leg. Almost concurrently, another woman, sitting a few spots away, straightened up, and her neighbor then took a deep, audible breath. In fact, once I became aware of this mutual influence of movement, I suddenly found myself, while in meditation, taking a heavy breath a second after the woman next to me let out a heavy breath.

This mutual effect on movement has a mirror image—the synchronization of nonmovement. Although Collins's (2004) definition of rhythmic coordination involves synchronized movement, we can extend this notion to capture the synchronized nonmovement that takes place in the meditation hall, when all bodies present are silent, still, and relaxed. In fact, in these moments of intense collective meditation, I sometimes found that a deep breath from a neighbor prompted us nearby to take a deep breath ourselves, leading to coordinated breathing. In these periods of intense meditation, those who had not been able to sit quietly suddenly found themselves able to sit for an entire hour while making only minimal movements. The silent and relaxed bodies influenced one another as people entered deeply into meditation together.

Jonathan recounted the transformation he experienced when comparing the beginning and the end of a vipassana retreat:

> In the beginning I felt very awkward. I kept looking around at other people in the meditation hall. I thought that my neighbor was probably annoyed about every little noise I made. By the end of the course this feeling completely disappeared. I remember sitting meditating in a room filled with people and it was very, very quiet, and I just sat and meditated, with complete concentration. It was an amazing experience.

In this described transformation, others move from being an audience to become "bodily co-dwellers," and the interactive focus moves from a feeling of "awkwardness" to being together quietly without direct and acknowledged focus on others. In resonance with Jack Katz's (1999) notions of "doing emotions" and "being done by emotions," the first stages of training in meditation require "doing meditation" in the sense of projecting the right self to others and spending time in their minds. However, for successful "deep" meditation to take place, one needs to move to the phase in which one is "done by meditation" and is no longer actively attending to others, but instead joins them in tacit social attunement (Pagis 2019, 63).

Extending the Meditative Interaction Mode

The unique mode of interaction that is revealed in the meditation hall is not limited to meditating together. In fact, it extends to interaction in the meditation center as a whole. Remember that in a meditation center people share the dining hall, sleeping rooms, and corridors. The presence of others can be comforting but can also be quite irritating. Thus, also outside of the meditation hall participants train in accepting the presence of others while reducing awareness of their judgments or interferences.

Take, for example, the following incident described by Aaron, an Israeli meditator, who participated in a ten-day vipassana retreat. During the retreat his roommate had an alarm clock that ticked, and this alarm clock was getting on Aaron's nerves. When Aaron realized that the roommate did not even use the clock (as it was facing the wall) he became angry, thinking that the roommate should have been more considerate and remove the unnecessary clock. Since he was not supposed to talk with the roommate, he asked permission from the meditation instructor to say something, yet "the instructor said it is better not to talk and that I should try to accept it." Then something changed:

> On the third day of the course I was trying to sleep during the break and that clock was ticking and I was trying to ignore it, and then I told myself, "Don't ignore it, just listen to it and feel whatever sensation comes." ... Every tick I feel anger building up ... for half an hour or so ... and I observe this anger ... but after an hour I felt a feeling I never felt in my life, a feeling of deep peace ... a feeling of kindness to everyone in the retreat.

Aaron's description reveals that there is more to the ticking clock than mere noise. For Aaron, the noise of the clock is not a natural entity like the noise of raindrops, as raindrops do not trigger anger. In everyday social reality, the noise of the clock represented the inconsideration of the roommate, the fact that he did not take Aaron's feelings and experiences into account.

If Aaron could have talked to his roommate, the anger would have come to an early end, as Aaron could have approached his roommate and explained his experience. But he was asked not to talk or signal. Instead he was asked to try to accept the sound. Such acceptance entails a shift in the mode of social interaction. When shifting the focus away from his roommate to the sound of the clock and the sensations on the body this sound produces, Aaron practiced in disattending conventional social order, turning the ticking from sounds that carry indications regarding injustice or lack of consideration, to random asocial disturbances. When Aaron was successful in dis-attending to his roommate and the relation between them, he experienced a "feeling I never felt in my life, a feeling of deep peace" that was accompanied by "a feeling of kindness to everyone in the retreat." Indeed, when practitioners succeed in shifting to the meditative interaction mode, they frequently encounter experiences deemed spiritual, such as equanimity, relaxation, and lovingkindness (see also Pagis 2015).

The lovingkindness that Aaron experienced resonates with what Weber (1946) dubbed "acosmic benevolence," or universal brotherliness, which, as opposed to worldly love, "which is always love for particular persons, is love for all, without distinction—love for whoever comes, friends, strangers, enemies" (Bellah 1999, 277). This type of love characterizes contemporary spiritual circles; it manifests a social relation that is oriented toward others, but it does not require engagement with a particular person. It is thus not surprising that the kind of interaction mode practiced in the meditation center, in which people are relieved from constant attention to others but are not isolated from the presence of others, facilitates this type of emotional experience.

One practitioner put it aptly when he remarked that meditation is a time in which "I don't have the need to be in a form. Just to sit and breathe and find a whole world in it." His use of the notion "form" alludes to the daily self that needs to be maintained in interaction, the projection of self into the world, the way others see me and respond to me. Of course, in meditation practitioners are actually in a form—that of a meditator, sitting with the legs crossed and the back straight without moving. Still, the form of a meditator represents a place outside of structured social roles, replicating, to borrow anthropologist Victor Turner's (1974) notion, the "liminoid" space of the meditation center, a space that offers a break from society.

In this context, the shift back to "being in a form" can be unsettling. Roy's experience illustrates the shift back to the conventional mode of interaction, and how this conventional mode was found to be destructive to meditation:

When the silence was over a few of us sat together outside on the grass, and I told some kind of joke and everybody laughed, and then after a while we entered the meditation hall to meditate together for an hour, and I just couldn't meditate! I kept going back to the interaction outside and how

188   MICHAL PAGIS

> I told that joke and the reactions of others. . . . It made me feel very elevated
> and excited but I completely lost my equanimity and could hardly meditate.

Roy describes a normal everyday interaction that includes shared excitement and elevation, or what Collins (2004) referred to as emotional energy. As social creatures, we would think that such excitement would be viewed as positive, and indeed Roy seemed to have enjoyed his social status and the positive self-reflection he received from others. But his comments reveal that for him, such excitement stands in sharp contrast with the meditative spirit.

For a successful joke-telling I must attend to the reaction of the listeners. I need to attend to the "me" that they perceive that emerges through their gestures, and adjust my conduct accordingly—through changing the tone of voice, expressions of face, hand movements. If I were to ignore their responses and focus on my breathing at the same time of telling a joke, the whole performance would most likely break down and I would fail to produce the shared excitement.

Roy's description illustrates the challenge to shift from one side of the interactive continuum to the other, to shift from carefully attending to others (and to myself through their responses) to pushing others to the background and "forgetting" their existence. Such challenge frequently emerges when retreat participants step out of the meditation center into their everyday life, a life where their friends and family expect "conventional" engaged interaction. Not surprisingly, when returning to everyday life, practitioners of vipassana frequently spoke of diminished calmness and equanimity, and how their "old self" returned.[4] They then try to replicate the experiences they encounter in the meditation retreat in their daily life, either in weekly group sittings or when meditating alone.

Solo Meditation

In the preceding discussion I illustrated how the practice of meditation is supported by the physical proximity of the group. But what happens in solo meditation at home? Meditators decrease their dependence on the physical proximity of others as they become more advanced in the practice. They start meditating alone in their homes, and meditation turns into a relatively solitary practice. However, solitary meditation practice is not disconnected from the silent community described above. In fact, home practice frequently

THE MICROINTERACTIVE ORDER OF SPIRITUALITY   189

recreates the original environment of the meditation center through the use of certain spatial and temporal arrangements.

Meditators practicing alone usually practice in dim lighting and in silence, as in the meditation center. They sit for an hour, which is the time frame for a sitting in the meditation center. They sit in the same posture, and though this is not required, the posture is usually the same for all meditators. Some use the same audio recording that is used in collective group sittings, which includes a few meditation instructions and a short piece of chanting and brings the community of meditation practice into their home. The recent use of meditation applications, such as Insight Timer, also helps to reconstruct a communal space. While using an application may seem like enhancing solitary practice (no need to be in the physical presence of others), the story is more complex. In the popular applications each session includes meditation instructions repeated in the same familiar voice, and in most sessions, you are consistently accompanied by that voice and thus are not left alone. You can see how many people are currently meditating using that specific application around the world, and some applications even list the names and locations of current users. Like other virtual networks, the application removes physical proximity while keeping you embedded in a social world.

Still, solitary meditation is reported as "less deep" than group meditation, indicating that the group has an important role in helping the meditator to let go of or bracket the outer world and go inward.[5] Practitioners of meditation, thus, find that they need to return to collective solitude, either in weekly groups sittings or in meditation retreats, in order to maintain their meditation practice.

Spirituality, Transcendence, and Modes of Interaction

When people meditate they are asked to shift attention to the relatively hidden parts of their selves and turn inward. Yet they are asked to do so in a group, where their bodies can be observed publicly, where they can track others and be tracked by others. In the presence of others, overt awareness of others becomes an obstacle that one must learn to overcome. Successful, "deep" meditation entails a mode of being together in which one relaxes one's attention to the self as viewed by others.

Spiritual practices are not just about the transformation of internal psychological states—they entail new modes of interaction. Scholars agree that the "subjective turn" that characterizes modernity is a cultural and social phenomenon (Taylor 1989). Yet many sociologists raise concerns that this turn inward represents a dissolution of the social fabric, with people becoming antisocial, overly individualistic, and perhaps even narcissistic (e.g., Lasch 1980; Madsen 2014; Rieff 1966). Such concerns have also been raised among leaders of the "contemplative movement" in regard to the growing secularization of meditation practice (Kucinskas 2018). However, these perspectives tend to ignore the growing institutionalization of looking inward in social spheres that are becoming a central part of our society, spheres that are weaving new social fabrics and even creating new communities.

These new communities are distinct from the classical notion of community. As we have seen in the case of meditation, these communities are not built on intensive social support or intimate friendship. Spiritual spheres offer unique spaces that balance "being together" and "being alone." They embrace rising individualization and secularization yet are based on collective, joint circles where affective effervescence is produced and where people search for experiences that can be categorized as mystical, transformative, or therapeutic.

I suggest that many collective spheres that are defined today as part of the "spiritual revolution" (Heelas and Woodhead 2005) are based on a shift in the mode of social interaction, and with it on some degree of collective solitude. When people gather together to practice yoga or collective chanting, to walk a pilgrimage together, or even to touch one another in a spiritual sex workshop, they are not searching for long-lasting ties or social commitment. In these spheres people gather together as a community of strangers and produce collective solitude that enhances personal emotional experiences that are frequently doomed spiritual. In many of these spheres the habitual, daily mode of interaction is discouraged, and people are asked to leave behind their everyday identities and selves. Instead of talk and overt communication, these spheres are based on bodily synchronization and bodily co-dwelling, thus offering people a way into "solitary" and "private" experiences of transcendence, without being isolated or excluded from the social fabric.

To borrow Merleau-Ponty's (1968) phrase, spirituality-related social spaces reveal a delicate balance between the visible and the invisible, the private and the public. Contemporary social life is extremely complex, as individuals constantly shift from one self to another, from one social role to another, and are required to keep constant awareness of the self as viewed by others, of the social form they perform for others. In contrast, spiritual

THE MICROINTERACTIVE ORDER OF SPIRITUALITY   191

spheres offer an alternative social order that enables participants to transcend the fragility of the self that is inherent to everyday social situations, to relax anxieties regarding how others perceive them, to relax anticipations regarding what they are. Such collective spheres offer practitioners a glimpse of a nonmundane form of existence where they can bracket their social identities and, at least temporarily, feel free from the need to perform a concrete social form.

Notes

1. Between 2005 and 2008, I conducted participant observation in Israeli and American meditation centers belonging to the same global meditation organization, Vipassana Meditation as Taught by S. N. Goenka. In addition, between 2009 and 2021 I sporadically tracked the vipassana social field in Israel through conversations and observations. Vipassana meditation, also known as insight meditation or mindfulness, originated in Theravada Buddhism and has become popular around the world. For full details see Pagis 2019.
2. I am here referring to the sociological understanding of self and identity, as developed by Cooley (1992) and Mead (1934). From a sociological point of view, our conception of ourselves is dependent on the responses we receive from others, as these responses serve as reflections that help us understand how others conceive us.
3. The vipassana school introduced in this chapter, vipassana meditation as taught by S. N. Goenka, is considered relatively conservative in terms of demands of silence and long meditation retreats. Still, meditation retreats offered by other meditation schools resemble the structure introduced here.
4. See Pagis 2019 for a detailed analysis of the tension between the meditative social order and everyday social relations and interactions.
5. This is in resonance with Kucinskas et al.'s (2017) study on spiritual awareness in everyday life, which found that people report higher spiritual awareness when in the company of others.

References

Bellah, Robert N. 1999. "Max Weber and World-Denying Love: A Look at the Historical Sociology of Religion." *Journal of the American Academy of Religion* 67(2): 277–304.
Bellah, Robert N., Richard Madsen, William M. Sullivan, Ann Swidler, and Steven M. Tipton. 1985. *Habits of the Heart: Individualism and Commitment in American Life.* Berkeley: University of California Press.
Bender, Courtney. 2010. *The New Metaphysicals: Spirituality and the American Religious Imagination.* Chicago: University of Chicago Press.

192 MICHAL PAGIS

Brown, Kirk Warren, and Richard M. Ryan. 2003. "The Benefits of Being Present: Mindfulness and Its Role in Psychological Well-Being." *Journal of Personality and Social Psychology* 84(4): 822–48.

Collins, Randall. 2004. *Interaction Ritual Chains*. Princeton, NJ: Princeton University Press.

Cooley, Charles Horton. 1992. *Human Nature and the Social Order*. New Brunswick, NJ: Transaction Publishers.

Goffman, Erving. 1981. *Forms of Talk*. Philadelphia: University of Pennsylvania Press.

Goffman, Erving. 1983. "The Interaction Order: American Sociological Association, 1982 Presidential Address." *American Sociological Review* 48(1): 1–17.

Gombrich, Richard. 1983. "From Monastery to Meditation Center: Lay Meditation in Modern Sri Lanka." Pp. 20–34 in *Buddhist Studies Ancient and Modern*, edited by Philip Denwood and Alexander Piatigorsky. London: Curzon Press.

Hatfield, Elaine, John T. Cacioppo, and Richard L. Rapson. 1994. *Emotional Contagion*. Cambridge: Cambridge University Press.

Heelas, Paul, and Linda Woodhead, with Benjamin Seel, Bronislaw Szerszynski, and Karin Tusting. 2005. *The Spiritual Revolution: Why Religion Is Giving Way to Spirituality*. Malden, MA: Blackwell.

Jordt, Ingrid. 2007. *Burma's Mass Lay Meditation Movement: Buddhism and the Cultural Construction of Power*. Athens: Ohio University Press.

Katz, Jack. 1999. *How Emotions Work*. Chicago: University of Chicago Press.

Kucinskas, Jaime. 2018. *The Mindful Elite: Mobilizing from the Inside Out*. New York: Oxford University Press.

Kucinskas, Jaime, Bradley R. E. Wright, D. Matthew Ray, and John Ortberg. 2017. "States of Spiritual Awareness by Time, Activity, and Social Interaction." *Journal for the Scientific Study of Religion* 56(2): 418–37.

Lasch, Christopher. 1980. *The Culture of Narcissism: American Life in an Age of Diminishing Expectations*. New York: Warner Books.

Luckmann, Thomas. 1967. *Invisible Religion: The Problem of Religion in Modern Society*. New York: Macmillan.

Lutz, Antoine, Julie Brefczynski-Lewis, Tom Johnstone, and Richard Davidson. 2008. "Regulation of the Neural Circuitry of Emotion by Compassion Meditation: Effects of Meditative Expertise." *PLoS ONE* 3(3): e1897.

Madsen, Ole Jacob. 2014. *The Therapeutic Turn: How Psychology Altered Western Culture*. New York: Routledge.

Mead, George Herbert. 1934. *Mind, Self and Society*. Chicago: University of Chicago Press.

Merleau-Ponty, Maurice. 1968. *The Visible and the Invisible*. Translated by Alphonso Lingis. Evanston, IL: Northwestern University Press.

Pagis, Michal. 2015. "Evoking Equanimity: Silent Interaction Rituals in Vipassana Meditation Retreats." *Qualitative Sociology* 38(1): 39–56.

Pagis, Michal. 2019. *Inward: Vipassana Meditation and the Embodiment of the Self*. Chicago: University of Chicago Press.

Rieff, Philip. 1966. *The Triumph of the Therapeutic*. Chicago: University of Chicago Press.

Saville-Troike, Muriel. 1985. "The Place of Silence in an Integrated Theory of Communication." Pp. 3–20 in *Perspectives on Silence*, edited by D. Tannen Deborah and Saville-Troike Muriel. Norwood, NJ: Ablex Publishing Corporation.

Taylor, Charles. 1989. *Sources of the Self: The Making of the Modern Identity*. Cambridge, MA: Harvard University Press.

Turner, Victor. 1974. "Liminal to Liminoid, in Play, Flow, and Ritual: An Essay in Comparative Symbology." *Rice Institute Pamphlet—Rice University Studies* 60(3): 43–92.

Weber, Max. 1946. "Religious Rejections of the World and Their Directions." Pp. 323–59 in *From Max Weber: Essays in Sociology*, edited and translated by H. H. Gerth and C. Wright Mills. Oxford: Oxford University Press.

Wilson, Jeff. 2013. *Mindful America: Meditation and the Mutual Transformation of Buddhism and American Culture*. Oxford: Oxford University Press.

Wuthnow, Robert. 1998. *After Heaven: Spirituality in America since the 1950s*. Berkeley: University of California Press.

9

Ecstasies

Or, the Limitations of Vanilla Spirituality Studies

Melissa M. Wilcox

Introduction: When Sheila's a Leatherdyke?

An undated article on Whosoever.org, "an online magazine for LGBT Christians," begins as follows:

> "When I get flogged, I go into a trance state. That's the only thing I know to call it. Outside stimuli are not present."
>
> A newcomer looks intently at the heavyset man speaking from the corner.
>
> Another voice breaks in, "It's like locking onto radar for me. I go on auto pilot and just let the Top take me away. Or at least until his arm gives out."
>
> The room breaks into laughter, and I glance at my watch. 9:15pm. We're running over, and they like the building cleared by nine, so I take the hands of my lover to my right and the newcomer to my left.
>
> "I hate to end this so soon, but some of us are going out for coffee afterward[.] If anyone wants to join us we can continue for a while there. Let's close in the usual manner."
>
> Before I close my eyes, I see a circle of 16 men, most dressed in leather or uniforms, grasp hands. Some bow their heads while others like myself turn [our] faces upward.
>
> After a few words of prayer, 16 strong voices join in a resonating, "In Jesus' name, Amen."
>
> What's wrong with this picture? Absolutely nothing, and that's what this is all about. (Haberman 1999)

This is not your grandmother's—or your doctoral adviser's—religious individualism. Or maybe it is; there are plenty of grandparents involved in these

---

Melissa M. Wilcox, *Ecstasies* In: *Situating Spirituality.* Edited by: Brian Steensland, Jaime Kucinskas, and Anna Sun, Oxford University Press. © Oxford University Press 2022. DOI: 10.1093/oso/9780197565001.003.0010

ECSTASIES   195

kinds of scenes, and some quite famous academics have been known for their involvement.

In 2002 I did not have the tools to write "When Sheila's a Leatherdyke," although the data would have been there had I thought to look; however, it is also interesting to consider whether that article would have been published at the time. All the same, in the article I did write, entitled "When Sheila's a Lesbian" (Wilcox 2002), and in many other forums, I have spent my career advocating for the full inclusion of queer and transgender communities and practices within the study of religion. More recently (e.g., Wilcox 2018, 2019), I have begun to make the argument that scholars' resistance to engaging with more specifically *queer* forms of religion—in the sense of queer communities, but also in the queer theoretical and political sense of the term as odd or disruptive—is detrimental to the study of religion, and demeaning and dangerous to queer and transgender people. In this exploratory chapter I consider one specific example of a queer form of religious practice whose serious study would benefit the field and (if done well) would offer greater respect and justice to its practitioners.

Embodiment in general, and especially sexuality, is often marginalized in the study of religion, particularly when the object of study is a mainstream tradition practiced by dominant groups in global North / global West cultures. Yet, despite the centrality of belief and the marginalization of practice in the lives of many who currently identify as spiritual, too close a focus on belief and identity to the neglect or exclusion of embodiment and practice risks forming an incomplete picture of spirituality as a phenomenon today. One site in which spirituality is explicitly constructed—even first realized—through embodiment is in the practice of spiritual BDSM (bondage/discipline, dominance/ submission, sadism/masochism). This chapter follows Fennell's (2018) work on sacred kink by arguing for the importance of queer and trans leather/BDSM spirituality to spirituality studies as a whole, not only for its contributions to established themes in the field but also for the new insights it offers on such topics as Fennell's concept of the postrational; practitioners' use of embodied and affective empiricism; the critical importance of embodied spiritual practices, including sexual ones; and the role of play for adults in contemporary global North / global West cultures.

Religion, Sexuality, and Queerness

To the credit of the many fields that come together to study religion, the past decades have seen a marked opening toward the study of religion in LGBTQ communities, moving from a common presumption in the 1990s that the study of "religion and homosexuality" meant studying what religious heterosexuals thought about when they heard the word "homosexuality," to a widening recognition that religion thrives in queer communities, to a more recent but steady growth in transgender studies in religion (e.g., re the latter, Cragun and Sumerau 2017; Crasnow 2017; Pritchard and Ott 2018; Strassfeld and Henderson-Espinoza 2019; Sumerau et al. 2018). Despite the promise of these developments, as the reductionist and medicalizing concept of studying "homosexuality" has opened up into more accurate and inclusive approaches to sexuality and has broadened to include trans people and communities as well as (occasionally) more intersectional approaches, the concept of religion has remained relatively static. Certainly it is a notable improvement that the growth of spirituality, or "SBNR," studies, as well as earlier avatars of such work (Sheilaism, secularization, religious individualism, and the like) has been paralleled by a growing attention to religion—including spirituality—in LGBTQ communities. The limitations that remain, however, reveal a broader limitation in these areas of study as a whole: both religion and sexuality continue to be understood in primarily cognitive modes, and bodies remain stubbornly absent.

"Religious" and "spiritual" are, of course, identity terms in the cultures most often addressed within spirituality studies; the acronym "LGBTQ" also indexes a series of sexual and gender identities. Both sets of terms are therefore definitively cognitive in nature. Furthermore, although identity may also be practiced (we often call this "expression"), studies of such practice commonly evade the body itself. Certainly, in the study of religion, they evade the body in the midst of sexual acts. This seems to be especially true, to date, for studies of religion in queer and transgender communities.

There are a number of possible reasons for such evasion. Fieldwork in this regard would be challenging (sociological flies-on-the-wall are often an awkward presence, but would be much more so in the bedroom), and survey developers would be hard-pressed to operationalize such fluid and complex social interactions. These are difficult questions to ask during interviews, especially if one is working with recently recruited participants or a team of researchers and the interpersonal connection is therefore short term and relatively shallow. But there may be other reasons, as well. How many of us think to take the "Oh, God!" of sexual ecstasy as a religious expression? In fact, most detailed studies of sexual activity and religion have addressed the practices of Orientalized or otherwise distanced, colonized others. There may be a lurking, perhaps Enlightenment-rooted, suspicion that "real" religion and sexual ecstasy have either no relationship or solely an antagonistic one (Ramberg 2014). Or, along the lines of the persistent undercurrent of misogyny that attends much scholarship on spirituality (e.g., Bellah et al. 1985; Carrette and King 2005; see Gauthier et al. 2013 for brief but incisive commentary in this regard), any relationship between sexuality and spirituality may seem impossibly shallow and inconsequential. It is this assumption, in particular, that should raise warning flags for us when it comes to studying spirituality and sexuality in queer and transgender communities, given those communities' persistent sexualization in the popular imaginary.

Both queer and trans communities and our straight and cisgender allies are keenly aware of the impact of scholarship on the legal and political standing of those under study. One need only look to the use of sociological and psychological research in recent Supreme Court cases on same-sex marriage (in which, it must be said, the sociology of religion found itself in part on the side of homophobic bigotry) to see glaring examples of the power—or perhaps the disingenuousness—of the ivory tower. With many in queer and transgender communities advocating an assimilative politics through the pursuit of marriage rights, military service, and other markers of normative national citizenship—an approach termed "homonormativity" by Lisa Duggan (2002) and, when married with patriotism, dubbed "homonationalism" by Jasbir Puar (2007)—both religious organizations and scholars of religion may be playing an important protective role. As both Duggan and Puar argue, however, such protections only extend to certain queer and (even more rarely) transgender people, and in advocating such assimilationist approaches those queer and trans people and their allies simultaneously promote the further marginalization, even the categorical erasure, of minoritized queer and transgender people and communities (see also Valentine 2007). Broadening our scope does not have to mean painting queer and trans people with a lurid brush; it means representing these communities, as we should represent all communities, in all of their breadth and complexity. It means attending to profoundly *queer* manifestations of the religious. One of these manifestations takes place in BDSM communities.

Prior Research on BDSM Spirituality

Although studies of BDSM have a striking tendency to scatter religious language throughout their narrative while failing entirely to acknowledge it (e.g., Newmahr 2011; Weiss 2011), and Tinsley's recent (2018) multidisciplinary cultural studies work has drawn religion and BDSM together in evocative ways, published qualitative or ethnographic research on leather spirituality, BDSM spirituality, and sacred kink is exceedingly rare. Some queer and transgender religious leaders have written about leather/BDSM spirituality from Christian (e.g., Shore-Goss 2018), Buddhist (e.g., Karuna 1998), and neopagan (e.g., Kaldera and Harrington 2006) perspectives, as have theologians more broadly (e.g., Carrette 2005), and a number of graduate students have taken up the issue in conference papers, again often from a theological perspective more than a descriptive-analytical one.

A 1998 article by Mira Zussman with the pseudonymous Anne Pierce, published in *Anthropology of Consciousness*, offers one of the earliest ethnographic explorations of leather spirituality, predominantly within a queer context and focused on the San Francisco Bay Area. Challenging the apparent double standard by which anthropology (we could add here the study of religion in general) nonchalantly accepts a wide variety of bodily practices in "other" cultures yet scorns similar practices that crop up close to home, Zussman and Pierce draw connections between leathersex and Christian, Jewish, and Muslim traditions, pointing for instance to the historic links between pain and sacred ecstasy in Christianity, the repeated theme of binding in Judaism, and the centrality of submission in Islam.[1] They also note, as does Peterson (2005) almost fifteen years later, a persistent emphasis among their interlocutors on describing BDSM experiences in religious language, including not only direct connections to Christianity and neopaganism but also the use of terms like "mindfulness." Interestingly if unsurprisingly, Zussman presents herself as a nonpractitioner of BDSM, while Pierce, also an academic, takes on a pseudonym because, in Pierce's own words, "Identification within this community could possibly be an obstacle for future academic pursuits such as fieldwork" (Zussman and Pierce 1998, 36).

Pierce goes on to articulate the "sincere hope that my participation in this project will contribute to the demystification and the increased acceptance of consensual play and those who engage in it so that future authors in my position will not need to use a pseudonym" (Zussman and Pierce 1998, 36). It seems to have taken far longer than Pierce hoped, but Fennell writes in her

ECSTASIES 199

2018 article on sacred kink that "to the best of my knowledge, I am the first publicly 'out' kinkster to study the American mainstream BDSM subculture ethnographically" (Fennell 2018, 1051). Critiquing Zussman and Pierce's study for what she finds to be inadequate and inaccurate coverage of "hetero-leaning" kinkster communities, and raising concerns about the absence of Neopaganism from Beckmann's (2007) study of transcendent experiences among British BDSM practitioners, Fennell offers the first in-depth, mixed-method study of spirituality in BDSM communities. Conducted over the course of several years and deeply grounded in her lengthier personal involvement in kinkster communities, Fennell's research draws on extensive fieldwork in the Washington, DC / Baltimore area kink scene and on an impressively large survey ($n > 1,100$) of self-identified kinksters in the United States and Canada whose participants were recruited primarily through the BDSM-focused social media site FetLife.

Fennell finds that "spirituality is a major motivating factor for why many kinksters participate in BDSM," adding that "the subculture . . . primarily envisions 'spirituality' in Pagan, and to a lesser degree American Buddhist, terms" (Fennell 2018, 1053). By "American Buddhist," she seems to mean not only US-based white Buddhist lineages but also popular cultural understandings and appropriations of Buddhism such as those promoted by John Kabat-Zinn and other marketers of mindfulness (see, e.g., Gleig 2019). Fennell also insightfully takes note of her interlocutors' discomfort with the ineffability of their transcendent experiences in the context of their firm commitment to science as the ultimate arbiter of knowledge and truth, describing a widespread "ambivalence . . . from people who find themselves confronted with what feels like disconcerting or uncomfortable spiritual realities that do not match their rational understanding of the world" (Fennell 2018, 1059). Her interlocutors call these realities (or claims to their reality) "woo"; she calls their ambivalence "post-rational" and frames the tools the kink subculture offers for navigating this ambivalence "secular-ish," evoking unintentionally but irresistibly for me Lynne Gerber's (2014) claim that ex-gay different-sex marriages involve a "queerish" form of celibacy.

Furthermore, Fennell notes that the Christian and Jewish participants in her survey were much less likely than the Neopagans and Buddhists to understand BDSM and spirituality as connected, and she even quotes a Christian interlocutor, Nathan, who opined that "BDSM is a lot more spiritual than religion." Nathan explained, "Religion for me is like, 'Oh, that's cool. I can believe that.' [. . .] But in the BDSM community you find a lot more spiritual people dealing with things such as energy or auras." Unlike with religion, Nathan struggles to believe in these "spiritual" phenomena and yet he has experienced them, "so I can't disbelieve [them] completely" (Fennell 2018, 1057). To Nathan, and apparently to a number of Fennell's interlocutors, religion indicates a creed that one may find credible and adhere to, whereas spirituality indicates not just practice but, more specifically, embodied experience.

As Fennell notes, though, there are distinctions between "hetero-leaning" kink communities and queer and trans leather/BDSM communities that deserve concerted attention. Despite the fact that these communities are hardly separated by a hermetic (or Hermetic) seal, and that their experiences of ecstasy in fact seem to have a great deal in common, because of the differences as well as the similarities in their members' historical relationships to religion and spirituality they deserve continued study in their diversities as well as in their connections. Strikingly, one of the sites of such diversity appears to be in Christianity. Whereas Nathan found no connection between Christianity and BDSM practice, for instance, queer and transgender Christian commentators have noted for years the obvious connections for them between the bound, wounded, and ecstatic sacred bodies of that religion—especially evident, for Western Christians, in Roman Catholicism—and the ecstasies they and their communities experience through binding and wounding. Similar insights seem less prevalent—in fact, apparently not present at all—among Fennell's interlocutors, perhaps because few of those in her study would have grown up gazing at the crucified Christ as the sole naked male body they were allowed and even encouraged to adore. Similarly, S. J. Crasnow (2019) has recently written about explorations of the connections between binding tefillin and BDSM binding at a Talmud camp run by the queer Jewish organization SVARA. From within simultaneous Jewish and leathersex spaces, it is difficult to avoid noticing that both traditions involve reverently winding black leather around human flesh. The precise contours of the convergences and divergences in kink and leathersex spiritualities cannot be fully predicted and have yet to be fully explained; they deserve ample additional exploration.

In practice, sacred kink and queer and trans BDSM/leather spirituality involve the evocation of a wide variety of traditional and innovated religious practices, and the invocation of any number of spirits, saints, and deities from traditions around the world. Some, such as the Jewish and Christian approaches described above, are rooted in religions that are often participants' own ancestral traditions; others are intertwined with traditions

ECSTASIES   201

to which the practitioners have converted; and still others draw widely on appropriated practices, typically from colonized peoples considered "tribal" (a term generally used as a slightly more respectful synonym for "primitive"). These categories, it should be noted, are not mutually exclusive. At the heights of practice, many kinksters and leatherfolk describe an ecstatic experience of oneness or disembodiment that they often term "transcendence" or, in a more New Age idiom, an "out-of-body experience." Some describe intense white light coming toward them, or emanating from the consensually wounded body of a play partner. They often interpret these experiences through their own world-concepts, just as those who experience other forms of religious ecstasy do. Many come to seek out these experiences intentionally, and respond to them by framing BDSM play as sacred. Both Zussman and Pierce in 1998 and Fennell (2018) twenty years later found length and depth of involvement in BDSM communities to be positively correlated with associating BDSM and spirituality.

The Importance of BDSM and Leather for the Study of Spirituality

Above all else, BDSM/leather spirituality matters because queer and transgender communities matter. There is a profound injustice in the constant, nagging insistence that scholars who study these communities must justify our work in terms of its relevance to the study of heterosexual and cisgender people. Queer and trans communities matter in and of themselves, not because of how they can aid in the self-understanding of straight and cis communities. Furthermore, though, if included as fully and taken as seriously as straight and cis communities, queer and trans communities have the potential to challenge and transform the inter- and transdisciplinary study of religion in unprecedented ways. I have made this argument in a variety of contexts and forms for years; here, I outline it in the context of the profoundly queer (in the capacious, not the identitarian, meaning of the term) religious form of queer and trans leather/BDSM spiritualities. In sum, leather and BDSM spirituality matters to spirituality studies both because of what it has in common with other forms of spirituality studied in this subfield and because of the new insights it has to offer.

Among the continuities between BDSM/leather spirituality and the larger field of spirituality under study are therapeutic narratives; the predominance of white practitioners; a common valorization of spirituality over against religion; an individualism that may be disengaged from traditional religion or routed through it; interpellation and sometimes active engagement within a neoliberal logic of spiritual marketing and consumption that draws on settler and franchise colonial and Orientalist frameworks; and the centrality of affect as a determinant of truth and "authenticity." As a specific site of study, leather/BDSM spirituality may offer new or unique insights into these patterns, and existing research may also afford significant insights into an understanding of BDSM/leather spirituality not as a culturally aberrant phenomenon but as a logical outcome of broader cultural patterns in the contemporary global North / global West. Potentially new directions of study suggested by leather spirituality, and in some cases by spiritual BDSM and leathersex as a whole, include Fennell's (2018) concept of the postrational; the role of embodied and affective empiricism in determining spiritual "truth" in a "postrational" world; the centrality of practice and, even more so, of embodiment; by extension, the necessity of attending to sexuality not just in theory, fantasy, or recollection—that is, cognitively—but also in its embodied form; and the role of play in neoliberal societies. Each of these could be the topic of a longer paper, so I unpack them only in the briefest of terms below.

Continuities

1. *Therapeutic narratives*: Just as many practitioners of spirituality extol its therapeutic effects and seek out spaces of religious or spiritual healing, many BDSM practitioners also understand their experiences as therapeutic. Though sensationalized by popular media and not recognized by the American Psychological Association, BDSM therapy is a form of healing practice recognized in these communities (Lindemann 2011).

2. *Whiteness*: Assertions about the whiteness of spiritual BDSM communities should not be construed to claim that all such practitioners are white or that there are no communities of color structured around spiritual BDSM. In fact, many BDSM communities include people of color; yet overall the scene seems to be particularly white, at least in its public face and in the United States (but see Cruz 2016). The same is true for the discourse of "spirituality" in general; although it certainly has its adherents of color, at least in public discourses whiteness predominates as an ever-present but unmarked category among consumers of

spirituality even as producers of spirituality are frequently cast as people of color (typically Asian and indigenous North, Central, and South American—all groups Orientalized by colonialist discourses; see Lucia 2020).

3. *Spiritual but not religious*: As Fennell notes in the case of kinksters, and as has been widely observed in queer and transgender communities, the language of spirituality carries a positive valence among many members of these communities, with religion being relegated to the negative realm of the dogmatic. Yet many studies of the "spiritual but not religious" phenomenon focus intently on the cognitive, and often on practice only as adjunct to the cognitive. What does it mean to be spiritual but not religious while being bound to a Saint Andrew's cross and flogged?

4. *Individualism*: We seem, at long last, to have moved at least partially beyond the misogyny and handwringing that attended earlier studies of individualism in general and of religious individualism as a whole; indeed, scholars like Meredith McGuire (e.g., 2008) have sharply reminded us to look beyond our contemporary noses to the fact that religious practice has long been regional, local, and individual. Yet what remains useful in studies of religious individualism may be the centrality of the self as the arbiter of truth in these contemporary discourses, and the neoliberal "pic 'n' mix" approach to religious consumption (cf. Gauthier et al. 2013) that seems to differ in important ways from the religious and cultural blending that takes place when those of different religions live together in relative equality, or the creative religious and cultural recombination that oppressed groups engage in when forced to take on a dominant group's practices.

5. *Marketing and consumption*: These combinative and appropriative practices derive both from broader spiritual practices in global North / global West cultures and from the influence in spiritual BDSM circles of the modern primitive movement. Zussman and Pierce, writing about queer and trans leather/BDSM spirituality in the context of the Bay Area, describe a ritual that clearly demonstrates the influence of both the modern primitive movement and neoliberal spiritual consumption: "The 'Piercing Wheel Ritual' appeared to be borrowed generously from the Lakota Sundance [*sic*] and was accompanied by Hindu chanting and Sufi trance dancing." They note, importantly, that "despite the ritual borrowings . . . there was no question that this was a

204 MELISSA M. WILCOX

serious religious event held by leather pagans attempting to create authentic, meaningful and effective ritual" (Zussman and Pierce 1998, 33). Working in the Bay Area a few years later, Weiss (2011) found such strong correlations between neoliberal capitalism and BDSM in the mainstream, pansexual communities she studied that she made those correlations the central focus of her book on the topic.

6. *Affect*: Although affect studies are still not widely engaged within the study of religion (and affect studies generally return the neglect in full), nonetheless many of us have noted at least in passing the presence of affect in discourses on spirituality. If affect is relevant to spirituality studies as a whole, how much more relevant must it be to the study of BDSM spirituality, whose practitioners explicitly set out in search of affect as their route to the sacred? This is one of the innovative aspects of these movements that takes us into the realm of new insights they might have to offer.

New Insights

In calling these "new insights," I do not mean to imply that they are unique to BDSM spiritualities. Instead, they are new angles on spirituality studies that may well resonate far beyond the world of BDSM.

1. *Post-rational:* Fennell's concept of the post-rational is an intriguing one, potentially relevant to a much broader discussion of contemporary societies but also not necessarily a particularly new phenomenon. In the nineteenth century, for example, the intersections of Enlightenment thought with the burgeoning Romantic movement led many highly educated elites to the conclusion that the next frontier in the scientific revolution was the empirical study of the world beyond the human. Far from being a credulous approach to a limited comprehension of science, as they are frequently made out to be, movements like Spiritualism, Mesmerism, Christian Science, Theosophy, and even chiropractics and osteopathy were rooted in sophisticated theories that posited the existence of the world beyond the human as an empirically verifiable and scientifically approachable natural phenomenon (Albanese 2007). Today's post-rational skeptics may not be cut from quite the same cloth as yesteryear's metaphysicals, but their resistance

ECSTASIES   205

to mystical explanations and their powerful draw to the scientific even when it fails to fully explain their experiences may be yet another manifestation of the "new metaphysicals" explored by Bender (2010).

2. *Embodied and affective empiricism*: Moreover, as Fennell notes, the twin foci of affect and scientific empiricism come together in spiritual BDSM through a reliance on embodied and affective empiricism. Although not interviewed in the context of BDSM, a member of the Sisters of Perpetual Indulgence who took part in my most recent book project described exactly this sort of perhaps-post-rational affective empiricism. Sister Unity Divine is a convert to a Hindu-based new religious movement; in describing the process of her conversion, she explained that, "*My* faith is like, 'Well, I poked at it with a stick, I kicked the tires, I stepped on it, and it bit me, so I know it's there, so as much as I know is there—the part with the teeth—I believe in that' " (Wilcox 2018, 181). Fennell's (2018) interlocutors who struggle to reconcile a belief that there is nothing beyond the human with their own experiences at the heights of BDSM practice seem to be caught between exactly these two poles: the belief in a rationally explainable, empirically verifiable world and an affective, embodied approach to empiricism that presents them with discomfiting empirical counterevidence to their beliefs.

3. *Practice and embodiment*: This empiricism, importantly, centers not on belief but on practice—and not on just any practice, but on resolutely *embodied* practice. The experiences that have left Fennell's interlocutors reluctantly convinced of the reality of phenomena they find irrational and scientifically unverifiable are profoundly embodied experiences; to whatever extent they may be cognitive, they are so in the context of an embodied mind and cannot be brought into being in the absence of intense bodily experiences. Yet spirituality studies has been insistently disembodied. Embodied beings practicing spirituality do so with their bodies, regardless of the extent to which they are cognizant of doing so. Therefore, practitioners who intentionally make use of their bodies to produce spiritual experiences and states of being may offer us particular insights into the embodiment of spirituality.

4. *Embodied sexuality*: In much of the study of religion, sexuality is also treated as a cognitive concept, and not a property—much less an activity—of bodies. Evangelical Christians may bring God into the bedroom by placing a Bible on the bedside table (see DeRogatis 2014), but although God might be watching, we scholars look away. As with

206 MELISSA M. WILCOX

embodied empiricism and embodied practice, spiritual BDSM refuses to let us look away from the sex that is taking place. The definition of sex, of course, is always in the eye of the beholder; in many BDSM communities, the connections between BDSM practices and sex are contested—are nipple clamps sexual? What about rows of clothespins aligned on an arm or down a torso? Yet, in a larger milieu in which at least some practices are fairly explicitly sexual, it seems fair to argue that spiritual BDSM makes it quite difficult for scholars to ignore the embodied practices of sex in the practice of spirituality. That we should be asking about such practices in other venues as well seems more obvious once we attend closely to their dynamics in kink, BDSM, and leather communities.

5. *Play*: BDSM practitioners regularly use the language of theater and recreation to describe their activities. Urination is termed "water sports"; a preplanned encounter (as many are) is called a "scene," and BDSM activities in general are referred to as "play." This offers three insights for spirituality studies. For one, as I have argued in the context of the Sisters of Perpetual Indulgence (Wilcox 2018), we often take religion and spirituality far too seriously. This is not to argue that we should disregard them, but rather that we should stop giving especial credence to religion in its most solemn forms. Second, the focus on play in BDSM spirituality should encourage spirituality studies to engage more with ritual studies, and to wonder about the relevance to our work of the concept of performativity (Butler 1990). Finally, the concept of grown-up (not specifically "adult," as in "sexual") play seems particularly present in contemporary US cultures, and perhaps in global North / global West cultures more broadly. Be it the ludic activism identified as central to queer communities by Benjamin Shepard and Sara Warner, performative street activism more broadly (Bread and Puppet Theater comes to mind for many people, along with lesser-known groups like CIRCA, the Clandestine Insurgent Radical Clown Army), adult enactment of childhood institutions like playgrounds and day care, cosplay, or any number of other grassroots cultural phenomena, play seems to hold a powerful contemporary importance that has not, to my knowledge, been adequately explored. How do grown-up play and spirituality come together? BDSM spiritualities may offer a route into thinking about this larger phenomenon.

ECSTASIES 207

Conclusion: Queering and Kinking Spirituality Studies

Regardless of the religious form it takes—Buddhist, Neopagan, Christian, Jewish, "post-rational," spiritual but not religious, or some combination of the above—spiritual BDSM has a wealth of insights to offer to scholars of spirituality studies. Because it developed and is practiced within communities that have already often been forced to engage in careful and incisive critique of traditional religious practices and doctrines, queer and trans leather/BDSM spirituality may offer especially important new perspectives on spirituality. Queering the study of religion or spirituality can no longer be—indeed, should never have been—limited to a homonormative "add queers and stir" approach. Instead, attending to truly queer forms of religion, whether or not they are practiced by people who themselves use the identity term "queer," can help us to better understand the full contours of religion in contemporary societies, including both the marked overlaps between leather spirituality, BDSM, sacred kink, and more quotidian forms of spirituality and the notable divergences between the three that offer us fresh insights and far greater depth in our research. New analytical directions await both sexuality studies scholars and scholars of religion who venture into this particular intersection of our fields.

Note

1. It may be worth stressing here that Zussman and Pierce are not making a reductionist argument that all of these religions are simply forms of BDSM; rather, they are attempting to challenge widespread cultural resistance to the idea that leathersex and religion could have anything in common.

References

Albanese, Catherine L. 2007. *A Republic of Mind and Spirit: A Cultural History of American Metaphysical Religion.* New Haven: Yale University Press.

Beckmann, Andrea. 2007. "The 'Bodily Practices' of Consensual 'SM,' Spirituality and 'Transcendence.'" Pp. 98–118 in *Safe, Sane and Consensual: Contemporary Perspectives on Sadomasochism,* edited by D. Langdridge and M. Barker. New York: Macmillan.

Bellah, Robert N., Richard Madsen, William M. Sullivan, Ann Swidler, and Steven M. Tipton. 1985. *Habits of the Heart: Individualism and Commitment in American Life.* Berkeley: University of California Press.

Bender, Courtney. 2010. *The New Metaphysicals: Spirituality and the American Religious Imagination*. Chicago: University of Chicago Press.

Butler, Judith. 1990. *Gender Trouble: Feminism and the Subversion of Identity*. New York: Routledge.

Carrette, Jeremy R. 2005. "Intense Exchange: Sadomasochism, Theology, and the Politics of Late Capitalism." *Theology and Sexuality* 11(2): 11–30.

Carrette, Jeremy R., and Richard King. 2005. *Selling Spirituality: The Silent Takeover of Religion*. New York: Routledge.

Cragun, Ryan T., and J. E. Sumerau. 2017. "No One Expects a Transgender Jew: Religious, Sexual and Gendered Intersections in the Evaluation of Religious and Nonreligious Others." *Secularism and Nonreligion* 6(1): 1–16.

Crasnow, S. J. 2017. "On Transition: Normative Judaism and Trans Innovation." *Journal of Contemporary Religion* 32(3): 403–15.

Crasnow, S. J. 2019. "SVARA's Queer Talmud Camp." Paper presented at the University of California, Riverside, Conference "Queer and Transgender Studies in Religion," February 24, Riverside, CA.

Cruz, Ariane. 2016. *The Color of Kink: Black Women, BDSM, and Pornography*. New York: New York University Press.

DeRogatis, Amy. 2014. *Saving Sex: Sexuality and Salvation in American Evangelicalism*. New York: Oxford University Press.

Duggan, Lisa. 2002. "The New Homonormativity: The Sexual Politics of Neoliberalism." Pp. 175–94 in *Materializing Democracy: Toward a Revitalized Cultural Politics*, edited by Russ Castronovo and Dana D. Nelson. Durham, NC: Duke University Press.

Fennell, Julie. 2018. "'It's All about the Journey': Skepticism and Spirituality in the BDSM Subculture." *Sociological Forum* 33(4): 1045–67.

Gauthier, François, Tuomas Martikainen, and Linda Woodhead. 2013. "Introduction: Religion in Market Society." Pp. 1–17 in *Religion in the Neoliberal Age: Political Economy and Modes of Governance*, edited by Tuomas Martikainen and François Gauthier. Burlington, VT: Ashgate.

Gerber, Lynne. 2014. "'Queerish' Celibacy: Reorienting Marriage in the Ex-Gay Movement." Pp. 25–36 in *Queer Christianities: Lived Religion in Transgressive Forms*, edited by Kathleen T. Talvacchia. New York: New York University Press.

Gleig, Ann. 2019. *American Dharma: Buddhism beyond Modernity*. New Haven: Yale University Press.

Haberman, Hardy. 1999. "Soul of a Second Skin: Spirituality, Christianity and the Leather Community." *Whosoever*, July 1. https://whosoever.org/soul-of-a-second-skin-spirituality-christianity-and-the-leather-community/.

Kaldera, Raven, and Bridgett Harrington. 2006. *Dark Moon Rising: Pagan BDSM and the Ordeal Path*. Hubbardston, MA: Asphodel Press.

Karuna, Vajra. 1998. "Zen in Black Leather." Pp. 247–52 in *Queer Dharma: Voices of Gay Buddhists*, vol. 1, edited by Winston Leyland. San Francisco: Gay Sunshine Press.

Lindemann, Danielle. 2011. "BDSM as Therapy?" *Sexualities* 14(2): 151–72.

Lucia, Amanda J. 2020. *White Utopias: The Religious Exoticism of Transformational Festivals*. Oakland: University of California Press.

McGuire, Meredith B. 2008. *Lived Religion: Faith and Practice in Everyday Life*. New York: Oxford University Press.

Newmahr, Staci. 2011. *Playing on the Edge: Sadomasochism, Risk, and Intimacy*. Bloomington: Indiana University Press.

ECSTASIES   209

Peterson, Thomas V. 2005. "Gay Men's Spiritual Experience in the Leather Community." Pp. 337–50 in *Gay Religion*, edited by Scott Thumma and Edward R. Gray. Walnut Creek, CA: AltaMira Press.

Pritchard, Elizabeth, and Kate M. Ott, eds. 2018. "Transing and Queering Feminist Studies and Practices of Religion." Special issue, *Journal of Feminist Studies in Religion* 34(1).

Puar, Jasbir. 2007. *Terrorist Assemblages: Homonationalism in Queer Times*. Durham: Duke University Press.

Ramberg, Lucinda. 2014. *Given to the Goddess: South Indian Devadasis and the Sexuality of Religion*. Durham, NC: Duke University Press.

Shore-Goss, Robert E. 2018. "Queer Incarnational Bedfellows: Christian Theology and BDSM Practices." Pp. 222–44 in *Contemporary Theological Approaches to Sexuality*, edited by Lisa Isherwood and Dirk von der Horst. New York: Routledge.

Strassfeld, Max, and Robyn Henderson-Espinoza, eds. 2019. "Trans*/Religion." Special issue, *TSQ: Transgender Studies Quarterly* 6(3): 283–96.

Sumerau, J. E., Lain A. B. Mathers, and Ryan T. Cragun. 2018. "Incorporating Transgender Experience toward a More Inclusive Gender Lens in the Sociology of Religion." *Sociology of Religion* 79(4): 425–48.

Tinsley, Omise'eke Natasha. 2018. *Ezili's Mirrors: Imagining Black Queer Genders*. Durham, NC: Duke University Press.

Valentine, David. 2007. *Imagining Transgender: An Ethnography of a Category*. Durham, NC: Duke University Press.

Weiss, Margot. 2011. *Techniques of Pleasure: BDSM and the Circuits of Sexuality*. Durham, NC: Duke University Press.

Wilcox, Melissa M. 2002. "When Sheila's a Lesbian: Religious Individualism among Lesbian, Gay, Bisexual, and Transgender Christians." *Sociology of Religion* 63(4): 497–513.

Wilcox, Melissa M. 2018. *Queer Nuns: Religion, Activism, and Serious Parody*. New York: New York University Press.

Wilcox, Melissa M. 2019. "Geographies of Ecstasy: Fakir Musafar and the Modern Primitive Movement." Paper presented at the Conference "Taking Exception: Queering American Religion III," March 28–30, Mexico City, Mexico.

Zussman, Mira, with Anne Pierce. 1998. "Shifts of Consciousness in Consensual S/M, Bondage, and Fetish Play." *Anthropology of Consciousness* 9(4): 15–38.

10

Textures of Spirituality in Rural Malawi

Ann Swidler

What does religion in rural Malawi have to teach us about spirituality more generally? On the one hand, "spirituality" is no mystery in Malawi.[1] Virtually everyone is religious. According to the CIA's World Factbook, only 1 percent of Malawians claim no religion.[2] Churches and mosques are vibrant local social institutions; religious language, religious experience, and religious interpretations of the world are intertwined with people's ordinary perceptions and explanations of everyday life. On the other hand, in a place where religion does so much, it can be hard to find the distinctively spiritual aspect of religious experience. If we manage to tease out that spiritual element, however, we may gain clues that are useful for understanding spirituality even in places where spirituality seems in some ways to have escaped, or subsumed, religion.

Let me first say what I mean by "spirituality." In a relatively simple, straightforward sense, spirituality is experience of the self as connected directly to the sacred, either through inner experience (as in meditation or sudden awareness of the unity of the universe) or through an experience of transcendence, whether in the midst of collective ritual, in a vision, or when praying to, or as Malawians would understand it, talking with, God. This sort of spirituality helps sustain or nourish the inner self, especially when it is drained or besieged by life's assaults. In a place like Malawi, spirituality is not separate from the complex of belief, ritual practice, and institutional organization (or, if we follow Geertz [1966]: ethos, worldview, and sacred symbol) that constitutes religion. Nonetheless, in the midst of all the practical, communal, and personal support religious leaders and religious communities provide—from healing and miracles to ethical guidance to material help—we find moments in which people seek the spiritual sustenance religion can provide.

In Malawi religious meanings are omnipresent, but what we would call the "spiritual" can be nearly drowned out. Personal names for both men and women invoke faith—Gift (Mpatso), Blessings (Madalitso), Mercy (Chifundo), Praise (Yamikan), Grace (Chisomo). A shop may be called Blessings Bakery or Trust

Ann Swidler, *Textures of Spirituality in Rural Malawi* In: *Situating Spirituality*. Edited by: Brian Steensland, Jaime Kucinskas, and Anna Sun, Oxford University Press. © Oxford University Press 2022.
DOI: 10.1093/oso/9780197565001.003.0011

in God Grocery or one of hundreds of other inventively faithful names. And many people, though not all, explain almost everything that happens to them as due to divine intervention, from getting a job, to surviving an illness, to being blessed with a child. Religious understandings and explanations are not limited to religious topics or settings, as in this beautiful exchange from one of the conversational journals that rural ethnographers collected in Malawi (Watkins and Swidler 2009, 176–77), recounting a discussion of AIDS among men attending a funeral who spent a long, rainy night outdoors under a shelter, while indoors people sang hymns to comfort the bereaved. Death, they suggested, "indeed started long time ago and as a punishment for what our forefather Adam did in the Eden and his wife Eve after [she was] bewitched by the Satan." They then considered the question of why death came into the world.

> Then the man who slept together with me said that God was clever enough. He knew all about this. He knew that if people could not be dying then the end result will be that the population will be [so] high that no place can be found uncovered, as we see nowadays that there [are] a lot of places uncovered like the national parks and game reserves. But had it been there were no deaths where could all people born everyday be living?

The men then turned to AIDS as a punishment from God:

> He went on saying that AIDS is killing a lot of people nowadays. Another one said indeed it's true, but of AIDS indeed God has really shown himself that He is above all. He is even more above the great scientists who are proudly boasting and claiming that they are wise enough to eradicate any kind of disease, but not in case of AIDS. AIDS came from God and He created it to minimize the population.

Despite this religious grounding of basic understandings of life, however, it is often hard to find something specifically spiritual in the religious lives of poor villagers in rural Malawi.

The Context

This chapter draws on more than 350 interviews conducted in June and July 2018 and 2019 in Malawi's rural south, almost entirely by local interviewers, recorded, and then translated and transcribed into English.[3] About 120 interviews were conducted in 2018 in a single large village with a mixed Christian and Muslim population, 46 interviews were with members of town-based mosques or Pentecostal churches, and almost 200 interviews were conducted in 2019 in a number of different villages.

Even by African standards, Malawi is very poor (ranking somewhere between the fifth and eighth poorest countries in the world in Purchasing Power Parity GDP) and very rural, with about 80 percent of the population engaged in subsistence agriculture. It nonetheless has a rich, dynamic religious ecology, with local churches and mosques competing and, as we shall see, an insistence that people choose, and can change, their congregation, denomination, or faith tradition.

As in many African societies, life in Malawi is always uncertain (see Johnson-Hanks 2006; Swidler and Watkins 2017): harvests fail, parents die young (so children leave school, sometimes in the early primary grades), disease threatens, small businesses fold, one's mud-brick house collapses in the rains. In such a situation, relations of generalized reciprocity, but also of unequal interdependence (Swidler and Watkins 2007), are crucial for survival. People depend on neighbors, relatives, various "well-wishers," and, often, their religious congregations for help, both spiritual and material.

It is against this background that we can understand both the central role that religion plays in most Malawians' lives and the ways spirituality gets squeezed out by the many practical demands, and the practical benefits, of religious life.

What Religion in Malawi Demands and What It Offers

In Malawi religious congregations, religiosity (one's reputation and sense of self as religiously committed), religious language (one's interpretation of events and their causes), religious obligations (especially ritual ones, and especially for Muslims), and religious experiences (prayer, song, hearing God speak, fighting with the Devil, experiencing miracles) are pervasive. Religion provides community and entertainment (music, singing, sermons, etc. [see Manglos 2011, 341–45]), heals illness, provides some material support in times of difficulty, saves one from bad behavior, resolves family disputes, fights witchcraft, and, as I've argued elsewhere (Swidler 2013), sustains hope in the face of endless setbacks.

TEXTURES OF SPIRITUALITY IN RURAL MALAWI 213

Practical Religion: Choosing and Changing

When Malawians are asked why they choose—or why they stick with—a particular "church" (used to describe a particular congregation, whether church or mosque, but also a denomination or a faith tradition), they most frequently answer in practical terms. The most common reason, by far, to join a new religion is marriage, since it is traditional that a wife follows her husband's faith. A twenty-two-year-old Muslim villager (#115), a husband and father who farms to feed his family and also works as a builder, said that his family members are all Muslim like himself, but "I have my half-sister . . . who was married by a Christian." Asked how the parents reacted, he said, "The parents were not bitter because their daughter had made a choice, and they respected her choice because, as you know, a woman should follow the religion of her husband; and whatever happens, we all worship the same God." This theme, that all worship the same God, is echoed almost everywhere, despite occasional negative comments about other denominations' ritual practices. A forty-year-old Muslim (#48), father of four, a better-educated villager with a business in town, put it differently, saying that he believes "everyone is born a Muslim." He then explained, "The reason is when you ask anyone who is the owner of your life, he will say that my life belongs to God; even if you ask anyone who brings the rains to the earth, he will tell you that it is God who brings the rains to the earth, which means we all belong to one religion. The only difference is what we are doing."

Healing and Miracles

The second major reason people change faith traditions, however, involves healing and the power of prayer. The concern with healing primarily encourages conversions from Islam to Christianity, especially to Pentecostal and African Independent churches. A woman I met said, quite simply, that she had been born and raised Muslim, but "when I fell sick, my fellow Muslims did not come to pray for me, while the Christians did. So I joined the Christians [Assemblies of God]." Another interviewee, the thirty-five-year-old sheikh at a local mosque (#9), averred that "through my faith in Islam I have seen that this is the only true religion which will take me to heaven." But when asked whether he knew anyone who had changed religions, he told of a man who "changed because he was sick, and people used to go to see him.

Both Muslims and Christians were going to see him, and I think his interest was that he was not satisfied with the way the Muslims were going to see him compared to Christians, so he decided to leave Islam and join Christianity." In the sheikh's view, it was not that the Christians offered more material help: "What he said was that when people came to pray for him, it was the Christians who would offer a prayer that was convincing to him, and he decided to join Christianity. So it might happen that when we were offering prayers, our prayers were done in Arabic, so it might have happened that the guardians and the relatives did not understand what we were praying."

Healing is not the only evidence of God's power. This Pentecostal Christian (#19), a member of Living Waters, described how his faith was rewarded:

> I have a testimony. When I got married we stayed for three years without having a child, and people were saying a lot of things, and they also suggested many things, like giving us fertility herbs, but we trusted in the Lord, and God showed us his greatest [gift] by giving us a child, whom we have now. God opened the womb of my wife.

A young woman, twenty-one (#144), remarried after her first husband left her with two children, joined her new husband's Church of Christ congregation. She reported:

> I was sick, and I was not eating anything because when I ate anything, I was vomiting. When I cough[ed], I was coughing bloody sputum. . . . The church sent a message that they will come to see me after the church service, but I told them that they should not come, but I will force myself to go to church. So I went to church though I was feeling sick. And when they had prayed for me at the church, I sweated profusely, and after that I came home and asked the people to prepare porridge for me to drink. That was how I got healed. I immediately knew that God loves me, and I prayed to thank him for healing me.

Our interviews contain many such examples of people who were healed after a pastor (or sometimes a group from the congregation) prayed for them. Some congregations also have rituals for driving out demons. But these ritual actions are less available to Muslim clerics (imams or sheikhs), since they violate Islam's rigorous theology of God's absolute transcendence (see Trinitapoli and Weinreb 2012, 172–73).

Ethical Regulation

Another crucial benefit of religious membership is what I call "ethical regulation." This involves both the direct advice, and sometimes supervision and chastisement, religious congregations offer, but also the internal discipline that can lead one to avoid dangers like alcohol or casual sex, or can improve one's behavior as a son or daughter, husband or wife.

A Christian husband and father (#19) reported that, through his Living Waters church,

> in my spiritual life, I have changed because in the past when I was praying, I would understand really the will of God, but now when I pray I can understand what God wants me to do, and I am always willing to [do] what God requires me to do. While in my physical life, or I can say in my family, we have had quarrels, as I said, when I received Jesus we were coming from a family dispute, but since that time our family has been living in peace and love.

In other cases, it is the specific ritual practices or the rules of conduct that matter. A young woman, twenty-one (#144), remarried after her first husband, a Muslim, left her with two children, explained why she then left Islam: "That religion it is not good; it has bad laws." "Like what?" the interviewer asked. "It allows a man to have polygamy. And also during the funeral they do not allow women to go to the graveyard." When she tried once to follow a body to the graveyard, "I was embarrassed and I knew that I was a member of a religion which I did not understand its teachings and principles. I therefore decided to leave the religion because I was not able to follow the laws of the religion." Her current church, the Church of Christ, does "not allow polygamy; members of the church do not drink beer nor have other extramarital sexual partners. All these are not allowed in the church." Her church also counsels couples who have trouble in their marriages. She offered an example of a husband who "was having another woman, and when his wife asked him about the issue, he said that he will divorce her and marry another woman." The pastor "invited the couple to come to church, and the pastor asked all the people who are married in the church to remain behind so that they can sort out the issue, and when they had discussed the issue with the couple and the church, the man [accepted] to change his decision" and continue the marriage. "They all accepted their mistakes and asked for forgiveness. The pastor helped them, and the family reconciled such that the man is now staying at [his wife's] home."

Peace in the Household, Harmony in the Village

Religion not only teaches personal ethics, it can help people regulate the emotions that can disturb their homes and their communities. The young husband and father (#19) who had converted to Living Waters with his wife explained, "My life changed at that time [when he received Jesus as his Lord and Saviour]. We had quarreled with my wife, and there came a pastor.... As he was preaching, I was touched, and at the end of the service I approached him and told him that I need Jesus in my life, and at that he helped. And together with my wife we received Jesus as our personal savior; that is what happened." He said that now he and his wife no longer quarrel, and also that "before I received Jesus, I was someone who was rude to my parents. I was not kind to people, and the moment I received Jesus it all changed."

Not only the household, but the village benefits from religion, which is believed to produce greater harmony among villagers. Chief Chirombo,[4] chief of the village where we did most of our 2018 interviews, said that he would not allow anyone to live in his village who was not a member of a church or mosque. He didn't care which because all worship the same God. When, at his chief's court, a rebellious teenager was accused of stealing, the chief, himself Muslim, decided that the Muslim children needed discipline. He decreed that all the Muslim children would now have to go to madrassa in the late afternoons. The next time I visited, I saw the town crier going down the road, calling out for the children to go to the mosque, and children ran toward the mosque, the girls with their headscarves flying behind them. I asked about the Christian children, and the chief insisted that they were better behaved because they "read with their parents." I assumed that he meant reading the Bible together after church.

A pastor, who had founded his own Pentecostal church, explained that he had begun with only eight members and now had over three hundred. When I asked how he had decided where to build his church, he said that he had persuaded a chief whose village had no church to let him preach there and to give him land for a church. The chief supported his effort at evangelizing because the chief believed that if the pastor established a church and preached to the people, there would be greater harmony in the village. Since village harmony is a prized achievement and one of chiefs' primary responsibilities (Wroe 2015, 54–60), the chief was persuaded.

Welfare Services

In addition to maintaining social peace, congregations are one of the many important redistributive or mutual insurance institutions that operate in these very poor communities. During famine periods, or the hunger season that comes almost every year before the new harvest is ready, neighbors will share with neighbors (Verheijen 2013). And many villagers count on their relatives when they need help, as the young mother quoted above (#144) explained: "It is my father-in-law who supports us when we do not have food because he is the one who is working. He works as a watchman." Nonetheless, most respondents also reported that their churches or mosques collect money for those who are ill or to give to the poor. For Muslims, donations of food are linked to the ritual calendar, such as providing food for the poor to break the Ramadan fast. Some Muslims also give *sadaq*, personal donations of alms for the poor. The rural poor also very occasionally benefit from donations of zakat, the obligatory donation of a percentage of one's wealth, although these villagers describe themselves as too poor to incur the obligation to make such donations themselves.

Identity/Individuality/Rationality

For some believers, doctrine really does matter, especially, for those Christians who are literate, fidelity to the Bible. This is less of an issue for Muslims, almost none of whom, even if they can chant the Koran in Arabic, can read and understand it. Indeed, Muslim respondents primarily emphasize the extent, and the correctness, of their ritual observance, rather than the quality of religious services, preaching, or even ethical guidance.

A Christian villager (#51), now forty-one, who farms and does odd jobs to support his family, began school only as a teenager because he was too poor to attend as a child, eventually completing Standard 6 (sixth grade). He joined the Seventh Day Adventist church after he learned to read:

218   ANN SWIDLER

> At first I was a member of Abraham Church [an African Independent denomination]. That was the time when I had not started school and after that there came the Jehovah's Witness.... But when I started school and was able to read, I discovered that what the Jehovah's Witnesses were telling me and what the Bible was saying was different.
>
> I chose Seventh Day because of their message which they preached to me was very convincing, and whatever they were preaching to me was in agreement with what was written in the Bible, so I knew that this church preaches the truth about the Bible. So I made a decision to join the church.

This man's religious quest was, however, not only intellectual. He spoke with feeling about what we might see as the moral or spiritual side of his experience:

> The word of God changes me from being a sinner to becoming someone closer to God; so whenever I am listening to the word of God, it changes me to become someone who is to do what pleases God. So whatever message I hear, either from the radio or at the church, it changes me.

His religion also provided ethical regulation, allowing him to overcome a violent, angry streak:

> I was someone who was asking my parents, "What should I do so that I should enjoy [life] in this world. Should I be drinking or practice witchcraft and fighting?" And my parents told me that when you will be drinking you can die easily, and when you will be practicing witchcraft, you will find other people more advanced than you and you will also die. And when it came to fighting . . . they said you can only fight when you have been provoked. So I used to pick up fights with people. . . . Later on, when I was home, there was a child making fun of me . . . so I went and slapped him and his cheeks were swollen and he could not eat for a week. I regretted my action, and from that time I made a decision that I should never engage myself in fighting people. I did that decision because I was now a Christian.

In at least one case, deep engagement with the Bible led to an independent quest for religious understanding, a quest that separated its bearer from any church. A poor villager, thirty-two (#39), married with three children, also farms, though he runs out of food during the hunger season and has to do piecework to feed his family. With a Form 2 (tenth grade) education, he is well educated by the standards of his village. He said, "I used to belong to a religion, but now I stopped." Born and raised in the village, he had been a member of the Anglican Church, and then one day, at a friend's house, he encountered a Bible, in English, with

> verses some in black and some in red. So I had an interest, so I borrowed the Bible so that I could read it at home and also I should go and ask my pastor about this Bible, which was strange to me. So I went and asked my pastor. His answers were not convincing; he was just telling me, "You are not reading this Bible with the help of the Holy Spirit. All what you are asking it is the work of Satan, who is telling you to be asking these questions. You are not supposed to ask these questions." And when I went home, I was disappointed, and I decided that I should stop going to church. And if God will allow it, I may start again later.

Far from reconciling himself with the church, however, his quest has led him further and further away. During the interview, he quoted one Bible verse after another, explaining the many ways in which the Christian churches do not really follow what the Bible says, leading him to think that perhaps the Muslims are closer to the Bible's commandments:

> Okay, we believe in one God. It is in Mark 12, verse 29, which says clearly about the oneness of God, while at Anglican, we do not have one God. We have some other forms in the Godhead. We were being taught the Godhead has three Persons; that was what we called Trinity. And also we have the form of worship which is Matthew 26, verse 39; and we also have the issue of offering, which is in Hebrews 10, verse 24.
>
> Muslims, when they are praying, they do wash their face and feet before praying. And I was interested when I found that we have verses which support these acts, like Leviticus 19, verse 27; Leviticus 21, verse 5; Jeremiah 29, verse 5; 1 Chronicle 19, verse 5; Exodus 30, verse 17; Exodus 30, verse 40; John 13, verse 4. And when I was reading these verses, it was giving an interest that the Bible is still talking to us.

This man's unusual intellectual quest might be seen as an assertion of individuality, an insistence on his own powers of understanding, in a situation where there are few avenues for such personal self-affirmation.

220 ANN SWIDLER

The Bible, of course, can have what we might regard as spiritual, as well as intellectual, uses. Another woman, forty-two years old with six children (#50), a member of the main missionary denomination, the Church of Central Africa Presbyterian, explained why she writes down the Bible verses that the pastor uses in his sermon: "The verses help me when I need encouragement when I am stressed or worried."

Glimmers of Spirituality

As we have seen, there are hints of spirituality even in the midst of the pressing concerns that otherwise undergird Malawians' religious life. But even these seem to differ between Muslims and Christians. For Muslims, closeness to God, or perhaps a sense of being personally right in the world, rests primarily on proper fulfillment of ritual obligations. The thirty-five-year-old sheikh quoted above (#9), when asked whether he feels "closer to God" during Ramadan, said,

> Yes, we do feel that we are closer to God because you can have people who have never slept in the mosque coming to sleep in the mosque during the month of Ramadan and also you may have people who have not been able to read the Quran reading it and even some people who have not been coming to mosque for prayers coming to mosque for prayers all the five times.

For many Muslims we interviewed, the key questions of religious life are those of ritual adherence, especially whether one has lived—both ritually and ethically—so as to go to heaven. But the practical, ethical, and spiritual benefits of religion are interconnected. The forty-year-old father of four quoted above (#48) described the benefits of prayer this way:

> Yes, they [prayers] do help me so much because for someone who prays to God it means he is closer to God. And in so doing you do not get sick or have other problems as people normally have. And when this happens, do not think that it is being done because you are clever. But God sends angels to come and protect you. God has special angels who are assigned to protect the people who give their time to pray to Him.

TEXTURES OF SPIRITUALITY IN RURAL MALAWI   221

Christians reported a more emotionally charged experience of spirituality. The young divorced and remarried mother of two (#144) quoted above hopes to join the Mavano, the woman's group at her Church of Christ congregation because "The songs which the women sing are captivating to the soul." Music and song are in turn tied to the experience of fellowship and communion.

This experience of spiritual power and the emotions that go with it seems especially important for members of Pentecostal churches, perhaps not surprising since, to quote Wikipedia (2019), Pentecostalism "is distinguished by belief in the baptism in the Holy Spirit that enables a Christian to live a Spirit-filled and empowered life. This empowerment includes the use of spiritual gifts such as speaking in tongues and divine healing." On the other hand, healing and prophecy, two of the central spiritual gifts recognized by Pentecostalism, have been critical to the success of Christianity in Africa more generally, and especially to the creation of the African Independent churches, which broke with the missionary denominations over precisely these issues (Horton 1971; Peel 1968).

A married father with one child (#19), a member of Living Waters Church, explained that although he switched to Living Waters from the Evangelical Presbyterian Church when he married so that he and his wife, who had been a member of the Ethiopian Church, could "as one body . . . all belong to one church," he found that

> sometimes things happen for a purpose because all along, though I have been going to churches, . . . I would not feel that I was praying. There was emptiness in my spirit. But when I decided to join Living Waters, there was a great change and even before we joined we had heard of the things that happen at Living Waters as a Pentecostal church and also that they do pray for the sick and things happen. And we decided to join the church and now we have been enlightened and we understand the Christian principles and character.

Where, then, is the room for—or the need for—"spirituality" in this picture? I would argue that spirituality is pervasive in these accounts, but mostly just below the surface. It is there largely because villagers, especially the poorest, endure so much tragedy, disappointment, and uncertainty that they constantly need both inner resources and external help. They depend on help from their kin, from neighbors, from their church or sometimes their

222 ANN SWIDLER

mosque, and from any other patrons who might help them. As the forty-two-year-old woman (#50) quoted above, whose husband left her with six children, said of her situation:

I: Do you ask for assistance from your relatives when you have a problem?
R: Yes, when I do not have food, I cannot let my children sleep on an empty stomach. I will go and ask for food from my relatives.
I: What about your neighbours?
R: I can also go and ask for assistance. My neighbours are the closest I have and my problems [are] theirs, and also their problems are also mine.
I: What about members of your church?
R: Yes, I do ask them to assist when I have a problem.

This woman is the same one who said that the Bible verses her pastor discusses in church "help me when I need encouragement when I am stressed or worried." What we would recognize as spirituality here is the shoring up of the inner resources of the self in times of trouble, as well as the increased vitality people report during religious services, or the sense of strength, hope, and fortitude with which they face illness and adversity. All these, whether experienced by an individual seeking comfort alone through prayer or Bible reading, or by individuals immersed in and transported by collective ritual, reach into the self and "up" toward some transcendent source of power in ways we would recognize as spiritual. But, as I have said, for poor Malawian villagers, these experiences are usually so embedded in organized religious life, and organized religious life has so many practical constraints and benefits, that specifically spiritual experiences seem only to leak out around the edges of religious life.

Spirituality and Religion in Malawi and the Modern West

Many Malawians experience closeness to God, gratitude for God as Creator, and dependence on divine power as ever-present realities. Asked why they pray, both Christians and Muslims tend to answer, as this Jehovah's Witness, did, "to praise God for what he is doing to me" (#266) or, as another woman, Anglican (#264), put it, laughing, "Who do you think wakes me up in the morning? It is God." A Muslim woman (#263) summed up: "I go for prayers because I did not create myself; it is God who made me and put me in this

TEXTURES OF SPIRITUALITY IN RURAL MALAWI   223

world, so I have an obligation to thank Him for creating me." For Malawians, however, there is little distinction between the institutional and practical benefits of religion and its spiritual aspects. Gratitude for "life" means both gratitude for physical life, for waking in the morning, and for the life of the spirit. As the distinguished anthropologist Harri Englund (2003, 89) has noted of the Assemblies of God in Malawi, "The perception [is] that spiritual progress of a church and its members is inseparable from enhanced material security."

If we take this perception further and reflect on the potential value of a distinction between *religion* and *spirituality*, we should start with Durkheim's ([1912] 1995) insistence that at the heart of religious experience lies the exaltation, the collective effervescence, the sense of dependence on a power greater than the self that collective ritual provides. This is the power that awes and overwhelms the individual, but also animates the individual self, enlivening, or indeed creating, its vitality, its sense of life, as Durkheim suggests in his discussion of the modern idea that the soul comes from God. For Durkheim, it is only this animating, collectively derived force that gives religion the authority to establish worldviews and to provide answers to the ultimate questions of existence, which Geertz ([1966] 1973) and especially Weber ([1922] 1968) saw as the hallmarks of religion. As Geertz argues, it is this authoritative power that allows institutional religions to require the very ritual practices that in turn reproduce sacred power.

So how does the "spiritual" come to be experienced as distinct from "religion," or at least to seem an analytically separable component of religious experience, so that in the modern West, at least, we see spirituality as independent of religion? The spiritual, I would submit, always requires an appeal to some source of energy, strength, vitality that can animate the self. But, as Durkheim anticipated, as the individual becomes the focus of the collective consciousness in modern societies, people can experience the source of the sacred as coming from within the self as well. If the "spiritual" is whatever animates or reinvigorates the self with energy that seems to come from a transcendent place, then it draws on the collective sense of the sacred, even if that sacredness is sought in the inner depths of the self. While people differ individually in their capacity for and their need for spiritual experience, it is when the profane, ordinary self is under unusual pressures that the longing for spiritual experience intensifies.

I have argued elsewhere (Swidler 2013) that Malawians who are upwardly mobile also seek spiritual support from religious experience, because they

224 ANN SWIDLER

need enormous inner strength to resist the sometimes unrelenting demands of kin and neighbors, to remain confident that their faith provides them immunity from witchcraft, and to overcome the crushing defeats and obstacles that threaten their aspirations for the future. For these Malawians, usually more urban and somewhat better educated, religious experience has a strong spiritual component. It offers inner confidence while it expands their sense of the powers of the self, by allying that self with what believers see as the source of ultimate power.

The relevance to our contemporary experiences of spirituality is, I think, that one part of the contemporary longing for spiritual experience is the desire to strengthen (or replenish) the inner resources of the self, in a social world that requires people to mobilize so much of themselves so intensively (see Swidler 2001). For us, it is not the terrible uncertainties of capricious death, unpredictable harvests, inexplicable malice, corruption, and injustice that tax our inner resources. More usually it is the draining sense that we have too much to do, too many demands on our time, and that we have to construct our own life paths without much guidance, that makes us seek time to renew the inner sense of self and seek connection with larger life forces that may or may not take religious form. But it is this need for inner strength and for renewal of our inner vitality that links contemporary spiritual quests to those of even the most spiritually depleted, or encumbered, Malawian villager.

There is an argument to be made that, as with personal intimacy, it is only when the pragmatic constraints that make people inescapably interdependent have loosened that such modern luxuries as pure intimacy, truly voluntary friendship, or pure spirituality can blossom (Fischer et al. 1977). But if spirituality fully flowers only when religion becomes less pragmatically central to everyday life, we see nonetheless how social conditions that place difficult demands on the self also lead people to search for sources of spiritual comfort and strength.

Notes

1. I would like to thank Laura Goy and Jacob Kendall, who accompanied me to Malawi and generously shared their data. We are indebted to superb interviewers: Violet Boilo, Shamilah Chimbalanga, Precious Cliff Diwa, Shamzay Mandala, and Janepher Matenje, and to Jonathan Kandodo for translating and transcribing the interviews and

TEXTURES OF SPIRITUALITY IN RURAL MALAWI   225

providing invaluable insights. Thanks to Abdallah Chilungo for managing the research and for his friendship and advice. I also thank the many Malawians who generously shared their time and their insights. Dick Madsen, Bill Sullivan, and Steve Tipton, as well as the editors and contributors to this volume, gave valuable feedback on the chapter.

2. The CIA World Factbook (2019) estimates Protestant 27.2 percent (includes Church of Central Africa Presbyterian 17.7 percent, Seventh Day Adventist / Baptist 6.9 percent, Anglican 2.6 percent), Catholic 18.4 percent, other Christian 41 percent (including African Independent churches and a variety of Pentecostal and evangelical churches, many unaffiliated), Muslim 12.1 percent, other 0.3 percent, none 1 percent. Muslims are concentrated in the Southern Region, where we did our interviews.

3. Jonathan Kandodo translated the interviews directly from audiotapes as he transcribed them. He is highly skilled, and his work remarkably accurate. Nonetheless, the vocabulary in which he translates local speech is probably influenced by his own broad knowledge. I doubt, for example, that the poor villager who described coughing up blood during an illness used a word as technical as the English word "sputum." I have not corrected the transcripts, except for obvious typos and to add commas or periods as appropriate.

4. A pseudonym for both chief and village. A chief takes the name of his (or occasionally her) village and is considered the "owner" of the village.

References

CIA World Factbook. 2019. "Africa: Malawi." Retrieved March 29, 2019. https://www.cia.gov/library/publications/the-world-factbook/geos/mi.html.

Durkheim, Émile. [1912] 1995. *The Elementary Forms of Religious Life*. Translated by K. Fields. New York: Free Press.

Englund, Harri. 2003. "Christian Independency and Global Membership: Pentecostal Extraversions in Malawi." *Journal of Religion in Africa* 33(1): 83–111.

Fischer, Claude S., Robert Max Jackson, C. Ann Stueve, Kathleen Gerson, and Lynne McCallister Jones, with Mark Baldassare. 1977. *Networks and Places: Social Relations in the Urban Setting*. New York: Free Press.

Geertz, Clifford. [1966] 1973. "Religion as a Cultural System." Pp. 87–125 in *The Interpretation of Cultures*. New York: Basic Books.

Horton, Robin. 1971. "African Conversion." *Africa: Journal of the International African Institute* 41(2): 85–108.

Johnson-Hanks, Jennifer. 2006. *Uncertain Honor: Modern Motherhood in an African Crisis*. Chicago: University of Chicago Press.

Manglos, Nicolette. 2011. "Brokerage in the Sacred Sphere: Religious Leaders as Community Problem-Solvers in Rural Malawi." *Sociological Forum* 26(2): 334–55.

Peel, J. D. Y. 1968. *Aladura: A Religious Movement among the Yoruba*. London: Oxford University Press.

Swidler, Ann. 2001. "Saving the Self: Endowment versus Depletion in American Institutions." Pp. 41–55 in *Meaning and Modernity: Religion, Polity, Self*, edited by R. Madsen, W. Sullivan, A. Swidler, and S. M. Tipton. Berkeley: University of California Press.

Swidler, Ann. 2013. "African Affirmations: The Religion of Modernity and the Modernity of Religion." *International Sociology* 28(6): 680–96.

Swidler, Ann, and Susan Cotts Watkins. 2007. "Ties of Dependence: AIDS and Transactional Sex in Rural Malawi." *Studies in Family Planning* 38(3): 147–62.

Swidler, Ann, and Susan Cotts Watkins. 2017. *A Fraught Embrace: The Romance and Reality of AIDS Altruism in Africa*. Princeton, NJ: Princeton University Press.

Trinitapoli, Jenny, and Alexander Weinreb. 2012. *Religion and AIDS in Africa*. New York: Oxford University Press.

Verheijen, Janneke. 2013. *Balancing Men, Morals, and Money: Women's Agency between HIV and Security in a Malawi Village*. Leiden: African Studies Centre.

Watkins, Susan Cotts, and Ann Swidler. 2009. "Hearsay Ethnography: Conversational Journals as a Method for Studying Culture in Action." *Poetics* 37(2): 162–84.

Weber, Max. [1922] 1968. *Economy and Society: An Outline of Interpretive Sociology*. 2 vols. Edited by Guenther Roth and Claus Wittich. New York: Bedminster Press.

Wikipedia. 2019. "Pentecostalism." Retrieved March 29, 2019. https://en.wikipedia.org/wiki/Pentecostalism.

Wroe, Daniel Gareth. 2015. "'What Can I Do?' Living with Doubt and Uncertainty in the Central Region of Malawi." PhD dissertation, School of International Development, University of East Anglia.

11

Gifts, Weapons, and Values

The Language of Spirituality in Twenty-First-Century Central America

Robert Brenneman

Discourses of spirituality, though shaped by global conversations and international conferences, are nevertheless informed by and arise out of local, national, and regional contexts. What we mean when we use terms like "spiritual" or "spirituality" can't help but be guided by the discursive interactions we have had as persons located in a particular time and place. For this reason, a book aimed at deepening our social scientific understanding of spirituality must be informed by more than mere reflections on the language of spirituality in twenty-first-century North America. For a more nuanced and multifaceted understanding of spirituality, we need to look beyond the economically prosperous nations of the North Atlantic. There is much to learn from examining the diverse approaches to these notions of spirituality in the "global South." What follows is an attempt by a North American sociologist to describe how Central Americans use terms like "spiritual" and "spirituality"—or, to be more precise, *lo espiritual y la espiritualidad*. Having traveled widely throughout Central America and lived, worked, and researched there at various times during my adult life, I am aware of both my outsider status and my privilege as a resident gringo. Recognizing the dangers inherent in purporting to speak on behalf of my neighbors from the global South, I must point out from the outset that what I have attempted to gather here are the thoughts of a participant-observer—a religious person (I would never attempt to call myself "spiritual") who has spent a great deal of time in religious communities—Protestant and Catholic as well as the occasional Mayan ceremony—throughout Central America but especially in Guatemala. Although I am a theorist of sorts, I will not be attempting to develop or define a theory of spirituality in Central America. Instead, my goal is to provide descriptive data in qualitative form aimed at exposing some of the most

Robert Brenneman, *Gifts, Weapons, and Values* In: *Situating Spirituality.* Edited by: Brian Steensland, Jaime Kucinskas, and Anna Sun, Oxford University Press. © Oxford University Press 2022. DOI: 10.1093/oso/9780197565001.003.0012

common contexts in which the *language* of spirituality is exercised in Central America. If there is an argument in this chapter, it might be summarized in the claim that the concept of spirituality is shaped by both religious tradition and social location. My data are drawn from a variety of sources related to my own research, especially my research on religious gang ministries late in the first decade of this century as well as my experiences participating with religious communities in Guatemala at various times during the past twenty-five years.

Gangs as a *Spiritual* Problem

My point of entry into this discussion is my book *Homies and Hermanos: God and Gangs in Central America* (Brenneman 2012). I begin here for two reasons. First, and most obviously, these are the data that are most available to me. But second, and more importantly, I believe that my discussions with gang ministers and converted ex-gang members provide a window into the way Central Americans actually *use* concepts relating to spirituality, and use them as tools—that is, as cultural means for getting things done. Or to borrow and expropriate Swidler's apt phrase, my interviews provide glimpses of "spirituality in action" (Swidler 1986) rather than mere reflections by academics.[1]

A good place to begin might be a discussion I had shortly after entering the field in December 2006. I was conducting initial interviews with persons involved in gang ministries and during an interview with Fr. Julio Coyoy, a priest who had helped to start a gang prevention center in a very tough neighborhood of Guatemala City, I asked him if any of the local Pentecostal churches had contributed to efforts to reduce gang violence. Father Coyoy was immediately dismissive, calling the Pentecostal churches nothing more than "spiritualists" who offered "song therapy" instead of a gospel that was "real and practical." His use of the term "spiritualists" was intended as a criticism of the airy escapism of Pentecostal faith in the difficult neighborhoods of urban Guatemala. It reminded me that many Central Americans, especially those with considerable formal training, religious or not, consider Pentecostal spirituality a complete and utter waste of time.

But the deeper I delved into my research, the more I came to believe that many Pentecostal churches were providing a lot more than "song therapy"—although vibrant, emotion-laden music was and is one of their trademarks—and in more than a few cases, Central American Pentecostal churches were offering a great deal of support that was "real and practical" even if that support tended to be focused on individual reform projects and was always soaked in the language of faith. And surely enough, the many Pentecostal pastors and lay leaders I would come to meet over the course of my research on pathways out of the gangs used the language of spirituality frequently in order to describe their own efforts at gang ministry. Below I describe some of the ways those Pentecostals used terms like "spirit" and "spiritual."

Pastor Luis Arreola, who headed up a ministry called "Gangs for Christ," provides a good example. During a lengthy interview, Pastor Arreola, a former gang member himself, described to me his own motives for ministering to gangs: "I don't wait for the government to help me. I hope that the church solves [the gang problem]. Because I think the church is the one with the solution to this problem—the church as a church—because this is a spiritual problem" (Brenneman 2012, 189). What he meant by defining the gang as "a spiritual problem" was not clear to me at first. Did he mean that it was a problem that could only be worked out in the heavens, by supernatural powerbrokers? I don't think so. Further analysis of that interview and many others with Pentecostal pastors, leaders, and converted former gang members led me to conclude that by defining the problem as a *spiritual* problem, Pastor Arreola and others like him were attempting to make gang violence the *church's* problem. They were attempting to bring the problem of gangs and gang violence into the realm of action for the Pentecostal church.[2] After all, it is the deep conviction of Pentecostal ministers like Arreola that their faith, training, and practice have given them spiritual tools, often called "gifts," that make them especially well prepared to deal with problems of a spiritual nature. Abner, a former gang member who had become an ordained Pentecostal minister after converting to Pentecostal Christianity, criticized Protestant congregations that don't provide ministry to gang members and other troubled youth. He agreed with Arreola that the church was the best-equipped organization to deal with gangs: "I think that the church is the first one with a solution in its hands... [T]he church should be the first one on the scene, changing the situation" (Brenneman 2012, 199).

But if spiritual problems look like gang violence, what do spiritual solutions look like? That is, what is unique about the capacities of Pentecostal gang ministers who understand themselves to be well equipped to deal with spiritual problems of this sort? Although this chapter uses the *discourse* of

230 ROBERT BRENNEMAN

spirituality as a sort of "paper trail" in order to understand how spirituality is experienced by Central Americans, it is clear that spirituality, for pastors and gang members alike, is a term that implies *action*. The Central American gang ministry coordinators and ministers I spoke with, as well as the ex-gang members who spoke so highly of them, tended to be highly involved in the religious, social, and economic lives of the youth and young adults they mentored. The ministers, most of whom were clergy but a few of whom worked as lay leaders, provided advice, accompaniment, and accountability via regular check-ins with ex-gang members and their family members. Additionally, it was not uncommon for a minister to have provided a letter of recommendation or a verbal reference for a former gang member struggling to find legal employment. This service was especially important due to the fact that few Central American employers are willing to trust a former gang member, least of all one who has not completed high school, as is the case for most youth who have joined a gang. In a few cases, a reference from a minister was the only means of buying enough trust to be given a chance in a formal job. The pastors in these contexts were only willing to provide such a reference after having spent considerable time—typically months—mentoring the former gang member during his process of extrication from gang life and the *vida loca* (crazy lifestyle). In effect, these pastors and gang ministry coordinators played a role not unlike that of a social worker or counselor in United States or Canada. They acted much like an advocate, albeit one with considerably more freedom to ask pointed personal questions and inquire with family, neighbors, and friends as to the habits and lifestyle of the young men who had come to them for help.[3]

Thus, to some extent, the solution offered by Central American Pentecostal pastors—the minority who are involved in gang ministry—to the "spiritual problem" of gang violence is not entirely different from that provided by a social worker or counselor. But neither is it the same. Central American pastors see their ministry as going beyond accompaniment, job support, and counseling. It consists of something more holistic than that provided by a social services agency. Pastor José Fernandez, whose church and gang ministries are situated in Chamelecón, Honduras, one of the hemisphere's most violent neighborhoods, described his ministry of "gang restoration" this way:

> We believe that the work that this title communicates has to do with returning to the person their quality of life—the quality of life in all senses, beginning with the spiritual but then continuing to include giving back

their emotional quality [of life] and their material quality. So in this sense we use the word "restoration" because we believe it's the most complete, right? It's the one that best sums up what we're trying to do for them.

Pastor José's point here and elsewhere seemed to be that purely social programs aimed at providing counseling or a job are not capable of addressing the full range of needs facing a gang member wanting to extricate himself from an all-consuming organization and lifestyle like the gang. He argued that any rehabilitation program that does not include a "spiritual" component cannot fully address the needs of a reforming gang member. That is, the work of the church includes but *must go beyond* social work to include a "spiritual" dimension. But what does that dimension look like and what might it address? On one level, addressing the "spiritual dimension" for these pastors involved helping them to effectively address *las cosas de Dios* ("things of God"), including seeking forgiveness from God, prayer, and Bible reading. Counseling these youth and young adults about such matters resembles what might be called the work of a "spiritual adviser" in a North American context. Yet there were hints in my research that seemed to imply that Central American Pentecostals are not describing an entirely "otherworldly" phenomenon when they use terms like "the spirit" and "spiritual." In a sermon I witnessed at a special open-air revival service created with the help of former gang members and aimed at current and aspiring gang youth, Carlos Tecerro, a Honduran ex-con turned Pentecostal minister preached a lively message geared toward persuading local youth to opt for the church instead of the gangs. He described the hypermacho gang disposition as a "spirit of inferiority" and a "sickness inside the soul" (Brenneman 2012, 203). Similarly, Camilo,[4] a converted former gang leader who often preached at revival meetings at the invitation of Pentecostal churches, used the language of "spirit" to describe the emotional struggles that led him to join the gang in the first place. Soon after being disowned by the couple he had thought were his parents, Camilo left his home and fled to the city, where he eventually found friends in the Eighteenth Street gang: "I started getting involved with them and started feeling hatred for my [former] family, and *a spirit of vengeance* entered me, of avenging my parents for all that had happened" (Field note 22).

In the language of "spirit" used by Camilo no less than by Pastor Carlos, we can catch a glimpse of the nature of the "spiritual problem" described by Pastor Luis. Here the word "spirit" seems to aim at an emotional or

232 ROBERT BRENNEMAN

psychological state. Psychologists in the North might describe Camilo's "spirit of vengeance" as "anger issues" and would probably use the term "low self-esteem" to describe what Pastor Carlos names a "spirit of inferiority" and perhaps treat either or both with cognitive behavior therapy or even prescription drugs. Sociologists like me are more apt to employ terms like "chronic shame" (Brenneman 2012) or "gang habitus" (Brenneman 2014). In any case, what is clear is that Central American Pentecostals employ the language of spirituality and the spirit to describe a range of emotional states that we in the Academic North would prefer to describe in sociological and psychological terms. Thus, part of the "spiritual work" of Pentecostal gang ministry has been aimed at helping former gang members exercise increased agency over such troublesome emotional states, by the power of the Holy Spirit, and in the context of a supportive congregation and a motivated pastor. After all, as several former gang members confessed to me, no matter how badly one wishes to make a clean break with the gang, it can be difficult to keep a steady job if you cannot manage your anger in the workplace.

From Gifts to Weapons

The vast majority of my interviews with converted former gang members in Central America took place in the context of small, neighborhood Pentecostal congregations. In these congregations, spirituality tends to be connected to a tradition of ecstatic worship in which the "gifts of the spirit" such as speaking in tongues, prophetic utterances, and faith healing equip the gathered community with a special set of tools for dealing with trauma, sickness, and grinding poverty (Chesnut 2003; Garrard-Burnett 1998, 2000). The *practice and experience* of these "gifts," in the context of the gathered community, help members and visitors to *feel* a sense of belonging, wholeness, and empowerment (Cox 2006; Miller and Yamamori 2007; Williams 1997). But a more recent wave of Central American Protestants worship in large congregations and megachurches typically described under the rubric of "neo-Pentecostalism." In these congregations, the earliest of which were founded or began to innovate in the 1970s, the term "spirituality" has been less closely tied to ecstatic manifestations of the "gifts" of the spirit. Instead, beginning in the 1980s and gathering steam in the 1990s, "spiritual warfare" became the predominant paradigm for spirituality. Undoubtedly tied to theological conversations with their counterparts in the North, this

GIFTS, WEAPONS, AND VALUES   233

language found especially fertile ground in Central America, and by the 1990s, Guatemala in particular was a net exporter of the language of spiritual warfare. The well-known megachurch pastor Harold Caballeros extended the metaphor of warfare to include the practice of "spiritual cartography," whereby believers could break down a whole city into territories that had been "won" for Christ and those that had yet to be conquered and remained in the control of Satan (Caballeros 2001). I would certainly not be the first to note that the "weaponization" of the language of spirituality coincided disconcertingly with the militarization of Central American society and the subsequent growth of private and public security following the signing of the peace accords in both Guatemala and El Salvador (Hurtado et al. 2007; O'Neill 2009; Smith and Higueros 2005). But what is even more interesting is the way a handful of Guatemalan neo-Pentecostal leaders were ready to adapt the language of spiritual conflict to crime-fighting and gang violence. In a 2007 televised broadcast of his own weekly call-in Christian talk show, former chief of police Erwin Sperisen admitted that his own forces had engaged in social cleansing—the extrajudicial killing of suspected gang members and other crime suspects without any trial or due process—and employed the language of religious duty as a justification for his own involvement in such "cleansing" (Hurtado et al. 2007; Smith 2007). Sperisen, who now serves time in a prison in Switzerland, having been convicted by a Swiss court of involvement in multiple murders of prisoners, was referring to an article in the *New York Times* that accused high-ranking evangelical government officials of engaging in social cleansing as part of their "holy work" to reduce crime (McKinley 2007). Sperisen not only admitted that the reports were true and the work justified, but went further to say that Caballeros, the megachurch minister and promoter of spiritual warfare, had provided the inspiration and motivation for his work as chief of police.

In short, whereas Guatemala's Pentecostal community tended to view the gangs as plagued by spirits of "inferiority" and "vengeance," some leaders in the neo-Pentecostal community seemed ready to identify their "spiritual enemies" as the very youth themselves.

Mayan Spirituality

Gangs and gang violence weren't the only spiritual "enemies" with whom the neo-Pentecostal spiritual warriors sought to do battle. An older, broader enemy involved indigenous Mayan practices and beliefs. Indeed, Pastor Caballeros's very successful book on the topic of spiritual warfare was inspired, according to the author himself, when the congregation's new building project had to be stopped due to the discovery of a pre-Columbian monument associated with Quetzalcoatl, the feathered, flying serpent of ancient Meso-American religious tradition. Although the congregation could not proceed with the building planned for that site, Caballeros considered the finding a fortuitous one in that it inspired him to conceptualize the city as made up of a vast spiritual terrain, some of which remained under the control of Satan, insofar as it had been dedicated to Quetzalcoatl and not yet won over for Christ. Since many Guatemalans continue to engage in a variety of traditional Mayan beliefs and practices, Caballeros and other leaders felt sure that such practices helped keep portions of the city and the nation in the firm grip of spiritual "principalities" intent on keeping the nation from prospering.

Thus we come to a third means of usage for the term "spirituality" in Central America, this one most common by far in Guatemala—that of Mayan spirituality. One way to think of Mayan spirituality is as an "adapted continuation" of pre-Columbian Mayan rites and beliefs (Bell 2012) and for neo-Pentecostals like Caballeros, it is precisely this connection to a pre-Christian past that makes the tradition both backward and idolatrous. Practices of Mayan spirituality include formal rites performed by Mayan priests and priestesses aimed at celebrating the creative forces at work in the cosmos, as well as everyday practices by the laity intended to maintain equilibrium between opposing cosmic forces. Although the term *la espiritualidad maya* is frequently used to describe these indigenous practices and beliefs passed down largely through male and female elders, this term probably owes as much to the influence of Western academics and other admirers as it does to the practicants themselves. Among Guatemalans who openly engage in these practices—often alongside or in synergistic combination with Catholic devotion—terms such as *la cosmovisión maya* ("the Mayan worldview") or *el costumbre* ("custom") are probably more common. Still, "spirituality" remains a common means of referring to these Mayan practices, especially by nonindigenous Guatemalans, including Catholics and Protestants alike.

This chapter is not the place to engage in an in-depth examination of Mayan spirituality and the many forms it takes today. That discussion is well deserving of the continued attention it receives by Mexican, Guatemalan, and North American anthropologists. Nevertheless, I bring it up here simply as a reminder of the ways in which the terms "spiritual" and "spirituality" are employed in the Central America of today and as a reminder that the Christian traditions do not have a monopoly on the marketplace of spiritual language and spiritual goods.

Spiritual "Values"

There is at least one more cluster of meanings associated with the term "spirituality" in Central America today. Catholics and nonreligious Central Americans with exposure to higher education can be heard using the terms "spiritual" and "spirituality" to refer to broadly ecumenical, often ambiguous forms of quasi-religious or meditative practice and values. For example, at a Jesuit-sponsored community youth center called Fe y Alegría (Faith and Joy) in San Salvador, I interviewed a director of gang outreach named Santos, who explained to me what was meant by the advertised "spiritual component" of his program: "We call it values formation," he said. "It's not catechistic or anything. It's more general than that. When we pray we want everyone to be able to participate, no matter what their religion is. We also try to help them to develop a personal project. . . . We try to help them think about what they want to do in life and how to get there" (Brenneman 2012, 222). Santos reported that prayers at the youth center typically take the form of a "moment of silence," and this approach allows the center to provide programming that is attractive to Catholics and non-Catholics alike.

During my time living and working in Central America, I have frequently encountered the term "spirituality" used in this way—as a means of attempting to acknowledge sacred realities without stepping on the toes of persons present who might not share the same practices or orientations as the leader, or simply as a form of addressing the "sacredness" of human lives, while also keeping the door wide open to those whose "names" for the sacred do not invoke Catholic or Christian tradition. For example, at a recent academic conference celebrating the canonization of Saint Romero, a well-known Catholic nun spoke enthusiastically about her organization's Center for Art and Peace, created out of the renovated shell of a former Catholic church building. Instead of a cross or any Christian symbols, the new center has a large sculpture of a tree trunk with its exposed roots, symbolizing the interconnectedness of all peoples and the importance of cultivating one's roots. Spirituality was a constant theme in the lively, well-received presentation about a postwar community that is seeking to create ecumenical space for expression.

I suspect that this expansive, somewhat ambiguous usage of the term "spirituality" comes closest to the way the term typically gets used by those of us in the academic community in the North, so it should come as no surprise that in Central America, this set of meanings is most commonly invoked by Catholic leaders, who typically possess a great deal more formal education than leaders in the Protestant, mostly Pentecostal community.

Discussion

By now it should be readily apparent that the language of "spirituality" is enormously pliable in Central America. Neo-Pentecostal megachurch pastors can mean something quite different than when a typical Catholic priest, or even, for that matter, a Pentecostal minister of a neighborhood church, uses it. Although it's always dangerous to try to categorize social life, the more so when we're talking about culture, I have exposed above at least four common clusters of meaning for the term "spiritual" in Central America:

1. A psycho-emotional state such as low self-esteem or violent anger
2. A supernatural entity or reality with bearing on personal and social life
3. A set of beliefs and practices rooted in pre-Columbian traditions, aimed at maintaining cosmic equilibrium
4. A catch-all term for corporate and individual rites open to all, regardless of religious commitment

A first observation is that, upon further examination, these four "clusters" of meanings are less exclusive than they appear. For example, while it would be easy to conclude that the first two meanings are in opposition to each other, since the first one (a psycho-emotional state) names something "real," while the second refers to something "supernatural," reality is considerably more complicated. In digging back through my field notes in preparation for writing this chapter, I discovered a comment that I hadn't noticed earlier. Pastor Henry, a young, up-and-coming pastor of a large congregation about an hour south of Guatemala City—one that was loosely affiliated with a megachurch in the capital—described to me some of the difficulties he had

GIFTS, WEAPONS, AND VALUES   237

faced a couple of years earlier when trying to mediate between two warring gangs in his hometown of Palín:

> Never in our history had we seen anything like this—[the two gangs] hated each other's guts, hated each other to death. They couldn't stand the sight of each other and were killing each other off. And there's something that— something from the outside, I don't know if it's spiritual or it's natural—but something puts it in their midst, and I would talk to them and tell them, "Look, if we keep up this hatred, what it's going to bring is nothing but hatred." In five years a vast amount of persons, tremendous, tremendous amount of persons [were killed] in the crossfire. (Field note 24)

Pastor Henry's description of "something from the outside"—something that is either "spiritual *or* natural"—offers a clue to suggest that what Guatemalan Pentecostals and neo-Pentecostals may be doing when they attach the term "spiritual" or "spirit" to aspects of personal and social life is, quite simply, attempting to "name" that which resists easy explanation, and in doing so, to make it graspable. After all, what do you do when you observe teens from your hometown—young men and boys who grew up down the street from one another—suddenly becoming "possessed" of a lethal hatred that has them competing for larger and larger weapons, and then scouring the streets for their neighbor-enemies so that they can kill them? Such a phenomenon must have seemed entirely outside their experience of social relations. Neighbors killing neighbors? And in the absence of a war? Utterly demonic.

Perhaps my beloved discipline of sociology could have "saved the day" by providing a toolkit of theoretical concepts that could have given Pastor Henry some cognitive purchase on what was going on. Sociologists like me could have apprised him of terms like Eli Anderson's "code of the street" (Anderson 1999), Thomas Scheff's "shame-rage spiral" (Scheff 2004), or Randall Collins's "tunnel of violence" (Collins 2007) in order to furnish him with conceptual purchase on the seeming senselessness of the violence afflicting these youth. But would a knowledge of such terms have enhanced Pastor Henry's ability to broker a truce between the warring gang factions? And would they have done so in a way that was *more effective* than simply considering such rage to be demonic? The answer to such a question, in the view of this author, escapes easy explanation and begs for far more investigation and embedded ethnography than could be provided by my research.

What is perhaps most interesting here is the fact that "spiritual" realities and "spiritual practices" appear to provide Pentecostal and neo-Pentecostal ministers with a means of describing *and addressing* complex and complicated social realities. That Pentecostal as well as neo-Pentecostal and even Catholic ecumenical spiritualities have been pressed into the service of gang violence reduction should come as no surprise given the frustrating intractability of Central American youth violence. Nor should we conclude for a moment that such language and such practices are useless or without impact in the face of "real" social and economic structures. Our own terms as sociologists—tunnels, codes, and spirals, no less than networks, structures, and toolkits—are themselves metaphors for helping us wrap our minds around similarly complicated realities. And like the language of spirituality, sociological terms are more or less useful depending on the degree to which sociologists can get buy-in from nonexperts. Do Introduction to Sociology students come to truly *believe* in the existence "social structures," and does such belief enable effective action toward reforming or eliminating unjust structures?

A second observation from observing Central American references to spirituality might be that in addition to religious tradition, *social location* plays an important role in the way Central Americans conceptualize the spiritual. For Pentecostals, most of whom occupy social space at the economic and racial margins of society, spiritual *gifts* guide life inside and immediately surrounding the community of faith itself. Such gifts benefit the gathered believers and anyone else who wishes to venture inside for a lively evening of catharsis and healing. For neo-Pentecostals, many of whom occupy the urban middle- and lower-middle-class rungs, spiritual *weapons* provide a language for discussing not only difficult matters of personal struggle such as addiction, but also complex political realities at the national level. After all, many members of these congregations have achieved enough social status to allow them to aspire to more than mere survival. Meanwhile, Mayan spirituality, with its ancient calendar-based set of personalities and forces, provides everyday Guatemalans, many of whom live outside the city, not only with a connection to their cultural heritage, but a means of entreating the forces of nature to cooperate for a good harvest and safe, healthy children. Ecumenical Catholics, whose positions of leadership require them to work with people from a variety of faith backgrounds, use the term as a way of eliding religious quarrels.

It is worth noting that Central America is not alone in its elastic use of terms surrounding spirituality. One can witness a variety in meanings attached to the language of spirituality here in the North, as evidenced by Nancy Ammerman's (2013) identification of four "packages" of meanings attached to spirituality in the United States. And yet the wide-ranging diversity of meanings, from a mood or psychological state to a means of identifying causes of social problems, to an indigenous practice, to a set of practices resembling "mindful" meditation, seems to suggest that the vast gulfs separating Central Americans by culture and socioeconomic status have engendered separate vocabularies of spirituality that exist simultaneously but largely in isolation from each other. Ironically, although one might expect conflict or miscommunication to result from such a diversity of meanings, it is my strong, but unprovable, impression that the employment of these clusters of meaning leads to fewer misunderstandings than one might imagine. After all, usage depends largely on social location in addition to religious tradition. Thus Central America's intense social stratification and the continuing distance between Catholics and Protestants mean that users and audience typically share a similar understanding of the meanings of what is "spiritual."

Conclusion

If one thing is clear from the foregoing discussion, it is that the variation in meanings of the term "spirituality" in Central America is vast and probably expanding. If academics hope to use the term as an etic, not just an emic, signifier, there is plenty of conceptual work yet to be done. One piece of evidence to support this claim is the fact that, while "spiritual" is a term used favorably by nearly every swath of Central American society, "religion" still has its proponents and detractors. For most Central American Protestants, and in particular for Pentecostals and neo-Pentecostals, the term "religion" is something that should be applied only to Catholicism. Most Pentecostals would say that what they practice is most definitely *not* a "religion." After all, religion, for the dyed-in-the-wool *hermano* (Pentecostal brother in the faith), is all of that mumbling, ritualistic, saint-infused claptrap that true believers leave behind when they exit Catholicism and convert to "true Christianity," that is Protestantism.

240   ROBERT BRENNEMAN

Of course, in this case we are dealing with an emic definition of religion, not religion as sociologists define it, which would certainly include Pentecostal Christianity. But the resistance to the word among Pentecostals should clue social scientists in to the fact that the term "religion" still has some sharp semantic edges, a fact that those who wish to see "spirituality" vindicated would do well to remember. At a minimum, if social scientists wish to use "spirituality" as an etic signifier—that is, as an analytically meaningful concept—we will need to be honest about its current ambiguity as well as its susceptibility to definition and utilization shaped by the religious tradition and social location of the person invoking the term. Or, to put it differently, if observing Central America's discourse of spirituality can make anything clear, it is that outside the North Atlantic no less than inside, the language of "spirituality" wears a diverse, multicolored cloak donned for a variety of occasions and contexts.

Notes

1. I don't wish to imply that spiritual practices and spiritual language are "nothing but" tools—that they are only a means to an end. Nothing could be further from the truth. But that they are employed as a means to get work done is, I think, a fact beyond dispute.
2. For the sake of simplicity, I will be using the term "Pentecostal" where others might use the term "evangelical" or "evangelical-Pentecostal." Although there are many Protestant congregations in Central America that are not formally or officially Pentecostal, and some of these congregations are involved in gang ministry, the vast majority of Christian non-Catholic congregations are either Pentecostal or have been largely Pentecostalized in their liturgy.
3. Of the sixty-three former gang members I spoke with, only four were women. Unlike the majority of men I spoke with, these women reported fewer struggles with addiction and employment, and none professed a religious conversion as part of their pathway out of the gang. The reasons for these differences have largely to do with separate pathways into and out of the gang for women versus men.
4. I have changed the name of former gang members in order to hide their identity.

References

Ammerman, Nancy. 2013. "Spiritual but Not Religious? Beyond Binary Choices in the Study of Religion." *Journal for the Scientific Study of Religion* 52(2): 258–78.

GIFTS, WEAPONS, AND VALUES   241

Anderson, Elijah. 1999. *Code of the Street: Decency, Violence and the Moral Life of the Inner City*. New York: W.W. Norton.

Bell, Elizabeth. 2012. "Sacred Inheritance: Cultural Resistance and Contemporary Kaqchikel-Maya Spiritual Practices." PhD dissertation, Ohio State University.

Brenneman, Robert. 2012. *Homies and Hermanos: God and the Gang in Central America*. New York: Oxford University Press.

Brenneman, Robert. 2014. "Wrestling the Devil: Conversion and Exit from the Central American Gangs." Special issue, *Latin American Research Review* 49: 112–28.

Caballeros, Harold. 2001. *Victorious Warfare: Discovering Your Rightful Place in God's Kingdom*. New York: Thomas Nelson.

Chesnut, R. Andrew. 2003. *Competitive Spirits: Latin America's New Religious Economy*. New York: Oxford University Press.

Collins, Randall. 2007. *Violence: A Micro-sociological Theory*. Princeton, NJ: Princeton University Press.

Cox, Harvey. 2006. "Spirits of Globalization: Pentecostalism and Experiential Spiritualities in a Global Era." Pp. 11–23 in *Spirits of Globalization: The Growth of Penteccostalism and Experiential Spritualities in a Global Age*, edited by S. J. Stalsett. London: SCM Press.

Garrard-Burnett, Virginia. 1998. *Protestantism in Guatemala: Living in the New Jerusalem*. Austin: University of Texas Press.

Garrard-Burnett, Virginia. 2000. "Introduction." Pp. xiii–xxiii in *On Earth as It Is in Heaven: Religion in Modern Latin America*, edited by V. Garrard-Burnett. Wilmington, DE: Scholarly Resources.

Hurtado, Paola, Claudia Méndez, and Mirja Valdés. 2007. "El último adios." *El periódico* (Guatemala City), April 15.

McKinley, James C., Jr. 2007. "In Guatemala, Officers' Killings Echo Dirty War." *New York Times*, March 5.

Miller, Donald, and Tetsunao Yamamori. 2007. *Global Pentecostalism: The New Face of Christian Social Engagement*. Berkeley: University of California Press.

O'Neill, Kevin. 2009. *City of God: Christian Citizenship in Postwar Guatemala*. Berkeley: University of California Press.

Scheff, Thomas. 2004. "Violent Males: A Theory of Their Emotional/Relational World." Pp. 117–39 in *Theory and Research on Human Emotions*, edited by J. Turner. Waltham: MA: Elsevier Press.

Smith, Dennis, and Mario Higueros. 2005. *Nuevas corrientes teologicos en Centroamerica y el Anabautismo biblico*. Guatemala City: Ediciones Semilla.

Smith, Dennis. 2007. "Communication, Politics, and Religious Fundamentalisms in Latin America." Paper presented at the Latin American Studies Association, September 2007, Montreal, Quebec.

Swidler, Ann. 1986. "Culture in Action: Symbols and Strategies." *American Sociological Review* 51(2): 273–86.

Williams, Philip J. 1997. "The Sound of Tambourines: The Politics of Pentecostal Growth in El Salvador." Pp. 179–200 in *Power, Politics and Pentecostals in Latin America*, edited by E. L. Cleary and H. W. Stewart-Gambino. Boulder, CO: Westview Press.

PART III
POWER

12

Everything Is Connected

Relocating Spiritual Power from Nature to Society

Stef Aupers

No less than a century after its formulation, Max Weber's analysis of the progressive "disenchantment of the world" continues to evoke intellectual debate (e.g., Asprem 2014; Campbell 2007; Partridge 2005). This process in Western society, Weber ([1919] 1948) famously argued in *Science as a Vocation*, "means that principally there are no mysterious incalculable forces that come into play, but rather that one can, in principle, master all things by calculation" (139). In ideal-typical contrast with premodern times and Eastern culture, modern society is governed by instrumental rationality—firmly institutionalized in capitalistic enterprises, modern science, technological devices, politics, and bureaucracy. The practice of magic is allegedly replaced by technology, since "Technical means and calculations perform the service" (Weber [1919] 1948, 139). In conformity with the Weberian thesis about "disenchantment," secularization theorists argue religion has now lost its social significance and explanatory value vis-à-vis the natural world (e.g., Berger 1967; Bruce 2002).

The argument of Max Weber on the disenchantment of the world and the thesis of secularization have been scrutinized since the 1960s by scholars working in the fields of anthropology, sociology, religious studies, and philosophy. *Theoretically*, it is often argued that secularization is problematic since religion is too much equated with Western (particularly North European), churched, Christian religion, whereas it should better be understood as a universal need for transcendence that manifests itself differently in time, space, and culture. Religion, Thomas Luckmann stated in *The Invisible Religion* (1967), has now become institutionally invisible. The decline of the Christian church in North European countries is not the end of religion as such, but made way for the rise of a pluriform "market of ultimate significance" where individuals construct

Stef Aupers, *Everything Is Connected* In: *Situating Spirituality*. Edited by: Brian Steensland, Jaime Kucinskas, and Anna Sun, Oxford University Press. © Oxford University Press 2022. DOI: 10.1093/oso/9780197565001.003.0013 strictly personal, eclectic packages of religious meaning. *Conceptually*, this noninstitutional and privatized type of religion has often been considered "post-traditional spirituality" (Heelas 1996), "alternative spirituality" (Sutcliffe and Bowman 2000), or "progressive spirituality" (Lynch 2007)—or a position empirically exemplified by individual people who are "not religious, but spiritual" (Ammerman 2013). In Europe, this type of spirituality is prominent in countries where Christian churches are in decline, that is, France, Sweden, and the Netherlands (Houtman and Aupers 2007)—a development that motivated the assumption that we are witnessing a "spiritual revolution" (Heelas and Woodhead 2005) or "Easternization of the West" (Campbell 2007). *Empirically* spiritual beliefs blossoming outside church and mosque are diverse and difficult to demarcate, which leads in turn to endless debates about conceptualization, operationalization, and measurement in the sociology of religion. The currents of contemporary spirituality range from New Age, esotericism, occultism, channeling, Gnosticism, paganism, and holistic healing to humanistic psychology, Eastern meditation practices, and mindfulness (e.g. Sutcliffe and Bowman 2000).

In this chapter, I develop a double argument in the debate on contemporary spirituality. On the one hand, the argument elaborates on the position scrutinizing the long-standing thesis of a progressive disenchantment and secularization in Western Europe. On the other hand, however, I develop a position that critiques and complements the academic work on post-Christian spirituality and re-enchantment. Much of the latter work focuses on alternative groups and individuals finding spiritual meaning in and through *the powers of nature* that have long been suppressed in modern, Western society. In this chapter I will instead theorize that spiritual forces are not necessarily located in the natural realm, but, perhaps increasingly, in modern society and its complex social systems. In critical dialogue with the ideas of the classics—that is, Weber, Marx, Mannheim—on modernity and religion, I will argue that undertheorized forms of modern re-enchantments should be understood as cultural responses to powerful, yet highly opaque systems that are beyond the control of contemporary citizens. Although various examples are used throughout this chapter, the main case used to build this argument is the growing phenomenon of conspiracy culture or, rather, the phenomenon of "conspirituality" (Ward and Voas 2011).

Modern Spirituality: A Double-Faced Phenomenon

Spiritual Power in/of Nature

In the conceptualization and empirical study of contemporary spirituality, the sacralization of *nature as a powerful, healing and meaningful force* is generally considered a key feature. From a historical perspective, it is telling in this respect that many contemporary beliefs, practices, and rituals in the spiritual milieu are rooted in the long-standing Western esoteric tradition (Hammer 2004; Hanegraaff 1996) and the romantic counterculture of the 1960s and 1970s (Campbell 2007; Heelas 1996). Modern institutions, typically capitalism, industrialism, and technology, are framed in these currents as the opposite of spirituality: they are destructive, alienating, and dehumanizing forces, whereas (human) nature is perceived as inherently spiritual, liberating, "healing," and meaningful. Indeed, notwithstanding their holistic premise that everything is connected, spiritual groups reproduce a strong ontological dualism between society and nature, connoting man-made reality versus natural reality; fake versus authentic; evil versus good; alienation versus salvation; and profane versus sacred. As Gordon Lynch (2007) argues in this respect: "Nature, within progressive spirituality, is typically seen as sacred, a site of divine life and activity," and this type of spiritual discourse "sees our only hope in a re-enchantment of the world, a renewed vision of the divine presence within the natural order that can generate new respect for nature and new ways of harmonious living within the natural order" (2007, 53–54). From New Age, holistic healing practices and paganism to people worshiping the "spirit of Gaia," spirituality is considered to reside immanently in the natural world. This sacralization of the forces of nature so typical of contemporary spirituality implies an imperative to return to nature on a political, social, and personal level. As to the latter—healing oneself by discovering the natural, authentic, or true self that is hidden underneath layers of socialization—is the lingua franca of what Heelas (1996) called "self-spirituality." In the spiritual milieu, he explains, modern people are essentially seen as "gods and goddesses in exile" (19) and "The great refrain, running throughout the New Age, is that we malfunction because we have been indoctrinated ... by mainstream society and culture" (18).

This then, is allegedly one of the binding doctrines of contemporary spirituality: the rediscovery of (human) nature that is imagined to be a mysterious, healing, and ultimately spiritual power (Aupers and Houtman 2006). From a sociological perspective, this celebration of (human) nature as an utterly spiritual power is often explained by progressive modernization as described by sociologists like Horkheimer and Adorno, Durkheim, or Weber. Empirical science, modern (culture) industries, the nation-state, bureaucracies, and technological artifacts have invaded the human lifeworld and, notwithstanding their contribution to efficiency and luxury, have contributed to a sense of "disenchantment," "anomie," and "alienation" (e.g., Heelas and Woodhead 2005). Such macrosociological, "etic" explanations converge with "emic" accounts of spokes(wo)men in the spiritual milieu. Already in his famous account of the US counterculture of the 1960s and 1970s, for instance, Theodore Roszak ([1968] 1995) pointed to the overpowering modern "technocracy"—an industrial society that "reaches the peak of its organizational integration" and, consequently, leaves "the citizen . . . confronted by bewildering bigness and complexity" (5, 7). Nature-oriented spirituality, from this perspective, is all too often constructed as the counter-part of modernity, as a multifaced ideology focused on the "rehabilitation of nature" (Campbell 2007) through a meaningful spiritual power outside modern institutions that, ultimately, seeks for a re-enchantment of the Western world.

Spiritual Power in/of Technology

In the academic debate on contemporary modern spirituality there is a blind spot with regard to another, complementary trend in the field of spirituality that remains empirically uncharted and undertheorized. Recent studies addressing the roots of spirituality in the counterculture of the 1960s and 1970s, for instance, argue that man-made products, science, and technology were *not* unambiguously considered as alienating in the milieu. In *From Satori to Silicon Valley* Theodore Roszak (2000) even revised his own interpretation: beside nature-celebrating "luddites," he argues, the counterculture featured many "technophiles"—hippies, hackers, and ICT gurus that projected the spiritual imagination on digital technology as a tool of salvation (e.g., Aupers et al. 2008; Rushkoff 1994). Key figures of the early Californian spiritual milieu, like Ken Kesey, Terrence McKenna, and Timothy Leary, fall within this category. The latter typically compared the personal computer to LSD (e.g., Dery 1996) and suggested in the 1990s that one can escape an "alienating" and "repressive" society by immersing oneself in the new otherworldly realm of cyberspace that

EVERYTHING IS CONNECTED 249

was opened up by complex computer networks: "Recite to yourself some of the traditional attributes of the word 'spiritual': mythic, magical, ethereal, incorporeal, intangible, non-material, disembodied, ideal, platonic. Is that not a definition of the electronic-digital? . . . These 'spiritual' realms, over [a] century imagined, may, perhaps, now be realized!" (Leary 1994, 81). Technology here is neither opposed to spirituality nor an irreligious power, as Max Weber would have it. From the "spiritual telegraph" in the nineteenth century (Davis 1999; Stolow 2008), to the PC in the 1970s (Dery 1996), and the World Wide Web in the 1990s (Aupers et al. 2008) to artificial intelligence in the 2000s (Geraci 2010)—technology has been an inspiration for the formation of spiritual communities and a veritable source of re-enchantment all along. Contemporary spiritual groups like Scientology, the Raelian movement, or "posthumanist" cults promising eternal life through the uploading of consciousness (Aupers and Houtman 2010) are not just considering technology a spiritual tool, but a source of re-enchantment in and of itself.

Based on my own fieldwork in Silicon Valley, I have demonstrated that influential ICT pioneers often frame artificial intelligence, virtual reality, viruses, algorithms, and our surrounding digital ecology in magical and animistic terms (Aupers 2002, 2009, 2010). Like nature, they are considered a mysterious, overpowering force that can be experienced as deeply spiritual. Exemplary are programmers referring to themselves as techno-pagans (e.g., Davis 1999; Dery 1996) arguing that "the force is great, and especially the programmers, laser jocks, scientists, and silicon architects can feel it. The technology has a spirit of its own, as valid as the spirit of any creature of the goddess" (in Aupers 2009, 163). And yet, whereas the opaque "spiritual power" of technology is often imagined to be a good, creative force, it can also, like nature, be considered a "dark" and "destructive" power. We can think in this respect to theories featuring the overpowering force of AI and robotics in the New Age of "spiritual machines" (Kurzweil 1999) and techno-apocalyptic and millennialist scenarios advocated by ICT gurus (Geraci 2010).

Modernist Theory Revisited

This shift of spiritual discourse from nature to our man-made technological environment opens up important theoretical questions in the debate on contemporary spirituality. The examples complement and problematize the

250 STEF AUPERS

common academic portrayal of "post-traditional" spirituality as sacralizing nature in opposition to modern, profane, "technocratic" society. Evidently, our technological environment is not seldom imagined to be imbued with mysterious powers.

How can this be explained sociologically? If we stay with the empirical case-study of technology we see that digital technology, like a force of nature, is often imagined to be extremely powerful, yet principally opaque and autonomous. This converges with contemporary theories on digital technology. It is, respectively, portrayed as a multilayered "black box" (Latour [1991] 1993), the inner workings being "unrepresentable" (Zizek [1996] 2001, 19), its manifestation as "disturbingly lively" (Haraway [1985] 2001, 30), and consequently "out of control" (Kelly 1994). Late-modern technologies can no longer unambiguously be understood as forces of "disenchantment." If we may paraphrase Weber ([1919] 1948), technologies have developed into "mysterious incalculable forces that come into play" that one can *no longer* "master . . . by calculation" (139). We may stretch this argument: modern social systems—from technology, the World Wide Web, and the culture industries to global capitalism, the state, and politics—are based on instrumental rational principles, but are, from a cultural perspective, experienced by more and more citizens as overly opaque and uncontrollable forces. This experience of alienation may motivate people to "return" to nature as spiritual power (as Roszak already noted fifty years ago), but social systems may also be considered to be a source of spirituality and enchantment in and of themselves.

If we revisit some of the classic social scientists writing on modernity (i.e., Durkheim, Weber and Mannheim), we already find in their accounts some of the seeds of this undertheorized re-enchantment of the system (e.g., Aupers and Houtman 2010; Pels 2003). Unlike artisanal production of goods, Karl Marx ([1844] 1964) argued famously, laborers in the industrial age are alienated from the industrial production process, the product, themselves, and their fellow workers. To explain the appeal of mass-made commodities to consumers, he took a "flight into the misty realm of religion" and dubbed it "commodity fetishism" since a commodity fundamentally *mystifies the real* circumstances under which it is produced—the social relations, exploitation, and production costs that remain hidden when we buy things (Marx [1867] 1990, 165). Commodities, Marx argued, are a modern fetish because people endow them "with a life of their own" (165).

EVERYTHING IS CONNECTED 251

And what about social systems, such as industries, governments, and the state? Particularly since the French Revolution, Émile Durkheim ([1897] 2002) argued in *Le Suicide*, cohesive communities in European countries made way for the state as a distant, opaque, but powerful force in the lives of individual citizens. He argues: "Individuals are made aware of society and their dependence upon it only through the State. But since it is far from them, it can exert only a distant, discontinuous influence over them" (Durkheim [1897] 2002, 356). The state, in other words, motivates sentiments of anomie since it is experienced and reified as a distant, alienating, yet highly powerful entity. Finally, theories of Weber and Mannheim make a related point. Notwithstanding his well-known assumptions that instrumental rationality in modern science, technology, politics, economics, and bureaucracies contributed to a "disenchantment of the world," Weber emphasized the autonomous and alienating aspects of these social systems. His famous metaphor of the "iron cage" communicates that since instrumental rationality's firm institutionalization from the seventeenth century onward, institutions came to follow their own internal logic and as such became experienced as external forces beyond human control. Karl Mannheim ([1935] 1946), in this respect, compared the anxieties aroused by these rationalized environments with those of premodern people facing nature: "Just as nature was unintelligible to primitive man, and his deepest feelings of anxiety arose from the incalculability of the forces of nature, so for modern industrialized man the incalculability of the forces at work in the social system under which he lives . . . has become a source of equally pervading fears" (59).

Such feelings of fear, anomie, and alienation—motivated by the "incalculability of the forces at work in the social system"—persist and, perhaps, accelerate in contemporary Western societies under the influence of globalization. Such macrosociological developments may explain a retreat to nature-oriented spirituality (i.e., New Age beliefs, healing practices, mindfulness) but, evidently, also motivate people to imbue technological and other social systems with spiritual power.

Re-Enchanting Political Power

To further elaborate and empirically "ground" this theoretical framework on modernity and spirituality, we will discuss another empirical case: the belief in invisible conspiracies that are part and parcel of a veritable conspiracy culture (e.g., Aupers 2012; Harambam and Aupers 2015; Harambam and Aupers 2017; Knight 2000; Melley 2000). From narratives about the coronavirus as a man-made biological weapon, chem-trails, Illuminati in the music industry, 9/11, political leaders as shapeshifting lizards, or QAnon theories about a corrupted "deep state" and Democrats sexually abusing young children and drinking their blood—contemporary conspiracy theories have become widely popular in the United States and Europe. In the United States alone, half of the public endorses at least one conspiracy theory, 20 percent believe the government is responsible for the attacks of 9/11, and 28 percent believe that a secret power elite is conspiring to establish a new world order (Oliver and Wood 2014). Such conspiracy theories, it will be demonstrated, show an elective affinity with religion and contemporary spirituality with one crucial difference: their advocates primarily detect mysterious patterns in the deeper layer of socials systems and re-enchant political power in society.

The Rise of Conspirituality

Ever since conspiracy theory as a particular discourse was picked up in the social sciences, its affinity with religious meaning-making has been emphasized. In the *Open Society and Its Enemies*, Karl Popper ([1945] 2013) already critically argued that "the conspiracy theory of society" is a primitive remnant from the premodern past and, particularly, "a typical result of the secularization of a religious superstition. The Gods are abandoned. But their place is filled by powerful men or groups—sinister pressure groups whose wickedness is responsible for all the evils we suffer from" (306).

Such arguments about conspiracy theory as religious belief have been a mainstay in the literature on conspiracy theory ever since (Dyrendal et al. 2018). More recently, however, it has been argued that there is a particular convergence between nature-oriented spirituality and conspiracy beliefs about society. Particularly in the spiritual wing of the milieu of conspiracy thinkers we are witnessing a hybrid ideology of "New Age conspiracism" (Barkun 2006), "conspirituality" (Ward and Voas 2011), or "millennial conspiracism" (Robertson 2016). This middle-ground position of "conspirituality," Ward and Voas (2011) explain, "appears to be a means by which political cynicism is tempered with spiritual optimism" (108). The popular British conspiracy theorist David Icke is an outstanding example of the fusion between spirituality and conspiracy thinking. Originally

EVERYTHING IS CONNECTED   253

motivated by spiritual experiences in Peru in the 1990s, he developed a highly complex "superconspiracy" (Barkun 2006) over the past years about countless, yet related, malicious groups (that is, Illuminati, the Rothschilds, the Brotherhood, shapeshifting aliens) that construct a fake reality to alienate humanity from their real spiritual nature and, in doing so, strive for a new world order (Robertson 2016). On the one hand, his work delves into dark and paranoid issue like "the Death of Bin Laden and other lies," "the fascist bloodline network," "shape-shifting, alien lizards," "global conspiracies," "mind programming," "brain washing," and "mass hypnosis," while it taps, on the other hand, in typical New Age themes like "astrology," "natural healing," "infinite love," and a "spiritual awakening."

Notwithstanding this seemingly arbitrary "bricolage" and empirical fusion of ideologies, there is an important analytic distinction between them: conspiracy theories are constructing "ultimate meaning" by attributing spirituality not so much to nature, but rather, in a paradoxical way, to society. In what follows, I will distinguish three ideal-typical strategies of ultimate meaning-making related to modern social systems and institutions. Ultimately, I will argue, conspiracy theories indicate a re-enchantment of secular political power.

Nothing Is What It Seems

The first assertion that characterizes the mindset of conspiracy theories is "nothing is what it seems" (Barkun 2006). This statement, like the others to follow, is typical for both conspiracy theorists and nature-celebrating spiritual advocates but, simultaneously, has a radically different meaning in the two fields. Spiritual believers locate meaningful forces unambiguously in the natural world—in the universe, the earth "Gaia," and all its mysterious manifestations. Nature is considered sacred: it contains an overpowering, yet invisible force or energy that permeates everything in the cosmos. This type of pantheistic spirituality is radically separated from society and modern culture. More than that: modern industrialism, science, and technology have undermined the meaningful relationship that people once had with nature.

Conspiracy theorists may share this critical analysis of modern society as corrupted and alienating to a large extent. And yet there's a crucial difference: invisible, yet immensely powerful forces are not primarily located in the natural realm but in the institutional world—they are to be found in mysterious groups that are operating *behind* the cultural screens, *underneath* and *beyond* the empirical surface of modern life. Conspiracy theorists, in other words, believe in a metaphysical *Hinterwelt* that is relocated from nature to the deeper layers of society. Nothing is what it seems: reality as we experience it is always a *staged* reality that conceals the awful truth that evil agents like politicians, scientists, CEOs, or other exponents of the "power elite" are de facto controlling our lives. Conspiracy theorists are thus not so much trying to discover the underlying forces of nature as aiming to uncover the hidden forces that control society— "secret" societies like the Illuminati, the "invisible government," a "deep state," or shapeshifting aliens sending subliminal messages on TV. This worldview is often illustrated in the milieu by reference to movies like *The Truman Show* (1999), *ExistenZ* (1999) or, most often, *The Matrix* (1999), where the protagonist "hacker," Neo, discovers that everyday reality is in fact a virtual reality constructed by artificially intelligent robots.

The mysterious "truth"—the underlying forces underneath empirical reality—in short, is not located in nature but in society. And it is not a good, but a fundamentally evil, force. The forces may be AIs, shapeshifting aliens, blood-drinking Democrats, mysterious Illuminati, Freemasons, Templars, the Bilderberg group, the CIA, FBI, NWO, or a sinister coalition between these, but such social groups are considered overpowering, mysterious forces exerting radical control over everyday life. Assumptions such as these are a manifestation of ultimate meaning-making: they can be understood as self-constructed "theodicies" explaining evil and suffering in the world.

Nothing Happens by Accident

Another assertion that both spiritual nature-worshipers and conspiracy theorists relate to is "Nothing happens by accident" (Barkun 2006). Spiritual seekers generally resist the modern assumption that the natural world is, essentially, devoid of meaning, direction, and intention. The process of evolution, for instance, may be typically understood by evolutionary biologists as governed by contingency, and human existence therefore is a mere lucky accident. Many spiritual seekers maintain that the evolution of life is motivated by an unfolding, spiritual logic and moves toward a higher, spiritual goal in the future. This teleological assumption results in the concept of an imminent New Age of light, peace, and stability (Hanegraaff 1996). Interestingly, it is often argued in the milieu that the universe "conspires" toward humans in a good and constructive way. There is a positive cosmic intention that is sometime called "pronoia," as the positive counterpart of "paranoia" (Zandbergen 2011). This implies that curious accidents in personal life should not be understood as accidental and should be read as what Carl Gustav Jung called "synchronicities": noncausal yet meaningful coincidences. In the narratives of conspiracy theorists, similar assumptions are made, but once again they generally do not apply to nature but to modern society. Whether we are talking about the attacks of 9/11, the assassination of JFK in 1963, or the auto accident in which Princess Diana lost her life in 1997, conspiracy theorists believe that nothing happens by accident: they seek human intention where others find coincidence; they detect structure where others see chaos; they find ultimate meaning where others meet the mundane. Every detail may be a piece of evidence that leads us to a grand scheme or plot: "Conspiracy implies a world based on intentionality, from which accident and coincidence have been removed. Anything that happens occurs because it has been willed" (Barkun 2006, 3–4).

An interesting illustration of the fact that conspiracy theorists believe that there is a (malicious) intention behind everything we see is the way they look at media messages. Particularly, they detect "signs" in mainstream texts and audiovisual material to prove that "things are not what they seem" and that "the truth is out there." Believers in the conspiracy theories about the death of Kennedy meticulously analyze visual details of the Zapruder film; 9/11 "truthers" study the televised events of the attack on the Twin Towers; QAnon members are relentlessly decoding cryptic messages of "Q" about the "deep state," Donald Trump, and the "Great Awakening" that were posted on 4chan and 8chan from October 2017 onward. In my work, I have demonstrated how conspiracy theorists on the internet provide a highly "oppositional reading" (Hall 1980) of the Grammy Awards (Aupers 2020). This televised form of entertainment is actually considered by one respondent "a performance in order to glorify the Illuminati"—a secret society that, allegedly, has enormous power in the music industry and strives for a new world order. In their oppositional readings, conspiracy theorists reinterpret every seemingly trivial detail in the performance, gestures, and clothing of the artist. They point out "hidden" signs and symbols that are allegedly used by the mysterious Illuminati in clips—like Jay-Z or Beyoncé making the "ritual" gesture of the "All-seeing Eye" with their hands or the "Eye of providence" (related to Freemasonry); they warn that Rihanna in her performance is actually

256   STEF AUPERS

posing as the satanic figure of "Baphomet"; they see the patterns of the dress of Lady Gaga conveying references to the Jewish mystic current of Kaballah or point out the use of pyramids, triangles, and occult symbols in clips from Katy Perry. Media texts, in these readings, become polysemic projection screens that, like Rorschach tests, are open to interpretations that clearly reflect the political-ideological position of the observer (Aupers 2020).

In general, such paranoid readings of media texts convey the underlying ideological assumption that, essentially, nothing happens by accident. Seemingly trivial choices in performance, clothing, or hairstyle of celebrities are taken as signs and symbols that represent a deeper, darker reality. Unlike in the discourse of many spiritual people, conspiracy theorists are not making that argument because they believe in the influence of an overpowering divine force in the natural world. There is no God, gods, or divine power involved. Rather, they believe that the evil "power elite" in society controls everything that happens. From this perspective, nothing happens by accident and everything has ultimate meaning.

Everything Is Connected

Finally, there is the common trope that "everything is connected"—a statement that, again, constitutes much of the discourse of spiritual seekers and conspiracy theorists. Spiritual seekers distinctly relate this statement to the natural world: it is an expression of their holistic worldview in which modern (Cartesian) dualism is rejected and the alleged connection between God and humans, nature and man, body and spirit is restored (Campbell 2007; Hanegraaff 1996; Heelas 1996). In this holistic universe, a transcendent God is replaced by an immanent spiritual force that permeates everything; humans are reconnected to the natural world and their "inner nature" once again while alternative treatments—yoga, reiki, holistic "healings," and so forth—approach individuals as an interconnected unity of "body-mind-spirit."

Among conspiracy theorists, the statement "Everything is connected" generally has a distinctly different meaning: instead of the holistic unity of nature, the adage points to the countless social connections, links, and coalitions that make up a global network of power. Contemporary conspiracy theories, after all, are seldom about scapegoating one, isolated, malicious organization. In expanded theories about a global "superconspiracy" (Barkun 2006), different societal organizations, actors, and (clusters of) coalitions are imagined to be part of the malicious cabal striving for a new world order (Knight 2000). For contemporary conspiracy theorists, the "truth is out there," always just out of sight; but, ultimately, "Everything is connected." Formulating a theory about evasive power in our society, or "connecting the dots," is imperative for every conspiracy theorist. She "must engage in a constant process of linkage and correlation in order to map the hidden connections" (Barkun 2006, 4). Like contacting nature, this activity may provide an out-of-the ordinary experience. As David Icke argues:

Connect the dots. There are dots like banking, government, all these different things, 9/11. Which in and of themselves are interesting. And you can see that something is not right. But when you connect the dots between apparently unconnected people, situations and organizations, that's when the tapestry appears and you go whooo. So that's what's happening.[1]

The holistic adage "Everything is connected," in short, can be a spiritual statement related to the force of nature, but it can also refer to the hidden organizations, elitist groups, actors, and power structures in society. People exemplifying the middle ground of "conspirituality" are involved in both. From a psychological perspective, this is not surprising. Research demonstrates that the tendency to "connect the dots" is a personal predisposition that strongly predicts conspiracy beliefs *and* supernatural assumptions about the natural environment. It is, they argue, a coping strategy: detecting hidden patterns reduces existential insecurity and increases a sense (or illusion) of control (Van Prooijen et al. 2017).

From the sociological perspective developed here, I argue that the contemporary spiritual search for hidden patterns is not primarily a psychological characteristic, but rather a cultural development motivated by a process of modernization. The search for hidden (and spiritual) patterns in nature is now massively complemented by pattern seeking in modern society because globalized social systems, the state, multinationals, organizations, actors, and, particularly, their *power structures*, have become way too complex to understand.

Conclusion

My point of departure in this chapter was the observation that "posttraditional spirituality" is generally understood in academia as a multifaced ideology focused on nature as a meaningful spiritual force outside modern institutions that, ultimately, seeks a re-enchantment of the Western world. There is, of course, no need to deny the numeral and theoretical significance of this nature-oriented form of spirituality. Already in Max Weber's time, at the beginning of the twentieth century, many of his fellow intellectuals took refuge in alternative spiritualities that promoted the return to (human) nature—like Steiner's anthroposophy, Blavatsky's theosophy, Romantic transcendentalism, or spiritualism (Asprem 2014; Aupers and Houtman 2010). Max Weber ([1919] 1948) was aware of this, but instead of incorporating this in his theories, he morally rejected such spiritual seeking as "plain humbug or self-deception," since one should "bear the fate of the times like a man" (149). Unfortunately, his personal moral aversion seems to have kept Weber from a systematic analysis of these trends of re-enchantment.

Whereas the interest in nature-spirituality is a long-standing historical trend that is by now well documented in academia (e.g., Asprem and Dyrendal 2015; Hammer 2004; Hanegraaff 1996) and is still prominent today, the main argument developed in this chapter is that there is another, by and large unacknowledged, spiritual trajectory that remains understudied and has implications for our conception of spiritual revival and re-enchantment. Most exemplary in this respect might be the spiritual adage that "everything is connected." Indeed, such a statement may refer to a powerful, spiritual and holistic connection with nature. But it may as well be a spiritual claim of an ICT-guru that we are 'now all connected' through technology on the expanding World Wide Web. Alternatively, it may be expressed by a conspiracy theorist arguing that dark political power, influential yet invisible to many, is "everywhere" in contemporary society and determines what we think and what we see. In addition to the more romantic forms of spirituality, then, we see that spirituality is relocated from nature to modern society. The case studies discussed here illustrate that "secular" modern social systems are not opposed to the spiritual imagination. Quite the contrary: the theoretical argument developed here is that modern social, political and technological systems—as envisioned by Marx, Weber, Durkheim, and others—have developed into autonomous, opaque, "incalculable forces." Confronted with such inexplicable forces, people may experience a sense of alienation, anomie, and disenchantment as these social theorists already noted. Evidently, however, people also develop all kinds of fantasies, narratives, and images to represent forces in / of modern society that seem neither representable nor controllable. Indeed, the conviction that "nothing is what it seems," "nothing happens by accident," and ultimately that "everything is connected" is widespread and constitutes veritable spiritual narratives about society. Such narratives about invisible power explain what has become inexplicable to many and do what traditional religious and spiritual worldviews have done all along: construct (ultimate) meaning in everyday life.

Note

1. Accessed 26 July 2021 http://www.youtube.com/watch?v = kRs-ke4Il5Y.

References

Ammerman, Nancy T. 2013. "Spiritual But Not Religious? Beyond Binary Choices in the Study of Religion." *Journal for the Scientific Study of Religion* 52(2): 258–78.

Asprem, Egil. 2014. *The Problem of Disenchantment: Scientific Naturalism and Esoteric Discourse, 1900–1939.* Leiden: Brill.

Asprem, Egil, and Asbjorn Dyrendal. 2015. "Conspirituality Reconsidered: How Surprising and How New Is the Confluence of Spirituality and Conspiracy Theory?" *Journal of Contemporary Religion* 30(3): 367–82.

Aupers, Stef. 2002. "The Revenge of the Machines: On Modernity, Digital Technology and Animism." *Asian Journal of Social Science* 30(2): 199–220.

Aupers, Stef. 2009. "'The Force Is Great': Enchantment and Magic in Silicon Valley."' *Masaryk University Journal of Law and Technology* 3(1): 153–73.

Aupers, Stef. 2010. "'Where the Zeroes Meet the Ones': Exploring the Affinity between Magic and Computer Technology." Pp. 219–38 in *Religions of Modernity: Relocating the Sacred to the Self and the Digital,* edited by Stef Aupers and Dick Houtman. Leiden: Brill.

Aupers, Stef. 2012. "'Trust No One': Modernization, Paranoia and Conspiracy Culture." *European Journal of Communication* 26(4): 22–34.

Aupers, Stef. 2020. "Decoding Mass Media / Encoding Conspiracy Theory." Pp. 469–82 in *Handbook of Conspiracy Theories,* edited by Michael Butter and Peter Knight. London: Routledge.

Aupers, Stef, and Dick Houtman. 2006. "Beyond the Spiritual Supermarket: The Social and Public Significance of New Age Spirituality." *Journal of Contemporary Religion* 21(2): 201–22.

Aupers, Stef, and Dick Houtman, eds. 2010. *Religions of Modernity: Relocating the Sacred to the Self and the Digital.* Leiden: Brill.

Aupers, Stef, Dick Houtman, and Peter Pels. 2008. "Cybergnosis: Technology, Religion and the Secular." Pp. 687–703 in *Religion: Beyond a Concept,* edited by Hent de Vries. New York: Fordham University Press.

Barkun, Michael. 2006. *A Culture of Conspiracy: Apocalyptic Visions in Contemporary America.* Berkeley: University of California Press.

Berger, Peter. 1967. *The Sacred Canopy: Elements of a Sociological Theory of Religion.* Garden City, NY: Doubleday.

Bruce, Steve. 2002. *God Is Dead: Secularisation in the West.* Oxford: Blackwell.

260 STEF AUPERS

Davis, Erik. 1999. *TechGnosis: Myth, Magic and Mysticism in the Age of Information*. London: Serpent's Tail.

Dery, Mark. 1996. *Escape Velocity: Cyberculture at the End of the Century*. New York: Grove Press.

Durkheim, Émile. [1897] 2002. *Suicide: A Study in Sociology*, translated by John A. Spaulding. London: Routledge.

Dyrendal, Asbjorn, David G. Robertson, and Egil Asprem, eds. 2018. *Handbook of Conspiracy Theory and Contemporary Religion*. Leiden: Brill.

Geraci, Robert. 2010. *Apocalyptic AI: Visions of Heaven in Robotics, Artificial Intelligence, and Virtual Reality*. Oxford: Oxford University Press.

Hall, Stuart. [1980] 2001. "Encoding/Decoding." Pp. 63–173 in *Media and Cultural Studies: Keyworks*, edited by M. G. Durham and D. M. Keller. Malden, MA: Wiley-Blackwell.

Hammer, Olav. 2004. *Claiming Knowledge: Strategies of Epistemology from Theosophy to the New Age*. Leiden: Brill.

Hanegraaff, Wouter. 1996. *New Age Religion and Western Culture: Esotericism in the Mirror of Secular Thought*. Albany: State University of New York Press.

Harambam, Jaron, and Stef Aupers. 2015. "Contesting Epistemic Authority: Conspiracy Theories on the Boundary of Science." *Public Understanding of Science* 24(4): 466–80.

Harambam, Jaron, and Stef Aupers. 2017. "'I Am Not a Conspiracy Theorist': Relational Identifications in the Dutch Conspiracy Milieu." *Cultural Sociology* 11(1): 113–29.

Haraway, Donna. [1985] 2001. "A Manifesto for Cyborgs: Science, Technology and Social Feminism in the 1980s." Pp. 28–37 in *Reading Digital Culture*, edited by D. Trend. Oxford: Blackwell.

Heelas, Paul. 1996. *The New Age Movement*. Oxford: Blackwell.

Heelas, Paul, and Linda Woodhead, with Benjamin Seel, Bronislaw Szerszynski, and Karin Tusting. 2005. *The Spiritual Revolution: Why Religion Is Giving Way to Spirituality*. Oxford: Blackwell.

Houtman, Dick, and Stef Aupers. 2007. "The Spiritual Turn and the Decline of Tradition: The Spread of Post-Christian Spirituality in Fourteen Western Countries (1981–2000)." *Journal for the Scientific Study of Religion* 46(3): 305–20.

Kelly, Kevin. 1994. *Out of Control: The New Biology of Machines, Social Systems and the Economic World*. Boston: Perseus Books.

Kurzweil, Ray. 1999. *The Age of Spiritual Machines: When Computers Exceed Human Intelligence*. New York: Penguin Books.

Knight, Peter. 2000. *Conspiracy Culture: From Kennedy to the X-Files*. New York: Routledge.

Latour, Bruno. [1991] 1993. *We Have Never Been Modern*. Cambridge, MA: Harvard University Press.

Leary, Timothy. [1994] 2014. *Chaos and Cyberculture*. Berkeley: Ronin Publishing.

Luckmann, Thomas. 1967. *The Invisible Religion: The Problem of Religion in Modern Society*. New York: Macmillan.

Lynch, Gordon. 2007. *The New Spirituality: An Introduction to Progressive Belief in the Twenty-First Century*. London: I.B. Tauris.

Mannheim, Karl. [1935] 1946. *Man and Society in an Age of Reconstruction: Studies in Modern Social Structures*. London: Kegan Paul, Trench, Trübner.

Marx, Karl. [1844] 1964. *Economic and Philosophic Manuscripts of 1844*. New York: International Publishers.

Marx, Karl. [1867] 1990. *Capital*. Vol. 1. London: Penguin Classics.

EVERYTHING IS CONNECTED 261

Melley, Timothy. 2000. *Empire of Conspiracy: The Culture of Paranoia in Postwar America.* Ithaca, NY: Cornell University Press.

Oliver, Eric J., and Thomas J. Wood. 2014. "Conspiracy Theories and the Paranoid Style(s) of Mass Opinion." *American Journal of Political Science* 58(4): 952–66.

Partridge, Chris. 2005. *The Re-enchantment of the West.* Vol. 1, *Alternative Spiritualities, Sacralization, Popular Culture, Occulture.* London: T&T Clark.

Pels, Peter. 2003. "Introduction." Pp. 1–38 in *Magic and Modernity: Interfaces of Revelation and Concealment,* edited by B. Meyer and P. Pels. Stanford, CA: Stanford University Press.

Popper, Karl R. [1945] 2013. *The Open Society and Its Enemies.* Princeton, NJ: Princeton University Press.

Prooijen, Jan-Willem van, Karen Douglas, and Clara De Inocencio. 2017. "'Connecting the Dots': Illusory Pattern Perception Predicts Belief in Conspiracies and the Supernatural." *European Journal of Social Psychology* 48(3): 320–35.

Robertson, David G. 2016. *UFOs, Conspiracy Theories and the New Age: Millennial Conspiracism.* London: Bloomsbury Publishers.

Roszak, Theodore. [1968] 1995. *The Making of a Counter Culture: Reflections on the Technocratic Society and Its Youthful Opposition.* Oakland: University of California Press.

Roszak, Theodore. 2000. *From Satori to Silicon Valley: San Francisco and the American Counterculture.* Palo Alto, CA: Stanford University Press.

Rushkoff, Douglas. 1994. *Cyberia: Life in the Trenches of Cyberspace.* San Francisco: HarperCollins.

Stolov, Jeremy. 2008. "Salvation by Electricity." Pp. 668–87 in *Religion: Beyond a Concept,* edited by H. de Vries. New York: Fordham University Press.

Sutcliffe, Steven, and Marion Bowman. 2000. *Beyond New Age: Exploring Alternative Spirituality.* Edinburgh: Edinburgh University Press.

Ward, Charlotte, and David Voas. 2011. "The Emergence of Conspirituality." *Journal of Contemporary Religion* 26(1): 103–21.

Wachowski, Andy and Larry Wachowski. 1999. "The Matrix." Burbank, CA: Warner Home Video.

Weber, Max. [1919] 1948. "Science as a Vocation." Pp. 129–56 in *From Max Weber: Essays in Sociology,* edited and translated by H. H. Gerth and C. W. Mills. London: Routledge.

Wertheim, Margaret. [1999] 2000. *The Pearly Gates of Cyberspace: A History of Space from Dante to the Internet.* London: Virago Press.

Zandbergen, Dorien. 2011. "New Edge: Technology and Spirituality in the San Francisco Bay Area." PhD dissertation, Faculty of Social and Behavioural Sciences, Leiden University.

Žižek, Slavoj. [1996] 2001. "From Virtual Reality to the Virtualization of Reality." Pp. 17–22 in *Reading Digital Culture,* edited by D. Trend. Oxford: Blackwell.

13

Yoga Spirituality in the Context of US Institutions

Candy Gunther Brown

Yoga provides a revealing example of a practice that many people understand as both spiritual and social, and of where the discourses surrounding a practice are sensitive to its institutional contexts. There are legal and financial consequences to describing yoga as both "spiritual" and "religious," as "spiritual but not religious," and/or as "secular." Accentuating or muting certain terms conveys benefits or limitations, depending on the setting. Such descriptors are not, as the historian of mindfulness Jeff Wilson explains, "mere statements of fact," but "markers of value employed strategically by agents" who are "making an argument" (2014, 9). Sometimes the same agents describe the same practices in very different ways as they move across institutional contexts—a strategy that linguists call "code-switching" and sociologists characterize as "frontstage/backstage" behavior (Goffman 1986; Gardner-Chloros 2009). This chapter examines yoga as a spiritual and a social practice. It considers three institutional contexts for interpreting yoga spirituality: religion, law, and education. The chapter argues that even as social practice reinforces yoga spirituality, religious, legal, and financial pressures either to link or distance yoga from religion influence how people talk and think about yoga spirituality.

Religious Institutions

The context of twentieth- and twenty-first-century US religious institutions fosters the differentiation of yoga spirituality from religion. For much of US history, Americans often used the words "religion" and "spirituality" interchangeably, as chronicled by the *Oxford English Dictionary*. The concept of "spirit," at the root of spirituality, shares with religion a metaphysical

Candy Gunther Brown, *Yoga Spirituality in the Context of US Institutions* In: *Situating Spirituality*. Edited by: Brian Steensland, Jaime Kucinskas, and Anna Sun, Oxford University Press. © Oxford University Press 2022. DOI: 10.1093/oso/9780197565001.003.0014

YOGA SPIRITUALITY AND US INSTITUTIONS   263

assumption: that living beings have an immaterial, or more than material, aspect that transcends the visible world.

By the 1960s, the term "religion" had accreted negative connotations as the province of powerful institutions that enforce adherence to doctrines and rules. Many Americans came to distance their own beliefs and practices from "religion," while using the term "spirituality" for metaphysical ideals—such as personal meaning and transcendence, and moral and ethical virtues—that they like (Fuller 2001, 6). Between 2007 and 2014, the proportion of the religiously unaffiliated climbed from 16 to 23 percent (Pew 2015, 4); only 18 percent of this group think of themselves as a "religious person," but 37 percent identify as "spiritual but not religious," or SBNR (Pew 2012, 22). Nearly three-quarters of millennials say they are "really more spiritual than religious" (Grossman 2010).

Yoga as a Spiritual Practice

The popularity of yoga has grown apace with the rise of SBNR America. Surveys report that the percentage of the US adult population practicing yoga rose from 3 percent (5 million people) in 1976, to 5.1 percent in 2002, 6.1 percent in 2007 (15.8 million), 9.5 percent (20.4 million) in 2012, and up to 15 percent (36.7 million people) by 2016 (Syman 2010, 256; Clarke et al. 2015, 13; *Yoga Journal* and Yoga Alliance 2016, 11). Between 2007 and 2017, the percentage of children practicing yoga grew from 2.1 to 8.4 percent—or from 1.3 to 4.9 million (Barnes 2008, 4; Black et al. 2018, 5).

Many Americans consider yoga to be a spiritual practice. According to the Pew Research Center, 23 percent of all Americans, and 28 percent of the religiously unaffiliated, "believe in" yoga as a "spiritual practice" (Pew 2012, 24). A 2013 survey of participants in beginner yoga classes ($N = 604$) found that 73 percent identify yoga as a "spiritual activity" and 37 percent are actively "seeking a spiritual experience" (Quilty et al. 2013, 45, 47, 48).

As practitioners engage in yoga over time, spirituality becomes increasingly motivational. A 2017 survey ($N = 2,628$) reported that although only 8.2 percent of practitioners start yoga primarily for "spiritual reasons," 53 percent end up exploring "spiritual values" through yoga, and 26.5 percent discover that yoga helps them feel "connected to God" (Keil 2017). A 2016 nationwide survey revealed that 62 percent of yoga students ($n = 360$) and 85 percent of teachers ($n = 156$) altered their primary reason for practice over

264 CANDY GUNTHER BROWN

time. The primary motive typically switched from "exercise and stress relief" to "spirituality." Of students who changed reasons for practicing, spirituality became the primary motive for 24 percent and an additional motive for 48 percent; for teachers, 50 percent attested that spirituality became their primary motive, and the other 50 percent identified spirituality as an additional motive (Park et al. 2016, 887, 891).

The *2016 Yoga in America Study* (*N* = 2,021 US adults; *n* = 1,707 practitioners) by *Yoga Journal* and Yoga Alliance observed that more practitioners (83 percent) than nonpractitioners (59 percent) agree that "yoga is spiritual" (26, 42). The prospect of "spiritual development" motivated 24 percent of new practitioners to begin yoga (30). While 26 percent of practitioners believe that a "great yoga teacher" should focus "on the spiritual aspect of yoga," this sentiment increases to 48 percent of instructors and 85 percent of studio owners, suggesting that those more invested in yoga are more likely to associate it with spirituality (30, 53, 72).

Americans tend to differentiate yoga spirituality from religion. A 2017 survey (*N* = 643) reported that 81 percent of practitioners do not "relate yoga to religion," yet 81 percent believe yoga helps them to "feel more connected to nature/universe/god/a higher power," and 73 percent believe "yoga has made them a better person" (Drughi 2017).

Despite disavowing yoga's relationship to religion, longer-term practitioners are less likely to identify as Christian and more likely to identify as SBNR or as Buddhist. In a survey conducted in Australia (*N* = 2,567), among respondents with less than one year of yoga exposure, 43 percent identified as Christian, 26 percent as secular, 23 percent as SBNR, and 4 percent as Buddhist. After six or seven years, 28 percent identified as Christian, 27 percent as secular, 31 percent as SBNR, and 9 percent as Buddhist. Although only 19 percent recalled beginning yoga for spiritual reasons, 43 percent said yoga became a "spiritual path" (Penman et al. 2012).

Yoga classes, and especially teacher trainings, incorporate teachings that are widely classified as "religious." Although only 30 percent of the US population is "familiar" with the "philosophy and history of yoga," 82 percent of practitioners claim familiarity (*Yoga Journal* and Yoga Alliance 2016, 17). Instruction in more than poses and breathing occurs relatively early—since most practitioners are at the beginner-intermediate level (98 percent) with less than five years' experience (74 percent) (*Yoga Journal* and Yoga Alliance 2016, 23).

The Yoga Alliance certifies 43 percent of all yoga instructors (*Yoga Journal and Yoga Alliance* 2016, 23). Certification requires "study of yoga philosophies and traditional texts (such as the Yoga Sutras, Hatha Yoga Pradipika or Bhagavad Gita)," a "yoga lifestyle, such as the precept of non-violence (ahimsa), and the concepts of dharma and karma," "energy anatomy and physiology (chakras, nadis, etc.)," and "chanting, mantra, meditation" (Yoga Alliance 2016). The Bhagavad Gita (ca. 200 BC–200 CE)—often identified as a Hindu text and studied in yoga trainings—can be read as conceptualizing yoga as devotion through meditation on a benevolent, omnipotent Supreme Being, here known as Krishna (Syman 2018). The *Yoga Sūtras* incorporate moral and ethical teachings from Hindu, Buddhist, and other traditions (Singleton 2010, 26). The Yoga Alliance Code of Conduct "centers on the principles of the yamas," negative "ethical guidelines of Patanjali's Yoga Sutras" for behaviors to restrain, such as ahimsa (nonviolence) and satya (avoidance of dishonesty) (Yoga Alliance 2020). As late as May 2019, this code also included adherence to the *niyamas*, positive ethical observances that encompass *svādhyāya* (self-study by reciting the Vedas), and *Īśvarapraṇidhāna* (surrender to God) (Jois [1962] 2010, 6–17; Yoga Alliance 2019).

Although the spiritual and religious connotations of yoga attract some people, such connotations deter others from practicing or motivate them to reconceptualize yoga spirituality as compatible with their own religion. *Yoga in America* asked nonpractitioners their reasons. Of those who have never tried yoga, 9 percent—and of those who stopped, 4 percent—said "the 'spirituality' aspect of the practice bothers me" (*Yoga Journal* 2012, 41). Critics of mandatory yoga—including Christians, Muslims, and Sikhs in the United States and India—interpret yoga as not only spiritual, but also religious. As one Muslim mother of school-aged children expressed her objection, yoga often begins with a sun salutations, or *Sūrya Namaskāra*, which "requires a person to bow to the Sun God," but "Islam being a monotheistic religion doesn't allow followers to bow before anyone except Allah" (Lal 2016).

Christians attracted to yoga are motivated to interpret the practice as spiritual but not religious, and therefore available to complement church attendance. As a "devoted Southern Baptist church member" explained, "I get much more out of yoga and meditation than I ever get out of a sermon in church" (quoted in Mohler 2010). An Amazon.com customer purchased a *Christoga: Faith in Fitness* DVD "because I was worried that my prayer life was lacking. This is an excellent way to incorporate Christ's Word into your soul" (Becca 2008). Christian yogis relabel sun salutations as "son salutations"—worshiping Jesus—and *prāṇāyāma* (controlled breathing to channel impersonal, vital energy) as breathing in the Holy Spirit. "Christian yoga alternatives" add Bible verses, relabel poses, and target Christian markets with program names such as Yahweh Yoga, WholyFit, Outstretched in Worship, and PraiseMoves (Brown 2018). None of these Christian variants frame yoga as mere physical exercise but as a spiritual discipline, rooted in non-Christian religion, that must be intentionally relabeled as Christian.

Yoga as a Social Practice

Despite the tendency of many Americans to think of spirituality as more individual than social, yoga is for many other Americans not only spiritual but also social. Of Americans who practice yoga, 48 percent do so in a gym, 45 percent in a yoga studio, 21 percent in a community center, 9 percent at a retreat center, and 9 percent in a school (*Yoga Journal* and Yoga Alliance 2016, 28). New practitioners come to yoga through friends (33 percent), free classes (24 percent), relatives (15 percent), healthcare providers (11 percent), and work colleagues (7 percent) (*Yoga Journal* and Yoga Alliance 2016, 29). A 2013 survey (N = 604) reported that 16 percent of beginners are seeking "social interaction" (Quilty et al. 2013, 45, 47, 48). Quality of "social interaction" influences class selection for 14 percent of practitioners, and 66 percent seek out teachers who are "warm and friendly" (*Yoga Journal* and Yoga Alliance 2016, 31, 32).

Although postural yoga practice is more individual, even in class settings, than participation in many sports teams, teachers and practice communities influence how individuals interpret their experiences. Even as human bodies receive sensory input individually, perceptions form as input filters through "frameworks of understanding" developed during social interactions (Goffman 1986, 10). Experiments show that participants in group sensorimotor activities (such as yoga classes) collaborate more after such activities, suggesting that social practice engenders communal bonding (Soliman et al. 2015, 853, 857). Practitioners report developing their understanding of yoga through social interactions with their yoga class (48 percent), friends (40 percent), and reading internet articles (36 percent) and yoga magazines (17 percent) (*Yoga Journal* and Yoga Alliance 2016, 38). Because many in the American "yoga community" interpret yoga as a spiritual practice (Bowman

2014b), participation in that community reinforces interpretation of yoga as spiritual.

Legal Institutions

The context of US legal institutions gives rise to dueling conceptualizations of yoga spirituality as "religious" or "secular." Legal protections or limitations on "spirituality" depend on its classification as a subcategory of "religion." The US Constitution makes no mention of spirituality. The First Amendment uses the word "religion" once to govern two clauses: protecting "free exercise" and prohibiting "establishment." Courts arbitrate disputes over whether practices are "religious" for the purpose of interpreting the First Amendment (*Malnak v. Yogi* 1979; *United States v. Meyers* 1996). Judicial decisions in turn shape how individuals and groups talk about beliefs, practices, and communities in relation to legal definitions.

Free Exercise of Religion

When "free exercise" is at stake, practitioners have reason to categorize yoga spirituality as religion. The three main contexts for free exercise claims involve rights for prisoners and employees and sales tax exemptions. Courts have interpreted yoga as religion in cases in which prisoners argued for their right to practice yoga (*Powell v. Perry* 1988; *Garvins v. Burnett* 2009; *Cotton v. Cate* 2014). Conversely, the US Equal Employment Opportunity Commission (EEOC) protects employees from being required to participate in workplace yoga programs, finding mandatory yoga to constitute "reverse religious discrimination" (EEOC 1994, 2008).

When state and local governments classify yoga as physical fitness for the purpose of collecting sales tax on fitness services, leaders in the yoga community seek religious exemptions.

Missouri yoga studios protested a 2009 tax because "yoga is a spiritual practice. It's not a purchase" (Huffstutter 2009). In 2012, New York's State Taxation and Finance Department exempted yoga studios from sales tax, because yoga is not "true exercise" but akin to religious "meditation and spiritual chanting" and is "meditative and spiritual rather than fitness" (Blain 2012; DNAinfo 2012). New York's yoga exemption came through lobbying by Yoga

268 CANDY GUNTHER BROWN

for New York. One of that group's principal members, Eddie Stern, the director of Ashtanga Yoga New York and president of the Hindu Broome Street Ganesha Temple, attributed the campaign's success to the god Ganesh: "He is a remover of obstacles, even obstacles like the tax department" (Beck 2012).

In 2014, the District of Columbia imposed taxes on yoga and other "health-club services" with "the purpose of physical exercise." Protests came not only from local yoga studios—which insisted that the "purpose" of yoga is "spirituality" rather than "exercise"—but also from nationally prominent leaders in the yoga community (Hallet 2014). President of the Universal Society of Hinduism Rajan Zed denounced the DC tax as "religious infringement" because yoga is "one of the six systems of orthodox Hindu philosophy" and "a mental and physical discipline by means of which the human-soul (jivatman) united with the universal-soul (paramatman)" (quoted in Bowman 2014a). Yoga Alliance president Richard Karpel urged DC officials to emulate New York's exemption, reaching the "same, indisputable conclusion" that the purpose of yoga is "spiritual rather than fitness" (Karpel 2014a, 2; Yoga Alliance 2014). Sales tax controversies prompt the argument that yoga is more spiritual than physical, that yoga spirituality is tantamount to religion, and thus that yoga should be protected by the free exercise clause of the First Amendment.

Establishment of Religion

When "establishment" is at stake, practitioners tend to describe yoga as physical exercise with secular health benefits and to differentiate universal spirituality and ethical virtues from institutional religion. The primary context for establishment clause claims is public education. Courts focus on public schools—the "symbol of our democracy"—because here the state exercises "coercive power" over young students whose attendance is "involuntary," and who are "impressionable" to the "authority" of teachers as "role models" and "peer pressure" (*Edwards v. Aguillard* 1987, 583–84, 595). The Supreme Court has disallowed schools from "coercion" or "endorsement" of religious practices such as prayer and devotional Bible reading, even if "denominationally neutral" and students are allowed to opt out (*Engel v. Vitale* 1962, 430; *Abington School District v. Schempp* 1963; *Lee v. Weisman* 1992).

Some of the *same* individuals and organizations who argue in free-exercise contexts that yoga is religious—for instance, Eddie Stern, Rajan Zed, and the Yoga Alliance—insist in establishment-clause contexts that yoga is devoid of religion. In *Sedlock v. Baird* (2013), parents sued the Encinitas Union School District of San Diego, California, alleging that the district's Ashtanga Yoga program establishes religion. The K. P. Jois USA Foundation, incorporated in 2011 to honor the Indian Hindu guru Krishna Pattabhi Jois (1915–2009), who developed modern Ashtanga yoga, funded (with an initial grant of $533,720, totaling over $4 million in five years) and co-developed the school program (Jois Yoga 2013; Brown 2019). According to Jois, "The reason we do yoga is to become one with God," and the sun salutations (*Sūrya Namaskāra*) that "form the foundation for the entire method of the practice of yoga" are a "prayer to the sun god" Surya (Jois Yoga 2004, 18; 2005, 7; 1995, 64).

The Jois Foundation's head of curriculum development, Eddie Stern, served as the Encinitas school district's "Health and Wellness Project Manager" (Regur 2013). Stern's Jois Foundation biosketch described him as "teaching yoga exercise," although the foundation's ".com" counterpart introduced Stern as an "avid devotee of the Hindu tradition" (Stern 2015; Atkins 2016; Brown 2019, 83–84). Like Stern, Zed reframed yoga as exercise versus religion when moving from a sales-tax to a public-school context. Zed (2016) urged California to "work towards formally introducing yoga as a part of curriculum in all the public schools of the state."

Yoga Alliance spokespersons similarly alternated between framing yoga as spiritual—and thus encompassed by religious protections, and as physical—and thus exempt from religious prohibitions, depending on the legal context. Yoga Alliance even cited the same *Yoga in America* (2012) survey data to support conflicting arguments. In May 2013, Yoga Alliance board of directors chair Brandon Hartsell submitted a legal declaration in support of the *Sedlock* defense. He attached a copy of *Yoga in America* (2012) to argue that none of "the top five reasons" people give for starting yoga "relate to a religious motive" (*Yoga Journal* 2012, 54; Hartsell 2013, 4).

Fourteen months later, in July 2014, Yoga Alliance president Richard Karpel submitted the same *Yoga in America* survey to the District of Columbia to protest its yoga tax—this time calling attention to the findings that "spiritual development" motivated 31.7 percent of practitioners to start yoga, and 40.2 percent of practitioners have, in the course of practice, come to identify "spiritual development" as a benefit (*Yoga Journal* 2012, 54–55;

Karpel 2014b). Citing the *Yoga Sūtras* as authoritative, Karpel (2014b) elaborated that yoga is an "eight-limbed path" that begins with "ethical principles" and culminates with "'samadhi,' often referred to as a state of bliss" (2). Karpel stressed that "none of us in the yoga community think the purpose is physical exercise" (Bowman 2014b). A Yoga Alliance statement explains that "if it takes the notion of a firm gluteus or a flatter tummy to get some people in the door, that's fine with us. Eventually they'll find great teachers who help them understand what yoga is really about." However, *misguided notions about the purpose of yoga become destructive when they lead to misplaced government burdens*" (2014).

Three months after arguing that yoga is "really about" spirituality, in October 2014, Yoga Alliance submitted an amicus curiae brief for the *Sedlock* appeal. Arguing that yoga "commonly is practiced free from religious ideology," the brief again cites *Yoga in America* to emphasize that "although a minority [40.2 percent] of survey participants identified spiritual development as a benefit of yoga, over half identified . . . physical health benefits" (Yoga Alliance 2014, 2, 6). The *Sedlock* appellate court identified Hartsell's declaration and *Yoga in America* as providing "abundant evidence that contemporary yoga is commonly practiced in the United States for reasons that are entirely distinct from religious ideology" (*Sedlock v. Baird* 2015). Three days after the appellate ruling for the defense, Yoga Alliance (2015) issued a statement calling it a "win for yoga" and taking credit for having "actively participated in the proceedings" to bring about this "victory."

Sedlock was not the first "victory" for public-school yoga won by disavowing religion. In 2002, Tara Guber, wife of movie producer Peter Guber, encountered resistance in marketing her Yoga Ed. program to Colorado public schools. When challenged, she denied that Yoga Ed. is a "religious-, dogma- or faith-based program" (Havlen 2002). Guber overcame objections from "Christian fundamentalists" on the school board by replacing the term *samādhi* with "oneness," "meditation" with "time in," and *prāṇāyāma* with "bunny breathing" (Associated Press 2007). Guber (2004) confided to an interviewer for *Hinduism Today* that, regardless of terms, she expected yoga practice to "go within, shift consciousness and alter beliefs"; the magazine credited her with winning a "Vedic Victory." Guber's willingness to relabel yoga practices reflects an experiential concept of religious transformation that contrasts with a Protestant Christian view that religion consists primarily of intentions and belief statements.

Like Guber, Pattabhi Jois considered it unnecessary to "talk about God" when teaching yoga, because "when you practice correctly, you come to experience God inside" whether you "want it or not" (Jois 2004, 18). Similarly, a yoga textbook, *Myths of the Asanas*, used in the Encinitas Union School District, attests that "when one enacts anjali mudra [praying hands, formed, among other times, at the start of sun salutations], for example, the actual feeling of reverence emerges within" (Kaivalya and van der Kooij 2010, 182). If reverential postures *produce* reverential feelings, then distilling yoga spirituality from broader religious contexts by intending or stating it to be something else may be more difficult than Christian or secular appropriators assume.

Both the Jois / Sonima / Pure Edge Foundation and Yoga Ed. programs helped schools financially (in the case of Yoga Ed. directing federal grant money to teacher training). By contrast, the North Penn School District in Pennsylvania stood to lose at least $1 million per year if a yoga-based charter school, Education for New Generations, were allowed to open (Brown 2019). To prevent financial bleeding, North Penn apprised the state board of education Charter Appeal Board of code-switching by charter-school cofounder Glenn Mendoza. In applying for a school charter in 2012, Mendoza and colleagues framed Pranic Healing and Arhatic Yoga (including Superbrain Yoga) as nonreligious, educational techniques. In 2011, Mendoza had sued the hospital that employed him as a pediatrician for seeking to terminate him because of his "religious and spiritual practice of Pranic Healing and Arhatic Yoga," which is "no different than being Jewish, Hindu, Buddhist, Catholic or Muslim." The Charter Appeal Board (2016) cited Mendoza's linguistic inconsistency as grounds for its decision to deny the charter because the school would have impermissibly established religion. In California and Colorado, school districts benefited financially by defining yoga as nonreligious, whereas in Pennsylvania a school district saved money by defining yoga as religious.

Educational Institutions

Most often, the context of US educational institutions encourages conceptualizing yoga as secular, in the sense of promoting physical, mental, and emotional health, and as spiritual in the sense of cultivating purportedly "universal" moral and ethical virtues. Americans have long idealized public schools as instilling moral and ethical character (McClellan 1999). In the wake of Supreme Court rulings on prayer and Bible reading, getting yoga into schools requires marketing it as nonreligious.

Yoga advocates have reason to seek access to schools to gain power to influence beliefs, values, and worldviews of the rising generations. Sonia Jones, wife of hedge fund billionaire Paul Tudor Jones and devotee of Krishna Pattabhi Jois, created the Jois Foundation with a mission of bringing the "philosophy, teaching, and values of Sri K. Pattabhi Jois to as many people as it is able to reach" through "outreach" to "youths in underserved communities" (Jois Yoga 2013). The objective of the Jois Foundation (later renamed Sonima and then Pure Edge) is for yoga and mindfulness training to be required for teacher credentialing and "essential" in school curricula on a national level (Sonima 2012).

Public school yoga is marketed as replacing disruptive with virtuous behavior. An article in *Teaching Tolerance: A Project of the Southern Poverty Law Center* lauds a "Title I" Atlanta school that uses yoga to quell "bickering, fussing and general behavior problems" and as a "strategy for proactively managing classroom behavior" (Williamson 2012). The Pure Edge (formerly Jois/Sonima) yoga and mindfulness curriculum instills "core values (e.g., being truthful, kind, compassionate, fair, responsible, respectful, generous, courageous, determined, forgiving)" (Stern et al. 2016, 28). Educators who can no longer use prayer and Bible reading to teach character are looking for nonreligious alternatives for cultivating morality and ethics. "Secular yoga" promises to do just that.

Conclusions

The classification of yoga as "spiritual," "religious," and/or "secular" depends in part on which terminology offers the most benefits with the fewest limitations in a given institutional context. For many Americans, yoga is both a spiritual and a social practice, and social interactions with others in the yoga community reinforce yoga's spiritual appeal. Practitioners who move across institutional contexts code-switch in how they talk about yoga, at certain times accentuating and at other times downplaying yoga's associations with religion. The ways people talk about yoga and spirituality in turn affect how they think about yoga and spirituality.

Strategic avoidance of religious and/or spiritual language when expedient may work better than intended, leading people to think about yoga—or other spiritual practices—less in terms of religious or spiritual categories. In other words, code-switching could prove unstable. The switch might stick in its last position, resulting in a depletion of religious and/or spiritual meanings as well as language. Education scholar Christopher McCaw (2020) distinguishes "thin" from "thick" mindfulness. Thick mindfulness is deeply integrated with Buddhist ethical and ontological concepts. The thinning of religious language allows mindfulness entrance into public institutions. As with yoga, once thin mindfulness has made it through the schoolhouse door, instructors have considerable latitude to teach thick mindfulness. But this assumes that instructors remain sufficiently agile to switch back and forth as needed. Otherwise, the thinning of language might lead to the thinning of experience. From the perspective of those who worry about the loss of thick mindfulness and/or yoga, code-switching amounts to a "Faustian bargain," entering school curricula at the cost of these practices' soul (Purser and Loy 2013). From other vantages, yoga practices contain their own "thickness," and thus instill spirituality and religion, regardless of terminology or intentions. It remains to be seen whether the institutional contexts of yoga, or other spiritual practices, will ultimately be more influential in thinning or thickening the connections between spirituality and religion in America.

References

Associated Press. 2007. "Yoga Causes Controversy in Public Schools." *NBC News*, January 28. http://www.nbcnews.com/id/16859368/.

Atkins, Shira. 2016. "100 Most Influential Yoga Teachers in America." *Sonima.com*, February 8. https://www.sonima.com/yoga/100-most-influential-yoga-teachers-in-america-2016/.

Barnes, Patricia M., Barbara E. Bloom, and Richard L. Nahin. 2008. "Complementary and Alternative Medicine Use among Adults and Children." *National Health Statistics Reports* 12: 1–23.

Becca. 2008. "Build Spiritual and Physical Strength with Christoga." Customer review, *Amazon*, March 13. https://tinyurl.com/ya8evoqu.

Beck, Sara. 2012. "Government Agencies Targeting Yoga Studios, Some Owners Say." *New York Times*, August 12. http://cityroom.blogs.nytimes.com/2012/08/12/government-agencies-are-taking-aim-at-yoga-studios-operators-say/?ref=nyregion&_r=0.

Black, Lindsey I., Patricia M. Barnes, Tainya C. Clarke, Barbara J. Stussman, and Richard L. Nahin. 2018. "Use of Yoga, Meditation, and Chiropractors among U.S. Children Aged 4–17 Years." *NCHS Data Brief*, November, 324: 1–8.

Blain, Glenn. 2012. "Yoga Ruled Not 'True Exercise' by State Tax Department." *NY Daily News*, July 27. http://www.nydailynews.com/new-york/yoga-ruled-not-true-exercise-state-tax-department-article-1.1123779.

Bowman, Bridget. 2014a. "Hindu Leader Condemns D.C. Yoga Tax." *Roll Call*, October 2. https://www.rollcall.com/2014/10/02/hindu-leader-condemns-d-c-yoga-tax/.

Bowman, Bridget. 2014b. "Yoga Community Argues 'Yoga Tax' Does Not Apply to Studios." *Roll Call*, September 25. https://www.rollcall.com/2014/09/25/yoga-community-argues-yoga-tax-does-not-apply-to-studios/.

Brown, Candy Gunther. 2018. "Christian Yoga: Something New under the Sun/Son?" *Church History* 87(3): 659–83.

Brown, Candy Gunther. 2019. *Debating Yoga and Mindfulness in Public Schools: Reforming Secular Education or Reestablishing Religion?* Chapel Hill: University of North Carolina Press.

Charter Appeal Board. 2016. "Opinion and Order." July 1. *Education for New Generations Charter School v. North Penn School District*, CAB No. 2013-10.

Clarke, Tainya C., Lindsey I. Black, Barbara J. Stussman, Patricia M. Barnes, and Richard L. Nahin. 2015. "Trends in the Use of Complementary Health Approaches among Adults: United States, 2002–2012." *National Health Statistics Reports* 79: 1–15.

District of Columbia Office of Tax and Revenue. 2014. "Effective October 1 the District of Columbia Sales Tax Extends to Additional Services." September 24. http://otr.cfo.dc.gov/release/effective-october-1-district-columbia-sales-tax-extends-additional-services.

DNAinfo. 2012. "Yoga Is Not Exercise, State Rules in Tax Decision." *DNAinfo*, July 26. https://www.dnainfo.com/new-york/20120726/new-york-city/yoga-exempt-from-sales-tax-because-its-not-exercise-state-rules.

Drughi, Octavia. 2017. "A Deeper Look into Yoga & Spirituality." *Book Yoga Retreats*, April 4. https://www.bookyogaretreats.com/news/yoga-and-spirituality-survey.

EEOC. 1994. "Best Practices of Private Sector Employers: Facts about Religious Discrimination." December. https://www.eeoc.gov/eeoc/task_reports/best_practices.cfm.

EEOC. 2008. "Section 12: Religious Discrimination." *Compliance Manual*. July 22. https://www.eeoc.gov/policy/docs/religion.html#_Toc203359487.

Fuller, Robert. 2001. *Spiritual, but Not Religious: Understanding Unchurched America*. New York: Oxford University Press.

Gardner-Chloros, Penelope. 2009. *Code-Switching*. New York: Cambridge University Press.

Goffman, Erving. 1986. *Frame Analysis: An Essay on the Organization of Experience*. Boston: Northeastern University Press.

Grossman, Cathy Lynn. 2010. "Survey: 72% of Millennials 'More Spiritual Than Religious.'" *USA Today*, April 27. https://usatoday30.usatoday.com/news/religion/2010-04-27-1Amillfaith27_ST_N.htm.

Guber, Tara. 2004. "Tara's Yoga for Kids: One Noble Soul Takes on the Public School System and Wins a Vedic Victory." *Hinduism Today*, April–June. https://www.hinduismtoday.com/modules/smartsection/item.php?itemid=1328.

Hallet, Vicky. 2014. "The Big Question about D.C.'s 'Yoga Tax': Should It Apply to Yoga?" *Washington Post*, September 30. https://www.washingtonpost.com/express/wp/2014/09/30/the-big-question-about-d-c-s-yoga-tax-should-it-apply-to-yoga/.

Havlen, Naomi. 2002. "Yoga in Classroom Brings Out Critics and Supporters." *Aspen Times*. Retrieved April 26, 2020. https://web.archive.org/web/20061121055249/http://yogaed.com/ye_new_site/pdfs/ASPEN/aspentimes2.pdf.

YOGA SPIRITUALITY AND US INSTITUTIONS   275

Huffstutter, P. J. 2009. "Missouri's Yoga Enthusiasts Go to the Mat over Sales Tax." *LA Times*, December 18. http://articles.latimes.com/2009/dec/18/nation/la-na-yoga-tax18-2009dec18.

Jois, Krishna Pattabhi. [1962] 2010. *Yoga Mala*. Maisuru, India: Astangayoganilaya; reprint, New York: North Point.

Jois, Krishna Pattabhi. 1995. "Wisdom of the Masters: Fourteen Distinguished Figures in the Yoga World Offer Advice to Those Starting Out on the Yoga Path As Well As to Seasoned Practitioners." Interview by *Yoga Journal*. *Yoga Journal* 6(122): 62–69.

Jois, Krishna Pattabhi. 2004. "3 Gurus, 48 Questions: Matching Interviews with Sri T. K. V. Desikachar, Sri B. K. S. Iyengar & Sri K. Pattabhi Jois." Interview by R. Alexander Medin. Edited by Deirdre Summerbell. *Namarupa*, Fall, 6–18.

Jois, Krishna Pattabhi. 2005. *Surya Namaskara*. Karnataka, India: Ashtanga Yoga Research Institute; New York: Ashtanga Yoga New York.

Jois Yoga. 2013. "Story." September 15. https://web.archive.org/web/20170113034729/http://joisyoga.com:80/about/story/.

Kaivalya, Alanna, and Arjuna van der Kooij. 2010. *Myths of the Asanas: The Stories at the Heart of the Yoga Tradition*. San Rafael, CA: Mandala.

Karpel, Richard. 2014a. "The DC 'Yoga Tax' Isn't Really a Yoga Tax." *Yoga Alliance*, July 30. https://www.yogaalliance.org/the_dc_yoga_tax_isnt_really_a_yoga_tax.

Karpel, Richard. 2014b. "Letter to Office of the Chief Financial Officer, DC." *Yoga Alliance*, July 18. https://www.yogaalliance.org/Portals/0/Articles/YA-Comment-Letter_DC-Budget-Health-Club-Tax.pdf.

Keil, David. 2017. "Assessing the Impacts of Yoga Asana—Survey Summary." *Yoga Anatomy*, March 21. https://www.yoganatomy.com/yoga-asana-survey-results-summary/.

Lal, Neeta. 2016. "The Politics of Yoga." *Diplomat*, April 4. http://thediplomat.com/2016/04/the-politics-of-yoga/.

McCaw, Christopher. 2020. "Mindfulness 'Thick' and 'Thin': A Critical Review of the Uses of Mindfulness in Education." *Oxford Review of Education* 46(2): 257–88.

McClellan, B. Edward. 1999. *Moral Education in America: Schools and the Shaping of Character from Colonial Times to the Present*. New York: Teachers College Press.

Mohler, R. Albert. 2010. "Yahoo, Yoga, and Yours Truly." *Albert Mohler*, October 7. http://www.albertmohler.com/2010/10/07/yahoo-yoga-and-yours-truly/.

Park, Crystal L., Kristen E. Riley, Elena Bedesin, and V. Michelle Stewart. 2016. "Why Practice Yoga? Practitioners' Motivations for Adopting and Maintaining Yoga Practice." *Journal of Health Psychology* 21(6): 887–96.

Penman, Stephen, Marc Cohen, Philip Stevens, and Sue Jackson. 2012. "Yoga in Australia: Results of a National Survey." *International Journal of Yoga* 5(2): 91–101.

Pew Research Center. 2012. *"Nones" on the Rise: One-in-Five Adults Have No Religious Affiliation*. Washington, DC: Pew Research Center. https://www.pewresearch.org/wp-content/uploads/sites/7/2012/10/NonesOnTheRise-full.pdf.

Pew Research Center. 2015. *America's Changing Religious Landscape: Christians Decline Sharply as Share of Population; Unaffiliated and Other Faiths Continue to Grow*. Washington, DC: Pew Research Center. https://www.pewforum.org/2015/05/12/americas-changing-religious-landscape/.

Purser, Ron, and David Loy. 2013. "Beyond McMindfulness." *Huffington Post*, August 31. http://www.huffingtonpost.com/ron-purser/beyond-mcmindfulness_b_3519289.html.

Quilty, Mary T., Robert B. Saper, Richard Goldstein, and Sat Bir S. Khalsa. 2013. "Yoga in the Real World: Perceptions, Motivators, Barriers, and Patterns of Use." *Global Advances in Health and Medicine* 2(1): 44–49.

Regur Development Group. 2013 (March). "EUSD Yoga." Video 1 of 4. In *Sedlock*.

Singleton, Mark. 2010. *Yoga Body: The Origins of Modern Posture Practice.* New York: Oxford University Press.

Soliman, Tamer M., Kathryn A. Johnson, and Hyunjin Song. 2015. "It's Not 'All in Your Head': Understanding Religion from an Embodied Cognition Perspective." *Perspectives on Psychological Science* 10(6): 852–64.

Sonima Health and Wellness Foundation, Inc. 2012. Form 990. Internal Revenue Service. Retrieved April 28, 2020 (https://projects.propublica.org/nonprofits/display_990/453182571/2013_12_EO%2F45-3182571_990_201212).

Stern, Eddie. 2015. Biographical sketch. *Sonima Foundation.* February 16. Removed by March 7, 2017. http://www.sonimafoundation.org/about-sonima-foundation/leadership/eddie-stern/.

Stern, Eddie, Courtney McDowell, Melanie Jane Parker, Christina Reich, and Barbara Verrochi. 2016. *Grades 3–5 Health & Wellness Course Unit 1 Session Plans.* Palm Beach, FL: Pure Edge.

Syman, Stefanie. 2010. *The Subtle Body: The Story of Yoga in America.* New York: Farrar, Straus & Giroux.

Syman, Stefanie. 2018. "The First Book of Yoga: The Enduring Influence of the Bhagavad Gita." *Yoga Journal*, October 12. https://www.yogajournal.com/yoga-101/first-book-yoga.

Williamson, L. A. 2012. "Yoga in Public Schools." *Teaching Tolerance: A Project of the Southern Poverty Law Center* 42 (Fall): 27–28.

Wilson, Jeff. 2014. *Mindful America: Meditation and the Mutual Transformation of Buddhism and American Culture.* New York: Oxford University Press.

Yoga Alliance. 2014. "The DC 'Yoga Tax' Isn't Really a Yoga Tax." *Yoga Alliance*, July 30. https://www.yogaalliance.org/the_dc_yoga_tax_isnt_really_a_yoga_tax.

Yoga Alliance. 2015. "Another Win for Yoga in Encinitas." April 6. https://www.yogaalliance.org/Learn/Article_Archive/Another_Win_for_Yoga_in_Encinitas.

Yoga Alliance. 2016. "Spirit of the Standards––RYS 200." July. https://www.yogaalliance.org/credentialing/standards/200-hourstandards.

Yoga Alliance. 2019. "Code of Conduct." May 28. https://web.archive.org/web/20190528175036/https://www.yogaalliance.org/AboutYA/OurPolicies/CodeofConduct.

Yoga Alliance. 2020. "Code of Conduct." February 27. https://www.yogaalliance.org/AboutYA/OurPolicies/CodeofConduct.

Yoga Journal, with Sports Marketing Surveys USA. 2012. *Yoga in America—2012.* Boulder, CO: Yoga Journal.

Yoga Journal and Yoga Alliance, with Ipsos Public Affairs. 2016. *The 2016 Yoga in America Study.* Boulder, CO: Yoga Journal. https://web.archive.org/web/20191207050802/http://media.yogajournal.com/wp-content/uploads/2016-Yoga-in-America-Study-Comprehensive-RESULTS.pdf.

Zed, Rajan. 2016. "Lauding Encinitas School Board for Funding Yoga, Hindus Urge Yoga in All California Schools." Press release, June 23. https://www.forpressrelease.com/forpressrelease/243331/19/lauding-encinitas-school-board-for-funding-yoga-hindus-urge-yoga-in-all-california-schools.

Cases

Abington School District v. Schempp. 1963. 374 U.S. 203.

Cotton v. Cate. 2014. 578. F. App'x 712. 9th Cir.

Edwards v. Aguillard. 1987. 482 U.S. 578.

Engel v. Vitale. 1962. 370 U.S. 422.

Garvins v. Burnett. 2009. No. 2:07-cv-174. WL 723888. W.D. Mich.

Lee v. Weisman. 1992. 505 U.S. 577.

Malnak v. Yogi. 1979. 592 F.2d 197. 3d Cir.

Mendoza v. Children's Women's Physicians of Westchester, LLP, Good Samaritan Hospital Medical Center. 2011. Supreme Court of the State of New York County of Rockland, Index No. SU-2011-3600, NYSCEF Doc. No. 8-12.

Powell v. Perry. 1988. No. PB-C-85-331. WL 93834. E.D. Ark.

Sedlock v. Baird. 2013. Superior Court of San Diego County, No. 37–2013–00035910–CU–MC–CTL.

Sedlock v. Baird. 2015. 235 Cal. App. 4th 874.

United States v. Meyers. 1996. 95 F.3d 1475. 10th Cir.

14

Training Spiritual Caregivers

Spirituality in Chaplaincy Programs
in Theological Education

Wendy Cadge, Beth Stroud, Patricia K. Palmer, George Fitchett,
Trace Haythorn, and Casey Clevenger

Numerous rabbinical and theological schools across the country offer courses in spiritual care, spiritual direction, spiritual integration, and the like. For example, the Claremont School of Theology currently offers a PhD in practical theology with a concentration in spiritual care and counseling, and the Iliff School of Theology offers a master of arts in pastoral and spiritual care. Yet scholars exploring trends toward spirituality and away from religion tend to overlook seminaries, theological schools, and other institutions that shape these discourses as they train religious leaders. Rather, scholars have favored individually oriented studies, case studies of seemingly spiritual groups, and a broad focus on consumers rather than producers of spiritual discourses and frames (Ammerman 2014; Roof 2003; Wuthnow 1998).

In the *New Metaphysicals*, Courtney Bender (2010) called for more attention to the sites where discourses of spirituality are produced and understandings of how they shape individuals' senses of spiritual and religious identification. We take Bender's call seriously in this chapter, exploring graduate theological education as a field that produces both discourses of spirituality and increasingly professionals—called chaplains or spiritual providers. While some might view this focus on theological education as counterintuitive, seeing these as the very institutions producing religious discourses that spiritual discourses push against, there is something more complicated at work here.

We focus narrowly on graduate education for chaplaincy, conceptualizing it as a site of transition (in a growing number of settings chaplaincy is being called spiritual care) and one of the few growth areas in light of long-term declines in theological education, as shown in Figure 14.1 (Meinzer 2018;

Wendy Cadge, Beth Stroud, Patricia K. Palmer, George Fitchett, Trace Haythorn, and Casey Clevenger, *Training Spiritual Caregivers* In: *Situating Spirituality.* Edited by: Brian Steensland, Jaime Kucinskas, and Anna Sun, Oxford University Press. © Oxford University Press 2022. DOI: 10.1093/oso/9780197565001.003.0015

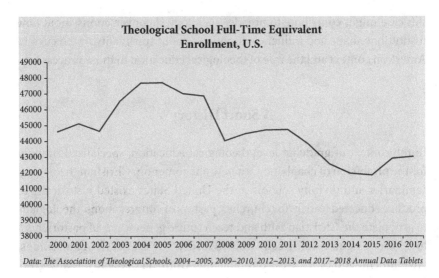

Figure 14.1 Theological school enrollments, 2000–2017

Tanner 2017). These educational institutions and the individuals they train are also reporting declining employment opportunities for full-time religious leaders, the growth of bivocational positions—in which a religious leader combines part-time positions—and growing numbers working outside of congregations where they undoubtedly encounter talk of spirituality (Schleifer and Cadge 2019; Vaters 2017; Wheeler 2014).

This chapter is one part of a broader project examining how theological schools, clinical training programs like the Association for Clinical Pastoral Education (ACPE), and professional associations train chaplains to work in healthcare.[1] About a quarter of theological schools, including those that offer accredited master's degrees, but are Jewish, Muslim, Buddhist, and interfaith institutions and *not* affiliated with Association of Theological Schools (ATS), have chaplaincy-focused programs or degrees. Most of these programs are relatively recent, that is, established after 2000, and new ones are emerging regularly. Many use languages of spirituality to describe the content and goals of their programs, with little standardization (Cadge et al. 2019; Cadge et al. 2020).

We briefly describe the history of graduate education for chaplaincy, the content of the curriculum, and approaches to religious diversity in this chapter, focusing on three distinct paths and sets of institutional contexts through which it emerged. We conclude with brief reflections about what this case might contribute to broader sociological conversations about how institutions shape and influence discourses about spirituality in the current American context and the role of theological education in those processes.

A Short History

In the context of graduate-level theological education, specialized training for the profession of chaplaincy is a new phenomenon. Christian theological seminaries and divinity schools in the United States existed historically to produce educated leaders for churches: pastors of congregations, theologians to articulate the Christian faith and teach future generations of pastors, and, to a lesser extent, theologically trained leaders for nonprofit organizations, government, and other areas of public life. Until very recently, few degree-granting theological schools conceived of chaplains as needing anything different from their academic programs than all their other students. In the Christian setting, the master of divinity, with its fourfold program of education in biblical studies, theology, history, and the various arts of ministry, was thought to be adequate for chaplains as well. In some sectors where chaplains work, such as the US armed forces, the MDiv is accepted as sufficient academic preparation (Stahl 2017).

Some chaplains, and particularly those in healthcare, have long pursued specialized education to supplement their graduate theological degrees. The clinical pastoral education (CPE) movement emerged in the mid-1920s when Anton Boisen, the chaplain at Worcester State Hospital in Massachusetts, began to experiment with using the mental hospital as a theological laboratory. He invited students to spend their summers in the hospital, serving as ward attendants by day and meeting for theological reflection at night. During those same years Richard Cabot, often called the "father of medical social work," wrote a plea titled "A Clinical Year for Theological Students," in which he urged theological schools to follow the example of medical education by integrating an internship year into the basic professional degree (Cadge 2012).

Due to the shared vision and energy of Cabot, Boisen, and Boisen's first students, the CPE movement grew and expanded rapidly. Cabot's proposal for integrating a clinical year into theological education was never realized. Instead, CPE developed its own organizations and centers, which operated parallel to theological seminaries and divinity schools. Some Protestant

TRAINING SPIRITUAL CAREGIVERS   281

denominations came to require or strongly recommend at least one unit of CPE for ordination, and most seminaries came to award academic credit toward the MDiv—generally the equivalent of one academic course—for a maximum of one unit of CPE. Further units of CPE, however, were often pursued only by specialists in pastoral care: congregational pastors who placed unusual value on their caring and healing functions, pastoral counselors and psychotherapists, and chaplains—especially healthcare chaplains. Until the 1970s, CPE remained an overwhelmingly mainline Protestant educational program, dominated by members of Protestant denominations that skewed white, male, and affluent and required a high level of education for ordination, particularly Presbyterians, Unitarians, Congregationalists, and Methodists. Lutherans developed their own CPE programs and organizations, as did Southern Baptists (long before the Southern Baptist Convention's conservative turn in the 1980s). Today, few seminaries require CPE, though most allow students to earn academic credit by taking one unit (Myers-Shirk 2008).

The oldest specialized chaplaincy program we know about *within* graduate theological education—as opposed to alongside or subsequent to it— was established in 1988 at Pentecostal Theological Seminary in Cleveland, Tennessee, the flagship school of the Church of God International.[2] Since then, our evidence suggests accelerating growth, as shown in Figure 14.2. In our sample of twenty academic chaplaincy programs, only the one at Pentecostal dates to before 1990. Three of the programs in our sample were established in the 1990s, eight were established between 2000 and 2009, and ten more since 2010. We continue to hear about new chaplaincy programs, and chaplaincy programs in development.

The chaplaincy program at Denver Theological Seminary, which first enrolled students in 1998, is among the oldest and best known in the United States. Its founder, Jan McCormack, had been a military chaplain for twenty years and was working on her doctorate of ministry at the seminary while serving as the senior chaplain at Buckley Guard Base (now Buckley Air Force Base) when administrators approached her about developing a way for students to specialize in chaplaincy. McCormack described chaplaincy as fundamentally different from congregational ministry in an interview, saying, "We chaplains don't wait for people to come to us. We go to them. And we're typically working in someone else's work center. . . . so in many ways we're all workplace chaplains. It's a whole different mindset for people to think that it isn't just taking what I do in the church, putting a new title on

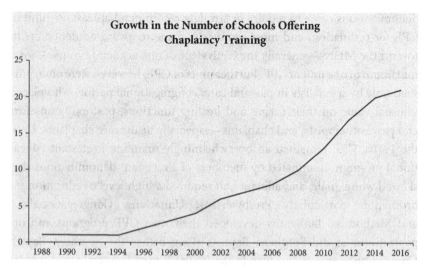

Figure 14.2 Growth in theological schools offering chaplaincy training in our sample, N = 21

it, and doing it somewhere else." From her military experience, McCormack knew that many people, particularly young people, were willing to trust chaplains even if they didn't trust organized religion or clergy in general. That knowledge motivated her to build a program that now includes multiple degree options and a fully accredited CPE center.

Three Historical Patterns

Across the twenty schools we examined in depth, we identified three major patterns that shaped the development of academic chaplaincy programs: a military chaplaincy pattern, a pastoral counseling pattern, and a minority religion pattern, which integrate discourses about spirituality to varying degrees.

Military Chaplaincy Pattern

The military chaplaincy pattern was most common in evangelical seminaries such as Pentecostal, Denver, Ashland Theological Seminary, and Columbia

Biblical Seminary, but we also saw it at the Seminary of the Southwest, an Episcopal school, and we see a variation on the theme at Boston University School of Theology, which is United Methodist. In this pattern, military chaplains themselves provided the energy and professional expertise for a new academic program. The programs at Denver, Ashland, Columbia Biblical, and Seminary of the Southwest are all directed by career military chaplains who retired from service with distinguished records. Like many who retire from the military, they retired at a relatively early age, which made it possible for them to pursue ambitious, long-term projects in retirement. Variations on Jan McCormack's story, described above, were repeated in interviews. David Scheider, the founding director of the chaplaincy program at Seminary of the Southwest, was an army chaplain for twenty-five years. William Payne, who designed and directs the program at Ashland, was a navy chaplain whose military career included serving at one point as deputy chaplain for all of Europe and, later on, all of Iraq. Michael Langston, who created the program at Columbia Biblical, began after retiring from a navy career including a tour as the commanding officer of the Navy Chaplain School and executive director of the Armed Forces Chaplaincy Center, as well as responsibilities in military diplomacy that included engaging religious leaders in Iraq and Afghanistan and mentoring some of Hamid Karzai's senior cabinet staff in religious leader engagement.

Talk of spirituality and spiritual care is present in the materials about some of these programs, but not others, likely related to the faculty who lead them. It should come as no surprise that seminary administrators have seen these retired military chaplains as resources, and looked to them to build programs. The retired chaplains, in turn, are profoundly motivated to design strong programs as a result of their military experience. For McCormack the motivation came from her sense that chaplains inspire trust. Payne was moved by the shortcomings of the chaplains he supervised in the navy: they were "woefully unprepared," he says, to serve in a pluralistic context. The military chaplaincy pattern also helps explain the emergence of the chaplaincy track at Boston University School of Theology, where Shelly Rambo, a pastoral theologian with a research interest in trauma, noticed the passion and focus of military chaplains who came to BU to pursue advanced theological training between deployments. "There was one year where I had several chaplains, and they made a very big impact on me," she says. They had come to BU, in particular, for its certificate program Religion and Conflict Transformation.

Their presence made Rambo think about what else BU could offer military chaplains.

The impact of military investment in higher education and professional advancement for its chaplains can hardly be underestimated, and this likely plays a role in how spiritual discourses are present in these programs. Traditionally the military views chaplains as the professionals who protect religious free exercise and has only slowly started to use the language of spirituality, mostly in terms of spiritual assessments that the military thinks chaplains should conduct on their colleagues (Cadge and Skaggs 2018; Stahl 2017; Sullivan 2014). The BU students who inspired Rambo were able to be there because their employer paid for them to obtain an additional year of schooling to help prepare them for more significant responsibilities, and they likely encountered more talk of spirituality in theological school than in the military. Other leaders of military chaplaincy programs in our sample received help from the army or navy in obtaining their doctorates, which enabled them to obtain their positions, in some cases, and provide leadership to the field.

Pastoral Counseling Pattern

The second way chaplaincy programs emerged in theological schools is through pastoral counseling, most common in mainline Protestant schools with a robust tradition of pastoral theology, such as Brite Divinity School and Iliff School of Theology, but also at Nazarene, which is more evangelical in character. In this pattern, a chaplaincy program develops under the guidance of a senior faculty member in the field of pastoral counseling or pastoral theology, often as a gradual shift in emphasis from counseling to chaplaincy within a program. This shift is evident in the work of Joretta Marshall at Brite Divinity School, who has seen the focus of her program switch from counseling to pastoral care in response to the development of licensing requirements for counseling professionals. Marshall says, "You can get licensed in Kentucky, for example, in Tennessee, and I think in North Carolina still, as a pastoral counselor. But everybody else mostly has to do LPC [licensed professional counselor] tracks to get licensure or an MSW or have some other kind of clinical degree." Although the program at Brite is now oriented toward pastoral care, students interested in pastoral counseling can pursue a dual track in collaboration with Texas Christian University's School of Social Work to earn an MSW along with their theological degree.

The teaching focus at Iliff School of Theology also reflects the shift away from counseling. Carrie Doehring says, "I'm trained both as a therapist and a pastor, but my writing and teaching has really focused on spiritual care, both [in] congregations and then intercultural spiritual care in multifaith settings," which reflects Iliff's commitment to preparing students for chaplaincy. Echoes of Judith Schwanz's background in counseling may remain in the chaplaincy certificate program at Nazarene, which requires Counseling for Grief and Loss as one of two key courses; nevertheless, the program provides certification of specialty training in chaplaincy rather than counseling. These guiding faculty members may have many years of professional counseling experience and may or may not have direct chaplaincy experience, but are often astute observers of the field. Aware of changes in licensing and reimbursement practice that have made it more difficult to make a living as a pastoral counselor than it was twenty years ago, these pastoral theologians have recognized chaplaincy as a profession in which the skills and values they teach continue to serve a critical need. They tend to move seamlessly between discourses of religion and spirituality, frequently using the term "spiritual care" to describe the work for which they are training.

Minority Religious Pattern

The third way chaplaincy programs have emerged is related to minority religions, and is common to schools and degree programs serving students from religious groups that represent small but growing percentages of the American population and have a less established institutional presence. In our sample, these include Islamic programs at Hartford Theological Seminary and Bayan Claremont, Buddhist programs at Naropa University and University of the West, and a program designed for persons with eclectic spiritual or religious identities and commitments at the Chaplaincy Institute in Berkeley, California.

What is unique about these programs is that a primary reason they offer a master's degree in the first place is to open up pathways into professional chaplaincy for their constituents. For members of the minority religious traditions, the benefit of an MDiv or equivalent degree is its legibility in civil society as a qualification for professional religious service. Hartford, Bayan, Naropa, and

University of the West all have graduates serving as chaplains in the armed forces—and without the degrees these schools make available, it would be very difficult for any Muslims or Buddhists to obtain those positions. Although Loyola University Chicago does not represent a minority religion (Catholic), its chaplaincy program developed to address some of these same limitations, in particular providing training to Catholic women religious who otherwise had limited avenues to enter leadership positions in ministry. Language of spirituality is evident in materials about all of these programs as well as interviews with their leaders.

Training Chaplains

Chaplaincy-related programs housed in theological schools and seminaries are diverse in form and content. They include short-term training courses for the general public, certificate programs, master of divinity degrees with a focus in chaplaincy, master of arts degrees in chaplaincy, doctorate of ministry degrees with a chaplaincy focus, and various combinations of the above. Some theological schools house ACPE-accredited centers within them, while others partner with CPE centers in their cities and states. In the United States and Canada, we identified about eighty theological schools that offer formal curriculum in chaplaincy, as shown in Figure 14.3. We excluded from these

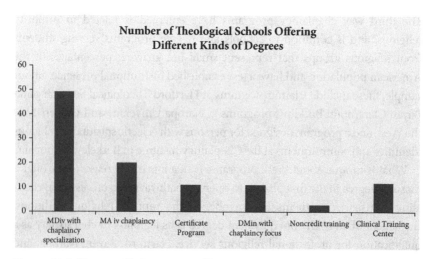

Figure 14.3 Degree offerings nationally, N = 83

counts schools that only offered courses in chaplaincy, focusing on specific programs making a concerted effort to train chaplains. The largest fraction of schools offers a master of divinity degree with a chaplaincy specialization. Growing numbers offer a master of arts degree in chaplaincy. Small numbers offer certificate programs and/or a DMin with a chaplaincy focus. Nationally we located about ten ACPE-accredited clinical training programs housed within theological schools. These broad patterns were replicated in our sample of twenty schools, as shown in Figure 14.4.

The most basic approaches—mostly at programs started through the military or pastoral care patterns—do little more than introduce students to the profession of chaplaincy and steer them toward existing courses in the curriculum thought to be most useful to chaplains. For example at Nazarene, MDiv students who wish to get a "certificate in chaplaincy ministry" are required to take two three-credit courses, Introduction to Chaplaincy and Counseling for Grief and Loss, and to use CPE for their field experience. At Boston University, Rambo points out, the chaplaincy track has involved no actual new courses so far: it consists of tweaks to existing distribution requirements. For example, all MDiv students must take two courses in an area called "Texts and Traditions," but chaplaincy students must choose a course in world religions for at least one of those.

Some of the other MDiv programs with chaplaincy concentrations require a longer list of courses, typically a combination of required courses

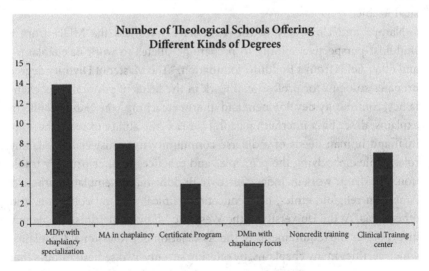

Figure 14.4 Degree offerings growth in our sample, N=21

and electives. At Brite, for example, students must complete a course titled Ministry of Pastoral Care as well as three hours of coursework in military chaplaincy and nine additional hours of coursework in pastoral care or courses related to war and peace. This program has a military focus, while a second focuses in pastoral care. Students at Denver Seminary take Issues in Counseling Ministries and electives from courses with titles such as Religious Pluralism, The Many Faces of Chaplaincy, Community-Based Clinical Pastoral Education, Crisis Counseling, and so forth. The extent to which these courses include language about spirituality in their titles and course descriptions of learning goals varies and seems to roughly parallel their history and which of the three trajectories informed their development.

Programs started through the minority religion pattern tend to have broader approaches to the curriculum and integrate more explicit discussion of spirituality. Claremont School of Theology has an Interfaith Track and an Islamic Chaplaincy Track in its MDiv that, according to the bulletin, "presupposes that men and women can exercise responsible leadership only when they combine an intimate knowledge of their own traditions, appreciation of other forms of spiritual practice and insight, a deep engagement with today's social and political realities, and strong dialogical and critical thinking skills." Coursework covers sacred texts, history of particular religious traditions, theology and teaching, and religious and/or faith-based ethics in addition to clinical pastoral education. Students in the Islamic Chaplaincy Track also must demonstrate intermediate proficiency in classical Arabic.

Naropa and University of the West have reworked the MDiv from a Buddhist perspective, aiming to prepare graduates to work in chaplaincy and other fields from a Buddhist foundation. "The Master of Divinity degree prepares students for professional work in the fields of pastoral care, chaplaincy, community development and dharma teaching," the Naropa Bulletin explains, describing interfaith pastoral care as "the ability to serve the spiritual and human needs of a diverse community in ministerial/chaplaincy roles while embodying the principles and practices of one's primary tradition." Academic work includes courses in Buddhism, contemplative practice, American religion, ethics, field education, clinical pastoral education, and other areas. At the University of the West, the MDiv in Buddhist chaplaincy incorporates the requirements of the Association of Professional Chaplains, which certifies many chaplains, by offering seventy-two semester hours that cover topics required for certification. Spiritual formation is emphasized throughout this curriculum, beginning with the first sentence of the learning objectives: "Spiritual formation in Buddhist chaplaincy is seen as the development of ethics, contemplative practice and wisdom." Students get hands-on experience in "spiritual care" as well as "spiritual care and counseling" throughout the program.

As a group, theological educators rarely agree and are not in sustained conversation across programs about what students need to be effective chaplains. There are few commonalities within or across programs regardless of the pattern that led to their formation and whether they are MDiv or MA programs. Learning goals similarly vary. Some faculties emphasize the centrality of self-reflection in the process of training to be a chaplain, while others emphasize experience with ritual, language, and ethics as central to the training. There are also varied approaches to clinical pastoral education. About three-quarters of the schools require at least one unit of CPE. Some require two units, and two programs require their students to complete the four units of CPE required to be board certified. Seven schools have ACPE-accredited centers connected to them, a number that seems to be growing over time.

Variation in curriculum is partially related to the pattern through which particular programs developed and mostly to the background of the faculty teaching in it and their own professional development and experience with chaplaincy. These faculty are as diverse as the programs they run. Two-thirds hold PhDs, and others hold DMin, EdD, or master's degrees. Four are also certified as ACPE educators—a credential that arguably represents as many years of advanced training as a doctorate. Quite a few are pastoral theologians, but the range of academic disciplines to which others belong is very wide and includes education, ethics, healthcare planning, interdisciplinary studies, intercultural studies, Islamic studies, psychology, religious studies, and sociology. Some of the faculty members in the sample have been in academia their whole professional lives. Others acquired their degrees during or subsequent to previous careers in military or healthcare chaplaincy, counseling, healthcare administration, or community organizing.

In interviews with the faculty who designed these programs, and who teach and mentor students in them, three major faculty commitments came into focus. Only one of those commitments—preparing their students to serve as spiritual helpers in a context of religious diversity—was one we specifically asked about in the interview. The other two major commitments were helping their students develop theological depth, and helping students develop a sense of identity and authority as chaplains. Not all the faculty expressed all three commitments, but most spoke about theological depth, expanded on the topic of religious diversity, or discussed identity and authority.

In speaking about identity and authority, faculty members expressed a concern that chaplains understand their unique place in society and the particular responsibilities that inhere in the chaplain's role. Some faculty members described who chaplains are and the power they have in terms of what other people look to them to do. For example, Rambo noted that the military chaplains in her program are often focused on getting further training in ethics, because commanders place a high value on chaplains' ethical advice. Garrett-Cobbina spoke about the transference and associations that attach to chaplains as soon as they introduce themselves as such: when the chaplain enters the room, she said, the patient responds out of whatever it is that the sacred or the holy represents to them.

Elaine Yuen, who directs the chaplaincy program at Naropa University, spoke about chaplains' identity and authority in relation to time. In the hospital setting, Yuen explained, where chaplains are uniquely unbound to the time pressure of billable hours, they are often more free than social workers or other staff members to develop a holistic understanding of patients' concerns, and to advocate for them. A number of the faculty members used metaphors about proximity to describe the chaplain's special identity and authority, describing the chaplain as the one who "comes alongside" or is good at "accompaniment." Jan McCormack says she always begins explaining chaplaincy to people who do not understand it by saying, "We chaplains don't wait for people to come to us. We go to them." The founder of the program at Pentecostal, recently retired, titled his book on chaplaincy *Outside the Gates*, and Oliver McMahan, who directs the program now, repeated that phrase a number of times in his interview, at moments trailing off between clearly articulated thoughts about the need for counseling skills and other practical ministry training to emphasize the extra-congregational nature of chaplaincy. "A chaplain needs to be willing to go . . . *outside the gates.*" Some located the chaplain's authority in the chaplain's ability to withstand the tensions of the curious social location chaplaincy requires, remaining true to several seemingly competing loyalties at once—faith community, employer, and the persons to whom care is provided.

Spiritual and Religious Differences

In current practice, most chaplains, by design, work with people who are spiritually and religiously different from them (Sullivan 2014). The faculty we interviewed emphasized that chaplaincy necessitates a stance of openness toward other faith traditions as well as knowledge about other traditions, and is incompatible with proselytization. This emphasis was nuanced differently from school to school. Two broad frames emerged that mapped loosely on to the pattern through which the program developed.

At evangelical schools mostly started through the *military or pastoral counseling patterns*, educators often began their discussion of religious diversity (typically religious, not spiritual) by describing the dilemma of the conservative evangelical seminarian who initially finds the idea of religious pluralism uncomfortable or even intolerable. When faculty at these schools spoke about religious diversity, one could almost imagine they had used the same words to talk with students. Chaplaincy at evangelical schools framed the chaplain's universal caregiving as a silent form of witness to the Christian faith, a witness that waits patiently for the moment when another person invites the chaplain to share this faith in a way that renders the exchange ethical. Of her young, conservative evangelical students, McCormack said:

> It isn't that they can't evangelize the way that they grew up if the person asks and the door is open, but that they don't necessarily have to do it that same way. They make it a dichotomy. Either I can't or I must. And I'm saying, it's always about the client. It's about their needs and their timing. It is not about you.

Evangelical chaplaincy faculty value knowledge about religious traditions other than Christianity, but their first educational task is sometimes persuading students that chaplaincy requires a certain evangelical reserve. "You have to hear and receive and not be offended, and then to be able to love and to take care of and come alongside of," said Mike Langston. "When you do that, later on they're going to come back to you and they might start asking you those theological questions that you want to dive into right now. But it might be ten weeks. It might be a whole year before they ever get to that point."

At the Buddhist and Muslim degree programs started with an interfaith focus, Jewish and Christian traditions remained a significant area of study in chaplaincy programs, and the faculty included scholars with substantial training and experience in those traditions. At University of the West, for example, the director of the chaplaincy program, Victor Gabriel, an ordained Tibetan Buddhist priest, is of Jewish and Asian ancestry, was raised Catholic, and was at a previous time in his life a Benedictine monk. Gabriel was recruited to University of the West specifically to teach the Abrahamic texts and traditions to Buddhist students, and freely uses his understanding of one tradition to teach his students something about another. He uses the Bible and the Koran to introduce his students to the principles of hermeneutics before inviting them to bring a critical lens to the study of Buddhism, connects the Five Precepts to the theologies of Jewish philosopher Martin Buber, and intentionally uses many of the same textbooks that his counterparts in Christian and Jewish schools would use. Gabriel says, "When I took over the program, we made it a rule that we would keep 50 percent what I call industry standards. That's how I market it to the students. Which, you know what it means, right? It means they are Christian. I told them that it's industry standards." As at Naropa, Bayan, and Hartford, the chaplaincy program at University of the West is focused on equipping students to navigate a landscape in which their own religious tradition, while it may represent a growing demographic in the United States, remains very much a vulnerable minority and spiritual discourse a language to bridge difference.

Initial Conclusions

Chaplaincy training programs are growing in theological schools, one of the few areas of growth amid declining enrollments. As faculty construct degree programs, talk about learning goals, and engage with their students, they simultaneously engage in discourse about spirituality that contribute to how spirituality is shaped inside and outside of religious organizations. As Courtney Bender and Nancy Ammerman remind us, spirituality is constructed in a wide range of ways across religious and nonreligious organizations and must be understood as such (Ammerman 2014; Bender and McRoberts 2012).

This chapter identifies three patterns through which chaplaincy education has emerged and begins to describe the contents of it and the presence and significance of various spiritual discourses in the process. On the evangelical and military side, spiritual discourses are more muted. On the mainline Protestant and interfaith side, they are more present, often serving as a bridge across people with different backgrounds and experiences. The pattern through which a program developed shapes the extent to which languages of spirituality are used as do the broadly diverse faculty that currently set learning goals and teach in the programs. It is the combined influence of programs histories and their faculty that shape the varied discourses about spirituality we identify in this chapter.

That said, these programs existing in the context of degree-accrediting institutions which are shaped by the policies of accrediting organizations, in many cases historical or current commitments to particular religious traditions, and other broader tensions in theological education today. Such factors combine to shape what is taught and how it is taught alongside the history of particular degree programs.

The programs we describe are young and small, and even in our sample some felt severe repercussions of the financial and political pressures facing their institutions. The faculty who administer these programs mostly work in isolation: a few have opportunities to collaborate with colleagues at nearby institutions. Nearly every chaplaincy department is a one-person shop. Findings from the larger study suggest that clinical educators in ACPE centers are only very marginally aware, if at all, of the work that is underway in theological schools to strengthen the theological education students receive prior to yearlong CPE residencies. Graduates of these academic programs also represent only a very small proportion of clinical residents and eventual chaplains. While we see some sites of extraordinary integration of the clinical and the academic aspects of chaplaincy education, for example at San Francisco Theological Seminary, where the director of the CPE center is a tenured member of the faculty, for the most part clinical chaplains in healthcare continue to be educated in a two distinct steps, one academic and the other clinical. The profession of chaplaincy, too, is in flux, with endorsement standards, competencies, academic requirements, and everything else subject to debate and possible change.

Some of our respondents hinted at a larger vision that, like the rest of this story, utilizes spiritual language in varied ways. Rochelle Robbins spoke of wanting her students to take more assertive roles with other members of their interdisciplinary teams, claiming the strengths they bring to the table in terms of understanding systems and groups, actively communicating, writing notes that doctors and nurses can act on, and intervening in the plan of care. Laurie Garrett-Cobbina anticipates seeing chaplaincy find a foothold

294 WENDY CADGE ET AL.

in more and more workplaces, from Google to Warner Brothers, and imagines that one day chaplains might be more important to the spiritual lives of Americans in general than the pastors of congregations. While those on the evangelical side continue to emphasize religion and those on the more progressive side speak more in terms of spirituality, spiritual discourses are present throughout the field, shaped by historical factors and the realities of institutional contexts, making an important component of how discourses of spirituality are being shaped in the contemporary United States.

Notes

1. We began by searching the websites of ATS member schools for any type of chaplaincy education program. Then we performed similar searches of the websites of schools accredited by TRACS (Transnational Association of Christian Colleges and Schools) and AARTS (the Association of Advanced Rabbinical and Talmudic Schools) to award master's degrees. Then, we searched the directories of the regional higher education accreditation agencies (the Higher Learning Commission, the Middle States Commission on Higher Education Accreditation, the New England Commission of Higher Education, the Southern Association of Colleges and Schools Commission on Colleges and Schools, and the Western Association of Colleges and Schools College and University Commission) for any other institutions that offered graduate-level degree programs for religious leaders, and performed a similar search of those institutions' websites. Two more programs (those at Brigham Young University and Western Michigan State University) were missed using this method and added later. This yielded a list of academic chaplaincy programs that, while it may not be comprehensive, is more comprehensive than any previous list. Because so many schools had chaplaincy programs, it was necessary to select a smaller sample where we would then interview faculty and gather more detailed enrollment and curriculum data. A large majority of the schools with chaplaincy programs were Protestant seminaries and divinity schools, so for the sample we chose schools that advertised two or more types of chaplaincy programs (for example, both an MA degree in chaplaincy and a chaplaincy track within an MDiv program), and tried to select roughly equal numbers of mainline and evangelical institutions. We then oversampled schools affiliated with all other religious traditions (Jewish, Muslim, Buddhist, Roman Catholic, and interreligious schools), including all the ones we could find that offered a chaplaincy program. A few schools were later eliminated from the study either because they chose not to participate, because they were not currently offering a chaplaincy program even though it may have appeared so from their institutional websites, or because after multiple attempts by telephone and email we were unable to reach anyone at the school.
2. The Church of God does not require a master's degree for ordination, and Pentecostals' degree programs thus serve not as academic gateways for students first contemplating

a call to ministry, but rather as advancement programs for persons the church has already identified as leaders. For Church of God pastors, the academic and training requirements for professional chaplaincy careers are much steeper than those for ordination, and interest in such careers often drives interest in the MDiv. In fact, according to Oliver McMahon, professor of clinical mental health counseling and the current director of the chaplaincy program, from earliest days the seminary's MDiv was envisioned as a path to professional chaplaincy in healthcare and the armed forces. Pentecostal offers several levels of chaplaincy training, from a one-week intensive course for persons interested in volunteering as chaplains with their local police or fire department or a disaster response team, to an MDiv with a chaplaincy focus including courses in trauma and crisis counseling, world religions, the theology of suffering, and extensive fieldwork.

References

Ammerman, Nancy T. 2014. *Sacred Stories, Spiritual Tribes: Finding Religion in Everyday Life*. New York: Oxford University Press.

Bender, Courtney. 2010. *The New Metaphysicals: Spirituality and the American Religious Imagination*. Chicago: University of Chicago Press.

Bender, Courtney, and Omar M. McRoberts. 2012. "Mapping a Field: Why and How to Study Spirituality." Social Science Research Council. https://tif.ssrc.org/wp-content/uploads/2010/05/Why-and-How-to-Study-Spirtuality.pdf

Cadge, Wendy. 2012. *Paging God: Religion in the Halls of Medicine*. Chicago: University of Chicago Press.

Cadge, Wendy, George Fitchett, Trace Haythorn, Patricia Palmer, Shelly Rambo, Casey Clevenger, and Irene Elizabeth Stroud. 2019. "Training Healthcare Chaplains: Yesterday, Today and Tomorrow." *Journal of Pastoral Care and Counseling* 73 (4): 211–21.

Cadge, Wendy, and Michael Skaggs. 2018. "Chaplaincy? Spiritual Care? Innovation? A Case Statement." Working Paper, Department of Sociology, Brandeis University.

Cadge, Wendy, Irene Elizabeth Stroud, Patricia K. Palmer, George Fitchett, Trace Haythorn, and Casey Clevenger. 2020. "Training Chaplains and Spiritual Caregivers: The Emergence and Growth of Chaplaincy Programs in Theological Education." *Pastoral Psychology* 69: 187–208.

Meinzer, Chris. 2018. "Master's Enrollment—a Changing Landscape." The American Theological Schools: The Commission on Accrediting, April.

Myers-Shirk, Susan E. 2008. *Helping the Good Shepherd: Pastoral Counselors in a Psychotherapeutic Culture, 1925–1975*. Baltimore: Johns Hopkins University Press.

Roof, Wade Clark. 2003. "Religion and Spirituality: Toward an Integrated Analysis." Pp. 137–50 in *Handbook of the Sociology of Religion*, edited by Michele Dillon. Cambridge: Cambridge University Press.

Schleifer, Cyrus, and Wendy Cadge. 2019. "Clergy Working outside of Congregations, 1976–2016." *Review of Religious Research* 61: 411–29.

Stahl, Ronit. 2017. *Enlisting Faith: How the Military Chaplaincy Shaped Religion and State in Modern America*. Cambridge, MA: Harvard University Press.

Sullivan, Winnifred Fallers. 2014. *A Ministry of Presence: Chaplaincy, Spiritual Care and the Law*. Chicago: University of Chicago Press.

Tanner, Tom. 2017. "Four Trends That May Portend the Future for ATS Enrollment: What the Last Decade Says about the Next Decade." *Journal of Christian Ministry*, 6: 22–26.

Vaters, Karl. 2017. "The New Normal: Realities and Trends in Bivocational Ministry." *Christianity Today*. https://www.christianitytoday.com/karl-vaters/2017/december/new-normal-9-realities-trends-bivocational-ministry.html

Wheeler, David R. 2014. "Higher Calling, Lower Wages: The Vanishing of the Middle-Class Clergy." *The Atlantic*, July 22.

Wuthnow, Robert. 1998. *After Heaven: Spirituality in America since the 1950s*. Berkeley: University of California Press.

15

Spirituality and Islam

Sufism in Indonesia

Rachel Rinaldo

How does spirituality manifest within Islamic traditions?[1] Muslim societies indeed have mystical and devotional traditions such as Sufism, which is today often referred to by both scholars and lay practitioners as a spiritual tradition. In common with other forms of spirituality, Sufism emphasizes the inner self and the individual relationship to the divine. Yet Sufism has a contested status in many contemporary Muslim majority societies.

This chapter examines Sufism in Indonesia, the world's largest majority Muslim country. It investigates how Sufism has intersected with other approaches to Islam and examines the social and political contours of the recent Sufi revival. Historically, Sufism has been both politically and theologically influential in Indonesia, but has also faced challenge and contestation from other Muslims. In recent years, the concept of spirituality has enjoyed new prominence in Indonesia and is often associated with Sufi approaches to Islam. Indonesian Sufism has revived, especially among the educated middle class, though it has also become closer to more conventional Islamic practice. Elements of Sufism have been taken up by contemporary Islamic preachers and activists seeking to broaden their appeal. These developments suggest a need for a more multifaceted understanding of the relationship between institutionalized religion and spirituality.

Spirituality and Sufism in Islam

Muslim societies have long-standing mystical, devotional, and esoteric traditions. There are terms in Arabic, Persian, Turkish, and other languages spoken by Muslims whose meaning is close to the Western meaning of spirituality. As the scholar Seyyed Hossein Nasr writes, "These terms refer to that

Rachel Rinaldo, *Spirituality and Islam* In: *Situating Spirituality*. Edited by: Brian Steensland, Jaime Kucinskas, and Anna Sun, Oxford University Press. © Oxford University Press 2022. DOI: 10.1093/oso/9780197565001.003.0016

which is related to the world of the Spirit, is in Divine Proximity, possesses inwardness and interiority, and is identified with this as real . . . permanent, and abiding, rather than the transient and passing" (Nasr 1987, xvii).

Perhaps the best-known of the Islamic mystical and devotional traditions is Sufism (also called *tasawwuf*). Sufism is best understood as not a specific philosophy or movement, but rather, as Sedgwick (2000) proposes, a set of emphases and practices. Sharing the main objectives of Islam such as submission to God, Sufis more strongly emphasize the struggle with temptation and desire, and for control of the self in order to come to know God while still on earth (10). Thus, Sufism can be understood as an Islamic form of spirituality. Sedgwick notes that Sufis tend to take a more pragmatic view of Islamic law in order to allow for a variety of actions in the struggle against temptation, which may account for the widespread but inaccurate perception that Sufis are unorthodox or theologically liberal. In fact, Sedgwick argues, Sufism is very heterogeneous and does not easily correspond to scholarly distinctions between theological conservatism and liberalism or scripturalism versus interpretivism. What really distinguishes Sufism is a heightened awareness of the presence of the divine and a strong emphasis on the teacher-follower relationship, usually involving a charismatic teacher-scholar (known as a *shaykh*, *wali*, or *pir* in various contexts) who is understood as possessing special proximity to the divine: "The end of the Sufi path, then, is mystical union with God, and the greatest Sufis . . . have experienced this proximity to God. . . . Most Sufis are ordinary believers with a special thirst for the divine, for something more than the day-to-day practice of Islam can provide" (Sedgwick 2000, 29). Like other Muslims, Sufis follow the standard practices of Islam, such as the five daily prayers and fasting, but they are more likely to be involved with tariqas, Sufi schools or orders with a spiritual leader that followers see as the path to becoming closer to God.

Sufis trace their origins back to the Koran. Some of Islam's most renowned thinkers, such as the Persian philosopher Al-Ghazali, and the Spanish philosopher Ibn al-'Arabi have been associated with Sufism. Scholars agree that Sufism began to flower in the eleventh century and became an important aspect of Islamic life throughout the Middle East, West Africa, and Asia in the medieval era (Danner 1987). Because Sufi sheikhs traveled widely and were often part of vast trade networks, they may have played a role in bringing Islam to Southeast Asia from the thirteenth to fifteenth centuries, and later contributed to Islamizing Southeast Asian regions such as Java (Sedgwick

2000; Feener and Laffan 2005; Kersten 2017). Yet Sufism has been contested and critiqued from within Islam. This is particularly true in Indonesia, where Sufism has been at times influential and other times marginalized, often related to shifting national and global religious and political contexts.

Sufism Contested

Sufism has long been contested. Nineteenth-century Western scholarship often positioned Sufism as opposed to Islamic orthodoxy. More recently Sufism has been held up by Western policymakers as well as governments of some majority Muslim societies as a model of peaceful, moderate, and pluralist Islam (Sedgwick 2000; Ewing 2020; Philippon 2020). This, along with the popularity of the Sufi poet Rumi, is probably the root of common, romanticized understandings of Sufism as mystical and unorthodox, and perhaps not even Islamic. Indeed, the late twentieth century saw the rise of Sufism in Western societies as a transnational new religious movement that is fairly disconnected from Sufism in Muslim-majority societies (Genn 2007).

Western perceptions of Sufism as romantic, mystical, and unorthodox have both influenced and in turn been influenced by reformist Muslim critiques of Sufism. Sufism has been subject to critique by a variety of Muslim reformist movements, such as Wahhabism and Salafism, as well as Muslim modernism.

Ibn 'Abd al-Wahhab, the founder of what has come to be known as Wahhabism, was not the first critic of Sufism, but has been one of the most influential. He sought to purify Islam of innovations, arguing for a return to Islam as it was practiced by the Prophet Muhammad and his companions. Ibn 'Abd al-Wahhab opposed Sufis and others who practiced Islam in ways he viewed as unorthodox. For example, he harshly criticized the common practice of visiting the tombs of Muslim saints, and his followers demolished shrines marking the birthplaces of the Prophet Muhammad and his first wife Khadija (Sedgwick 2000). As the Kingdom of Saudi Arabia emerged in the twentieth century, it adopted Ibn 'Abd al-Wahhab's views as the core of its official practice. Ibn 'Abd al-Wahhab's views have been disseminated through Saudi Arabia's global educational and religious programs backed by its oil wealth (Varagur 2020).

However, an arguably greater challenge to Sufism came with the rise of Salafism in the twentieth century. Intellectual ferment and longings for reform in the Middle East, and especially in Cairo, resulted in a Muslim modernist movement in the late nineteenth century, which sought to reconcile Islam with aspects of modern society and Western science. Taking their cue from the modernist movement but extending far beyond it, Salafis sought to return Islam to the pure practices of the first Muslims. Salafis tended to have a narrower perspective on Islamic jurisprudential interpretation (*fiqh*), while also encouraging Muslims to study the Koran for themselves. The extent to which Salafi and modernist Islamic thinkers rejected Sufism varies, but what does seem clear is that they both were harshly critical of popular Sufi practices such as shrine culture and festivals (Sedgwick 2000; Ewing 2020). Similarly, some prominent Western scholars of Islam in the twentieth century, such as Clifford Geertz, viewed Sufism as a mystical tradition in decline due to the rise of the rationalist scripturalism of Muslim reformists and modernists (Howell and Bruinessen 2007).

Over the course of the twentieth century, both Salafist and modernist Muslim perspectives became more influential in the major Islamic institutions, such as al-Azhar University in Cairo. Modernists were especially critical of what they saw as the secrecy and exclusivity of Sufi orders and their deference to charismatic masters (Howell and Bruinessen 2007:7). More recently, contemporary Salafist movements have sometimes militantly opposed Sufism. Extremist movements such as the Islamic State have attacked Sufi shrines. Yet some scholars argue that this is less about theological differences than about the global positioning of Sufism as a moderate form of Islam. This has led Sufism in some countries to be identified with governments viewed with antipathy by extremist Muslims (Ewing 2020; Philippon 2020).

Sedgwick writes that by the end of the twentieth century, "Sufism was in partial eclipse in the Islamic world" (2000, 97). And yet other scholars suggest that the Islamic resurgence that began in the late 1960s in the Middle East not only invigorated the well-known Islamist and neofundamentalist movements, but also a lesser-known resurgence of Sufism. This development calls into question both Muslim modernist and Western assumptions about Sufism's association with tradition rather than modernity (Howell and Bruinessen 2007). The case of Sufism in Indonesia illuminates this complex trajectory.

Sufi Spirituality in Indonesia: Challenges and Uncertainty

Sufism has had a prominent influence on Indonesian Islam. While historians are not sure exactly when or how Sufism first reached Southeast Asia, there is increasing evidence that Sufism may have played a role in the gradual Islamization of the region. Certainly, from the sixteenth century, the regions that have become modern Malaysia and Indonesia were enmeshed in Indian Ocean Islamic trade and religious networks (Kersten 2017). By the seventeenth century, Sufist currents were evident in the writings of Acehnese and Javanese Islamic scholars. Recent historical scholarship suggests that the seventeenth and eighteenth centuries produced extensive cross-fertilization of more sharia-oriented (Islamic law) Islam and Sufism in several of the sultanates of the region. Historian M. C. Ricklefs describes the Mataram court of Central Java as developing a "mystic synthesis" involving "reconciliation of Javanese martial traditions of kingship with Islamic traditions of mystic piety (Ricklefs 2006, 49). Kersten (2017) argues that Malay-speaking Sufis "played a role in bringing the Javanese-speaking heartlands of central and east Java under the sway of more sober forms of Sufism and within the ambit of wider Islamic religious learning" (51). The Indonesian archipelago became known for Islamic practices that included visiting the tombs of saints, deep respect for teacher scholars (known as *kyai* in Java), and the development of Islamic boarding schools led by *kyai*s and structured around the teacher-student relationship. Muslim thinkers in Java and other regions were also very much engaged with the leading Middle Eastern Islamic scholars of the time, often via the networks of religious scholars who traveled the Indian Ocean region (Kersten 2017).

In the early twentieth century, the intellectual currents of Muslim reformism and modernism reached Indonesia. Founded in Java in 1912, Muhammadiyah was Indonesia's first mass Muslim organization. Strongly influenced by Muslim modernists and an emerging urban Muslim class, Muhammadiyah focused on educational and social welfare provision, and sought to disseminate more modern and rationalistic religious understandings throughout Indonesia. Muhammadiyah has always seen itself as adhering to Islamic orthodoxy, and as such has sought to weed out what it sees as un-Islamic innovation, syncretism, and superstition. It leaned toward a more scripturalist approach to interpreting religious texts.

However, one of the key Islamic scholars associated with Muhammadiyah, Hamka, who also became one of Indonesia's leading public intellectuals in the mid-twentieth century, sought to reconcile Sufism with modernist Islam. In his work, he reinterpreted key Sufi concepts and encouraged Sufis to shed their superstition and irrationality, emphasizing what he saw as the positive aspects of spirituality for Muslims (Aljunied 2016). Thus, while many Muhammadiyah thinkers have been suspicious of Sufism as representing an overly syncretic approach to Islam, Hamka stands as an early proponent of a synthesis of Sufism and more orthodox Islam that has become more prominent in recent years.

In 1926, traditionalist religious scholars in Java, seeking to counter the influence of modernizers, established Nahdlatul Ulama, another large Muslim organization. While Nahdlatul Ulama also sees itself as adhering to Islamic orthodoxy, it has long been known for its greater tolerance of Javanese cultural practices, its traditional Islamic boarding schools, recitation of sacred texts, and its emphasis on interpretation of *fiqh* (Rinaldo 2013). Nahdlatul Ulama has also long drawn its adherents from more rural parts of Java.

Sufi teachers were important in the formation of Nahdlatul Ulama, and their influence has long been evident in the practices and philosophy of the organization. Yet, by the 1990s, Sufism within Nahdlatul Ulama changed into a more orthodox and sharia-oriented Islam, reflecting a broader shift in Indonesia toward more orthodox practice and understandings of Islam (Bruinessen 2007).

Sufi influences are also very evident in the *kebatinan* (search for inner truth) movements that arose in Indonesia in the early twentieth century. Many of these movements presented themselves as Muslim alternatives to more scripturalist versions of Islam, while others strayed beyond the conventional boundaries of Islam. These syncretistic mystical movements usually followed a particular spiritual teacher and had doctrine and rituals strongly influenced by Sufism (Aljunied 2016; Bruinessen 2007). Many of these movements focused especially on meditation as a means of acquiring spiritual power. *Kebatinan* movements drew their followers from a range of social classes—some were popular among peasants, while others attracted urban elites. Additionally, there were other mystical movements that considered themselves Muslim and Sufi but were viewed as heretical by more established Sufis.

The relationships to power of these different movements have been diverse. Muslim intellectuals associated with both Muhammadiyah and Nahdlatul Ulama were politically influential over the course of the twentieth century, often jockeying for favor as government advisers. For example, Nadhlatul

Ulama's Kiai Mustafa cultivated strong relationships with the authoritarian regime of Suharto in the 1970s, even publicly emphasizing the role of Sufism and spiritual growth for the government's development efforts. These efforts produced conflict within his organization, and in 1984 Nahdlatul Ulama decided to withdraw from formal politics. But as a result of the accommodation between NU and the regime, some Sufi teachers became spiritual counselors of Suharto government officials, and NU-oriented civil servants became influential in the Ministry of Religious Affairs (Bruinessen 2007).

Kebatinan and other mystical and heterodox movements did not fare as well over the course of the twentieth century. Although they gained widespread popularity after the country gained independence in 1945 and through the 1960s, they failed to gain legal recognition as religions, and eventually faced accusations of illegitimacy (Howell 2007). The Indonesian state since independence has recognized Islam, Protestantism, Catholicism, Hinduism, and Buddhism as official religions (with Confucianism a later addition). The country's founding philosophy, Pancasila, includes belief in one God as its first principle, instituting a "Godly nationalism" that is not secular but also not defined by Islam (Menchik 2015). Membership in the nation is thus synonymous with membership in an official religion.

Toward the end of his regime, President Sukarno (president of Indonesia from 1945 to 1967) directed the government to recognize other religions but urged the *kebatinan* groups to return to their legitimate religions (Howell 2007, 223). During the 1950s and 1960s, many followers of *kebatinan* and mystical groups were allied with the Left, and they were targeted as communists during the mass killings of 1965–66 (Bruinessen 2007). Some of these movements survived by disavowing claims to be religions. Proclaiming their support for the new Suharto regime (1967–98), they were given the status of "faiths" and placed under the supervision of the Ministry of Education and Culture rather than the Ministry of Religion (Howell 2007). Under the Suharto regime Indonesian citizens were required to specify one of the official religions on their identity cards, leading in some cases to conversions of nominal Muslims to Christianity, and in other cases, of adherents of spiritualist movements to Islam (Hefner 2001). While *kebatinan* movements still exist, their popular appeal in recent years has been much more limited. And as scholars have chronicled, from the 1970s onward there has been a trend for more orthodox religious practice, particularly among Muslims (Ricklefs 2012). As Howell observes, "The normative standard for religion embodied in legislation and public administration of the modernizing state had come

304 RACHEL RINALDO

to embody the Enlightenment ideals of highly rationalized social forms and scripturalist religious expression" (2007, 226).

But spirituality more generally and Sufism in particular did not disappear from Indonesia. Despite the trend for orthodoxy, charismatic mystics have continued to proliferate, even from within established religious institutions (Bruinessen 2007). Over the years, some have become politically influential. And along with Indonesia's Islamic revival in the 1980s and 1990s came a grassroots revival of Sufism, particularly among the growing urban middle class, and an incorporation of Sufi elements by more conventional Islamic actors and institutions. Thus, as Bruinessen (2007) comments, "Urbanization, globalization, economic growth, and the education revolution have not led to the marginalization of Sufism in Indonesia but rather to increased social and political prominence" (Bruinessen 2007, 111).

The Sufi Revival in Indonesia

The Islamic revival in Indonesia became very evident in the 1990s and especially after the country democratized in 1998. It has been marked by the widespread adoption of headscarves and Muslim dress by women, the proliferation of Muslim religious study groups and private schools, visibly Muslim political actors, the building of Arabic-style mosques across the country, and even the adoption of more Arabic-sounding names. Along with this, many scholars argue, has come a more conservative approach to understanding and practicing Islam, marked by greater adherence to orthodox pious practices, increased emphasis on gender difference, and more differentiation between Muslims and non-Muslims (Hefner 2001; Bruinessen 2013). And yet this Islamic revival is multifaceted—it has also fostered the rise of progressive Muslim scholarship and activism, including a lively Muslim feminist movement (Rinaldo 2013, 2014).

A lesser-known aspect of the Indonesian Islamic revival is the revitalization of Sufism, or what some have called the Sufi Renewal. As Howell (2001, 2012, 2015) has chronicled, the modernist Muslim intellectual Nurcholish Madjid popularized the term "neo-Sufism" in the 1990s. He was known for establishing for the Paramadina Foundation in an affluent Jakarta suburb in 1986—an organization that offered workshops, lectures, and other educational activities for an audience of educated urban Muslims. Madjid and his circle were critical of both fundamentalist Islam and what he saw as "new

SPIRITUALITY AND ISLAM   305

age cults" that were outside of organized religion (most likely he was referring to *kebatinan* and other mystical movements). Instead, starting with a landmark 1993 lecture that was later published as a booklet, Madjid encouraged Muslims to cultivate their inner spiritual lives. Madjid's neo-Sufism condemned what he viewed as folk Sufism and traditions of deference to spiritual masters but also found great value in Sufi practices such as spiritual retreat and efforts toward intimacy with God. Most important, Madjid called for Muslim spirituality to contribute to society. Neo-Sufism thus set the stage for Indonesian Sufism's evolution to become more socially acceptable as well as more socially engaged (Howell 2012).

Through the 1990s, Paradamina was an influential organization, and Sufi-inflected mass media such as pamphlets, self-help books, and videos became widespread. Now a full-fledged university, Paramadina has come to be seen as part of a network of progressive Islamic institutions and organizations. In addition to its degree programs, Paramadina continues to hold religious courses, seminars, and workshops for the public, and its many prominent faculty and alumni have become identified with an inclusive and pluralist approach to Islam. Paramadina's success also led the way for Sufi spirituality to be adapted in surprising new ways.[2] New expressions of Sufism have been especially popular with younger and more educated Indonesians.

Sufism and Spirituality in Contemporary Indonesia

In the last twenty years, Indonesia has seen a fusion of more scripturalist Islam with Sufi spiritualist practices. This has been pioneered by a cohort of "televangelist" Muslim preachers who are extremely savvy about attracting mass audiences and whose preaching styles are strongly emotive, humorous, and generally entertaining. Howell (2012, 2015) discusses the examples of Arifin Ilham and Abdullah Gymnastiar (Aa Gym) who lead televised mass prayer services and outdoor rallies that include Sufi praise songs and litanies. Aa Gym's preaching, which often has a confessional element, emphasizes purifying the heart, while Arifin Ilham emphasizes that becoming closer to God will help believers become more pious and better practitioners of Islam. As Howell (2015) observes, "Both preachers linked religious emotion to the work of personal moral reform presented in their sermons and in their books" (22).

What makes this incorporation of Sufism particularly intriguing is that Arifin Ilham's and Aa Gym's approaches to Islam generally emphasize a more conservative and scripturalist interpretation of texts. Neither comes directly from the traditionalist Nahdlatul Ulama milieu, where we might expect to find such incorporations of Sufism. Arifin Ilham refers to his approach as Salafi Sufism, which he distinguishes from Sunni Salafism, which he criticizes for being influenced by foreign, impure practices. What exactly constitutes Salafi Sufism is somewhat ambiguous, but Arifin's statement suggests that he seeks to distance himself from Middle Eastern Salafism, not because he disagrees with such an interpretation of Islam, but rather because it strikes him as alien to Indonesia. According to Howell (2012), Arifin Ilham is sympathetic to those who have tried to make Indonesia a state ruled by sharia law. He has associated with some of Indonesia's more extremist Islamic preachers, but also has cultural connections to the Nahdlatul Ulama milieu. Arifin Ilham and Aa Gym point toward a surprising new fusion of Sufism and Salafism, somewhat reminiscent of Hamka, in which Salafi preachers use Sufis spiritual exercises, recitations, and litanies to develop resonance and mass appeal. These and other Sufi renewal movements apparently "offer Muslims ways to cultivate an experientially rich religious practice" (27) that can broaden and deepen Islam's attractiveness.

Arifin Ilham and Aa Gym have both become rich and influential through sales of their programs. Aa Gym has been extremely successful in marketing his programs for spiritual development as a form of human resources training (known as *Manajemen Qolbu*—or Heart Management) to corporations and other institutions. This popular program fuses Sufi spirituality with Western pop psychology and management theory (Hoesterey 2015). Aa Gym's popular appeal faded somewhat after he took a second wife, but newer celebrity preachers with similar styles have emerged in his place.

Manajemen Qolbu is just one of several Sufi-inflected spiritual development programs that became popular with Indonesian companies and corporations starting in the early 2000s. Another training program that has been perhaps even more successful and influential is the Emotional Spiritual Quotient (ESQ) developed by the businessman Ary Ginanjar. Studying ESQ trainings at the state-owned company Krakatau Steel, Rudnyckyj (2010) found that the trainings included an emphasis on changing the self through self-reflection, emotional accounts of personal transformation, collective Muslim prayer and recitations, physical activities to produce connection and embodiment, as well as an emphasis on the personal charisma of Ginanjar as a master trainer. While Rudnyckyj (2010) does not specifically discuss the Sufi elements of ESQ, widely available descriptions of the training on the internet describe it as combining science, Sufism, Islam, psychology, and management theory. Ginanjar has also been vocal about his view that Indonesia is undergoing a moral crisis because most Indonesians do not adhere to Islam and Islam needs spirituality in order to avoid being merely "ritualistic" (Rudnyckyj 2010, 8).

There are also more free-flowing expressions of Sufi renewal, particularly in urban settings. Arifin (2019) observes that a growing number of young people are becoming involved in the activities of the long-standing Naqshabandya Sufi order. They seem to be especially drawn to practices such as dance and music as ways to express love for God, and many of their events take place in upscale cafes and coffee shops, which have proliferated in urban areas in Indonesia. Nevertheless, according to Arifin (2019), Sufi orders such as Naqshabandya have gone through a process of change, deemphasizing the sheikh-student relationship, simplifying recruitment, and encouraging reflection on political issues such as nationalism and democracy. Indeed, Umar and Woodward (2020) propose that efforts to promote Salafism have actually led to a resurgence of Sufi-oriented piety in Indonesia and Nigeria. They argue that Sufis have successfully used "cultural strategies" such as music, theater, and festivals to counter the influence of Salafism, and that Salafism's weakness is its conflation of Islam and Arab culture as well as its strident opposition to local cultural expressions of Islam.

Similarly, Muttaqin (2012) has tracked the shifting meanings of the Indonesian word *spiritualitas* and the English word "spiritual," finding that both are now commonly used in Indonesia. He proposes that their recent usage demonstrates a trend for Islam to absorb expressions of spirituality. Muttaqin (2012) argues that previously, the Indonesian word *spiritualitas* was associated with *kebatinan* and other groups viewed as not true religions, and increasingly as heterodox by Muslims. But the Sufi renewal movements, as well as the televangelists and the Sufi-inflected religious management trainings have lent the concept of spirituality a new and positive connotation. According to Muttaqin (2012, 48), "This indicates a shift in the meaning of spirituality from the ideas and practices related to the indigenous and eclectic-cultural expressions outside official religions to one that is closely associated with religion." For Muttaqin, this suggests that rather than spirituality being understood as an alternative to religion, in Indonesia institutionalized religion, especially Islam, has taken over spirituality. As the most well-known and accessible form of Islamic spirituality, Sufism has been key to this process.

However, despite these freewheeling and often creative expressions of Sufism among urban elites, the incorporation of Sufi spirituality into tele-vangelism and corporate training programs may ultimately have greater consequences than simply making Islam appealing to the masses. Such programs seem to use a very broad definition of Sufi spirituality, inviting people to be closer to God and emotionally expressive in their piety, but not drawing them into Sufi orders. Rudnyckyj (2010) argues that such trainings represent a shift to mobilize religion to address the economic and cultural challenges of globalization by fusing Islam with human resources management techniques. In a religiously and ethnically diverse country, the proliferation of Islamic spiritual trainings, particularly at state-owned corporations, redefines national belonging in much more religious terms. Thus, the stakes of the appropriation of Sufi spirituality may be high. The widespread adoption of spiritual training programs risks marginalizing both non-Muslims and those who may seek to be Muslim in a different way. As Rudnyckyj concludes, the introduction of "explicitly Islamic spiritual reform . . . called into question the religious pluralism that was a founding principle of the nation" (2010, 220). Although Sufism has a reputation for being more tolerant, it would be a mistake to assume that Sufism promotes political or cultural liberalism. A recent study found that Islamist protests in Jakarta in 2016 intentionally created an atmosphere similar to Sufi assemblies and also mobilized Sufi associations to participate by framing the rallies as religious rather than political events (Miichi 2019). Thus, Sufism can be incorporated into Islamist political efforts.

Insights for the Study of Spirituality and Religion

Sufism has been a leading form of Islamic spirituality for centuries. But the ascendance of modernist and scripturalist approaches to Islam in many Muslim-majority societies has meant that Sufism, especially with its focus on the personal connection to divinity and its relationship to popular mystical Islamic practices, risks being perceived as heterodox and impure. And yet, while Sufism may no longer be closely connected to centers of Islamic power in many countries, it has survived. In fact, its "eclipse" may have been overstated (Sedgwick 2000). Especially in countries such as Mali, Morocco,

SPIRITUALITY AND ISLAM 309

and Indonesia, Sufism has adapted to changing religious and political contexts, and also found new practitioners, particularly among the growing urban middle classes (Bruinessen and Howell 2007).

The case of Indonesia suggests several important insights as well as possible new directions for the study of spirituality. First, the relationship between institutional religion and spirituality may not necessarily be dichotomous. The rise of more modernist and scripturalist approaches to Islam has indeed been a challenge for Sufism and more spiritualist ways of practicing Islam. Some elements of the Sufi renewal in Indonesia may represent a backlash or at least a need for an alternative to scripturalist Islam. But the dynamic between scripturalist and Sufi spirituality also deserves attention for highlighting how these seemingly incompatible ways of being Muslim can sometimes be reconciled. In Indonesia, Sufi spirituality has become an important means of adding emotional depth and richness to scripturalist practice, and Sufi-inflected religious preaching and trainings may be contributing to the mass appeal of Islam in Indonesia.

Second, Sufism's shifting status in Indonesia suggests the importance of understanding the political dimensions of spirituality. In a country where the government actively manages religion and polices the boundaries both between religions and between religion and nonreligion, spirituality can easily become politicized. During the twentieth century, at times scripturalist Islam has been marginalized and Sufi Islam and even mystical Islamic movements were closer to power, while at other times scripturalist Islam's ascendance has posed challenges for Sufism. More recently, institutionalized Islam may be drawing on Sufism to broaden its appeal, while Sufi movements have also become more orthodox in their practice, drawing away from more mystical Islamic movements viewed by religious and political authorities as merely "faiths" or cultural movements. Thus, scholars should consider how spirituality is understood politically with respect to institutional religion in different contexts. How and when does a dichotomy form between spirituality and institutionalized religion? And when does spirituality come to be a source of political contestation or accommodation?

Finally, the transnational dimensions of spirituality also deserve greater investigation. As the historical discussion in this chapter shows, not only did Sufism historically spread through transnational religious networks, but so did its challengers such as Salafism. Contemporary Sufi renewal movements also have transnational dimensions. Ary Ginanjar has exported his ESQ programs to a number of countries, and Sufi orders originally based in the

Middle East and South Asia have followed Muslim immigrants to the West. More recently, Western religious seekers have also been attracted to Sufi spirituality (Sedgwick 2000; Genn 2007).

When considering these transnational dimensions of Sufism, the case of Indonesia shows how Sufism and its relationship to politics is highly contextual. While Sufism can be found across the world, its trajectories differ greatly in various Muslim contexts. For example, while Sufism was once an important aspect of Muslim religious life in Saudi Arabia, during the twentieth century, Sufi shrines were attacked and Sufi practitioners persecuted. While the Saudi government has become more tolerant of Sufism, Sufism remains marginal in the kingdom (Ambah 2006).

The country of Pakistan bears stronger similarities to Indonesia, with a long history of both popular and intellectual Sufism. However, Pakistan's inception as a republic in which Islam plays a central role, and the country's deep involvement in geopolitics since 9/11, have had significant impacts on Sufism. Thus, "Debates about Islamic reform and the legitimacy of Sufi Islam have been intertwined with struggles to negotiate the type of Islamic state and society that Pakistan aspires intertwined with struggles to negotiate the type of Islamic state and society that Pakistan aspires to be" (Ewing 2020, 12). While Sufi shrines and tariqa have been mainstays of religious life in Pakistan, South Asian Muslim reformists with Salafist leanings such as the Deobandi movement and the scholar Abul A'la Maududi harshly critiqued such practices as aberrant, primitive, and syncretic, and they have been an important influence on both the Pakistani state and on popular understandings of Islam. Nevertheless, while some scholars suggest that popular religious practice in Pakistan has shifted away from Sufism, others observe that these more Salafist-oriented movements embrace certain aspects of Sufi tradition while condemning others (Zaman 2018). In recent years, the Pakistani state has embraced Sufi organizations and thinkers to position itself as a locus of moderate Islam. But these Sufi-leaning organizations and thinkers do not necessarily fit stereotypes of Sufism as "liberal" or "peaceful." At the same time, militants such as the Islamic State have violently attacked Sufi shrines. Whether such attacks arise from beliefs about how Islam should be practiced or from conflicts with the Pakistani government, Ewing (2020) maintains that in South Asia "a chasm has developed between something that has come to be called Salafi or 'fundamentalist' Islam and Sufism, and this chasm has come to shape the understandings and practices of Muslims themselves" (1).

Social movement scholars highlight the importance of political opportunity structures in expanding or constraining the possibilities for collective action, and thereby also influencing the actions of social movement actors. Similarly, the divergent paths of Sufism in different Muslim contexts suggest that *religious opportunity structures* influence religious practices, identities, and actors. Religious opportunity structures could include the relationship between religion and the state as well as the nature of the elite's religious commitments. The cases of Indonesia, Pakistan, and Saudi Arabia in the twentieth century suggest that the relationship between religion and the state has shaped both the trajectory of Sufism and Islamic spirituality more generally. Thus, in Indonesia and Pakistan, republican states that incorporate aspects of Islam as well as secular governance have often sought to incorporate Sufism. The popularity of Sufism and Sufi Salafism among middle class and elite Indonesians suggests a more heterogeneous and autonomous religious field that allows for religious bricolage.

Meanwhile in Saudi Arabia, the monarchy's embrace of Wahhabism and governance by Islamic law has made it hostile to Sufism. Salafism and Sufism seem to be more strongly dichotomized in contemporary Pakistan than Indonesia, due to the widespread influence in Pakistan of reformist movements such as the Deobandi, militant movements that lean toward Salafism and have a hostile relationship to the state, and the state's embrace of Sufism during the war on terror. These examples point to the need for sociologists of religion to consider how religious opportunity structures shape spiritual practices and movements.

Much remains to be understood about contemporary Islamic forms of spirituality, but following the complex trajectory of Sufism in Indonesia and elsewhere can help us to better understand how Islamic spirituality is influenced by both cultural contexts and religious and political power relations.

Notes

1. The author would like to thank Eva F. Nisa (Australian National University) for insightful comments on this chapter.
2. The Sufi renewal in Indonesia has certainly not been without critics. Some Salafis continue to express virulent opposition to such practices, connecting them to heterodoxy and moral crisis (Laffan 2007).

References

Aljunied, Khairuddin. 2016. "Reorienting Sufism: Hamka and Islamic Mysticism in the Malay World. *Indonesia* 101: 67–84.

Ambah, Faizeh Saleh. 2006. "In Saudi Arabia, a Resurgence of Sufism." *Washington Post*, May 2.

Arifin, Achmad Zainal. 2019. "From Magics, Dances, to Cafes: The Role of Sufism in Constructing Identity among the Urban Youth." *Advances in Social Science, Education and Humanities Research* 339. https://doi.org/10.2991/aicosh-19.2019.35.

Bruinessen, Martin van. 2007. "Saints, Politicians and Sufi Bureaucrats: Mysticism and Politics in Indonesia's New Order." Pp. 92–112 Chapter 6 in *Sufism and the "Modern" in Islam*, edited by Martin van Bruinessen and Julia Day Howell. London: I.B. Tauris.

Bruinessen, Martin van, ed. 2013. *Contemporary Developments in Indonesian Islam: Explaining the "Conservative Turn"*. Singapore: Institute of Southeast Asian Studies.

Bruinessen, Martin van, and Julia Day Howell, eds. 2007. *Sufism and the "Modern" in Islam*. London: I.B. Tauris.

Danner, Victor. 1987. "The Early Development of Sufism." Pp. 438–79 Chapter 13 in *Islamic Spirituality: Foundations*, edited by Seyyed Hossein Nasr. New York: Crossroad Publishing Company.

Ewing, Katherine Pratt. 2020. "Introduction. Sufis and the State: The Politics of Islam in South Asia and Beyond." Pp. 1–24 in *Modern Sufis and the State: The Politics of Islam in South Asia and Beyond*, edited by Katherine Pratt Ewing and Rosemary R. Corbett. New York: Columbia University Press.

Feener, R. Michael, and Michael F. Laffan. 2005. "Sufi Scents across the Indian Ocean: Yemeni Hagiography and the Earliest History of Southeast Asian Islam." *Archipel* 70: 185–208.

Genn, Celia A. 2007. "The Development of a Modern Western Sufism." Pp. 257–78 Chapter 14 in *Sufism and the "Modern" in Islam*, edited by Martin van Bruinessen and Julia Day Howell. London: I.B. Tauris.

Hefner, Robert W. 2001. *Civil Islam: Muslims and Democratization in Indonesia*. Princeton, NJ: Princeton University Press.

Hoesterey, James Bourk. 2015. *Rebranding Islam: Piety, Prosperity, and a Self-Help Guru*. Palo Alto, CA: Stanford University Press.

Howell, Julia Day. 2001. "Sufism and the Indonesian Islamic Revival." *Journal of Asian Studies* 60(3): 701–29.

Howell, Julia Day and Martin van Bruinessen. 2007. "Sufism and 'the modern' in Islam." Pp. 3–18 Chapter 3 in *Sufism and the "Modern" in Islam*, edited by Martin van Bruinessen and Julia Day Howell. London: I.B. Tauris.

Howell, Julia Day. 2007. "Modernity and Islamic Spirituality in Indonesia's New Sufi Networks." Pp. 217–40 Chapter 12 in *Sufism and the "Modern" in Islam*, edited by Martin van Bruinessen and Julia Day Howell. London: I.B. Tauris.

Howell, Julia Day. 2010. "Indonesia's Salafist Sufis." *Modern Asian Studies* 44(5): 1029–51.

Howell, Julia Day. 2012. "Introduction: Sufism and Neo-Sufism in Indonesia Today." *Review of Indonesian and Malaysian Affairs* 46(2): 1–24.

Howell, Julia Day. 2015. "Revitalised Sufism and the New Piety Movements in Islamic Southeast Asia." Pp. 276–92 Chapter 18 in the *Routledge Handbook of Religions in Asia*, edited by Bryan S. Turner and Oscar Salemink. London: Routledge.

SPIRITUALITY AND ISLAM 313

Kersten, Carool. 2017. *A History of Islam in Indonesia: Unity in Diversity*. Edinburgh: Edinburgh University Press.

Laffan, Michael F. 2007. "National Crisis and the Representation of Traditional Sufism in Indonesia: The Periodicals *Salafy* and *Sufi*." Pp. 149–71 Chapter 9 in in *Sufism and the "Modern" in Islam*, edited by Martin van Bruinessen and Julia Day Howell. London: I.B. Tauris.

Menchik, Jeremy. 2015. *Islam and Democracy in Indonesia: Tolerance without Liberalism*. Cambridge: Cambridge University Press.

Miichi, Ken. 2019. "Urban Sufi and Politics in Contemporary Indonesia: The Role of Dhikr Associations in the Anti-'Ahok' Rallies." *Southeast Asia Research* 27(3). https://doi.org/10.1090/0967828X.2019.1667110.

Muttaqin, Ahmad. 2012. "Islam and the Changing Meaning of *Spiritualitas* and *Spiritual*." *Al-Jamiah: Journal of Islamic Studies* 50(1): 23–56.

Nasr, Seyyed Hossein. 1987. *Islamic Spirituality: Foundations*. New York: Crossroad Publishing Company.

Philippon, Alix. 2020. "Sufi Politics and the War on Terror in Pakistan: Looking for an Alternative to Radical Islamism?" Pp. 140–60 Chapter 8 in *Modern Sufis and the State: The Politics of Islam in South Asia and Beyond*, edited by Katherine Pratt Ewing and Rosemary R. Corbett. New York: Columbia University Press.

Ricklefs, M. C. 2006. *Mystic Synthesis in Java: A History of Islamization from the Fourteenth to the Early Nineteenth Centuries*. Norwalk, CT: East Bridge Signature Books.

Ricklefs, M. C. 2012. *Islamisation and its Opponents in Java: C. 1930 to the Present*. Singapore: National University of Singapore Press.

Rinaldo, Rachel. 2013. *Mobilizing Piety: Islam and Feminism in Indonesia*. New York: Oxford University Press.

Rinaldo, Rachel. 2014. "Pious and Critical: Muslim Women Activists and the Question of Agency." *Gender & Society* 28(6): 824–46.

Rudnyckyj, Daromir. 2010. *Spiritual Economies: Islam, Globalization, and the Afterlife of Development*. Ithaca, NY: Cornell University Press.

Sedgwick, Mark J. 2000. *Sufism: The Essentials*. Cairo: American University in Cairo Press.

Umar, Muhammad Sani, and Mark Woodward. 2020. "The Izala Effect: Unintended Consequences of Salafi Radicalism in Indonesia and Nigeria." *Contemporary Islam* 14: 49–73.

Varagur, Krithika. 2020. *The Call: Inside the Global Saudi Religious Project*. New York: Columbia Global Reports.

Zaman, Muhammad Qasim. 2018. *Islam in Pakistan: A History*. Princeton, NJ: Princeton University Press.

16

The Transmission of Spirituality in Broader Landscapes of Power

Jaime Kucinskas

In thinking of spiritual practice in the United States, many people conjure images of serene, isolated meditators sitting cross-legged on zafu cushions, calming yoga classes at sparsely decorated yoga studios, or peaceful walks in nature, which offer practitioners respite from the hectic vicissitudes of everyday life. Such images abound in the scholarly literature on spirituality as well. For example, Michal Pagis (2010) describes Buddhist vipassana daily meditation sessions as

> semi-sterile environments in which one can renounce social interaction and resurrect Buddhist wisdom. The semi-sterile environment is based on an imitation of the conditions of the meditation center: a temporal and spatial renunciation from daily life through sitting in an isolated corner, turning off the phone, dimming the lights, and concentrating on sensations. (485)

Descriptions such as these depict spiritual practices as occurring in intentionally bounded places, which are in certain physical and cognitive ways "set apart and forbidden," in the canonical words of Émile Durkheim (1995).

Yet, in the midst of people's deeply social lives, how set apart are spiritual practices and experiences? Even when people try to set their daily life aside, influence from greater social structures and cultures can seep in, in sometimes unexpected ways. In this chapter, in an effort to sensitize scholars and practitioners to the dynamic, relational, and socially situated nature of spirituality (Stanley 2012), I put forth a framework to study spirituality as a particularly adaptable cultural form, shaped by practitioners and the cultural and structural forces around them in manifold ways. At the heart of this framework is the conceptualization of spirituality as a "porous cultural

Jaime Kucinskas, *The Transmission of Spirituality in Broader Landscapes of Power* In: *Situating Spirituality.* Edited by: Brian Steensland, Jaime Kucinskas, and Anna Sun, Oxford University Press. © Oxford University Press 2022. DOI: 10.1093/oso/9780197565001.003.0017

object," which senders transmit and translate for receivers across social space and time (Pagis et al. 2018). It also can serve as a placeholder of sorts, or an "empty signifier," in the words of Laclau (1996), which draws upon and encodes elements of "oppositional organizational elements" and ultimately may tilt to support hegemonic cultures (Islam et al. 2017).

As Peter Beyer (2020) theorizes, as traditional religions lose power and influence, spirituality is on the rise. He attributes the latter's increasing appeal in part to how adaptable and individualistic it seems, unconstrained by the obligations and formal regulatory mechanisms of religious institutions that control how traditions are maintained, conveyed, and passed on—such as through powerful, hierarchical, clearly delineated authority structures, official doctrine, and other normative constraints specifying who, when, and how practices can be taught.

Spiritual practices are constituted and transmitted in ever more syncretic incarnations as they are carried into new areas. They may arise at the interstices of religious organizations and private life (Sigalow 2016), other secular institutions, or public life (Kucinskas 2019; Pagis et al. 2018). They can be promoted by commercial or nonprofit organizations, such as mindfulness or yoga classes, which seek to attract secular audiences. Given the varying institutional boundaries that spirituality may span, and the cultural contradictions and multiplex, multilayered meanings possible in such locations, each of these different forms of spiritual transmission is likely to vary from the others, as well as contain substantial internal variance.

By paying more attention to foundational elements of the process of spiritual transmission, such as *transmitters* and how they convey the practices, *the audience*, and *both the local and larger contexts* in which they are located, scholars of spirituality can better illustrate the socially embedded, dynamic nature of spiritual phenomena. As cultural theorist Wendy Griswold articulates in her "cultural diamond" (2012), there is a lot to be gained by examining the relationships between the four points of culture, which include cultural objects, cultural creators, cultural receivers, and the social world in which they are situated. Spiritual transmission occurs as people or organizations convey information about a special practice to others, who learn it and may alter it. Alterations are based on who is receiving the practice and how they interpret it; this new practitioner then shares what they learned about the practice with someone else, and the dynamic process of communication continues on.

However, rather than occur in a social vacuum, this process occurs in a context of multiple, overlapping, and hierarchical social fields. Applying this framework to spirituality studies, and extending it based on insights from field theory, sensitizing scholars to the multiple overlapping social hierarchies and fields in which spirituality is embedded (Fligstein and McAdam 2012), not only heightens sensitivity to the dynamic nature of spirituality, but also attunes us to how powerful interests and institutions can infuse and shape spiritual content. Media portrayals of spiritual practices and practitioners, and others—who learn about spiritual practices secondhand through word of mouth, the media, and other sources outside of spiritual spaces, yet hold positions of influence and power—further shape the development of the practices, who does them, why they do them, and who avoids them.

As spirituality moves, its transmitters may wrestle with different aims, such as maintaining a sense of spiritual legitimacy and authenticity or altering spirituality to fit in new locations and appeal to new audiences.[1] While transmitters may seek to incorporate more "authentic" or earnest spiritual practices, values or references from their own spiritual lineages, some studies suggest that influences from their larger cultural and institutional contexts can tilt the balance of the oppositional mix of spiritual and secular elements to reinforce rather than transform the institutional and normative status quo (Islam et al. 2017).

I illustrate the key elements of my framework of the cultural transmission of spirituality using examples from my (2019) research on leaders of the mindfulness movement in the United States as well as from a collaborative research project on students' spiritual practices at a small elite liberal arts college.[2] I first show how spiritual *transmitters* adapt practices in manifold strategic and subtle ways, as evident in the spread of mindfulness in the United States. By adapting mindful practices and ideology to appeal to new institutional audiences (across healthcare, education, business, and the military) while also incorporating elements from their own secular, spiritual, and religious backgrounds, mindful leaders created a vast new field composed of differentiated mindful programs and practices. Next, I show how mindfulness continued to develop based on *media coverage* and by *others outside the movement* who learned about it secondhand in varied *powerful institutional contexts*. Lastly, through an example from a power yoga class at a small residential college, I show how *audiences* embedded in certain social locations can interpret spiritual practices quite differently than teachers convey, based

THE TRANSMISSION OF SPIRITUALITY 317

on where they are socially situated in terms of their age, peer culture, and institutional setting.

Based on all of these above mechanisms and tensions shaping spiritual transmission, spiritual meanings and practices gradually change. They change in part due to certain strategic actions on the part of transmitters, in part due to less conscious alterations made on the behalf of both the senders and receivers of practices, and in part due to powerful influences from broad social institutions and cultures, such as that portrayed and amplified in the media—to result in the transformation of practices as they move across time and institutions. In short, the larger social and institutional settings people are a part of permeate and infuse their spiritual experiences, in ways sometimes unbeknownst to practitioners. By paying heed to these processes of spiritual transmission, practitioners and scholars alike will become much more aware of the fundamentally relational and institutionally and culturally embedded nature of spirituality.

The Transmitters: Leaders of the Mindfulness Movement in the United States, 1979–2019

Since 1979, with the establishment of Jon Kabat-Zinn's Mindfulness Based Stress Reduction (MBSR) program at the University of Massachusetts Medical School in Shrewsbury, Massachusetts, a movement of intellectual, social, and economic elites have established a variety of organizations to spread mindfulness and other Buddhist-inspired contemplative meditation practices across professional institutions in the United States. However, rather than establish a single regulatory body to oversee the training and certification of mindful educators, founding members of the movement, such as Kabat-Zinn, instead advocated that mindfulness teachers should be allowed to adapt their programs as they see fit to appeal new audiences across institutional settings:

It is important to point out that there should and can be no fixed form for this to happen. Meditative pathways, teachers, and programs cannot be cloned, although effective models might be adapted and modified, as has been the case in medical and educational settings with mindfulness-based stress reduction. Appropriate forms and vehicles need to develop out of the personal contemplative experiences, meditation practices, and visions

318   JAIME KUCINSKAS

for what might be possible of the individuals who undertake to bring the
contemplative dimension into mainstream life in society. These forms will
have to interface in appropriate ways with the social terrain and be sensitive
to professional, institutional, generational, and ethnic cultures and their
values. (Kabat-Zinn 1994, 6)

Consequently, mindfulness differentiated in countless ways as it spread
into higher education, K–12 education, healthcare, the military, sports, law,
business, prisons, and elsewhere. In many programs, direct references to
Buddhist religion—such as to deities, cosmology, and rituals like chanting—
were removed. Transmitters adapted Buddhist-inspired mindfulness
practices further, based on their personal religious, spiritual, and professional backgrounds, and to resonate with intended audiences' professional
cultures, preferences, and needs.

This leaves us with a wide-ranging breadth of mindfulness programs. For
example, in one mindful education program for small children, educator
Julia Martin drew from her prior experiences working in education, from
feedback from a top Buddhist vipassana Insight Meditation teacher, and from
exercises she found online in the media to develop her mindfulness program
for kids. In doing so, she deliberately tried to create Buddhist-inspired mindfulness programs that would be age appropriate for kids, as understood from
a Western perspective on childhood development.

Martin's curriculum included various mindful lessons intended to teach
attention, kindness, and caring in alignment with Buddhist ethics. For example, she had small children use "kindness wands" in pairs: one student held a heart wand and spoke from the heart, while a second student,
holding a star wand, was a "star listener." Older children used a "Just Like
Me" practice, which I've seen used at Buddhist and mindfulness trainings
alike: Martin picked it up from a *Huffington Post* article. For the Just Like Me
practice, students paired with a partner they did not know well, closed their
eyes, imagined their partner and contemplated statements Martin read, such
as "So notice that this person has a body and a mind just like me. . . . Notice
that this person has hopes and wishes and dreams just like me. Notice that
this person has suffering in their life, in their families, in their school, in their
community."

Like other mindful educators of children, Martin took care to secularize the language used in her program. Mindful educators only seemed
vaguely aware of legal limitations of bringing religion into public schools,

THE TRANSMISSION OF SPIRITUALITY   319

as stipulated by the Establishment Clause of the First Amendment to the Constitution, which regulates church-state relations and prohibits government institutions, such as public schools, from supporting a particular religion. But they nonetheless took seriously the need to secularize programs. Most K–12 mindful educators were more worried about provoking a negative response from parents of other faith traditions or teachers than violating the Establishment Clause. As a result, they took care to translate their practices into secular language that kids, teachers, administrators, and parents would understand and not be offended by. "Meditation . . . really triggers people," Martin told me. "So I don't usually say meditation. I usually say mindfulness practice. And then the other is lovingkindness, because that sounds really religious. And what I say is caring practice."

By contrast, mindfulness emerged quite differently in a program targeting law enforcement officers and veterans. Michael Taylor, a former air force pilot who had studied Karma Kagyu Buddhism at Naropa University, created his program to appeal to "blue-collar, git 'er done kind of guys." Taylor drew from Tibetan Buddhist practices as well as a "mission oriented," "operational perspective" commonly used in the military and sports performance language. Similar to Martin, even as he acknowledged that his program was "very much" based in Karma Kagyu Buddhism, he removed explicit references to Buddhism and brought in language familiar and resonant with his intended audience. In his 'mind training" program he was

> not talking about meditation, not doing anything that they would consider weird or unusual. . . . Don't ever use the word "meditation." Don't even use the word "mindfulness." It's all couched in science, in terms of the neuroscience and the nervous system regulation. . . . It's all under the rubric of peak performance to some degree, in terms of what we present to 'em.

Taylor admitted his training program, which brought in combat practice from military and law enforcement training—using real guns and multiple assailants—would give "ordinary meditation teachers and a lot of therapists a conniption fit." Furthermore, some might question from a Buddhist ethical perspective whether Taylor had deviated from the central Buddhist tenets not to kill or incite harm to others in his effort to appeal to, train, and be of use to law enforcement and the military.

The preceding examples reveal how the transmission of spirituality is influenced by teachers—and their professional, spiritual, and religious

320 JAIME KUCINSKAS

backgrounds—as well as their institutional audiences—and the structural, normative, and linguistic limitations of the institution in which they are embedded. Through these processes, the arc of cultural transmission and adaptation shifts in deliberate and unconscious ways to maintain authentic claims to spiritual lineages while also accommodating the powerful interests of larger social institutions. As Gazi Islam and his colleagues (2017) find in their study of corporate mindfulness programs, mindfulness operates as an "empty signifier." As theorized by Ernesto Laclau (1996), empty signifiers operate as a space in which discourse containing oppositional elements in a system can be held and negotiated, "even as they attempt to capture the wholeness of the organization in its 'absent communitarian fullness'" (Laclau 1996, 43; cf. Islam et al. 2017, 4).

At their base, such signifiers are inherently political: both Laclau and Islam and his colleagues (2017) conclude that, over time, they come to represent hegemonic cultural interests. In the case of the corporate mindfulness programs Islam et al. (2017) studied, which ostensibly represented multiple competing interests such as employee well-being and performance, contemplation and action, and the interests of the greater good, most of the time practitioners and companies hosting the programs particularly valued the business-friendly stated benefits of mindfulness, with their emphasis on individual development, action, and increased productivity.

The Media: Mindfulness in the Public Eye

Accounts of mindfulness have appeared across wide-ranging, influential, national and international media outlets, such as the *New York Times*, *Washington Post*, *CNN*, *Time*, ABC News, *CBS Sunday Morning*, Fox News, *Daily Mail*, *Wired*, *Forbes*, *Scientific American*, and *Business Insider*. Many reports champion the benefits of mindfulness practice. For example, David Gelles's columns (2018a) at the *New York Times* inform people "How to Be More Mindful at Work." He interviews CEOs that meditate, extoling the benefits of their mindful practices and influences on their organizations. CNN anchor Anderson Cooper and *Huffington Post* founder Arianna Huffington have also promoted meditation across various media outlets and conferences.

In response to the mainstream popularity of mindfulness and its incorporation into powerful institutions, a chorus of critiques have arisen among other journalists in mainstream media (e.g., Burton and Effinger's 2014 "To Make a Killing on Wall Street, Start Meditating") academics, and religious practitioners (Purser and Loy's 2013 critique of "McMindfulness" on *Huffington Post*) about mindfulness's role in supporting capitalism, white supremacy, and other hegemonic cultures.

For the most part though, mainstream media tends to depict mindfulness in a positive but vague manner. In this stream of reporting, the practices seem to have lost definition, their distinctiveness, and their roots in Buddhism. Todd Essig's (2012) *Forbes* article on the Search Inside Yourself program at Google, which actually directly draws upon Buddhist tenets and practices, exhibits this trend in describing the program as

> a rock-solid business-friendly mindfulness course in three acts: train your attention, develop self-knowledge and self-mastery, and create useful mental habits.... All Mindfulness is Good Mindfulness. It doesn't matter where or how you develop mindfulness. Doesn't matter why. Doesn't even matter what you do: meditation, yoga, prayer, therapy, gratitude, science-help practices, hiking, painting, exercise, etc. It's all *good.*

Essig's reporting shows how easily spiritual traditions can be interpreted by journalists in mainstream media as positive, vague, nondescript secularized traditions. This then teaches readers that this is what these traditions, such as mindfulness, are: they are popular, secular, good, and business-friendly. This is despite the fact that the ethical roots of Buddhism seek to counter selfish, materialistic pursuits and that oftentimes Buddhist ethics and practices are seamlessly woven into mindfulness programs. At this point, through the process of diffusion through varied institutions and sources, spiritual meanings, ethics, and practices become ever more diffuse, open to interpretation, and accommodating to the interests, norms, and structures of their host organizations.

The effect of such reporting is that perceptions of spiritual traditions and subsequent spiritual practices transform as they move. Later generations of practitioners may fail to learn earlier religious and ethical nuances of the practices, and they may get increasingly secularized, and aligned with dominant institutions as they are transmitted.

Social Context: Institutionally "Approved" Spiritual Practices

In recent years, new critiques have surfaced from people outside of mindfulness circles, who have been told by their supervisors—who likely have little background in contemplative practices—that they should meditate so that they will be more socially skilled and agreeable at work. In a *Humans of New York* episode, a middle-aged black woman lodges one such complaint:

> Everyone's looking in and doing all of this inward reflection. If you're unhappy, it's because of you. Your unhappiness isn't a reflection of any systemic imbalance that we could address together. It's a "you" problem. I worked the most shit job when I moved back to New York last year. I was told instead of me becoming upset, because someone's spoken to me in a way that's horrifically disrespectful, unprofessional, and above all probably illegal, I was told, "Just take a few deep breaths. Maybe you should get the Mindful app, the meditation app." Are you serious? The things you are saying are not only not relevant to the job. Why are you commenting on my body? Why are you commenting on my weight? Why are you commenting on my hair? Don't tell me to meditate my frustration away because my frustration is valid and it's real and it's coming from a genuine place. I wouldn't be frustrated if it didn't matter.[3]

For this working-class black woman, rather than appropriately addressing her legitimate grievances about systemic problems in her workplace, like discriminatory statements from superiors based on her race and body, her supervisor instructed her to try a meditation app to calm down. In doing so, this supervisor put the onus on his employee to individually find a way to be happy at work, even when facing gendered and racial prejudice, rather than addressing the underlying problem of prejudice. Thus, he appropriated mindfulness as a practice to quell confrontation from a frustrated employee who was treated unfairly in the interests of keeping the peace and perpetuating the status quo of his leadership—and the white hegemonic culture in the larger organization.

This example shows how far afield mindfulness can move from its early proponents' progressive, countercultural aims to liberate individuals through the practices to create a more egalitarian, less materialistic society. It got to this place, where it aids the larger white capitalist system gradually, through all of the subtle incremental changes noted above, and in the absence of sufficient regulation in how mindfulness is transmitted. As Islam et al. (2017) conclude for the corporate mindfulness programs they examined, ultimately the manner in which mindfulness is framed comes to align "with dominant managerial perspectives" in the larger organizations in which they are embedded (1).

The Audience: Audiences' Selective Learning

New adopters of spiritual practices interpret spiritual transmitters' lessons in notably selective ways, due to the cultural and institutional settings in which they are embedded. While contemporary yoga is rooted in an admixture of Hindu, Buddhist, and secular cultural influences (Brown, this volume; Jain 2014), practitioners' experiences vary a great deal based on their contexts. Below I show how undergraduate students' experiences doing power yoga at a selective liberal arts college are shaped by their peer culture and the secular academic setting in which they live.

When I arrived at the college's evening yoga class, the fitness center exercise room was jam-packed with nearly fifty students. Practitioners sat on brightly colored mats covering nearly all available floor space, chatting casually with others sitting beside them. Mirrors lined the front and right walls, showcasing a few young women in the front row in pricy Lululemon sports bra tops and three-quarter-length Lycra pants. Most attendees were young women, wearing tank tops and tight pants in a variety of colors. Four bulky, muscular men of different races/ethnicities in T-shirts and baggy shorts or sweatpants sat next to each other in the center of the room; they appeared to be athletes.

Tanya Sterling, an energetic, trim, middle-aged brunette with long hair pulled back in a ponytail, led the class from the front of the room. She wore bright blue Lycra pants and a blue-and-black tank top, which seemed to fit in with what the students were wearing. Sterling began the class, in a surprisingly low, gravelly voice, noting the inclement weather outdoors: "My pants get brighter when the weather is worse," she said.

Then she gave a brief spiritual introduction to the class. She said there are three parts to life at this school, "school, social life, and sleep." "And," she said, "students say you can't have it all." But, she said, you have to figure out what you want and need. "We cannot have everything, but we can have it all," she

324 JAIME KUCINSKAS

said cryptically. "We have to define what it all is for us. . . . We have to find a balance. But balance isn't having equal proportions of everything." She used a metaphor of a cookie. "A cookie isn't balanced with equal parts sugar and salt," she said.

She then noted a husky, muscular young man in the center of the room, saying he was probably thinking they should "get to the ab workout" and "cut out the chatter." I looked at the clock, and she had been talking for four minutes. The student laughed. She joked with him that he was going to get the ab workout.

Sterling turned up the music and after a few yogic stretching poses, we transitioned into the promised sit-ups. I looked around and everyone seemed focused. A large male athlete was struggling with the sit-ups. Next Sterling initiated a standing posture on one crouched leg, with the other outstretched with an upturned foot. This balance pose was very challenging. While Sterling did it with ease, her arms outstretched in the air, every student placed their hands on the ground to hold themselves up. The class clearly had a challenging fitness component. Sterling stood out in seeming to do such difficult exercises effortlessly, while the students—male and female, and athlete and nonathlete alike—struggled.

Following this warmup, Sterling led a sun salutation sequence—a common series of standing yoga poses—followed by a series of twist poses stretching the back, and several standing balance poses on a single foot. At this point, Sterling was modeling the poses less frequently. Students seemed familiar with the common poses, but were also looking now and then at their classmates to see what they were doing, likely to make sure their poses were accurate.

During the last few minutes of the class, we all did the final yogic resting pose, savasana, lying prone on the ground. Sterling reiterated her earlier message: "You can't have everything, but you can have it all." She said to "listen to the wisdom mind to be still." Then she gently repeated to "listen to the wisdom mind to be healthy. To listen to the wisdom mind to take time for joy."

She then led two breath exercises, having everyone breathe in deeply through their nose and breathe out through their mouth. All the students enthusiastically breathed in and let out loud outbreaths. Students could choose to do it a third time "if they had something extra sticky" from their day. A handful breathed in and out across the room.

Sterling ended the class with a Buddhist-inspired blessing for equanimity: "May you be happy. May you be healthy. May you have lovingkindness, *metta*," she said, "and may everyone you know, and everyone you'll meet, have it too." She solemnly bowed her head, and brought her hands, palm to palm to heart center. Nearly everyone else did the same. "Namaste," she said. "Namaste," everyone else repeated. In leaving the class, I reflected that Sterling had struck a seemingly delicate balance between seeming tough—to attract the athletes and students seeking a challenging physical workout—and earnestly spiritual in how she taught the class. The class was clearly very popular. The students seemed to love her, enjoy the class, take the class seriously, and regularly attend it, despite their demanding academic course load at the college.

Two of my student researchers also attended Sterling's class and interviewed student participants about their experiences doing yoga immediately after the class. The students they spoke with enjoyed the class, and took away both social and physical benefits from attending it. The students seemed drawn to the class because it was a popular activity on campus that their friends attended, and because they loved Sterling, rather than because of its spiritual components. Interestingly, some students described having experiences that some people would identify as spiritual. But without a richer spiritual background, the students were hesitant to recognize and interpret such experiences as spiritual.

As largely middle- and upper-class American youths immersed in an intense secular collegiate environment in which nearly all students lived on a small, isolated campus, the students were more attuned to the yoga class's social and fitness functions. Moreover, the students interviewed were members of a select social subset of all students on campus: they were mainly athletes and members of Greek societies, who tended to frequent the campus's party scene more than most.

Because their socially esteemed peers also attended the class, these young people were acutely aware of its social pressures. For example, several students mentioned feeling pressured to attend the class with friends, because they would feel uncomfortable entering the crowded, popular class alone. Students also reported watching themselves and their peers in the mirror on the front wall of the room as they practiced, which contributed to their sense that it was an intimidating, competitive, but also a motivating place to practice yoga. Jane, for example, described feeling "weird" and self-conscious at times during the class, because her peers, and even people with whom she had been romantically involved, frequented the class. "It is intimidating!" she said, especially when "your butt is in everyone's face."

The majority of the students interviewed had first tried yoga elsewhere, such as at athletic or dance practice sessions. They enjoyed Sterling's class and talked about it with friends afterward. They largely described the class in an extremely secular way, which did not include Sterling's spiritual components. Instead, they focused on the class's fitness benefits. Dale, a fraternity member and former athlete, appreciated the physical elements of the class the most. He said he liked "how rapidly you improved" in the class and "how hard it is and the struggle aspect of it. It reminded me of the grind of sports from back in the day." Another student, Jenna, distinguished between typical yoga classes and the campus power yoga class, saying the latter was "much more physical, and I like that aspect of it." She said she was not that good at holding poses for extending periods of time, and in typical yoga classes got "frustrated . . . and a little bored." Elsewhere she had struggled to focus on her breath as told to do, which made her all the more frustrated.

Dale had also tried other yoga classes and concluded that he liked Sterling's class in particular, not yoga more generally. He felt alienated when "most yoga teachers . . . say 'Namaste.'" That had turned him off from the practices elsewhere. "Ugh," he said. "I don't really care about the stuff besides the physical aspect of it.'" However, because he liked Sterling so much, he did not seem bothered when she included spiritual components. Sterling, he thought, was "so genuine and good at talking and leading a class," which made him want to attend it more.

A few students said that attending the yoga class made them feel more connected to their body, but not necessarily in a spiritual way. For Rose, lying in savasana, listening to calming music, made her feel more connected to her body and the space around her. It gave her pause and space to ask the big questions, such as "What is life?" After reflecting further, she said this was a spiritual experience for her. In contrast, Jane felt more connected to her body after practicing yoga and said the practices helped in "clearing her headspace." However, she did not view this as a spiritual experience. Other students similarly drew upon secular language to describe their experiences during savasana: they said it was like "sleeping."

Students identified different benefits from the yoga class that they took with them into their everyday interactions with friends. Interestingly, they described these benefits in secular ways. Rose said that she often left the class feeling inspired, and that Sterling's wisdom came up "when I'm comforting other people." She would tell her friends to "remember what Sterling says!'" Similarly, Jenna said that Sterling "says the best things. And you're like, 'You

THE TRANSMISSION OF SPIRITUALITY   327

know what? You're right.'" In a striking admission, Dale admitted that power yoga had helped him win at drinking games: "So in beer dice there's a rule that if you kick it to your partner that's a point," he said. "Because of yoga, my hips are really flexible," which helped him to get those additional points.

Importantly, these students were not particularly spiritual before attending the yoga class. It seemed that attending the class had not noticeably affected their relationship with spirituality. The students did not have rich spiritual lives outside of the class and were hesitant to identify as spiritual. When asked if he considered himself a spiritual person, Dale began saying yes, but then changed to a no. Another student described herself as "open-minded." Two others who identified as "culturally Jewish" said that they "got" spirituality, but that they did not do spiritual practices.

When asked if power yoga was different from other kinds of physical activity, the students were similarly unclear. They struggled to find resonant language to compare and explain their experiences. Dale said that after power yoga, he experiences a "euphoric state," which many spiritual people might see as a spiritual experience directly tied to the yoga practice. However, when asked if yoga feels different from other practices, like working out or smoking marijuana, he struggled to find an answer. Although he initially admitted that it was more mentally relaxing than other practices, he caught himself midsentence before completing a statement that yoga felt different than lifting weights. Instead, he concluded that he "does not know."

The college students' experiences in the campus power yoga class reveal how much spirituality can change as it moves from one group to another, and how attenuated spirituality can become in some secular contexts. In particular, when new practitioners are part of a strong secular subculture, they are likely to take from the practices what is useful to them, which may be only the practices' secular components. Their applications of spiritual practices' benefits may cut against spiritual traditions' prior ethical commitments—such as using yogic benefits to improve performance in drinking games, when drinking alcohol is discouraged in some yogic texts and schools (Holthaus 2004). Rather than transform individuals and the groups and settings they are a part of, spiritual practice then becomes a mere tool that reinforces the status quo. Furthermore, even if the students experienced phenomena that the spiritually attuned would interpret as spiritual experiences, without having a larger supportive network in the practices, and lacking sufficient spiritual language, new adopters may struggle to make sense of such potentially spiritual experiences and instead turn their focus elsewhere.

328 JAIME KUCINSKAS

This further detracts from potential transformative impacts of spiritual experiences.

Conclusion

When spiritual practices spread across groups and institutions, as boundary-spanning objects, they are porous cultural forms or "empty signifiers," likely to undergo change in the process of transmission (Islam et al. 2017; Laclau 1996; Pagis et al. 2018). In this chapter, drawing on cultural theory, I highlighted some of the many situational factors that can shape spiritual transmission, altering spirituality as it moves. My framework of key factors affecting the spiritual transmission process highlights the importance of paying close attention to who transmits spiritual culture, who receives it, their intentions for doing the practice and cultural backgrounds, and the broader local, institutional, and macro-level contexts in which these groups are situated.

The powerful social settings and hegemonic cultures in which practitioners live shape spirituality in manifold ways. Even as practitioners seek to maintain key elements from their spiritual lineages, they adapt spiritual culture to resonate with new audiences, and fit within the latter's existing subcultures and institutions. Spiritual teachers aspiring to provide authentic lessons based on their own personal and professional backgrounds can also unconsciously shape spiritual traditions in their own image. Secondary sources, such as the media or others who have heard about the practices secondhand further contribute to shaping, spreading, and distorting spiritual culture. The media can be strategically deployed by spiritual proponents to spread word of the benefits of their practices. Alternatively, the media or other people can more indirectly learn about a spiritual tradition and pass on their understandings of it to others. Through all of these paths, spiritual forms morph and change as they move. As shown with the case of the spread of mindfulness in the United States, spiritual forms can change in countless subtle and bold ways, to align with cultural and structural forces at many levels, including local, institutional, state, and national contexts. While these many alterations can help cultures to spread quickly, this velocity may come at the cost of control over the content transmitted. By taking into account broader social contextual forces, scholars can more fully understand the transmission of spirituality and both its intended and its unintended, negative consequences (which practitioners may not be able to see).

Spiritual transmission is further affected by how new practitioners receive and understand spiritual practices. As shown by the example of the college student yoga class, how spiritual practices are received and understood can vary considerably in the eye of the beholder. For college students living on a small, isolated, academic-minded campus, their yoga experiences were filtered through a lens of their peer culture, their larger secular institutional culture, and their personal athletic and spiritual backgrounds, which left them mainly with the physical and social benefits of the yoga class, rather than spiritual development.

The brief examples and scholarship included in this chapter reveal how contemporary American spirituality contains far more variance than many practitioners and scholars may suppose. It arises across religious and secular institutions (Ammerman 2013), in public and in private life, and among various groups one might not expect, such as among public school kids, corporate business people, athletic teams, law enforcement, and veteran groups. Although assumed by many to be comprised of therapeutic, calming, transcendent practices, the practices can be used for various other utilitarian purposes, which in some cases may align more with hegemonic social forces, like capitalism or white supremacy, than personal development and emancipation, as many practitioners may presume.

By more fully recognizing the dynamic and nuanced nature of spiritual transmission in the contemporary United States—and by continuing to unearth and identify the many conscious and unconscious factors and mechanisms through which spirituality adapts as it moves, scholars can better comprehend both the complexity and the socially patterned nature of spirituality. To capture such cultures in transition, more in-depth qualitative studies, using combinations of process-tracing, ethnography, interviews, and comparative methods are needed.

My examples also carry a cautionary message to quantitative scholars relying on typical measures of spirituality—as oversimplistic categorical measures of spirituality may conceal as much as they reveal, and fail to capture changing, complex pluralistic cultural traditions, which can be interpreted in multiple, seemingly contradictory ways by study participants. The languaging of questions on spirituality, which tend to draw from particular secularized spiritual or religious traditions, may resonate and/or repel practitioners of the same tradition or of different traditions, depending on

330 JAIME KUCINSKAS

their own personal, professional, spiritual, and religious backgrounds. This makes multimethod studies all the more important in future research.

Notes

1. As a very insightful reviewer mentioned, transmitters may incorporate authenticity claims for a number of reasons. They may do so to justify to themselves that what they are doing is authentic. They may also do so in an effort to address a "specter of inauthenticity," which arises as traditions are moved and adapted. Consciously including spiritual content, motivations, or practices from their spiritual lineage can operate as a neutralization technique, which may, from the words of our helpful reviewer, "inspire confidence (even faith) in the 'legitimacy' of a spiritual discipline."

2. Data included in this chapter are drawn from a larger project on the development of the mindfulness movement I conducted from 2008 to 2016, which culminated in *The Mindful Elite: Mobilizing from the Inside Out* (2019), and from a Hamilton College Levitt Center–funded student research project on situated spirituality among yoga and meditation practitioners in upstate New York, New York City, Chicago, and Santa Barbara, California, that I conducted with Hamilton College Sociology of Religion students during the spring and summer of 2018. I am particularly grateful to Rachel Schooler and Emily Steates for their work collecting and analyzing data on the latter project. For both projects we used an inductive, emic-based approach, asking study participants to describe what spirituality meant to them.

3. From *Humans of New York, The Series*, uploaded on Facebook November 26, 2017, at 6:41 p.m., https://www.facebook.com/humansofnewyork.

References

Ammerman, Nancy T. 2013. *Sacred Stories, Spiritual Tribes: Finding Religion in Everyday Life*. New York: Oxford University Press.

Beyer, Peter. 2020. "Religion in Interesting Times: Contesting Form, Function, and Future." *Sociology of Religion* 81(1): 1–19.

Burton, Katherine, and Anthony Effinger. 2014. "To Make a Killing in the Markets, Start Meditating." *Financial Post*, May 29. http://business.financialpost.com/investing/to-make-a-killing-in-the-markets-start-meditating.

Durkheim, Émile. 1995. *The Elementary Forms of Religious Life*. Translated by K. E. Fields.

Essig, Todd. 2012. "Google Teaches Employees to 'Search inside Yourself.'" *Forbes*, April 30. https://www.forbes.com/sites/toddessig/2012/04/30/google-teaches-employees-to-search-inside-yourself/#488c50e1a820.

Fligstein, Neil, and Doug McAdam. 2012. *A Theory of Fields*. New York: Oxford University Press.

Gelles, David. 2018a. "How to Be More Mindful at Work." *New York Times*. Retrieved February 19, 2019. https://www.nytimes.com/guides/well/be-more-mindful-at-work.

THE TRANSMISSION OF SPIRITUALITY   331

Gelles, David. 2018b. "Talking Mindfulness on the CEO Beat." *New York Times*, November 28. https://www.nytimes.com/2018/11/28/reader-center/ceos-mindfulness-meditation.html.

Griswold, Wendy. 2012. *Cultures and Societies in a Changing World*. Thousand Oaks, CA: Sage.

Holthaus, Stephanie M. 2004. *A Phenomenological Study: Yoga during Recovery from Drugs or Alcohol*. Pacifica Graduate Institute.

Islam, Gazi, Marie Holm, and Mira Karjalainen. 2017. "Sign of the Times: Workplace Mindfulness as an Empty Signifier." *Organization*, 1350508417740643.

Jain, Andrea. 2014. *Selling Yoga: From Counterculture to Pop Culture*. New York: Oxford University Press.

Kabat-Zinn, Jon. 1994. *Catalyzing Movement towards a More Contemplative / Sacred Appreciating / Non-Dualistic Society*. Pocantico, NY: The Center for Contemplative Mind in Society.

Kucinskas, Jaime. 2019. *The Mindful Elite: Mobilizing from the Inside Out*. New York: Oxford University Press.

Laclau, E. 1996. *Emancipation(s)*. London: Verso Books.

Pagis, Michal. 2010. "From Abstract Concepts to Experiential Knowledge: Embodying Enlightenment in a Meditation Center." *Qualitative Sociology* 33(4): 469–89.

Pagis, Michal, Wendy Cadge, and Orly Tal. 2018. "Translating Spirituality: Universalism and Particularism in the Diffusion of Spiritual Care from the United States to Israel." *Sociological Forum* 33: 596–618.

Purser, Ron, and David Loy. 2013. "Beyond McMindfulness." *Huffington Post*, August 31. http://www.huffingtonpost.com/ron-purser/beyond-mcmindfulness_b_3519289.html.

Sigalow, Emily. 2016. "Towards a Sociological Framework of Religious Syncretism in the United States." *Journal of the American Academy of Religion* 84(4): 1029–55.

Stanley, Steven. 2012. "Mindfulness: Towards a Critical Relational Perspective." *Social and Personality Psychology Compass* 6(9): 631–41.

CONCLUSION

17

Three Questions about Spirituality

Its Meaning, Influence, and Future

Brian Steensland

In the early twentieth century, Émile Durkheim made the influential case that religion was a social phenomenon. Against the dominant views of his day that religion was a natural response to awe or a psychological feature of consciousness, he argued that religion was "an eminently social thing" (Durkheim [1912] 1995, 9). It comprises beliefs and practices oriented toward the sacred that create the basis for moral community. Durkheim helped establish a sociological approach to the human dimension of religion, one focused on explaining religion's dynamics, variations, and trajectory.

A similar impulse motivates this volume. In contrast to commonplace views that spirituality is individuated and idiosyncratic on the one hand or largely homogenous in its modern diffusion on the other, we show that spirituality—both the conceptual category and as lived experience—is sociologically influenced and patterned. Spirituality too is eminently social. Other collections have focused on the sociological dimensions of spirituality, such as work by Flanagan and Jupp (2009), but have not offered a general analytic framework for better apprehending contemporary spirituality. Our approach foregrounds how spirituality is shaped by the interplay of context and practice, and influenced by the distribution of material and symbolic resources.[1] This concluding chapter addresses three questions about contemporary spirituality and offers guidance for answers that are informed by our framework.

What Is Spirituality? A Relational Approach

Greater awareness of the social dimension of spirituality provides points of entrée for thinking about spirituality in richer ways, such how its meanings are patterned across social locations. To be sure, other commentators have

Brian Steensland, *Three Questions about Spirituality* In: *Situating Spirituality*. Edited by: Brian Steensland, Jaime Kucinskas, and Anna Sun, Oxford University Press. © Oxford University Press 2022. DOI: 10.1093/oso/9780197565001.003.0018

336 BRIAN STEENSLAND

also observed that spirituality is "inherently related to culture and context" (Sheldrake 2012, 22). We take this recognition a step further to explain why. Spirituality is defined and experienced relationally. It is a reservoir of attributes given shape in particular contexts by explicit or implicit oppositions. Thus, spirituality is not a stable category or essence. It takes on meaning in contrast to its "others."

This relational way of thinking about entities and boundaries will be familiar to many scholars of religion. It is similar to the approach Talal Asad has taken in tracing the genealogies of "religion" and "secular" as conceptual categories. Neither religion nor secularity has a singular or consistent meaning. Both take on a variety of meanings and have different boundaries depending on their historical and societal contexts. Asad (1993, 2003) illustrates this by comparing the evolution and usage of these concepts in Christian and Muslim contexts, showing how they are grounded in specific social, cultural, and geopolitical locations rather than being universal, value-free, and apolitical.

We take a related approach to understanding the meaning of spirituality, though informed more specifically by Gieryn's (1999) analysis of science. Gieryn shows that science is not one thing; it is many things. Rather than having permanent qualities, its qualities depend on the relevant stakes and audiences in particular settings. The content of "science" varies as it is engaged in struggles with other domains of authority—for instance, religion, applied science (engineering), pseudoscience, or politicized knowledge. Gieryn's approach highlights not only the malleable and multidimensional attributes of science, but how its shape and meaning is formed through pragmatic action and contestation. In his analysis, these patterns are rendered visible through systematic comparison across cases. They are less apparent to participants in the action.

Similar dynamics hold for spirituality. As anyone knows who has tried to locate a fixed or widely used definition, spirituality's meaning is hard to pin down. This is not because it is vague or empty; it's because the meanings are multiple. From this reservoir of meanings, the nature of spirituality emerges in particular contexts through oppositions and contrasts to spirituality's "others." In some contexts, spirituality is contrasted implicitly or explicitly with other cultural systems: religion, secularism, scientific naturalism, consumerism, nihilism, and so forth. Or it is contrasted with characteristics associated with those systems: collective, coercive, dogmatic, immanent, reductive, mundane, isolated, or meaningless. As a function of these contrasts, the attributes associated with spirituality in a particular instance vary widely. One implication is that stable definitions of spirituality, where they exist, are due to stable oppositions and contexts. Another implication is that the permeability of spirituality's boundaries is variable. In some settings, they may be porous because spirituality is used in an inclusive or bridging way (see Pagis et al. 2018), such as when a lingua franca or cooperation is sought. In other contexts, the boundaries are rigid, such as those involving legal decisions, governance, and state power (see Brown, this volume).

While there is no singular meaning of spirituality, our framework offers insights for understanding why there are particular meanings. Our relational perspective takes into consideration three analytical dimensions: how features of context delimit the meaning and practice of spirituality; how the practice of spirituality creates, sustains, and potentially transforms it; and how the distribution of resources and incentives shapes the language and experience of spirituality. Peter Beyer's (2020) recent account of contestation over the form and function of smudging as a "spiritual" practice among the indigenous people of Canada (in contrast to being a religious practice or a cultural practice) illustrates elements of this three-way interplay of context, practice, and power.

How Does Spirituality Influence?

Recognizing spirituality's inherent sociality expands our understanding of how it works. Here we highlight some implications for studies of health, spiritual consciousness and projects, and social engagement.

There is now a considerable body of research that examines the links between spirituality and mental and physical health (see Koenig 2012). While there are ongoing questions about conceptual and measurement issues, findings suggest that spirituality often has a positive impact on health. Taking a more sociological view on spirituality's impact and its causal pathways would acknowledge the potentially important collective features of spirituality. This would move studies beyond conceptualizing spirituality as an internal state toward a broader incorporation of relationships and practices. Existing research on the effects of religion suggests this will matter. Studies that include both internalized and social features of religion often find a more robust impact of the latter. In a sophisticated study, for instance, Lim and Putnam (2010) explored the well-documented links between religion and

338 BRIAN STEENSLAND

life satisfaction (which is one aspect of mental health). They found that the most robust religious predictors of life satisfaction were social and participatory. People with higher levels of satisfaction were regular church attenders and had friendship networks within their congregations. This impact was stronger than measures of religious belief or other internal factors.

In existing research on health, a complicating factor in capturing the sociological dimensions of spirituality is that empirical studies and meta-analyses often combine analyses of "religion" and "spirituality." When they are differentiated, religion is associated with shared and collective attributes, while spirituality denotes internal and psychological characteristics, such as virtues and dispositions. Future work would benefit from measuring and assessing the social dimensions of spirituality per se that do not necessarily bear upon organized religion, such as communities of practice, material affordances (books and other media), and shared cultural resources (narratives of hope, sentiments of belonging), to name a few. Doing so would recognize that a central feature of most all types of spirituality is a sense of connection, which is both cultivated through and actualized with others.

This aligns with one of Ammerman's key findings in her study of spirituality in everyday life—namely, that the seedbeds of spiritual consciousness are found in real and virtual conversations, "produced in interaction, carried by conversants from one place to another, and redeployed and reworked in each new telling" (Ammerman 2014, 300). She draws on the social theorist George Herbert Mead to illustrate how these types of conversations, both in-person and internalized, contribute to identity formation and, more broadly, the formation of the spiritual self. The role of the social in this process is fundamental, even though it often results in a sense of self-authorship and autonomy.

Further research on the formation of spiritual consciousness and the social elements of what we would call "spiritual projects" is needed. Philosophers have recently turned their attention to processes of "transformative experience" (e.g., Collard 2018), yet their general approach is atomistic, and their orientation toward individual agency is psychological. A more sociological perspective would incorporate at least two things. First, it would be based on a sociological action theory that takes interaction, habit, and temporality into account (e.g., Emirbayer and Mische 1998), thereby bringing the social, iterative, and projective nature of spiritual formation to the foreground. Second, it would look at the recursive effects of spiritual discourses on the formation of spiritual selves. For instance, Ian Hacking has elaborated on the process of

THREE QUESTIONS ABOUT SPIRITUALITY   339

"looping," that is, the way that authoritative discourses create new "human kinds"—categories of people and actions that come to feel natural rather than products of concepts and language. To understand how people come to see themselves as "spiritual," it is crucial to understand the looping processes through which discourses (via books, religious leaders, social relationships, and media) contribute to the experience of spirituality. This relates to our call to situate spirituality at the intersection of system and practice. One element of the broader system is the discourse that practitioners draw upon and reproduce through the formation and practice of their spiritual selves.

A common sentiment among scholars and cultural commentators is that the trend toward a more ostensibly individualistic spirituality will diminish the public presence of organized religion to the detriment of civic life. This concern can be seen in Jason Shelton's chapter on African American spirituality in this volume. If the trend toward spirituality means a move away from religion, what are the prospects for civic engagement in years to come, since historically the Black Church has been so central in social movement mobilization and black community life? Charles Taylor's perspective on the ethics of authenticity provides an orienting framework for addressing this challenge, since the pursuit of authenticity is so interconnected to the movement toward spirituality in the modern West. Taylor (1991) argues that a life lived authentically, properly understood, is a social accomplishment. The pursuit of faithfulness to oneself is only possible through a vast network of (unrecognized) collaboration. Discovering one's identity is intimately related to being recognized by others. Discovering what is good and worthwhile is only possible by reference to a socially stipulated hierarchy of values. Discovering one's place in the world involves learning social roles and adopting social scripts. A proper understanding of the social architecture upon which authenticity is built lays the groundwork for participating in its collective maintenance and betterment. Without much modification, these same observations could be applied to spirituality (see, e.g., Kucinskas 2019 on collective spiritual authenticity). Like the ethics of authenticity, spirituality has a social architecture that, when recognized, can point toward outward-facing spiritual engagement.

What might a socially engaged spirituality look like on the ground? Here more closely observed research is needed, but an emerging body of knowledge is suggestive. Stanczak (2006) interviewed seventy-six progressive religious activists in California to flesh out the connections between their spiritual lives and their civic engagement. He identified a number of linkages having to do with being called to new social roles, the reassessment of the costs and benefits of activism, spiritual practices that lead toward engagement, and emotional dynamics that reconfigure the ways people perceive and act in the world. While Stanczak's research delves into motivations and aspirations, it focuses less on the mobilizing structures that facilitate engagement. Most of his interviewees were ministers of various types, and thus had the social networks, resources, and organizational connections of institutional religion available to them. What is the potential for spiritual social engagement outside organized religion? Here we find Lichterman's (2005) concept of "bridging" social practices useful. Bridging practices include customs that orient people outward and intentional relationships that connect in-groups to out-groups. These types of customs and relationships enhance well-intentioned people's ability to engage beyond themselves and their immediate spheres. Lichterman found bridging practices to be important for civic engagement even inside church-based settings that have a robust outreach infrastructure already established. Outside organized religion, other types of concrete mobilizing structures are critical for engagement, such as the "social movement schools" Isaac and colleagues (2020) identified as important in mindfulness meditation movements.

A broader point is this: spirituality in the modern West is often associated with inwardness, harmony, and equipoise. On its face, the pursuit of spiritual fulfillment does not seem oriented toward public engagement. But as Christian Smith (2017) observes, the symbolic valence and social implications of spiritual practices are always context-bound; thus they can be reconfigured. He uses the example of "engaged Buddhism" as a case in point. Buddhist practices are commonly associated with detachment from the world. But when they are coupled with cultural frames of injustice and social infrastructures of mobilization, these same Buddhist practices can foster engagement and activism.

Where Is Spirituality Heading?

The growing attention to spirituality is driven by a host of factors. Attention from scholars stems from interest in the changing nature of authority, community, and the sacred. Interest from the broader public stems from the pursuit of transcendent experience and meaningful connection outside (or at the intersections of) religious institutions and authorized by the self. A key question about spirituality is where it is headed in the future. Our framework suggests two broad likelihoods.

THREE QUESTIONS ABOUT SPIRITUALITY 341

The first involves spirituality's relationship to secularism. In first-wave scholarship, much attention was devoted to the relationships between religion and spirituality. Now that spirituality is firmly on the agenda, attention is shifting to the relationship between spirituality and the secular. One perspective is that spirituality is a way station on the road from religion to secularism. Illustrative of this view is Steve Bruce's book *Secular Beats Spiritual* (2017), which focuses on spirituality in the United Kingdom. Bruce points to a variety of patterns in support of his argument: the most popular forms of spirituality are the least religious in nature; the religious elements of common spiritual practices are often downplayed; and interest in spiritualty has increased more slowly than the decline in religiosity.

One way of evaluating this argument is to focus on terminology. Bruce admits that the definition of spirituality is slippery and variable, but he defines it for his purposes as beliefs and practices that reference a supernatural power that is no longer external to us but inherent within us (Bruce 2017, 16). Much hinges on this definition. Whether the attribution of supernatural power to the self should be considered spiritual or secular is not clear cut. But what is clearer is that a variety of commentators do not see a sharp opposition between secularism and spirituality, and, moreover, are entirely comfortable with atheistic and wholly immanent forms of spirituality. In his volume *The Little Book of Atheist Spirituality*, Comte-Sponville (2007) addresses the question of secular spirituality head on, affirming that there can be an atheistic, godless spirituality oriented toward mystery in the universe and balance and harmony within the self. Ter Kuile (2020) draws lessons from the Harvard Divinity School to describe an immanent spirituality founded on rituals rooted in connection to self, others, and nature. Thus, to describe spirituality as a way station leading to secularism requires making a mutually exclusive distinction between spirituality and secularism. It makes little sense to describe spirituality as leading down the path to secularism when secularism itself can contain the spiritual.

This relates to spirituality's fundamentally relational nature, one whose essence is defined by contrasts with "not spirituality." The disagreement above is based on different perspectives on what spirituality is defined against: God, religious doctrine, scientific naturalism, meaninglessness, and so on. There are stakes in the definitions of religion, spirituality, and secularism. But beyond the terminological point is a conceptual one. If there come to be contexts where the boundaries between spirituality and not spirituality no longer need to be drawn, then the language of "spirituality" may recede. Yet the referents of spirituality will endure by other names. Take China as a counterexample to the historically Christian West. Exclusivist, monotheistic religion was never dominant in Chinese society. Because Western notions of spirituality have developed in relation to, and often in opposition with, Christianity, the term "spirituality" does not have a direct analogue in China. Spirituality per se is not a prominent concept because the religious and secular contexts are quite different. But this does not mean that the Chinese are less spiritual in the sense of their engagement in practices oriented to transcendence, others, or the natural world (see Sun, this volume). The question of the relationship between spirituality and secularism should itself be subjected to analysis in order to better understand how context shapes the question and the stakes. Predictions about spirituality based on easy juxtapositions between spirituality and secularism are themselves too easy.

The contrast between the West and China, and elsewhere in the volume to African contexts, points toward to our second likelihood: just as there is now a prominent view that the contemporary world contains "multiple modernities" (Eisenstadt 2000), in contrast to a singular path that all societies take toward modernity, there are and will be multiple spiritual milieux. Varied contexts lead to different spiritual experience, terminology, and boundaries. Work on global religions and multiple consciousness points toward what an analysis of multiple spiritualities would look like.

Seen from a global perspective, it is apparent that the forces of modernity exert similar pressures on major religious traditions such as Christianity, Hinduism, and Islam throughout the world. They are all impacted by institutional differentiation, standardization, scientific reasoning, human rights regimes, and the like. Yet because of the particularities of the traditions and their geographical and societal contexts, religious systems strike different balances with the modern world (Hefner 1998). Mirroring these multiple religious responses are variations in consciousness at the group and individual level. Drawing from the phenomenology of Alfred Schutz, Steets (2014) addresses how people differentially navigate religious and secular realms. Modernity opens up many different navigational paths via the multiple institutional spheres people encounter in their everyday life. Where spirituality explicitly enters the picture is in Schutz's notion of multiple realities, wherein people toggle between everyday and transcendent or spiritual realities with relative ease. Peter Berger (2014) discusses this in detail in his reflections on religious consciousness in varied pluralistic settings, and Ammerman (2014) has documented it in empirical detail in her study of everyday spirituality in the United States. The new analytic framework Ammerman presents in this

THREE QUESTIONS ABOUT SPIRITUALITY   343

volume describes four ideal-typical contexts that shape spirituality in different ways. It is a promising point of departure for systematically examining variations in spirituality across nations, religious traditions, and subgroups. Along related lines, Woodhead in her chapter looks at the current trend toward the deregulation of the "theosphere" in the anglophone West with the suggestion that contemporary spiritualities—whether monotheist, mystic, or polytheistic—will proliferate, coexist, and mutually influence one other.

What seems clear enough is that the pursuit of the spiritual will continue apace because the demands of modern life create the conditions that call it forth. Ann Swidler's chapter closes with an eloquent parallel between her African field site and the contemporary West. Though the challenges found in rural Malawi and, say, the United States may be different, and though the manifestations of spirituality may vary across these regions, people look to spiritual experience for similar reasons: to strengthen the inner resources of the self in the face of depletion. As the chapters collected here have endeavored to show, people do not do this alone or outside of formative social contexts, whether situated inside, outside, or at the intersections of institutional religion. In foregrounding spirituality's social dimensions, we hope not only to shed light on the collective aspects of spirituality that its individualistic discourse obscures, but to create more space for recognizing the collective obligations and opportunities that are part and parcel of spiritual formation.

Note

1. Here we are draw from Sewell's (1999) broader analysis of culture being mutually constituted by systems and practices, a framework that closely aligns with Ammerman's in this volume.

References

Ammerman, Nancy T. 2014. *Sacred Stories, Spiritual Tribes: Finding Religion in Everyday Life*. New York: Oxford University Press.

Asad, Talal. 1993. *Genealogies of Religion: Discipline and Reasons of Power in Christianity and Islam*. Baltimore: Johns Hopkins University Press.

Asad, Talal. 2003. *Formations of the Secular: Christianity, Islam, Modernity*. Stanford, CA: Stanford University Press.

Berger, Peter L. 2014. *The Many Altars of Modernity: Toward a Paradigm for Religion in a Pluralistic Age*. Boston: de Gruyter.

344 BRIAN STEENSLAND

Beyer, Peter. 2020. "Religion in Interesting Times: Contesting Form, Function, and Future." *Sociology of Religion* 81: 1–19.

Bruce, Steve. 2017. *Secular Beats Spiritual: The Westernization of the Easternization of the West*. New York: Oxford University Press.

Collard, Agnes. 2018. *Aspiration: The Agency of Becoming*. New York: Oxford University Press.

Comte-Sponville, Andre. 2007. *The Little Book of Atheist Spirituality*. New York: Penguin Books.

Durkheim, Émile. [1912] 1995. *The Elementary Forms of Religious Life*, translated by Karen E. Fields. New York: Free Press.

Eisenstadt, S. N. 2000. "Multiple Modernities." *Daedalus* 129(1): 1–29.

Emirbayer, Mustafa, and Ann Mische. 1998. "What Is Agency?" *American Journal of Sociology* 103(4): 962–1023.

Flanagan, Kieran, and Peter C. Jupp, eds. 2009. *A Sociology of Spirituality*. Farnham, UK: Ashgate.

Gieryn, Thomas F. 1999. *Cultural Boundaries of Science: Credibility on the Line*. Chicago: University of Chicago Press.

Hefner, Robert W. 1998. "Multiple Modernities: Christianity, Islam, and Hinduism in a Globalizing Age." *Annual Review of Anthropology* 27: 83–104.

Isaac, Larry W., Anna W. Jacobs, Jaime Kucinskas, and Allison R. McGrath. 2020. "Social Movement Schools: Sites for Consciousness Transformation, Training, and Prefigurative Social Development." *Social Movement Studies* 19(2): 160–82.

Koenig, Harold G. 2012. "Religion, Spirituality, and Health: The Research and Clinical Implications." *International Scholarly Research Network: Psychiatry* 1–33.

Kucinskas, Jaime. 2019. *The Mindful Elite: Mobilizing from the Inside Out*. New York: Oxford University Press.

Kuile, Casper ter. 2020. *The Power of Ritual: Turning Everyday Activities into Soulful Practices*. New York: HarperOne.

Lichterman, Paul. 2005. *Elusive Togetherness: Church Groups Trying to Bridge America's Divisions*. Princeton, NJ: Princeton University Press.

Lim, Chaeyoon, and Robert D. Putnam. 2010. "Religion, Social Networks, and Life Satisfaction." *American Sociological Review* 75(6): 914–33.

Pagis, Michal, Wendy Cadge, and Orly Tal. 2018. "Translating Spirituality: Universalism and Particularism in the Diffusion of Spiritual Care from the United States to Israel." *Sociological Forum* 33(3): 596–618.

Sewell, William H., Jr. 1999. "The Concept(s) of Culture." Pp. 35–61 in *Beyond the Cultural Turn: New Directions in the Study of Society and Culture*, edited by Victoria E. Bonnell and Lynn Hunt. Berkeley: University of California Press.

Sheldrake, Philip. 2012. *Spirituality: A Very Short Introduction*. Oxford: Oxford University Press.

Smith, Christian. 2017. *Religion: What It Is, How It Works, and Why It Matters*. Princeton, NJ: Princeton University Press.

Stanczak, Gregory. 2006. *Engaged Spirituality: Social Change and American Religion*. New Brunswick, NJ: Rutgers University Press.

Steets, Silke. 2014. "Multiple Realities and Religion: A Sociological Approach." *Society* 51: 140–44.

Taylor, Charles. 1991. *The Ethics of Authenticity*. Cambridge, MA: Harvard University Press.

Index

For the benefit of digital users, indexed terms that span two pages (e.g., 52–53) may, on occasion, appear on only one of those pages.

ABC News, 320

Abington School District v. Schempp, 268

Abraham Church, 218

acosmic benevolence, 187

ACPE. *See* Association for Clinical Pastoral Education

aesthetics, 35, 43–44

affect, 201–2, 204

affective empiricism, 195, 205

Africa, 11–12, 22–23, 38–39, 97–111

  historicizing and deconstructing spiritualities and epistemologies, 104–6

  marketplace of religion and spirituality in, 97–98, 99, 101, 111

  memory in spirituality, 102–3

  redefining spiritualities and epistemologies in, 101–4

  triple religious heritage of, 98

Africa as Object, 105

Africa as Subject, 105

African Americans, 12–13, 22–23, 154–73, 339. *See also* Black Church

  existing research on spirituality among, 156–57

  individualized conceptualizations of spirituality in, 154–55, 157–60

  interracial variation among, 154–55, 168*t*, 171–72

  intraracial diversity and, 155, 165–70, 172

African diaspora, 22–23, 99–100, 101, 107–10

  affinities within, 109–10

  contributions of, 109

  uniqueness of, 107

African Independent churches, 213–14, 221, 225n.2

African Spirituality (Olupona), 102

After Heaven (Wuthnow), 5

ahimsa, 265

AIDS, 210–11

alienation, 247–48, 250, 251

ancestor veneration, 103–4

Anglican Church, 218–19, 222–23, 225n.2

anomie, 247–48, 251

Anthropology of Consciousness, 198

anti-Semitism, 61–62

apophatic theology, 64, 65

Arhatic Yoga, 271

Armed Forces Chaplaincy Center, 282–83

Asatru, 59, 61–62. *See also* heathenism

Asheville, North Carolina, 57, 68n.3

Ashland Theological Seminary, 282–83

Ashtanga Yoga, 267–68, 269

Asians, 115, 144–45, 147

Assemblies of God, 222–23

Association for Clinical Pastoral Education (ACPE), 279, 286–87, 289, 293

Association of Professional Chaplains, 288–89

Association of Theological Schools (ATS), 279, 294n.1

asymmetry. *See* symmetry/asymmetry

atheism, 145, 148

ATS. *See* Association of Theological Schools

audience (for spiritual practices), 316–17, 323–28

Australia, 264

authenticity, 3, 5, 128, 247, 339

  BDSM and, 201–2

  spiritual transmission and, 316, 330n.1

al-Azhar University, 300

Azusa Street Revival, 174n.7

346 INDEX

baby boomers, 5
Baptist religion
 African Americans and, 155, 164t, 165–
  69, 171
 in Malawi, 225n.2
Barrows, John Henry, 50–51
Bayan Claremont School of Theology, 278,
 285–86, 288, 291–92
BDSM, 23, 197–207
 continuities, 202–4
 defined, 195
 importance of for study of
  spirituality, 201–2
 new insights, 204–6
 prior research on spirituality and,
  198–201
belief and belonging spirituality, 75–76
Besant, Annie, 52
Beyoncé, 99, 255–56
Bhagavad Gita, 265
Bible, 154–55, 217, 218–20, 268, 271–72
big data, 121–25
Black Atlantic, 107
Black Church, 21–22, 156–57, 172–73,
 339. *See also* African Americans
 Christianity in, 154–55
 denominational nucleus of, 166
 institutional importance of, 173
"Black Reltrad" syntax, 162–63
Blacks and Whites in Christian America
 (Shelton and Emerson), 156–
 57, 159–60
Blake, William, 72, 73
bodily co-dwelling, 185, 190
Boston University School of Theology,
 282–84, 287
both religious and spiritual, 133, 134–38,
 137t, 138t, 139–44, 139t, 140t, 146
boundary objects, 21, 24
 porous objects, 10, 21, 24, 75–76, 78–79,
  128–29, 314–15, 328, 336–37
boundary work, 11–12, 22–23, 74–
 77, 128–29
Brazil, 107–8
Bread and Puppet Theater, 206
bricolage, 5, 41, 105, 179, 253, 311
Brigham Young University, 294n.1
Brite Divinity School, 284–85, 287–88

Buber, Martin, 291–92
Buckley Guard Base, 281–82
Buddhism, 319, 321, 323
 African Americans and, 159–60
 BDSM and, 198, 199–200, 207
 chaplaincy education and, 285–86, 288–
  89, 291–92
 in China, 78–79, 83–84, 86–87
 engaged, 340
 in Indonesia, 303
 Karma Kagyu, 319
 mindfulness and, 317, 318
 Tibetan, 19–20, 319
 yoga and, 264, 265
 Zen, 52–53, 90
Business Insider, 320

California, 271, 339–40
Canada, 286–87, 337
Candomblé, 107–8
capitalism, 19–20, 22, 329
Cat and Cauldron, 59
cataphatic theology, 64
Catholicism, 10, 57
 in Africa, 98
 African Americans and, 155, 166–69,
  167t, 171
 in the African diaspora, 107–8
 BDSM and, 200
 in Central America, 234, 235–36,
  238, 239
 chaplaincy education and, 285–86
 in China, 79, 83–84
 college students and, 130–31
 formless mysticism and, 53
 in Indonesia, 303
 in Malawi, 225n.2
CBS Sunday Morning, 320
Central America, 23, 227–40
 gangs in, 227–34, 236–38,
  240n.4, 240n.3
 gifts (spiritual) in, 229, 232–33, 238
 Mayan spirituality in, 233–35, 238
 spiritual values in, 235–36
 weapons (spiritual) in, 232–33, 238
Chaplaincy Institute, 285
chaplaincy programs, 20, 24, 278–94
 degree offerings growth, 287f

degree offerings nationally, 286*f*
growth in theological schools
  offering, 282*f*
short history of, 280–82
spiritual and religious differences
  in, 291–92
theological school enrollments 2000-
  2017, 279*f*
three historical patterns in, 282–86
  (*see also* military chaplaincy pattern;
  minority religion pattern; pastoral
  counseling pattern)
training in, 286–90
charisma, 37
Charlottesville, Virginia, 61–62
China, 11–12, 22–23, 76, 77–89, 341–42
field notes, 77–82
historical context of, 82–83
looking for spirituality in context
  of, 85–87
spirituality as a relational concept
  in, 82–85
spiritual milieu of, 86–89
Chinese Communist Party, 81, 83
Christianity, 8–9, 10, 19, 21–22, 57, 67–68,
  73, 245–46, 336, 341–43
in Africa, 97, 98, 99–100, 104–5
African Americans and, 154–55, 157,
  158–59, 171
BDSM and, 198, 199–201, 207
chaplaincy education and, 280, 291–92
in China, 77, 78–79, 84–85
formless mysticism and, 53
Goddess spirituality compared
  with, 58–59
heathenism and, 62
in Indonesia, 303–4
in Malawi, 211–12, 213–14, 215, 216,
  217, 220, 221, 222–23, 225n.2
mindfulness and, 120–21
polytheism and, 64
World's Parliament of Religions and, 52
yoga and, 265–66, 270
church attendance. *See* religious service
  attendance
Church of Central Africa Presbyterian,
  220, 225n.2
Church of Christ, 214, 215–16, 221

Church of God in Christ (COGIC), 174n.7
Church of God International, 281,
  294–95n.2
CIA World Factbook, 210, 225n.2
CIRCA (Clandestine Insurgent Radical
  Clown Army), 206
City God Temple, 79
civil rights movement, 16, 21–22
classification concepts, 13–14
clinical pastoral education (CPE)
  movement, 280–81, 286–87, 289, 293
"Clinical Year for Theological Students, A"
  (Cabot), 280
CNN, 320
code-switching, 262, 271, 272, 273
collective solitude, 23, 180, 182
collectivity, 8, 15, 16–17, 40
college students, 128–51
change in religious/spiritual
  identification, 129–32, 139*t*
frequency distribution of religious/
  spiritual identification, 137*t*, 138*t*
multilevel models of religious/spiritual
  identification change, 140*t*
study descriptive statistics, 135*t*
study instrumentation and data
  collection, 133–34
study methodology, 133–34
study research questions and conceptual
  framework, 132–33
study results, 134–46
study variables and data analysis, 134
colonialism, 9–10, 50, 51, 83, 105, 106
Colorado, 271
Columbia Biblical Seminary, 282–83
commodity fetishism, 250
Communist Party of China. *See* Chinese
  Communist Party
conceptual context, 9–12
Confucianism, 77, 80, 82–84, 86–87, 91–92
Confucius, 79
Confucius Temple, 78, 79
Congregationalism, 280–81
conspiracy theories, 246, 251–57
"everything is connected," 256–57
"nothing happens by accident," 254–56
"nothing is what it seems," 253–54
rise of, 252–53

contemplative movement, 189–90
contestation, 337
   African spirituality and, 105–6
   of boundary objects, 21
   of Sufism, 297, 298–300, 301–4
context, 8–9, 22–23, 335
   in China (*see under* China)
   conceptual, 9–12
   cultural, 33, 38, 44
   entangled, 13, 38–40
   established, 13, 39–40, 41
   explained, 9–13
   institutionalized, 13, 41
   institutionally "approved" spiritual
      practices, 322–23
   interstitial, 13, 41–43
   macro (*see* macrocontexts)
   in Malawi, 211–12
   micro (*see* microcontexts)
   practice and, 38–44
   substantive, 9, 12
Cotton v. Cate, 267
counterculture of 1960s, 3, 5, 247–48
CPE movement. *See* clinical pastoral
   education movement
creolization, 108–9
cultural appropriation, 60
cultural context, 33, 38, 44
cultural creators, 315
cultural diamond, 315
cultural objects, 315
cultural receivers, 315
Cultural Revolution, 84
culture, 63, 130, 131

Daily Mail, 320
Daoism, 52–53, 77, 78–79, 83–84, 86–
   87, 90
Datong, China, 78
death rituals and ceremonies, 103, 104
deities/gods
   in Chinese religions, 78–79, 88
   pagan, 59–61
Denver Theological Seminary, 281–
   83, 287–88
Deobandi movement, 310, 311
Devil/Satan, 97–98, 232–34
dharma, 265

Diana, Princess, 254–55
diffused religion, 84–85
discourse, 16–17, 35, 227–28, 229–30
disenchantment, 245–46, 247–48, 250, 251
District of Columbia, 268, 269–70
divination, 159
divine rescue, 157–58
Durkheim, Émile, 3, 11, 92n.2, 223, 247–
   48, 250, 251, 258–59, 314, 335

ecstasies, 194–207. *See also* BDSM;
   leathersex
educational institutions. *see* public schools
Education for New Generations, 271
Edwards v. Aguillard, 268
8chan, 255–56
El Salvador, 232–33
embodied empiricism, 195, 205–6
embodied practice, 195, 205–6
embodied sexuality, 205–6
embodiment, 16–17, 33–34, 35, 36, 42–44
   aspects of, 15–16
   BDSM and, 23, 195, 201–2, 205–6
emic approach, 36, 239, 240, 247–48
emotion, 35, 42–43, 44
Emotional Spiritual Quotient (ESQ), 306–
   7, 309–10
empty signifiers, 21, 24, 314–15, 319–
   20, 328
enchanted feminism, 58–59
Encinitas Union School District, 269, 271
Energetic spirituality, 49–50, 55–56, 59–
   60, 61–62, 63, 67
engaged Buddhism, 340
Engel v. Vitale, 268
Enlightenment, 42, 50, 83, 105–6, 196–
   97, 204–5
entangled context, 13, 38–40
epistemology. *See* religious epistemology
Equal Employment Opportunity
   Commission (EEOC), 267
equanimity, 128, 129, 131
ESQ. *See* Emotional Spiritual Quotient
established context, 13, 39–40, 41
Establishment Clause of the First
   Amendment, 318–19
ethical regulation, 215–16
ethical spirituality, 75–76

Ethiopian Church, 221
ethnic paganism, 49, 59
etic approach, 36, 239, 247–48
Europe, 5–6, 8–9, 13, 22–23, 245–46. *See also* colonialism
evangelicalism, 22
  African Americans and, 164t, 165–69, 171
  chaplaincy education and, 291, 292–93
  college students and, 144–46, 148
Evangelical Presbyterian Church, 221
experience-sampling methodology (ESM). *See* smartphone-based experience-sampling method
Extinction Rebellion, 21–22
extra-theistic package, 75–76

Facebook, 121–22
Fasti, 88
Father God, 63, 65–66, 67
FetLife, 198–99
Fe y Alegría, 235
field experiments, 118–21, 124–25
fiqh, 300, 302
First Amendment, 267, 318–19. *See also* free exercise of religion
first-wave perspective, 4–8, 14, 341
Five Major Religions (of China), 83–84
Forbes, 320, 321
formless mysticism, 49–50, 52–55, 56, 58–62, 63
  Christianity and, 53
  in typology, 64–65, 65t
  World's Parliament of Religions and, 51–52
4chan, 255–56
Fox News, 320
France, 11–12, 19, 245–46
free exercise of religion, 267–68
French Revolution, 251
From Satori to Silicon Valley (Roszak), 248–49
frontstage/backstage behavior, 262

Galilei, Galileo, 114
Gandhi, 21–22
gangs, 227–34, 236–38, 240n.3, 240n.4

Gangs for Christ ministry, 229
Garvins v. Burnett, 267
General Social Surveys (GSS), 160–61, 162, 165, 169, 172–73, 173n.5
Al-Ghazali, 298–99
gifts (spiritual), 229, 232–33, 238
Ginanjar, Ary, 306–7, 309–10
Glastonbury, England, 57–62, 65–66, 67
god-belief matrix, 65f, 65, 66
Goddess Festival, 58
Goddess spirituality, 58–59, 61–62
Goddess Temple, 58
God of Fortune, 79
gods. *See* deities/gods
Goenka, S. N., 191n.1, 191n.3
Google, 121–22, 321
GPS, 123
Grammy Awards, 255–56
grave rituals, 80–82
Great Britain/United Kingdom, 5, 19, 22–23, 49, 53–54, 66–68, 341
Greek religion, 10
GSS. *See* General Social Surveys
Guatemala, 227–28, 232–35, 237, 238
Gymnastiar, Abdullah (Aa Gym), 305–6

Hamka, 301–2, 306
Hartford Theological Seminary, 285–86, 291–92
Harvard Divinity School, 341
Hatha Yoga Pradipika, 265
healing
  BDSM and, 202
  in Malawi, 213–14
health, 6, 7, 337–38
heathenism, 61–62
Hegel, Georg, 11
hegemonic power, 21
Hindu Broome Street Ganesha Temple, 267–68
Hinduism, 51, 90, 159–60, 265, 303, 323, 342–43
Hinduism Today, 270
Holiness religions, 162–63, 164t, 165–69, 171–72, 174n.7
Homies and Hermanos: God and Gangs in Central America (Brenneman), 228
homonationalism, 197
homonormativity, 197

350 INDEX

homophobia, 197
Honest to God (Robinson), 53
Horizon survey, 84
Huffington Post, 99, 318, 320, 321
Humans of New York, 322

Ibn 'Abd al-Wahhab, 299
Ibn al-'Arabi, 298–99
Icke, David, 252–53, 256–57
IDEALS. *See* Interfaith Diversity
    Experiences and Attitudes
    Longitudinal Survey
ideal types of theology, 65t
identity. *See* religious identity
Ignatius of Loyola, 10
Ilham, Arifin, 305–6
Iliff School of Theology, 278, 284–85
immigrants, 40, 42, 90
India, 22, 265
indigenous religions, 40–41, 97, 98, 99–
    100, 104–5, 337
individualism/individualization, 3, 4, 5, 6,
    19, 41, 179
    African Americans and, 154–55, 157–
        60, 339
    BDSM and, 201–2, 203
    in Malawi, 217–20
    meditation and, 179, 189–90
Indonesia, 19, 24, 297, 298–99, 300, 301–9,
    310, 311
Insight Timer, 189
institutionalized context, 13, 41
interconnecteness, 128
Interfaith Diversity Experiences and
    Attitudes Longitudinal Survey
    (IDEALS), 133–34, 146
interstitial context, 13, 41–43
Invisible Religion, The (Luckmann), 245–46
Ireland, 64
iron cage metaphor, 251
Islam, 8–9, 63, 73, 336, 342–43. *See also*
    Salafism; Sufism; Wahhabism
    in Africa, 97, 98, 99–100, 104–5
    African Americans and, 159–60
    BDSM and, 198
    chaplaincy education and, 285–86,
        288, 291–92
    in China, 77, 78–79, 83–85

in Malawi, 211–12, 213–14, 215–16,
    217, 219, 220, 222–23, 225n.2
yoga and, 265
Islamic law, 298, 301
Islamic State, 300, 310
Israel, 180, 181, 191n.1
Iśvarapraṇidhāna, 265
Italy, 13

Jakarta, 308
James, William, 8
Java, 301, 302
Jay-Z, 255–56
Jehovah's Witness religion, 218, 222–23
Jesus Christ, 62, 76, 159, 200, 216, 232–
    34, 265–66
jingshen, 85–86
Jois, Krishna Pattabhi, 269, 271, 272
Journal for the Study of Spirituality, 53–54
Jubilee Community, 57, 68n.4
Judaism, 8–9, 73
    African Americans and, 159–60
    BDSM and, 198, 199–201, 207
    chaplaincy education and, 291–92
    college students and, 145–46, 147
Jung, Carl Gustav, 254–55

K. P. Jois USA Foundation, 269, 271, 272
Kang Youwei, 82–83
karma, 159–60, 265
Karma Kagyu Buddhism, 319
Karzai, Hamid, 282–83
kebatinan, 302, 303–5, 307–8
Kendal, England, 49, 53–54, 57–58, 61,
    65–66, 67, 68n.1
Kennedy, John F., 254–56
Kesey, Ken, 248–49
Khadija, 299
King, Martin Luther, 21–22
kink, 198–99, 200, 205–6, 207. *See also*
    sacred kink
Kitchen Gods, 79
Koran, 217, 298–99, 300
Krishna, 265
kyais, 301

L. County, Shanxi Province, China, 77–
    78, 79–80

Laclau, Ernesto, 21, 314–15, 319–20, 328.
    See also empty signifiers
Lady Gaga, 255–56
Lady of Avalon, 58
law. *See* legal context; legal institutions
law enforcement, 319
Leary, Timothy, 248–49
leathersex, 23, 194–95, 198, 200–2, 203–4,
    205–6, 207
Lee v. Weisman, 268
legal context, 33, 38, 44
legal institutions, 267–71
Lemonade (album), 99
Le Suicide (Durkheim), 251
LGBTQ community, 146–47, 196
liberation theology, 157–58
Library of Avalon, 59
liminoid space, 187
lingxing, 86
Literary Expressions of African Spirituality
    (Marsh-Locket and West), 110
Little Book of Atheist Spirituality, The
    (Comte-Spoonville), 341
lived religion, 8, 22–23, 35–37, 38,
    43, 44, 90
    boundary work and, 74–76
    methodological innovations
        and, 114–15
    plausibility structures and, 43–44
Living Waters Church, 214, 215, 216, 221
looping, 338–39
Loyola University Chicago, 285–86
Lunar New Year, 79
Lutheranism, 280–81

macrocontexts, 12, 13, 33
    big data and, 125
    power and, 17–18
    practice and, 38–43, 44
Madjid, Nurcholish, 304–5
magic, 58–59, 60–61, 245
Malawi, 23, 210–24, 343
    the context, 211–12
    demands and offerings of religion
        in, 212–20
    ethical regulation in, 215–16
    glimmers of spirituality, 220–22
    healing and miracles in, 213–14

household peace, village
    harmony, 216–17
identity/individuality/rationality
    and, 217–20
practical religion in, 213
welfare services in, 217
West compared with, 222–24
Malaysia, 301
Mali, 308–9
Malnak v. Yogi, 267
Man, Myth and Magick, 59
Manajemen Qolbu, 306–7
Mannheim, Karl, 246, 250, 251
marketing and consumption, 201–
    2, 203–4
Marx, Karl, 11, 246, 250, 258–59
master of divinity (MDiv), 280–81, 285–
    86, 287–89
materiality, 35, 36, 42–44
Maududi, Abul A'la, 310
Mayan spirituality, 233–35, 238
May Fourth Movement, 83
McKenna, Terrence, 248–49
Mead, George Herbert, 338
meaning and purpose, 128
media, 316, 328–29
    conspiracy theories and, 255–56
    on mindfulness movement, 316–
        17, 320–21
meditation, 10, 179–91. *See also*
    mindfulness; vipassana meditation
    solo, 188–89
    spirituality, transcendence, and modes
        of interaction, 189–91
    Sufi, 302
metaphysical religion, 66, 66*t*
metaphysical spirituality, 8
Methodism, 155–56, 166, 167*t*,
    171, 280–81
methodological innovations, 113–25
    big data, 121–25
    field experiments, 118–21, 124–25
    smartphone-based experience
        sampling, 114–18, 123–25
    value of, 113–14
microcontexts, 12, 13
    power and, 17–18
    practice and, 38, 43, 44

352 INDEX

military chaplaincy pattern, 282–84, 287, 291, 292–93

Mindful Elite, The: Mobilizing from the Inside Out (Kucinskas), 330n.2

mindfulness, 7, 19–20, 22, 90, 179, 339–40
  Christian, 120–21
  critiques of, 322–23
  leaders of, 317–20
  the media on, 316–17, 320–21
  thin *vs.* thick, 273

ming, 88

Ming Dynasty, 78

minority religion pattern, 282, 285–86, 288–89

miracles, 213–14

Missouri, 267–68

modernist theory, 249–51

modernity/modernization, 7, 19
  Africa and, 106
  China and, 77, 82–84
  conspiracy theories and (*see* conspiracy theories)
  double-faced spirituality and, 247–51
  Islam and, 299, 300, 301–2, 309
  multiple modernities, 342–43
  subjective turn, 189–90

monotheism, 58, 60–61, 62, 73, 74, 76–77
  paternalist, 49–50, 51, 52–53, 54–55, 58–59
  in typology, 63–65, 65t

moral judgment, 35, 44

Morocco, 308–9

Mother Goddess, 58

Muhammad, 299

Muhammadiyah, 301–3

multi-institutional fields, 20–21

multiple modernities, 342–43

mysticism. *See* formless mysticism

Mysticism (Besant), 52

Mysticism (Underhill), 53

myths, 102–3

Myths of the Asanas (textbook), 271

Nahdlatul Ulama, 302–3, 306

Naqshabandya, 307

Naropa University, 285, 288–89, 290, 291–92

narrative, 35, 44, 114–15. *See also* therapeutic narratives

National Study of Youth and Religion, 130

Native Americans, 139–44

nature, 249–50, 251, 257–59
  conspiracy theories and, 252–57
  power of, 246, 247–48

Navy Chaplain School, 282–83

Nazarene, 284–85, 287

neither spiritual nor religious, 133, 134–38, 137t, 138t, 139t, 140t, 145–46, 149–50

neo-heathenism, 61–62

neoliberalism, 42–43, 203–4

neopaganism, 198, 199–200, 207

neo-Pentecostalism, 232–34, 236, 237, 238, 239

neo-Sufism, 304–5

Netherlands, 13, 245–46

New Age movements, 8, 49, 54–55, 57, 68n.2, 247

new metaphysicals, 8, 10, 204–5

New Metaphysicals (Bender), 278

New York, 267–68

New York Times, 232–33, 320

Nietzsche, Friedrich, 9–10

Nigeria, 107–8, 307

9/11 attacks, 254–56, 310

niyamas, 265

nonaffiliates. *See* religious nonaffiliates

Nones. *See* not religious

nonviolence, 21–22, 265

North Africa, 99–100

Northern Wei Dynasty, 78

North Penn School District, 271

not religious (Nones), 72, 74, 75

observational methods, 118–19

Odin, 61–62

On Genealogy of Morals (Nietzsche), 9–10

opaque power, 17

Open Society and Its Enemies (Popper), 252

Opium Wars, 83

organizational climates, 20–21

Orientalism, 89, 201–2

orthodoxy, 13–14, 53

orthopraxy, 13–14

Orunmila, 103

Outside the Gates, 290

Outstretched in Worship, 265–66

overt power, 17

Pacific Islanders, 144–45, 147
Pagan Census, 59
paganism
  ethnic, 49, 59
  neo-, 198, 199–200, 207
  techno-, 249
pagan polytheism, 49–50, 57–62, 67
Pakistan, 310, 311
Pancasila, 303
Paramadina Foundation, 304–5
pastoral counseling pattern, 282, 284–85,
    287, 291
paternalist monotheism, 49–50, 51, 52–53,
    54–55, 58–59
Pennsylvania, 271
Pentecostalism, 40–41, 221
  in Africa, 98
  African Americans and, 155, 162–63,
    164t, 166–69, 171–72
  in Central America, 228–29, 230, 231–
    34, 236, 237, 238, 239–40, 240n.2
  in Malawi, 211–12, 214, 216–17, 225n.2
  neo-, 232–34, 236, 237, 238, 239
Pentecostal Theological Seminary, 281,
    282–83, 290
Perry, Katy, 255–56
Pew Research Center polls, 154–55, 263
Ping Yao, China, 78–80
pir, 298
plausibility structures, 43–44
play, 195, 206
pneumatikos, 10
political power, 251–57
polytheism, 22–23, 63–64, 76–77
  in China, 76, 77
  pagan, 49–50, 57–62, 67
  in typology, 64–65, 65t
post-Christian spirituality, 5–6
postcolonial world, 9, 40–41, 89–90
postrationalism, 195, 199, 201–2, 204–
    5, 207
post-traditional spirituality, 245–46, 249–
    50, 257–58
Powell v. Perry, 267
power, 8–9, 16–17, 37
  capitalism and, 19–20
  contestation of boundary objects
    and, 21

explained, 17–22
hegemonic, 21
Malawian view of, 223
of nature, 246, 247–48
opaque, 17
organizational climates and multi-
    institutional fields, 20–21
overt, 17
political, re-enchantment of, 251–57
secularization and, 18–19
social movements and social
    change, 21–22
spiritual transmission in landscapes of
    (see spiritual transmission)
of technology, 248–49
power yoga, 316–17, 323–28, 329
practical religion, 66, 66t, 213
practice (spiritual), 8–9, 23, 335
  contexts of, 38–44
  embodied, 195, 205–6
  explained, 13–17
  institutionally "approved," 322–23
  multidimensional, 33–35
  spirituality in religious, 35–37
  yoga as (see under yoga)
pragmatism, 16–17
PraiseMoves, 265–66
prāṇāyāma, 265–66, 270
Pranic Healing, 271
Presbyterianism, 280–81
prisons, 7, 53–54
pronoia, 254–55
Protestantism, 22, 57, 76
  African Americans and, 154–55, 162–
    63, 165–69, 167t, 171–72
  in Central America, 239
  chaplaincy education and, 280–81, 284–
    85, 292–93
  in China, 83–84, 89
  college students and, 130–31, 139–
    46, 147
  formless mysticism and, 53
  in Indonesia, 303
  in Malawi, 225n.2
  moderate, 162–63
  World's Parliament of Religions
    and, 50
provincializing concepts, 90

354 INDEX

public schools
mindfulness training in, 7, 318–19
yoga in, 7, 268–72
Pure Edge Foundation, 271, 272

QAnon, 251–52, 255–56
Quakerism, 57
qualitative methods, 115, 118–19
quantitative methods, 115, 118–19
Quebec, Canada, 75–76
queer community/queerness, 195, 200–1, 203–4
religion, sexuality, and, 196–97
sexuality studies and, 207
Quetzalcoatl, 233–34

racism, 61–62, 107–8
Ramadan, 217, 220
rationality, 217–20
REALINC, 162, 173–74n.6
re-enchantment, 246, 247–49, 250, 251–59
reiki, 55–56
reincarnation, 103–4
relational approach, 9, 10, 54–55, 73, 341–42
in China, 82–85
explained, 335–37
religion
decline in traditional and organized, 3, 4–5
defined, 128, 156
establishment of, 268–71
free exercise of, 267–68
as multidimensional practice, 33–35
practical, 66, 66t, 213
as a social phenomenon, 335
spirituality in practice of, 35–37
spirituality overlap with, 6, 13
spirituality vs., 6, 223, 338
the state and, 39–41
varying meanings of, 336
yoga relationship with, 262–63, 264, 265, 267–71
Religion, Culture and Spirituality in Africa and the African Diaspora (Ackah, Dodson, and Smith), 110
religious affiliation, 75–77
in African Americans, 154–56, 162–63

in China, 84
in college students, 130, 131, 149, 150–51
religious but not spiritual, 133, 134–38, 137t, 138t, 139t, 140t, 144–45, 146, 148
religious commitment, 128, 130, 131
religious conversion, 131
religious engagement, 128, 130, 131
religious epistemology, 76
historicizing and deconstructing, 104–6
redefining, 101–4
religious identity, 75–77
in China, 77
in college students (*see under* college students)
in Malawi, 217–20
religious institutions, 262–63
religious nonaffiliates
African American, 155–56, 159–60, 166–69, 170–72, 173
yoga practice and, 263
religious reinforcers, 131, 145–46, 149–50
religious service attendance, 20–21, 117, 165, 170–71, 337–38
revellion, 107–8
Rihanna, 255–56
rites of passage, 103–4
rodas, 107–8
Romantic movement, 56–57, 204–5, 257–58
Rumi, 299

Sacred Cove Hoodoo, 59
sacred kink, 195, 198–99, 200–1, 207. *See also* kink
sacredness, 3, 73, 74, 92n.2
African Americans and, 154
in African spirituality, 102
BDSM and, 200–1
in China, 77
in Malawi, 210
of nature, 247, 253
sadaq, 217
Salafism, 299, 300, 306, 307, 309–10, 311
Salafi Sufism, 306
samādhi, 270
same-sex marriage, 197

San Francisco Theological Seminary, 293
saomu, 82
Satan. *See* Devil/Satan
satya, 265
Saudi Arabia, 299, 310, 311
SBNR. *See* spiritual but not religious
schools. *See* public schools
science, 336
Science as a Vocation (Weber), 245
Scientific American, 320
Search Inside Yourself, 321
second-wave perspective, 7–22
Secular Beats Spiritual (Bruce), 341
secularism, 7, 72–73, 245, 246, 341
  in Africa, 102
  boundary work and, 11–12, 75–77
  in China, 82–83
  meditation and, 189–90
  power and, 18–19
  varying meanings of, 336
  yoga and, 262, 264, 271–72
Sedlock v. Baird, 268, 269, 270
Sekhmet, 59–60
Seminary of the Southwest, 282–83
S-ESM. *See* smartphone-based
  experience-sampling method
Seventh Day Adventist religion, 217–18, 225n.2
sharia, 301, 302
shaykh, 298
Sikhism, 265
Sisters of Perpetual Indulgence, 205, 206
situated spirituality (explained), 4, 12–13
slavery, 109–10, 154
smartphone-based experience-sampling
  method (S-ESM), 114–18, 123–25
smartphone GPS function, 123
social boundaries, 74
social change, 21–22
social cleansing, 232–33
social location, 238
social movements, 21–22
social movement schools, 339–40
social world, 315
sociologization, 8
Sonima, 271, 272
SoulPulse study, 115–18
Southern Baptist Religion, 280–81

spirit money, 81, 82
spiritual but not religious (SBNR), 5–6,
  13–14, 22–23, 72, 75–76, 196, 245–46
  African Americans as, 154–56, 162,
  169–71, 170t, 172
  BDSM and, 201–2, 203, 207
  college students as, 133, 134–38, 137t,
  138t, 139t, 140t, 145, 146, 148–50
  increase in population, 3, 75
  yoga practice and, 262, 263, 264, 265–66
spiritual exercise, 10, 86
spiritual experience, 8
  capacity and need for, 223
  power and, 17
  social influences and, 12–13, 180
  yoga and, 263, 326, 327
spirituality
  belief and belonging, 75–76
  as compartmentalized, 41
  defined, 156, 210
  definition elusiveness, 9, 128, 336–37
  ethical, 75–76
  first-wave perspective on, 4–8, 14, 341
  fused with action, 38–39
  future directions of, 340–43
  influences of, 337–40
  meaning of, 335–37
  as optional, 39–40
  porous, 10, 21, 24, 75–76, 78–79, 128–29, 314–15, 328, 336–37
  religion overlap with, 6, 13
  religion *vs.*, 6, 223, 338
  in religious practice, 35–37
  rise in, 3, 315
  second-wave perspective on, 7–22
  situated (explained), 4, 12–13
  as a social phenomenon, 4, 8–9,
  335, 338–40
spiritual language, 227–29, 231–33, 234–35, 236–40
Spiritual Marketplace, The (Roof), 5
spiritual milieus, 49, 54–55, 90–92, 247–49
  of China, 86–89
  multiple, 342
spiritual quest, 128, 129, 131
spiritual revolution, 3, 5, 190, 245–46
Spiritual Revolution, The (Heelas and
  Woodhead), 5, 54

356 INDEX

spiritual transmission, 314–30
  audiences and, 316–17, 323–28
  leaders of, 317–20
  the media and, 316–17, 320–21, 328–29
spiritual values, 235–36
standpoint theory, 9
Stoics, 10
structuring processes, 13–14
subjective turn, 189–90
substantive context, 9, 12
Sufi Salafism, 311
Sufism, 19, 24, 297–311
  contestation, 297, 298–300
  contestation and uncertainty, 301–4
  explained, 298
  insights for the study of spirituality and
    religion, 308–11
  neo-, 304–5
  revival of, 304–5, 311n.2
  spirituality and, in Indonesia, 305–8
  spirituality and, in Islam, 297–99
Suharto regime, 302–4
Sukarno regime, 303–4
Sunni Salafism, 306
sun salutations, 265–66, 269, 271, 324
Superbrain Yoga, 271
Supreme Court, 197, 268, 271–72
Sūrya Namaskāra, 265, 269
svādhyāya, 265
SVARA, 200
Sweden, 245–46
symbolic boundaries, 74
symmetry/asymmetry, 72–73, 89
synchronicity, 254–55
synchronized movement, 184–85, 190

Taiwan, 19, 20
tariqas, 298, 310
tasawwuf, 298
*Teaching Tolerance: A Project of the
  Southern Poverty Law Center,* 272
technology, 245, 248–49, 250
techno-pagans, 249
Texas Christian University, 284–85
theism, 13, 52, 57, 58–59, 63, 67, 75
theistic package, 75–76
theosophy, 52–53
theosphere, 49, 57–58, 64, 67–68, 342–43

therapeutic narratives, 201–2
thick mindfulness, 273
thin mindfulness, 273
tian, 88
Tibetan Buddhism, 19–20, 319
Time, 320
tongling, 86
transcendence, 5, 128, 189–91, 200–1
transcendentalism, 10
transgender community, 196–97, 198,
  200–1, 203–4, 207
Trump, Donald, 255–56
Twitter, 121–22
"Tyger, The" (Blake), 72
typologies, 62–66

Ukraine, 61–62
Umbanda, 107–8
Union Theological Seminary, 156–57
Unitarianism, 57, 280–81
United Kingdom. *See* Great Britain/United
  Kingdom
United States, 5–6, 8–9, 11–13, 18–19,
  33, 41, 49, 53–54, 66–68, 74–75, 77,
  90, 342–43
  Capitol storming, 61–62
  chaplaincy programs in, 286–87
  conspiracy theory prevalence
    in, 251–52
  educational institutions in (*see* public
    schools)
  heathenism in, 61–62
  legal institutions in, 267–71
  mindfulness movement in, 316–
    20, 328–29
  religious institutions in, 262–63
  vipassana meditation in, 180, 191n.1
  yoga in, 19–20, 24, 262–72 (*see
    also* yoga)
United States v. Meyers, 267
Unite the Right rally, 61–62
Universal Society of Hinduism, 268
University of Massachusetts Medical
  School, 317
University of the West, 285–86, 288–
  89, 291–92
UPG (unverified personal gnosis), 61–62
Uyghur Muslims, 84

Vedas, 265
Versailles Treaty, 83
veterans, 319
vipassana meditation, 8, 23, 180–88,
    191n.1, 191n.3, 314, 318
    extending the interaction mode, 186–88
    interaction mode, 182–85
    the puzzle, 180
    retreats, 181–82
Virgin Mary, 64
Virgin of Guadalupe, 40
Vivekananda, Swami, 51–52, 53, 54–55

Wahhabism, 299, 311
wali, 298
Washington Post, 320
Watts, Alan, 52–53, 54–55
weapons (spiritual), 232–33, 238
Weber, Max, 37, 187, 223, 245–46, 247–49,
    250, 251, 257–59
welfare services, 217
West, 245–46, 339, 340, 342–43
    Africa and, 106
    China compared with, 341–42
    Malawi compared with, 222–24
West Africa, 103–4
Western Europe, 5–6, 8–9, 13, 246
Western Michigan State University, 294n.1
"When Sheila's a Leatherdyke?"
    (article), 194–95
White Clouds Temple, 78–79
Whites
    African Americans compared with,
        12–13, 22–23, 155–56, 160–61, 161*t*,
        162–63, 166, 171–72
    BDSM and, 201–3
    college students, 139–44, 145, 147
    methodological innovations and, 115

White supremacy, 50, 61–62, 329
wholeness, 128
WholyFit, 265–66
Whosoever.org, 194
Wicca, 49, 59–60, 62, 65
Wired, 320
women, 7, 51–52, 54, 55
Worcester State Hospital, 280
workplace, 7, 20–21
World's Parliament of Religions, 50–52,
    62, 63–64, 67
World War II, 3, 5, 67
Wyrdraven, 59

Yahweh Yoga, 265–66
yamas, 265
yinqi, 80
yoga, 7, 10, 19–20, 22, 24, 55–56, 262–72
    instructor certification, 265
    legal institutions and, 267–71
    percentage of US population
        practicing, 263
    power, 316–17, 323–28, 329
    as a social practice, 266–67
    as a spiritual practice, 263–66
Yoga Alliance, 265, 268, 269–70
Yoga Alliance Code of Conduct, 265
Yoga Ed., 270, 271
Yoga for New York, 267–68
Yoga in America Study, 264, 265, 269–70
Yoga Sūtras, 265, 269–70
Yorubans, 97, 99, 103–4
youling, 86
Yungang Grottoes, 78

zakat, 217
Zen Buddhism, 52–53, 90
zhengming, 91–92

Printed in the USA/Agawam, MA
October 31, 2022

800538.010